Beyond Rationalism

Beyond Rationalism

Rethinking Magic, Witchcraft and Sorcery

edited by

Bruce Kapferer

Berghahn Books
New York • Oxford

First published in 2002 by

Berghahn Books

Social Analysis, Volume 46, Issue 3, Fall 2002

Paperback edition published in 2003 by

Berghahn Books

www.berghahnbooks.com

Library of Congress Cataloging-in-Publication Data

A C.I.P. catalogue record for this book is
available from the Library of Congress.

ISBN 1-57181-418-3 (pbk.: alk. paper)

Printed in the United States on acid-free paper.

Contents

Acknowledgements

The idea for this volume developed in the course of a series of seminars among post-graduates and staff at the University of Bergen in which Bawa Yamba, Michael Lambek and René Devisch also participated. In organising the essays for the collection, I have had the advantage of extended discussions at Bergen with Knut Rio, Kari Telle, Marit Brendbekken and Ørnulf Gulbrandsen, all of whom have contributed essays. Outside Bergen, Bawa Yamba has always engaged me in challenging discussion, as have Rohan Bastin, Roland Kapferer and, in particular, Jadran Mimica, whose views are always inspiring. Kingsley Garbett, Marion Berghahn and Vivian Berghahn were keen that this volume should see the light of day, and applied the necessary pressure as well as providing insight. Without the efforts of Shawn Kendrick and her patient copy-editing, this volume could not have appeared. All of the contributors join me in extending our thanks to her.

Chapter 1

INTRODUCTION
Outside All Reason: Magic, Sorcery and Epistemology in Anthropology

Bruce Kapferer

Magic, sorcery and witchcraft are at the epistemological centre of anthropology. They embed matters at the heart of the definition of modern anthropology, and the critical issues that they raise are of enduring significance for the discipline. But the questions these phenomena highlight expand beyond mere disciplinary or scholastic interest. They point to matters of deep existential concern in a general quest for an understanding of the human forces engaged in the human construction of lived realities. Anthropology in the embracing Kantian sense is involved. The phenomena that are deemed to be magic and sorcery (including all that which such scholars as Durkheim (1915) and Mauss (1972) would include under the label 'profane') project towards the far shores of human possibility and potentiality. The human profundities to which they might lead are already there in the imagery and metaphors of thinkers, both abstract and concretely pragmatic, worldwide. Within European traditions the world of the magician and the sorcerer is routinely evoked to explore the continuing crisis that is faced by humankind, more recently, for example, in the works of Dante, Goethe and Nietzsche right through to the most contemporary philosophers and social commentators. The essays in these pages contend with some of the overarching existential issues towards which a concern with the magical must extend.

This introduction begins with a consideration of the somewhat narrower confines that have developed in the discipline of anthropology. But this should not obscure the fact that at the outset, the anthropology of magic and sorcery dealt with weighty issues – the foundations of religion, the underlying features of the human psyche and, indeed, the very nature of science. While these interests have persisted, over time they became narrowed or deflected onto smaller, more empirically manageable concerns. However, of late, via a renewed interest in magic and sorcery, anthropology is once more opening up to the larger questions. These include the significance of sorcery and magic as revelations of the fabulations and transmutations of capital in globalising circumstances, and the magical character of nationalist discourses of the modern and post-colonial state (Comaroff and Comaroff 2001, 1993; Coronil 1997; Kapferer 1997, 1988; Taussig 1997, 1980). Even so, anthropology largely remains bound to the problem of reason, confined to re-examining well-answered questions rather than exploring new horizons of interest to which the phenomena themselves point.

Territories of the Strange: Magic, Sorcery and the Realms of Unreason

Geertz once poignantly remarked that anthropologists are 'merchants of the strange'; magic and sorcery fill this bill of trade. Contemporary attacks on anthropological exoticism from several quarters of the discipline and elsewhere in intellectual and scholarly circles might have predicted a shrinkage of interest, especially in a subject as self-critical as anthropology. Anthropologists are acutely self-conscious of their colonialist past and the risks of a voyeuristic exoticism that have accompanied what a few commentators (Clifford 1997, Clifford and Marcus 1986, Fabian 1983) have described as their traveller's search for the ethnographic Other. But against the odds (especially given that anthropology as much as other disciplines in the social sciences and humanities is driven by intellectual fashions), sorcery and witchcraft – indeed, the occult as a whole – are reattracting anthropological attention (Comaroff and Comaroff 1999). Many insist that this is because empirically such practice is globally on the rise, a not unproblematic observation. However, I stress the vital epistemological status of occultic phenomena in the conceptual and theoretical imaginary of anthropological thought.

Reason and rationality, the central questions and themes at the centre of the philosophy of the Enlightenment and at the root of all dominant post-Enlightenment enquiry in the sciences and humanities, were and still are integral to the formation of modern anthropology. They are vital to defining the object of the discipline and in the construction of theory and methodology. The very history of anthropology may be described as an enduring crisis driven by shifting certainties/uncertainties as to what constitutes reason and rationality and the appropriate perspectives for their revelation. These issues achieve, perhaps, their sharpest focus in the occult – that which is mystical and stands outside, or is opposed to, science and the rule of reason. Anthropology established itself as the science of unreason, initially at least. This constituted its principal object. Indeed, unreason, or apparent unreason, defines the Other, the conventional region of anthropological enquiry. Once territorially confined to cultures and societies dominated by colonial and imperial power (whose rule of reason defined the legitimacy of such control and conquest), the Other, for contemporary anthropologists, is now deterritorialised. Everywhere, the unreason of the Other is the possibility of human action and vital even in the orders and structures composed by those authorities who would lay claim to a legitimacy ordained by reason's rule. If reason (now a thoroughly relativised reason and implicated in the excesses and devastations of power) is at the apex of systems of authority and domination, it is the unreason of this reason that has attracted much recent anthropological attention. Occultic metaphors – magic, sorcery, witchcraft – highlight these processes (Comaroff and Comaroff 1999).

The general point, then, is that magic, sorcery and witchcraft (among various other related concepts) address a central problematic in anthropology. It is to be expected that they would be among the key tropes at critical moments of debate or redefinition when epistemological questions at the heart of the discipline are likely to surface.

The Significance of Evans-Pritchard's Contribution

Evans-Pritchard's *Witchcraft, Oracles and Magic Among the Azande* (1937) defined major directions in modern anthropology. There are other works published about the same time that could be discussed, such as Kluckhohn's *Navaho Witchcraft* (1967) and especially Reo Fortune's *Sorcerers of Dobu* (1932). The former examines magical and sorcery practices from sociological and psychological angles demonstrating, among numerous other aspects, their role in the expression of conflict. Fortune extends more towards the importance of grasping the cosmological worlds of magic and sorcery. Geza Roheim's *The Riddle of the Sphinx* (1934), based on Australian Aboriginal materials, demonstrates early on the significance of a psychoanalytic approach. But I focus on Evans-Pritchard's path-breaking work because it is generally recognised by most anthropologists as the key study of significance and is the major reference for cognate fields. This is more than deservedly so.

Not only does the work itself contain an abundance of ethnographic material integral to a plethora of questions (many still to be seriously explored in anthropology) that might be provoked from a diversity of disciplinary or subject standpoints, but also there is an engaging lack of self-consciousness, a seductive naivety that draws the reader into an intellectually challenging reality. However, by far the greatest significance of Evans-Pritchard's study is that it opens up new horizons of understanding that are embedded in magical practices. He redirects the course and import of the anthropological exploration of ethnography.

Overall, *Witchcraft, Oracles and Magic Among the Azande* is a critical methodological and theoretical work in anthropology. It demonstrates a fundamental anthropological aim to de-exoticise what may otherwise be deemed as exotic and strange, but without destroying the nature of the phenomena in question. Magical practice is not here reduced to terms that are external to it. Furthermore, the work is significant because it implicitly overcomes what has become an issue in anthropology, that of relativism versus universalism. Written before the matter became acutely problematic for anthropology (perhaps fuelled by discourse in a postmodern anthropology dismissing its past and consumed by a need to be pragmatically relevant), Evans-Pritchard's study transcends the matter, demonstrating that a deep concern with phenomena as they are practised and in their terms is in every way thoroughly consistent with general understanding. Universalism and relativism are not opposed terms as they came to be treated in later anthropological debate. Possibly of greatest importance, Evans-Pritchard gave the anthropological Other a position in exploring issues of wide import. Azande practice was not a mere passive object for the demonstration of alien knowledge and theory, but was itself a source of knowledge and made active in both opening up horizons of understanding and challenging other analytic constructions of the nature of human experience. This direction in Evans-Pritchard's work – what should be regarded as a central project of anthropology – is being carried further in the work of contemporary African scholars (see, for example, Hallen and Sodipo 1997, Appiah 1992, Mudimbe 1988, Sodipo 1983).

Evans-Pritchard's important move in his Azande ethnography was to bracket off the thought and practice of the Azande from Western conceptions. He effectively disconnected or decentred practices glossed as magic and witchcraft – particularly those so conceived in the colonial or imperialised territories of the Other – from their submission to forms of thought and judgment constituted out of a Western history. This lay the groundwork for Evans-Pritchard's claim that Azande witchcraft was not the same as European witchcraft. Here he quite explicitly refused to identify Zande practice with the occult as the latter has become defined in Western contexts.

The word 'occult' is laden with the sense of the mystical and is the obverse of reason and scientific rationality. Indeed, what is broadly described as the occult, and largely a Western (especially Victorian) fascination with magic and witchcraft (*wicca*) together with the understanding of them, is the invention of a post-Enlightenment secularism. In fact, magic and witchcraft conceived as practices of the occult were created as alternative rationalisms to that of science (see Brendbekken, chapter 2, on Rudolf Steiner's anthroposophical movement), and, as if in obedience to the law of dialectics, the occultic vision drew into its practice aspects of the scientific rationalism it opposed. The mystical occultism of that which is glossed as New Age (recognised by some as the religion of postmodern globalisation) is an extension of the very Western-centred (and often highly Christian-influenced) perspectives within which not a few anthropological approaches were shaped. Indeed, this continues in much of anthropology, but Evans-Pritchard indicated a concern to distance Zande practice and conception from such approaches and, therefore, to avoid interpretations from the viewpoint of a history that was not that of the Azande. Furthermore, Evans-Pritchard's decentring strategy carried an implicit critique of anthropological approaches up to (and after) his work to the effect that they were insufficiently reflective on the logic of their own thought and practice whereby they constituted the realities of others. This resulted in the construction of anthropological Others that were merely inversions or obversions of the reality of the analyst or ethnographer's Self: the territory of the Other was invented as a zone for the free play of prejudices which resulted in neither a challenging of the assumptions of the Other nor, indeed, those of the Self.

Here, in my view, Evans-Pritchard prefigured recent criticisms of the anthropological method of 'othering' whereby the construction of difference disguises a similarity that is integral to the very procedures through which the ethnographic Other is invented. Difference and similarity are ultimately to be resolved at the empirical ethnographic level in the context of the perceptual and conceptual procedures involved. Their assertion is dependent on the evidence and not upon superficial or unexamined assumptions. The ethnographic bracketing that Evans-Pritchard pursued is directed towards exploring the circumstances in which the magical practices of the Azande establish similarities with and differences from other kinds of practices elsewhere. A common orientation in much anthropology is to make the realities of other peoples 'sensible' by demonstrating equivalences in the everyday reality of the ethnographer. This process of 'translation', often immediately satisfying and capable of drawing astounding associations, not infrequently encourages a refusal to examine the evidence and, therefore, derails the production of that careful understanding necessary for the establishment of new horizons of knowledge. Undoubtedly, Evans-Pritchard, as anyone, is likely to be found wanting, but the Azande ethnography displays a careful rigour that does not leap to unexamined comparisons. There is a constant reflective dialogue in the study between Evans-Pritchard's own encounter with phenomena and that of the Azande.

More immediately, Evans-Pritchard, by the bracketing or decentring of Zande magical practice, loosened the hold of post-Enlightenment European thought that unselfcritically submitted others to the authority of its own ideas and obscured vital dimensions of the phenomena encountered. Therein lay the difficulty with the intellectualist perspectives of Sir James Frazer's *The Golden Bough*, which celebrated modernist secularism and its scientific rationalism. Here the question was begged concerning the genealogical connection between non-Western magical practice and science, assuming that magical practices constituted a lower and preliminary form of the Western rational intellect. Magical practices were conceived as addressing the same kinds of problems as modern science and, thus, were viewed as pre-modern and inferior. Malinowski's (1954, 1922) approach towards Trobriand magic is an extension of such Frazerian intellectualism, as is Lévi-Strauss's (1966) description of non-Western magical practices as 'the science of the concrete'. However, I hasten to add that Lévi-Strauss, unlike the others, does not imply a hierarchialisation of thought. He stresses that the same intellectual capacities are involved, but that they are directed towards different problems and concerns. Magical thought (or mythic thought) is thoroughly empirical. In this sense it is a precursor to science, but otherwise its forms of abstraction, which deal with the problematics of existence within the limits of particular cultural and social constructions, are entirely different from science. In Lévi-Strauss's approach, magic and science are still different sides of the same coin.

Evans-Pritchard effectively questioned the intellectualist implication that science (and associated logical rationalism) and magical practice necessarily can be aligned along the same axis. Here he shared much with the earlier argument of the French philosopher, Lévy-Bruhl. Evans-Pritchard rejected what he took to be Lévy-Bruhl's racist suggestion that distinctions in mentality underpinned the different logical practice involved in Western rationalism as distinguished from others. This was possibly a misreading of Lévy-Bruhl. However, both refused scientific rationalist claims, such as those by the anthropologist Edward Tylor, that magical practice in non-Western societies was illogical because beliefs and ideas subverted the real relation between cause and effect. As later generations of anthropologists (and philosophers of science, especially) were to demonstrate, if this was so, then this was also the case with rational and scientific understanding. Lévy-Bruhl (1923) located the distinction between magic and science in different structures of reasoning altogether, stressing the notion of 'participation' or the thoroughgoing identity of human existence with its natural and cosmic environment, taking up dimensions that Lévi-Strauss (1968a, 1968b) was later to explore more complexly. Nonetheless, the externalist perspective from the position of science still dictated the understanding of the magical. Here Evans-Pritchard made a further innovation. He showed that Azande magical practice was directed towards specific matters at hand. It was an everyday, practical knowledge, thoroughly different from scientific rationalism as idealised – a practice completely unconcerned with contradiction and system coherence of the scientific sort.

In other words, when all was said and done and the ethnographic evidence was in, there was a unity between practices of the Azande and those of others. Magical practice is akin to what Husserl (1988), Schutz (1970) and other phenomenologists refer to as the 'natural attitude' and is grounded in ordinary experience mediated through cultural categories. Basically, this is what Evans-Pritchard meant when he insisted that witchcraft was simply part of routine Zande expectations. To the Azande, magic, sorcery and especially witchcraft are not concerned with the extraordinary in the sense conveyed by the term 'occult', which is increasingly being used to describe contemporary manifestations in metropolitan and peripheral territories. The comparison between Azande and Western scientific rationalism is a false family resemblance (Wittgenstein 1979, Winch 1958) and, although pursued by some (e.g. Horton 1993), achieves an inaccurate opposition that denies a unity or similarity with diverse practices elsewhere as a formation of common sense founded in different historical and cultural constructions of reality.

This is not to suggest that in his Azande ethnography Evans-Pritchard somehow broke anthropology away from its Enlightenment roots. His work is directed towards the question of reason and towards exploring the varieties and limits of practical reason or rationality. There is no singular or ultimate form of practical reason, and this is because of its thoroughly social character. This social grounding, extending from the ideas of Durkheim and Mauss, is vital in the psychological dimensions of magical, and especially witchcraft, experience.

As Evans-Pritchard describes, the troubled dreams that Zande have are populated with everyday social problematics. The apparent illogicality (to the external observer) of magical and witchcraft practice reveals its logic in the complexities and specificities of social practice. To put it another way, magic and witchcraft derive the logic of their illogicality in social processes. Reason, always a social practice, is limited by this self-same social factuality and can never establish a 'pure' perfect form in social contexts. Magic and witchcraft are particular manifestations of this fact.

Furthermore, the limitation of practical reason is in its totalising character. The magical and witchcraft practices of the Azande are specific instances of widespread forms of totalisation. Paradoxically, such totalisation lies in the hyperrationalism of magic and witchcraft, not in its irrationalism. Thus, the Azande assert the thorough interconnection of existential events as these relate to human experience. This totalisation emerges in the human-centric, person-centred and social nature of witchcraft's practical reason that gives prime force to human agency. That is, human agency is the factor which brings otherwise independently caused events into conjunction. A famous Zande instance that Evans-Pritchard uses concerns the grain bin that collapses, killing those Zande who chose just that moment to seek its shade. In witchcraft reasoning, it is human agency that effects such a conjunction, an agency that is so totalising that it can operate independently of the conscious awareness of the witch. In Evans-Pritchard's account, it is the unconscious dimension of witchcraft that distinguishes it from sorcery, which is motivated by conscious intent.

One of the more important implications of Evans-Pritchard's study is that magic and witchcraft are not part of a clearly bounded and internally consistent 'system' of knowledge. If anything, they are vital in a continually expanding and incorporating system of open horizons. Magic and witchcraft are always contextually relative, situationally adaptive, never abstract. The 'system' of ideas and practices of which they are part is constantly immanent, enduringly emergent, differentiating and shifting in response to new circumstance. Thus, in Evans-Pritchard's study of magical and witchcraft practices are the seeds of a dynamic approach to social life as a whole, even an asystemic perspective, which was to break beyond the more static Durkheimian vision that nonetheless gave the work its initial impetus.

Overall, it is easy to see why the Azande work became so inspirational for a relatively fledgling discipline such as anthropology, and why, also, it should be a major reference for an anthropology that is in the throes of reinventing itself. The Azande study, as well as its subject matter of magic, sorcery and witchcraft, refuses neat categorisation. In many ways it transgressed established conventions in the discipline and, in hindsight, threatened other perspectives that were yet to be made; even now, it presents new avenues of investigation and interpretation. Above all, it moved in the direction of liberating the Other (the Azande as a generic Other) from the chains of a Western intellectual hegemony: from either being that which was to be transcended or being that which was the ill-fated precursor of what was to come. With Evans-Pritchard, phenomena such as magic and sorcery and those peoples conceived as being at the periphery of metropolitan and scientific knowledge who continued to practise them were given positive place as well as authority and an active role in the advancement of human understanding.

Expansions and Retreats

Since Evans-Pritchard, magic and sorcery have continued to be engaged in discourses concerning rationality, especially with regard to questions in the philosophy of science. In some respects the critical implications of Evans-Pritchard's study have been ignored or deflected. Horton (1993), for example, has sustained the science-witchcraft axis of discussion. So too did Gluckman (1972, 1971, 1956), although he broadened magic and witchcraft into general metaphors for faulty reasoning or bad thinking, whether this be in science or in politics. A student of Evans-Pritchard, and following Michael Polanyi (1998), Gluckman applied Azande witchcraft logic to explain why poor scientific theories were upheld despite contradictory evidence. The answer was in the biasing and selection of evidence, the fact that the theory as a whole was never put into question, and so on. There was perhaps an anticipation of Thomas Kuhn's (1962) famous work, *The Structure of Scientific Revolutions*, in Gluckman's approach. However, he was chiefly interested in moments of systemic transformation through which new forms of thought and practice would come into play. Gluckman had in mind the shameful commitment to unreason of his native South Africa, then bound by the chains of apartheid. He was concerned with the circumstances whereby it would come to its rational senses and escape the prison of its particular logic of the absurd. But the main features of witchcraft and magic upon which he concentrated were their appearance at points of social conflict or in the fissures of social and political contradictions and disjunctions. They were the forms of reason which appeared in those spaces where other modes of reasoning failed. For Gluckman, 'magic' and 'witchcraft' were generalised forms of reasoning that were the privilege of any and every social reality. They were not located in the conventional anthropological territories of the peripheralised Other; rather, they were vital in all systems – functional simultaneously in their reproduction and in their failure. Gluckman in many ways destroyed the aura of exoticism that surrounded the subjects of magic and witchcraft and revealed further their social dynamics, which were sometimes obscured by the concern with their exotic features.

A major orientation pursued by Gluckman, his students and colleagues, and in different ways by many other anthropologists, was the social basis of belief. The factuality of belief (and of culture conceived as an organisation of belief) and the commitment of human beings to beliefs (including those relating to magic, witchcraft and sorcery) are properties of social processes. They are not to be reduced to the character of beliefs in and of themselves. In other words, no belief is necessarily absurd, true or false in itself but achieves such characteristics in the contexts of the structuring of social relations. Furthermore, for the kind of anthropology that Gluckman and other social anthropologists advocated, this social understanding created a form of comprehension that was missed in other disciplines, such as an individually centred psychology.

The Durkheimianism that underscored such a position (as well as the academic politics of a young discipline, especially in the British context, desirous of demonstrating its specific theoretical expertise) undoubtedly influenced a neglect of psychological factors, especially the importance of the psychoanalytic contribution. Obeyesekere (1981) presented a well-known trenchant critique in favour of the importance of a psychoanalytic perspective, a point well demonstrated by other anthropological work (Spiro 1979; Devereux 1974, 1970). There is, however, always the intensification and exacerbation of a discourse of pathology that continues to dominate most discussions of magical and sorcery practice, as Obeyesekere's (1981, 1975) own research illustrates. An orientation towards pathology, especially with regard to sorcery and witchcraft, of course, is also strong in social perspectives of a Durkheimian kind, as well as others. These, too, are prone to psychologism, especially that which continues the nineteenth-century concern with origins, as Durkheim's *The Elementary Forms of the Religious Life* (1915) well demonstrates.

In their understanding of witchcraft practice, many anthropologists have pursued as a sociological argument one that is essentially psychologistic. An example is Marwick's (1965) view of Chewa sorcery as a mechanism for the release of social tensions. Such psychologism is probably integral to the enduring functionalism of much anthropology; this is particularly evident in the field of magic and sorcery, given their powerful pragmatic intent. But obviously psychoanalysis should not be confused with psychologism. Psychoanalytic themes, such as the dynamics of desire, the imaginary and fantasy, which are of direct relevance to the social construction and force of magical forms, are to be neglected at considerable cost to an anthropological understanding. Some anthropologists are developing understanding from psychoanalytic perspectives (e.g. Lambek, chapter 8; Taussig 1997), though they remain in the minority.

A Neo-Durkheimian Intervention

Mary Douglas (1973, 1970), also Durkheimian in her emphasis, nonetheless pushed the understanding of magical practices in innovative ways. She reaffirmed the social foundation of sorcery and witchcraft practices, further shifting the anthropological gaze away from the problematics of reason and rationality. She also helped to keep studies of sorcery and witchcraft from being bogged down in a kind of microsociology of group conflict and tension, a major legacy of the Manchester tradition in social anthropology and a still continuing focus of many anthropologists. These redirections may have been impelled by her anti-psychologism, with psychologism perhaps being viewed as a risk in discussions of rationality and reason as well as in a sociology that becomes focused on individual intentions and motivations (as did much Manchester anthropology). Douglas returned to a primary concern with the social structures and frames within which certain kinds of personal practice and cultural strategies are associated and produced.

Adopting a comparative approach (the strength of both Durkheim and especially Mauss), she aimed to build greater understanding using detailed ethnographic findings but without becoming trapped in the specific case, as happens in so much anthropology. Simultaneously, she was concerned to avoid the traps of comparativism, for example, what Leach (1961) described as Frazerian 'butterfly collecting' in which disparate bits of ethnographic information were brought together willy nilly without attention to differences of form and context to illustrate and compound either trivial understanding or knowledge that was already assumed or accepted. Her interest, too, was to avoid the risks of cultural essentialism and social homogenising whereby societies or practices were lumped together in boxes or categories without attention to internal diversity and complexities of mix. These aims underlie Douglas's (1973) comparative constructs of grid (e.g. degrees of shared social classification) and group (e.g. degrees of boundedness, social distinction, separation), which she presented as two intersecting continua forming a topological space into which could be plotted kinds of practices and their structural associations. The final, general success of Douglas's efforts is due to her imaginative exercise which opened up possibilities for categorising practices such as witchcraft and sorcery in a sociologically meaningful way. She was able to reveal similar social processes underlying ethnographically distinct sorcery and witchcraft practices.

The Grid and Group of Witchcraft and Sorcery Practice

Witchcraft and sorcery are concepts that are frequently used interchangeably, and some anthropologists have challenged the validity of their distinction, seeing them as different aspects of an often obsessive concern with human agency (Kapferer 1997, Turner 1964). However, Douglas's grid-group schema suggests why a sociological distinction between sorcery and witchcraft may be significant and useful, or at least why such a distinction may be 'good to think with', even if it is not easily workable in diverse empirical contexts.

Actions can be attributed to sorcery or witchcraft at different moments in the social process or dependent on one's standpoint, as Victor Turner (1964) suggested. Nevertheless, it is worth considering some of the important dynamics that a conceptual distinction can highlight.

Douglas's concepts of grid and group are especially sensitive to different dynamics of bounding (of body, person and group) and, therefore, of transgression. These achieve further significance in relation to her concerns with such aspects as degrees of personal control and freedom, as these are affected by rules and other restrictions on conduct. As Douglas herself recognised, not only does her orientation point up salient features permitting a useful, sociological definitional distinction to be drawn between sorcery and witchcraft (one which is not overly absolutist or exclusionary), but also, and perhaps more importantly, Douglas's approach indicates in what spheres of social action witchcraft or sorcery-like forms are likely to be present, as well as the social conditions and processes for their creation or production. The perspective is suggestive as to why certain forms might appear to be prevalent in certain contexts or situations. Influenced by Douglas's approach, it is possible to construct a distinction between witchcraft and sorcery as Weberian ideal-types, which may assist in extending an understanding of their differential cultural, social and historical significance.

Typifications of sorcery, real or imagined, might include more than the fact that it is conscious, intentional action usually performed by specialists in the arts of magical rite. Such specialists are often socially marginal or in some way external to or outside of the populations that they serve. Kings are often described as supreme sorcerers in the ethnographic literature and can be conceived as outside the polities they determine or encompass (see de Heusch 1985, 1982; Kuper 1969; Gluckman 1971, 1954). Skilled sorcerers and magical practitioners often come from low status or outcast communities. A major feature of sorcery is its ambivalence. It is typically protective and destructive, the conjunction of these forces being integral to its potency. This is an aspect of the sorcery of healing practices, for example, that engage poisons to cure. Connected with the potent ambiguity of sorcery is its common figuration as intensely transgressive and violent, a force that is capable of crossing boundaries between persons and groups as well as enforcing them. Sorcerers sometimes achieve this by changing shape and by overcoming the ordinary barriers of time and space.

Witchcraft, unlike sorcery, often involves little in the way of overt magical or ritual practice (some European traditions aside, which I would typify rather as sorcery). It is unambiguously malevolent and death-dealing and highly immoral rather than amoral, amorality being an aspect of sorcery's ambiguity. Moreover, witchcraft is a potential quality of everyone and is deeply integral to the person. The Zande provide the model with their notion that witchcraft is a physically recognisable substance (*mangu*), located somewhere near the lower intestine, which is activated in the course of social action. Witchcraft as a dimension of the person is also deeply part of ordinary, ongoing social relations and courses along them (see Rio, chapter 5). It is intrinsic to the 'magicality' of social forces (the emotional and psychological energies that flow with them) that draw human beings into social relations (Kapferer 1997: 231–2, Sartre 1966) and hence necessitates little in the way of overt magical manipulation, as in the magical practice of sorcery. While, like sorcery, witchcraft is thoroughly transgressive, it is generated from the ambiguities and contradictions of sociality (rather than being ambiguous in itself) and is thoroughly integral to the social patterns of exchange and reciprocity (which witchcraft reveals as being themselves potentially transgressive). Whereas sorcery may be engaged to force reciprocity and exchange (the Trobriand *kula* provides illustration; see Munn 1986, Malinowski 1922) and comes from outside, witchcraft, more typically, is already integral to social relations and arises from them. Witchcraft is frequently conceived as emerging from within the community, fragmenting it from the inside.

I should emphasise that sorcery and witchcraft so typified are not mutually exclusive. Indeed, in ethnographic contexts their character as typified here is often intimately related. What is seen to be sorcery is often being presented as the openly violent and legitimate response to a more covert or hidden aggression against the person or community. Witchcraft can become sorcery in the process of its exclusion and the redefining of community bounds. Sorcery is a public reaction, and the dangerous, volatile, potentially rebounding quality of its revengeful force (sorcery, in effect, embodies the dangers of reciprocity and the transgressive potentiality of sociality) is one impetus behind both its ritual control and the social marginalisation of its practitioners who must bear sorcery's risks. Ordinary people who practise sorcery in Sri Lanka, for example, typically go outside their everyday contexts to practise it. This going outside is also part of sorcery's potency (see Kapferer 1997, 1988).

As the foregoing indicates, the forms of sorcery and witchcraft are likely to occur in different social dynamics and social space within the one broad social context. Sorcery action is hedged about with protective practices and involves, in some way or another, going outside, that is, becoming removed from the ordinary, routine lived-in world. Witchcraft or witchcraft-like effects, such as the 'evil eye', emerge in the intense spaces of everyday sociality and often involve close kin. Harrison's (1993) excellent study of a Sepik people in Papua New Guinea demonstrates a similar pattern, with powerful sorcery and magic occurring in the highly ritualised occasions of male cults organised for war and the assertion of communal boundaries. Contrastingly, what I refer to as witchcraft flows along the lines of marriage and kinship, cross-cutting communities and catching victims unawares in the vulnerability of their openness to others (in the magicality of sociality).

Following Douglas's lead, it is possible that the proportional mix of sorcery to witchcraft beliefs and practices within societies, and in comparison between them, is related to the kinds of social forces that determine their structural dynamics and processes. Douglas suggests that socio-cultural and historical realities that are highly differentiated internally, that manifest strong internal divisions and boundaries, and that express widely shared schemes and codes of social and personal control (often restrictively so) are likely to have sorcery as a major mode of practice rather than witchcraft. In societies that are relatively flexible and are not highly socially differentiated, in which the boundaries and divisions between persons and communities are not strongly marked, and in which personal and social codes of conduct are diverse and relatively non-restrictive, witchcraft is likely to be common.

There is much ethnography that might appear to give some support to the kind of thesis that can be developed from Douglas's approach. Thus, in various societies in Central and Southern Africa, witchcraft rather than sorcery appears to be the dominant form, and this appears to be associated with social forces, for example, that encourage movement and the regular break-up and formation of new settlements; fairly weak social boundaries crossed by kinship ties that articulate diverse localities; and little in the way of powerfully socially differentiated hierarchies. Witchcraft, as many ethnographies have indicated, is both a function and a cause of the socially labile character of many Central African contexts, being integral to a constant process of redefining and restructuring social and political relations (see Douglas 1973, 1970; Marwick 1965; Van Velsen 1964; Mitchell 1956). There are aspects of the Central African contexts that bear some resemblance to Melanesian materials as others have noted (especially Kelly 1993), despite the fact that it is often described as sorcery.

I note the emphasis that several ethnographers of witchcraft/sorcery in Melanesia place on the notion of the person (Strathern 1990) and what may be called the 'permeable Self' whereby persons are continually open to being intruded upon, usually by kin within their communities but also from outside. Dreaming is often an indication of this permeation of the Self by others (Lattas 1998). Intense fear of sickness and suspicions of death motivated by persons with whom one is socially involved are routine expressions. Witchcraft is the potentiality of 'good company' (Knauft 1985). Such ideas support frequent stigmatising accusations of witchcraft which, as elsewhere, provoke revenge and demands for compensation. Most people are potentially open to accusation, but widely feared sorcerers are somewhat different. They are loners, highly individuated and to some extent set apart from others. Among the Mekeo (Stephen 1996), these are persons who have hardened, bounded selves, who are not easily permeated and who intentionally and by magical means invade and destroy others (see also Knauft 1985).

Some groups among Australian Aborigines may be more oriented to magical action that can be typified as sorcery. Such groups manifest complex hierarchies of finely discriminated kinship relations, widely shared codes controlling kin activity and relations with strangers, and forms of authority powerfully backed by rituals of social and territorial regulation. All of this seems to be associated with the kind of sorcery that is practised: frequently highly ritualised, involving shape-changing and the capacity of the sorcerer to act simultaneously in more than one place at once, entering the bodies of his victims unbeknownst to them. Remarkable in this sorcery is its extreme transgressive character, with sorcerers describing the terrible physical-sexual destruction they visit on the victims they kill (see, for example, Burbank 2000, Berndt and Berndt 1989, Warner 1937).

Elaborate forms of magic and highly visible forms of sorcery are apparent throughout a number of contexts in South and South-East Asia. Here, social, political and religious hierarchies strongly differentiate communities, influencing the formation of sharp social and physical boundaries between them (of caste, class and ethnicity) that are often mutually reinforcing. In addition, there are widely shared codes and rules regulating social intercourse which also produce considerable social distance. Hindu India and Buddhist Sri Lanka provide numerous examples. Frequently, the beings of sorcery in these contexts are transcendent god-like or demonic figures who are extraordinarily violent, amoral beings. Janus-faced creatures of the boundary and of the margins, they are oriented simultaneously as destroyers, protectors and creators (see Obeyesekere 1984; in these pages, Kapferer, chapter 4; Bastin, chapter 6).

Other histories and other places are fertile in the construction of the images and imaginaries of the sorcerer and of demonic forms and practices. These appear to be associated with the destruction and formation of social and political hierarchies; the production of huge social cleavages founded in slavery or built upon transmutations of, for instance, feudalism; and the generation of modes of class domination together with the erection of all kinds of social and political barriers. Well-known examples relate to the fears and imaginaries of sorcery and the demonic in Europe during the 'witch craze' (Ginzburg 1983, Cohn 1975, Harris 1974). *Vodou* (also *candomblé, santaria*) in South and Central America and the Caribbean, formed from the practices of West African slaves, constituted its potencies in the social forces of despair, degradation and annihilating revolution (see Brendbekken, chapter 2). Contemporary practices of demon exorcism that take place in some Pentecostalist churches in North America and Europe or the exculpation of sorcerers in the Zionist African churches of southern Africa refract forces of social differentiation, exclusion and marginalisation (Csordas 1994, Pauw 1975).

A major contribution of Douglas's perspective is that it opens up the exploration of magic, sorcery and witchcraft to an anthropological understanding of social processes as formations of force and power. Their imaginal structure reflects this, and it is where psychoanalytic interpretations, for example, should be important (see Devisch, chapter 7; Lambek, chapter 8). However, Douglas points not just to the social grounding of sorcery and witchcraft constructions of the imaginary, but also to the distinctive force and even appeal that such imaginary may have. Here I concentrate on the magical practice of sorcery.

Sorcery as the Imaginal Face of Power

As indicated here, sorcery is that imaginal formation of force and power that is to be expected in social circumstances that are disjunctive or in some sense discontinuous. Its concept in many different ethnographic contexts revolves around its magical capacity to work with the very potencies of difference, differentiation, division, opposition, contradiction and transgression. It gathers the force of such potencies, harnessing them to the purpose of destruction or to conjunction. Sorcery makes the disjunctive conjunctive, the discontinuous continuous, the weak powerful. As Mary Douglas's work suggests, sorcery builds its force in the gaps, exclusions and marginalisations of social processes. These have potency; they are the positive of the negative. In this sense, sorcery is a thoroughgoing force of the social and the political. It is there in what is excluded, in remainders, in what is cast out, in dirt, in what social and cultural energies generate as disgust, as the terrible infraction of moral code and personal conduct (see Telle, chapter 3; Kapferer, chapter 4; Devisch, chapter 7).

Pursuing such observations further, extreme forms of sorcery and the demonic are likely to be highly apparent in contexts of state power. They are forces acutely generated in the social and political conditions of the state – the state as a centralised, differentiating and bounded entity – and represent its dreadful force. This is very apparent in cosmic states. In mediaeval Sri Lanka, only the king was able to exercise the magical potencies of sorcery (Peiris 1956). Among the Zulu, the supreme sorcerer is the king (Gluckman 1954). That this is so indicates the nature of the power of the king, who creates or re-creates the social order (as in the annual rites of kingship in Asia, Polynesia and Africa) and does so through fearful acts of exclusion and inclusion. The power of the king as sorcerer, I suggest, is in what he can force together in spite of the socially differentiating and divisive potencies that may fragment the king's order. Such potency is not merely in the king's capacity to order, but in the way he orders. Ordering is a hierarchialising and territorialising phenomenon, specifically when involved in state formation (see Deleuze and Guattari 1988). Its totalising dynamic involves a process of systemic inclusion and also systemic exclusion, a divisive and separating process. In some societies this is a sacrificial dynamic which is not only central to the kingship but also a dimension of the sorcerer. In these situations the power of the sorcerer is in what is excluded and in what is remaindered. King and sorcerer are alternative images of each other (the mythologies of Europe and of Asia often resonate with such themes). I stress that the force of king and state is in the sacrificial and sorcerous dynamic of destruction, division (differentiation) and exclusion, out of which order (sometimes conceptualised as the order of society) is created (see Kapferer, chapter 4, also 1997). Acts of violent destruction are integral to the (re)formation of king and state. By destroying, dividing and cutting, the power of the king as the sorcerer is generated. Thus, the sorcery of the power of king and state is oriented towards violence. Contemporary states are very different from cosmic states, which are the main contexts for the observations I make here (see de Heusch 1985, 1982; Valeri 1985), but perhaps they too have a sorcerous power in which their constitutive ordering force must be bound with the energies of destruction and exclusion (see Gulbrandsen, chapter 9; Feldman, chapter 10). Such destruction must be a recurring phenomenon as the sorcerous potential is generated in what is excluded. That which is excluded is re-created as a force that reactively threatens to rejoin that from which it has been separated, and therefore to destroy that whose very order or coherence depends upon the exclusion.

The Magic of Modernity: Fragmentations of Power

Most recent studies of magic and cultic practice, of sorcery and witchcraft, powerfully insist that these practices are thoroughly modern. The point has particular poignancy in a discipline often accused of traditionalism and exoticism. Magic, sorcery and ritual are virtually synonymous with the exotic and the 'traditional' past. Therefore, those scholars who assert that current practices of sorcery and magic are not merely addressing current crises but are often the inventions of these selfsame crises are not only making a valid empirical observation, they are making a point in the politics of a discipline frequently criticised as indulging in exoticism. Such a view is particularly relevant in a postmodern and post-colonial discourse – especially given the subject matter – in which anthropologists are anxious to rid themselves of their colonialist past. However, there is also a concern to change the focus of theoretical orientations in anthropology, to address magic, sorcery and witchcraft in postmodern and deconstructionist terms. The reorientation is away from the modernist visions of coherent systems, bounded cultures and societies that apparently demonstrated little internal diversity and an opposition to us/them contrasts that divided humanity from itself and, too often, appeared to serve the dominant interests of metropolitan power. But above all, in anthropology the drive has been towards understanding contemporary processes that an older, antiquarian and modernist anthropology – one concerned with witchcraft, sorcery and other exotic practices – might appear to threaten.

The apparent anti- or asystemic aspects of witchcraft and sorcery, including their anti-rationalism, have been picked up by deconstructionists and post-structuralists as anti-modernist and, in particular, antagonistic to the modernist state (Nietzsche 1961, 1954; Bataille 1993). Anthropologists have followed suit, and usefully so. However, certain risks are entailed. Paradoxically, the vision of magic and sorcery that Bataille (1988) and others drew upon is in itself a modernist one, and the approaches to magic and sorcery that scholars such as Frazer and Lévy-Bruhl put forward at the turn of the last century are being replayed. In other words, there is a danger of reintroducing modernist thought of an extraordinarily rationalist kind under the guise of being up to the minute and currently relevant. This is perhaps less problematic if it can be demonstrated that the postmodern modernism of current ideas and practices engaging such kinds of analysis or understanding are thoroughly integral to present-day contexts. While the world is modern everywhere, even in those regions that may still count as remote, there are multiple ways of being modern, and different conceptions of magic and sorcery may nonetheless hold sway despite a historical intertwining (see Brendbekken, chapter 2; Kapferer, chapter 4; Gulbrandsen, chapter 9). But even so, the reintroduction of a rationalist modernism in a new form threatens a degree of superficiality, an anti-anthropology, which pays insufficient attention to the diverse structures and processes in which differential modernities are constructed and which form various kinds of magical, sorcery and witchcraft practices.

The foregoing observations in no way reduce the importance of empirical recognitions that much sorcery and witchcraft now current in Africa (notwithstanding problematic assertions that it is on the increase) were fomented in the discourses of colonialism and post-colonialism. Legal proscriptions, part of the modernising project of colonialism, were a factor in reinventing sorcery as a potent force of modernity, a force resistant to colonial authority and alive in the ambiguities of post-coloniality. Brought within the legal system, sorcery and witchcraft have now become legitimate references before the law (see Geschiere 1997). This move was opposed by anthropologists at the time, although from the standpoint of a modernist modernising position rather than a post-colonial or postmodern one. Elsewhere, as in Indonesia, sorcery was not proscribed yet is no less modern; that sorcery was not proscribed may account for some of the differences from those practices described for Africa (Ellen 1993). An analysis of witch cleansing cults in Africa, both towards the end of colonial rule and now in an era of globalisation, reveals them as refracting major moments of redefinition of state political orders. In certain instances today, they are part of a dynamic of what is called 'villagisation' or the creation of communities outside the order of the state, which in many African contexts is in crisis and collapsing violently into itself (see Devisch 1996). Some of these and other African religious movements (Zionist churches in South Africa, the Lenshina movement in Zambia) can be seen as engaged in a 'de-sorcelling' of the state. They address the state effects of abjection, recognising in sorcery and witchcraft the destructive force of power.

In southern Africa, and especially in post-apartheid South Africa, the combination of intensified hope (an excess of desire) and the end of racial barriers is contradicted by the creation of stronger class hierarchies and boundaries within the African population. This is a process complicated by growing economic distress in the global context of transformations in capital and the creation of new aspects of foreign imperial control. Sorcery encapsulates the violence of new politically and economically conditioned fears and struggles. Its monstrous symbolism and matching practices at once assume the phantom shape of the destructive, implacable and apparently irresolute forces of everyday life, and attempt to strike directly at them (see Ashforth 2000; Niehaus et al. 2001; Comaroff and Comaroff 1999, 1993).

The terrible shape of the Sinhala god of sorcery, Suniyam, a being largely created in the circumstance of British rule and burgeoning in popularity in the reformations of post-coloniality, is another illustration of the modernity of witchcraft. Supplicants visit him to appeal to his violent 'justice' to punish enemies and to force remote government bureaucrats to act in their behalf (see Kapferer, chapter 4, also 1997, 1988; Bastin, chapter 6). Taussig's (1980) classic study of commodity fetishism and the Faustian dangers of devil pacts in Colombia (see also Nash 1979) presents these practices as a refraction of the intensities of social and economic contradictions at the margins of the expansion and transformation of metropolitan-based power. Taussig's work prefigures the more recent studies of African sorcery that stress the explosion of what Lacanian psychoanalysis would recognise as a politics of desire, a 'politics of the belly', and an overdetermination of consumption (see Bayart 1999, 1993; Friedman 1994). These studies also describe sorcery as having been refigured as the magical means for the protection of elite and vested class interests, as in Mobutu's Zaire or Papa Doc's Haiti.

Post-colonial Rationalities

Such processes, despite their localised symbolic forms and specificities of practice, are stressed in much postmodern and post-colonial anthropology as being
particular manifestations of more general political processes. They are as much
present at the centre as at the periphery, where the general forces driving them
(contradiction in capital, the failure of the modernist state) may be more
extremely manifest (Taussig 1980). The local often appears 'exotic' because it is
seen from the perspective of another local context. The critical point is that the
apparent 'otherness' constructed in a previous and modernist anthropology obscures the underlying political and economic processes of a general kind that, in
particular historical and social contexts, drive the differences (see Kapferer 2001,
1997, 1988; Geschiere 1997). However, in the contemporary redemptive mood of
anthropology there is a further push to demonstrate that surface differences are
also part of the underlying similarities. More than being a metaphor of practices
in the metropolitan centres of modernity (a method of self-exoticisation via the
Other), the magical is thoroughly integral in the modern or modernity everywhere: the magical structures of the surface are working at depth.

  Thus, the power of the modern state springs from the magical force of a hegemony forged through state constructions of nationalism, whereby populations
achieve an immediate unity with its objects – what Sir James Frazer described
as 'sympathetic magic' (see Coronil 1997, Taussig 1997). Here is located the
unreason of the modern, its own absurdity. More expansively, Jean and John
Comaroff (2001, 1999, 1993) suggest that the forms of sorcery and other magical practices they find in South Africa are replicated elsewhere in New Age mysticism, in the Satanic cult scares involving child abuse in England, even in the
fantasies surrounding the markets in stocks and shares. All this and much more
is part of what they describe as 'millennial capitalism' and 'occult economies',
making implicit references to highly problematic anthropological arguments
concerning the 'proto-rationalist modernism' of millenarian cults in Papua New
Guinea and other places (see Worsley 1970). There is a strong tension in their
analyses to reproduce earlier functionalisms, given their stand that such practices – modern sorcery and occultism especially – are conditioned in contemporary circumstances of vulnerability and uncertainty. This skirts close to earlier
positions that treated sorcery and witchcraft as pathological indicators of social
breakdown (see Redfield 1941) rather than being generated in specific kinds of
structural dynamics which, as part of their ordering or structurating process,
generate forces that are embodied in the forms that magical beliefs and practices
take (see Bastin, chapter 6). The reduction to arguments based on notions of
'vulnerability' and 'uncertainty' reintroduces the psychologism of functionalism
and reinsists a foundationalism that deflects analysis away from considering
mediating structural dynamics. Moreover, there is a turning away from the particularities of the phenomena, a tendency to lump them together under the
sign of the irrational which must await the true understanding of the anthropologist, the author of the rational. For all the insight, it may be wondered if

anthropology has not remained the same despite heralded changes. In the study of magic, sorcery and witchcraft, the nineteenth-century issue of the problem of reason has returned to centre stage. Whereas much current work (e.g. Taussig 1999) reconfigures such a problematic into a critique of reason and its tyrannies and aims to escape its rule, the Comaroffs reinstate the value of previous perspectives, though to necessarily weaker effect.

The old divide between the anthropological Self and the anthropological Other may have disappeared, the potential differences having been largely flattened out in a homogenising, globalising sweep. This contradicts the significance of the postmodern notion of multiple modernities, namely that there are many different ways of being modern, involving distinct histories and cultural and social orientations to reality, as well as the effects of intermingling and hybridising. The contradiction is even more problematic when diversity is subjected once more to the hegemony of dominant assumptions about the nature of reason and rationality in social practices. This is an important criticism that Bourdieu (2000) casts at both modernist and postmodernist anthropologists who leave unexamined the assumptions and logics implicated in their own analytical categories. Such was the major problem in Frazer's functionalism in which he applied his assumptions concerning others unreflexively and uncritically. To reverse and generalise the rational equation (humanity is united in a common irrationality), as is currently being done, sustains the hegemony of metropolitan assumptions rather than decentring them.

The crucial argument regarding modern magical practices concerns their disjunction from pasts (histories and cosmologies prior to modern periods, basically before the imperial expansions of the West) and the radical reconfiguration of the ideas and practices of the past in terms of the circumstances of the present. This position represents a major corrective to those orientations that see magical practices as survivals of tradition and refuse to attend to the import of their current reformulations in the political and social contexts of their use. It was an argument, excellently pursued by Gluckman and the Manchester school, which effectively indicated that the very appearance of traditional continuities was primarily a function of the political and social structural processes of the present. That they were reproduced in the present demanded a focus on their social situatedness rather than an approach that in effect dislocated them into contexts that were no longer in existence (primordialism) or reduced them to mentalistic predispositions (essentialism, psychologism). The force of this argument is one to which I personally and largely adhere.

However, this approach can threaten an oversociologisation of the phenomena in question or an excessive rationalisation of practices to the terms of an external view, a position that can effectively deny the very differences vital to the distinct modernity of practices and the particular articulation they form with broader structural processes. There is a seeming refusal to address the practices themselves, which even today are too often left exposed as anthropological exotica (of the very kind that has been disparaged) without much in the way of an attempt to enter within the terms of the symbolic structures that are manifested. A fuller consideration of what they are is avoided, while they are boxed away into familiar sociological and rational categories: witchcraft as resistance, witchcraft as the folk explanation of misfortune, or witchcraft and sorcery as types of 'social diagnosis' (Moore and Sanders 2001). The practices are domesticated to the analysts' own sensibilities. There is a tendency towards a too easy glossing of the phenomena in question, a brushing aside of dynamics that are not immediately and externally self-evident. Furthermore, such oversociologising and rationalising can disregard dimensions of practices – part of a 'sociology' already inherent in them – that are critical in the production of their distinct modernity (see Rio, chapter 5).

At the very great hazard of being misinterpreted, I suggest that there may be critical features of old practices that make them modern (beyond such generalities of the kind that they embed ambiguities, or make the abstract personal) and, indeed, impel them towards the present. Much sorcery practice in Sri Lanka, and ritual practice elsewhere (e.g. as reported for Papua New Guinea), derives its force from the fact that it fuses old practices onto the new, hybridises, and is 'foreign' and borrowed. Sorcery that is well tried loses its strength; its potency inheres in the new and in its fusion force (the most widely reported dynamic of sorcery). However, I cannot stress enough that the concept of 'traditional' – a thoroughly modernist notion – subverts the recognition that some practices which do have historical depth, and maybe because of it, possess internal dynamics that make them always already modern. Understanding how and why this may be so requires an analysis of their cosmologies and structural dynamics, the mythopoeia of their process (see Kapferer, chapter 4; Devisch, chapter 7). An externalist sociologising can encourage a turning away from such matters, thus overlooking the features of their dynamics that may, nonetheless, disclose 'sociological' aspects of the contexts within which they form an original articulation (Crick 1976).

Negative Cosmologies

The cosmologies that are implicated in much that is recognised as magical practice, sorcery and witchcraft are part of their contemporary force. They are often practices of cosmological fusion, in which all that is brought together has intensified or enlarged their innate potency in the potencies of that to which they are joined. In such fusion, cosmologies are frequently reconfigured and achieve their force in such restructuring. By cosmology I refer to a process whereby events, objects and practices are brought into a compositional unity, are conceived and patterned as existing together, and are in mutual relation. In this sense, magical practices and the conceptions and practices of sorcery and witchcraft constitute metacosmologies, that is, methods of patterning or bringing together acts, events or practices that may normally be expected to exist in different or separate cosmological frames. Their metacosmology is one that bridges or crosses different registers of meaning and practice (their hybridising energy) and frequently is a dynamic of negation. Much sorcery, for example, gathers its force by systematically negating dominant cosmological forms (the terror of its destructive agency) or else by breaking apart elements of other cosmological schemes in order to effect unions or crossovers that might otherwise be impossible. Magical practice and sorcery are major sites of invention, and their method of invention (a cosmology of invention) is to attack the very ways in which human beings routinely are seen or conceived to construct their realities. They work simultaneously on the basis of surface appearances and at depth, often constraining that which they address to the cosmological form which is emergent mythopoetically in the method of their constructive practice, frequently a dynamic of negation and appropriation.

Magical practices are rites in themselves (rites of the imagination and of abstract conception, as well as actual practices) and seldom come out of thin air. They work intuitively, which contributes to the explosion of the imaginary that is so often their feature. But they also do so by extending and adapting already available cosmologies, modes of constructing and patterning, to the pragmatics at issue, to the particularities of the case. Magic and sorcery may routinely be seen to operate at the boundaries of understanding, imaginatively and inventively so, but oriented, nonetheless, through structurating dynamics (even if radically negating them) that work with already conventional cosmologically patterned procedures.

The rites that are performed to counteract sorcery and witchcraft reveal the cosmologies (as negations) that are integral both to their conception and to their practice (see Telle, chapter 3; Kapferer, chapter 4; or Feldman's account of police torture in chapter 10). To put the case more strongly, the very cosmologies apparent in the diverse modernities of any ethnographic region, which already engage notions of witchcraft and sorcery as their negative discourse, may in certain situations of their reassertion or reinvention further enliven sorcery and witchcraft practices, though of course in original directions. This is Gulbrandsen's point (chapter 9) with reference to Botswana. Here, state ideological assertions stress a continuity with cosmologies of the past that are still contemporaneous in village practice. Contradictions are thus exposed which bring forth not only a relevant critical discourse of sorcery inherent in such cosmology, but also a regeneration of the fear of sorcery and of the violence that is associated with it.

An understanding of the cosmologies involved in sorcery, leaving aside the issue of their modernity, may also further an understanding of the violence associated with sorcery. As mentioned earlier in relation to the institutions of kingship and state, some practical cosmologies of sorcery indicate a sacrificial dynamic. Or, alternatively, the destructive actions of the sorcerer develop what is explicit in cosmologies that are founded in sacrifice. The sorcerer is a figure of both destruction and regeneration. His actions are centred in the differentiating crux of origination, from which life and death are produced. It is in the sorcerer's acts of destruction that life is also created or again made possible. The violent dismembering that often marks his practices is a mirroring in reverse of the differentiating, life-growth process.

Outside Reason: Virtuality and Magical Phantasmagoria

The importance of attending to the cosmologies of magical practice is that forms of reason or rationality that are not integral to the taken-for-granted understandings of the analyst may be revealed that better account for the practices being reviewed (Englund and Leach 2000). This perspective, one which is most developed in a relativist anthropology, is still committed to the problem of reason, if not a metropolitan or scientific reason. Distinct rationalities are discovered that may not be mutually reducible, but they are nonetheless systems of reason and in many anthropological perspectives are treated as being roughly equivalent, though approached in a different way. Reason – usually in a form with which the anthropologist is comfortable – is maintained.

However, it is possible that different cosmologies, particularly those connected with magic and sorcery, are not reducible in such ways. They may stand radically apart from reason, even outside reason. This is their maddening challenge to a discipline founded in the problem of reason. The labelling of these cosmologies as irrational, or what I have termed 'unreason', is paradoxically a way of forcing them within the bounds of reason, which may deny to magical practices and especially to much sorcery key qualities of their potency.

Much sorcery and magic are hybrid forms par excellence. They work at the boundaries and margins, in what Turner (1969) described as liminal spaces. Either they force together things that are normally held apart or they break apart that which is normally whole. This is refracted in the monstrous dimensions of sorcery objects, which are frequently an amalgam of different forms, or something in the process of changing shape – a being or object frozen in a transmogrifying instant, in the process of becoming-other, becoming-animal (see Deleuze and Guattari 1988). This process is one that is not yet subordinate to any system of reason or rule. Rather, it is a process at the moment of fusing or crossing different registers of meaning and reasoning. Such observations are problematic to a rationalising approach of anthropology that routinely conceives of sorcery and the magical as representations of social and political realities. The connection may at times be less direct; as I have suggested, magic and sorcery may be symbolisations of processes or dynamics that, in effect, reach beyond the limits of reason.

The very force of magic, sorcery and witchcraft (as could be said of a considerable amount of religious activity) is connected to their emergence in spaces apart from everyday life. Not only is their practice or occurrence motivated in spaces of disjunction, dislocation and discontinuity – in the breaks, blockages and resistances in the flow of everyday life – but also they elaborate their power and potentialities in such disjunctions, discontinuities and breaks. Magic and sorcery and the fear of witchcraft are imaginative irruptions formed in such processes. While oriented to overcome such breaks, they may yet elaborate further what can be called their own phantasmagoric space, an imaginal field whose force derives not so much by what it is representative of external to itself, but in the potentialities, generative forces, linkages and redirections that it opens up within itself (see Devisch, chapter 7).

My suggestion develops from Deleuze and Guattari's concept of virtuality. This is not to be seen as modular or representational of external realities but rather as a reality all its own, a dynamic space entirely to itself and subject to its own emergent logics. The cosmology in which its inner praxis is articulated has no necessary connection to realities external to it and no necessary internal consistency. Indeed, the imagery of what I call the phantasmagoric (virtual) space of magic and sorcery (and, also, much ritual) is likely to build out of numerous sources, both personal and historical (including that of other rites from the past and present). What I stress is that the potency of much magical practice is in this virtuality, which stands outside of all reason – even, perhaps, its own. As such it contains its own 'truth', which is not subject to any kind of falsification that exists independently of it. Furthermore, the potency of such phantasmagoric space, and of its practices, lies in its very irreducibility to externalities, which is achieved and effected through its imaginal formation.

Durkheim and Mauss consigned what they viewed as magic and sorcery to the realm of the profane. But as is implicit in their sacred-profane dichotomy, the force of the sacred, as well as the profane, is in the tension of their connection or in the forces generated by the dynamics of attraction and rejection, of formation and deformation created at the point of their intersection. Thus, these spaces often engage acts or substances that embody or produce such energies – faecal matter, intoxicating or hallucinogenic materials, objects of disgust and repulsion, acts of mutilation (see Telle, chapter 3; Gulbrandsen, chapter 9; Taussig 1987). What I describe as the virtual, phantasmagoric space of magic and of the sorcerer is a volatile site of structuration, neither essentially sacred nor profane. The terms 'sacred' and 'profane', of course, are largely rooted in a Judaeo-Christian discourse of good and evil, a discourse that has tended to dominate recent discussions of sorcery and witchcraft (see Moore and Sanders 2001). I wish to avoid such concerns here and to suggest further that the phantasmagoric or virtual spaces in which magical and sorcery practice work are largely amoral, the morality that may come to be applied to them being highly relative and contingent on a diversity of contextual considerations.

But to return to the key point, symbolic and interpretive anthropology is occasionally overdetermined in its commitment to match symbolic forms to empirical reality, to treat symbols as representations of the real. This overlooks the possibility that it is the lack of fit that is significant and the source of some potency. A consequence of the bizarre character of magical practice or the concern to sustain practices that appear to have no outward relevance to modernity is to force a distance between the symbolic and the lived-in world and, perhaps, to expand their pragmatic efficiency through a great diversity of contingencies – that is, to create a virtual or phantasmagoric space (Lambek, chapter 8; Obeyesekere 1981). In the context of such phantasmagoric space (clear examples are Buddhist and Hindu temples, which are the loci of much magical practice often relating to sorcery), people are able to establish their own original relation to existential reality and to reorient themselves into surrounding realities. Such phantasmagoric spaces enable individuals to form their own anxieties and concerns to the dynamic potencies of the spaces they enter. Here they can join and charge these potencies with their own intentional force, directing them towards objectives in the ordinary, daily world. The vital feature of such spaces, and of magical and sorcery practice as well, is that it is always already modern.

Perhaps we have reached a stage when the cycle of debate about the nature of reason with which much anthropology is still obsessed might be suspended, if not broken. This is not to ignore the insights that such interest has produced, as this discussion has indicated. But there is a limit to the understanding of reason, as Kant recognised long ago. A continuous commitment to the problems of reason and rationality can lead to an endless repetition of the same insights; occasionally, the observations are less penetrating than the first time around (compare statements made in the 1950s with those being made now).

Certainly, the phenomena of magic and sorcery have much bearing on reason and rationality, but their potential is much greater when released from the prison of reason. Evans-Pritchard's path-breaking work suggests as much. In his pages, magic and sorcery reveal qualities of the human imaginary in dream and in daily waking practice. These in their specifics broach serious questions as to the role of the imaginary or imaginal in the construction of realities and in the intuitive orientation of human beings to the processes of their ongoing existence. I refer here not to the imaginary or to intuition founded in a discourse of truth and falsity (to which a preliminary assertion that sorcery is fundamentally concerned with a universe of unreason and the illogical must return), but rather to their force as ever-present and necessary dimensions of human activity whereby reality, as always a human construction, takes shape. Magical and sorcery practices, which are thoroughly integral to the dynamic of human invention, acutely throw up the question of the imaginary: they are a major domain for the objectivated formation of the imaginary. This undoubtedly is constituted in socio-historical processes which in diverse ways embed memories – another field that the exploration of magical, cultic and sorcery practice opens up (see Feldman, chapter 10). But as forces of the imaginary, they press to the limits of human experience and beyond, breaking through the barriers of language and concept. They are among those human practices at the very centre of human creativity (positive or negative) and should be grasped more firmly in this regard than hitherto. As Lévi-Strauss recognised, sorcery and magic are the domains of the bricoleur in which novel constructions of reality are fashioned, where, indeed, 'cosmologies are in the making' (Barth 1987).

Magical practices are not merely the plane for the demonstration of a sociological or psychological theory – a folk instance of what we already know – but, for want of a better description, they display a 'machinery' of their own, a naive (unselfconscious) critique and investigation of the way human beings put themselves together socially and psychologically. In this way, they may extend towards a reconsideration of fundamental categories of understanding in the anthropological armoury: of reciprocity, the gift, sociality, and so forth. Furthermore, magical practices open out to a consideration of the formations of power, the dynamics of their cruelty and destructiveness. They may provide their own commentary on such matters, and it is to this possibility that anthropologists should be open (see Rio, chapter 5); in other words, they should accept the challenge of what they encounter and learn from it.

Nothing that I have said involves abandoning already established trajectories of anthropological analysis. Magical practice, sorcery, witchcraft, the cultic and ritual are fertile regions for the elaboration of perspectives developed in a variety of disciplines. These disciplines provide insight into the nature of these phenomena and, I think, dissolve them as forms of action, as somehow part of all human experience everywhere. But how this is so must not be done as some kind of article of faith or as merely an illustrative dimension of orientations – when all is said and done – that are radically antagonistic to the phenomena in question (see Feyerabend 1987). To do this is to shut away the potentialities encased in such practices that may be critical to the expansion and, indeed, the development of sociological theory and understanding.

I have been concerned to set the study of magical practice within an epistemological history of the social sciences and particularly anthropology. It is an area of vital interest because it embeds the thoroughgoing concern – that of the problematics of human reason and rationality – that has been, and remains, at the heart of anthropology's contribution. Magic and sorcery expose issues that are at the centre of the definition and redefinition of anthropology's project. They occupy critical turning points in the direction of the subject no less today than at the very beginning of the discipline. My aim here has been to outline an approach towards magic and sorcery that encourages a redrawing of their significance – not for an anthropology that mindlessly and resolutely holds on to a traditionalist exoticism, but rather for an anthropology that is committed to radically questioning conventional understandings of what it is to be a human being and to extend towards new horizons of knowledge. This was the adventure that began modern anthropology – and why I spent some time considering Evans-Pritchard's work – and it is crucially important that it should continue.

The Essays

These essays address and in numerous ways extend beyond the arguments in this introduction. The idea that underpins all of the essays is the concern to explore the potentially distinct insights that magical practices, sorcery and rite, and other rituals that appear to take their form, throw upon the social and political processes that give rise to them. The aim is to penetrate into the practices themselves in a way that reveals possibilities which a different anthropological approach might easily avoid, especially one that is still bound by the problems of rationality and is anxious to affirm the authority of metropolitan opinion. The essays here refuse to be limited by an anthropology of the surface.

Marit Brendbekken's (chapter 2) and Allen Feldman's (chapter 10) essays start and close this work. Both explore the effects of imperial history and the forces that joined the imperialists with those they dominated, as well as the creative, often terrible, forces that were unleashed. This is apparent in the *vodou* of the Dominican-Haitian borderlands that Brendbekken explores and in the inversionary forces and transmutations of historical memory that power magical practice. One of the exciting themes that Brendbekken pursues relates to the intertwining and mirroring of Self and Other that emerge in the hybridising spaces of the borderlands. This is a process that shows clearly how, for example, European conceptions of others are already bound up with themselves, that they are already generatively conjoined in the very differences they assert. Brendbekken concentrates on the mutual recognition and subversive relation of European anthroposophists and the *vodou*-practising peasants among whom the former conduct NGO work. The points she develops reflect back upon a critical understanding of anthropological approaches to the magical. Allen Feldman's essay draws us into the not dissimilar situation of South Africa and the work of the Truth and Reconciliation Commission, which must deal with the memories and pain of the state oppression of the apartheid years. He explores the sorcerous aspects, the impossible cruelties, that are associated with the tortures of the violent state. A feature of sorcery is that its fear and its violence also build and engage the banalities of ordinary existence; the commonplaceness of sorcery and sorcery-like practices is integral to their brutality.

Kari Telle (chapter 3) and Bruce Kapferer (chapter 4) explore rites that deal with transgression and its overcoming. Telle addresses directly the hidden and thoroughly transgressive dimensions of the sorcerous. Concentrating on theft (and notions that draw thieves within conceptions of witches) within a Muslim community in Lombok, she takes up the theme of smell (see also Feldman, chapter 10) and the dynamics of disgust as ambiguous potencies, disclosing the destructive agencies within communities, forcing their boundaries and also engaging in their ritual reconstitution. Telle expands on the ideas of Douglas, Kristeva, Taussig and others to reveal the threat and violence of subtle forces that permeate and dissolve boundaries rather than break them down. Kapferer focuses his discussion on the cosmology of sorcery among Sinhala Buddhists in Sri Lanka as this is revealed in a major anti-sorcery rite and in the urban sorcery shrines. The cosmologies connected with sorcery show how sorcery must always be more than mere sorcery and is centred in the heart of social and political processes and in the aporias of their constitution. He examines the sacrificial dynamic of sorcery, the critical aspects of its 'instituting imaginary' and the implicit critique of the state and its social orders to which sorcery practice directs attention.

Knut Rio (chapter 5) opens up, through Vanuatu materials, what I see as a new way of conceiving the lurking presence of sorcery and the terror that it conjures. Developing from Sartre, he demonstrates how sorcery operates like the absent third person who nonetheless conditions the circumstances and relations of the other parties. In this sense, sorcery is far more integral to the formation and structuring of social and political relations than many representational or symbolic perspectives in anthropology that concentrate on sorcery as expressing social problematics would indicate. Sorcery is attached to the very generative dynamics of the social and, as Rio shows, is a historical force as much as a product of history. This essay has strong resonances with others in this publication (especially those by Brendbekken and Feldman) that consider the issue of memory.

Rohan Bastin (chapter 6) returns the reader to Sri Lanka where he explores the technology of sorcery practice among Hindus and Buddhists. Bastin shows the differentiated character of sorcery and its distribution across a plethora of different sites, as well as its constantly cross-fertilising process, its hybridising and its rhizomic capacity to change domains and generate original meanings. Taking issue with approaches that continue to pathologise sorcery and related magical practices, he addresses directly their historically grounded 'creative dynamism'.

René Devisch (chapter 7) and Michael Lambek (chapter 8), both developing distinctive twists on overly neglected psychoanalytic themes, address the imaginary of sorcery. Devisch marvellously penetrates into the reality of the fetish among the Yaka in Kinshasa and Southwestern Congo. He reveals its potency to reside in its totalising force whereby it effects a complex link between the sensuous imaginary and other subliminal processes. Carefully articulating how the fetish is formed within its world and is able to enter into the whole existential realm of its victim, Devisch discloses how, through its 'economy of affect', the fetish kills. Lambek, too, draws us into the reality of the imaginary and the potency of its force. He takes anthropology to task (as did Obeyesekere before him) for too easily and simplistically dismissing Freud. One reason is the anthropological stress on the social and its lack of interest in arguments about fundamental drives, perhaps all the more problematic in a discipline currently critically alert to essentialism. But Lambek, through his Mayotte ethnography, demonstrates the imaginal formation of the social relational and how this relates to witchcraft and possession. He develops Obeyesekere's important work on the nature of public fantasies or what I have called phantasmagoric spaces.

With Ørnulf Gulbrandsen's essay (chapter 9) we turn explicitly to sorcery discourse and the structural and ideological dynamics of the state, themes that run through a number of the other essays. The essay directly addresses highly influential questions raised by the Comaroffs and others on the basis of African ethnography concerning the modernity of witchcraft and sorcery. Dealing with ritual murders in Botswana, Gulbrandsen demonstrates their thorough connection with globalising forces that throw up contradictions in a modernising discourse of the state. He shows the fear of ritual murders to be part of a cosmology of crisis, in which sorcery is a key discourse, connected with the modernist state's 'invention of tradition'.

The essays as a whole attempt to push the anthropological discussions of magical practices in new directions. They address epistemological issues at the heart of anthropological understanding and indicate how the worlds in which anthropologists work must force anthropology not only constantly to re-examine the value of past work, but also to extend towards new horizons of understanding.

ACKNOWLEDGEMENTS

I wish to thank the participants in a regular graduate seminar in the Department of Social Anthropology, University of Bergen, for the exciting context they provided in which the ideas that have formed part of this essay were discussed. It is among members of this seminar that the idea for this publication developed. Some of those who participated have also contributed essays. A preliminary version of this essay was presented before the School seminar in the School of Social Sciences, James Cook University. I wish to thank Rohan Bastin and also Dundi Mitchell for their comments, as well as the seminar as a whole. Olaf Smedal, Kari Telle, Tom Ernst, Judith Kapferer and Roland Kapferer have read through the final draft, and I am most grateful to them for their insightful comments.

BIBLIOGRAPHY

Appiah, A.K. *In My Father's House: Africa in the Philosophy of Culture*. Oxford, 1992.
Ashforth, A. *Madumo: A Man Bewitched*. Chicago, 2000.
Barth, F. *Cosmologies in the Making*. Cambridge, 1987.
Bataille, G. *Theory of Religion*. Trans. R. Hurley. New York, 1993.
———. *The Accursed Share*. Vols. 1–3. Trans. R. Hurley. New York, 1988.
Bayart, J.-F. *The Criminalization of the State in Africa*. Bloomington, Indiana, 1999.
———. *The State in Africa*. London, 1993.
Berndt, R., and C. Berndt. *The Speaking Land: Myth and Story in Aboriginal Australia*. Ringwood, Victoria, 1989.
Bourdieu, P. *Participant Objectivation: Breaching the Boundary Between Anthropology and Sociology – How?* Huxley Memorial Lecture, 2000. The Royal Anthropological Institute, London. http://www.stocton.co.uk/pb/huxley.pdf.
Burbank, V.K. '"The Lust to Kill" and the Arnhem Land Sorcerer: An Exercise in Integrative Anthropology.' *Ethos* 28, no. 3 (2000): 410–44.
Clifford, J. *Routes: Travel and Translation in the Late Twentieth Century*. Cambridge, Mass., 1997.
Clifford, J., and G. Marcus, eds. *Writing Culture: The Poetics and Politics of Ethnography*. Berkeley, 1986.
Cohn, N. *Europe's Inner Demons: An Inquiry Inspired by the Great Witch Hunt*. London, 1975.
Comaroff, J., and J.L. Comaroff. 'Introduction.' In *Millennial Capitalism and the Culture of Neo-Liberalism*. Durham, N.C., 2001.
———. 'Occult Economies and the Violence of Abstraction.' *American Ethnologist* 26, no. 2 (1999): 279–303.
———. 'Introduction.' In *Modernity and Its Malcontents: Ritual and Power in Postcolonial Africa*, ed. J. Comaroff and J.L. Comaroff. Chicago, 1993.
Coronil, F. *The Magical State: Nature, Money and Modernity in Venezuela*. Chicago, 1997.
Crick, M. *Explorations in Language Meaning: Towards a Semantic Anthropology*. London, 1976.
Csordas, T.J. *The Sacred Self*. Berkeley, 1994.
Deleuze, G., and F. Guattari. *A Thousand Plateaus*. Trans. B. Massumi. London, 1988.
Devereux, G. *Mohave Ethnopsychiatry*. Washington, D.C., 1970.
———, ed. *Psychoanalysis and the Occult*. New York, 1974.

Douglas, M. *Natural Symbols*. London, 1973.
———. *Purity and Danger*. London, 1970.
Durkheim, E. *The Elementary Forms of the Religious Life*. London, 1915.
Ellen, R. 'Introduction.' In *Understanding Witchcraft and Sorcery in Southeast Asia,* ed. C.W. Watson and R. Ellen. Honolulu, 1993.
Englund, H., and J. Leach. 'Ethnography and the Meta-Narratives of Modernity.' *Current Anthropology* 41, no. 2 (2000): 225–48.
Evans-Pritchard, E.E. *Witchcraft, Oracles and Magic Among the Azande*. Oxford, 1937.
Fortune, R. *Sorcerers of Dobu*. London, 1932.
Fabian, J. *Time and the Other: How Anthropology Makes Its Object*. New York, 1983.
Feyerabend, Paul. *Farewell to Reason*. London, 1987.
Friedman, J. 'The Political Economy of Elegance: An African Cult of Beauty.' In *Consumption and Identity,* ed. J. Friedman, 167–87. London, 1994.
Geschiere, P. *The Modernity of Witchcraft*. Charlottesville, 1997.
Ginzburg, C. *The Night Battles*. Trans. J. Tredeschi and A. Tredeschi. Baltimore, 1983 [1966].
Gluckman, M. *Politics, Law and Ritual in Tribal Society*. Oxford, 1971.
———. *Custom and Conflict in Africa*. Oxford, 1956.
———. *Rituals of Rebellion in South-East Africa*. Manchester, 1954.
———, ed. *The Allocation of Responsibility*. Manchester, 1972.
Gombrich, R., and G. Obeyesekere. *Buddhism Transformed*. Princeton, 1988.
Hallen, B., and J. Olubi Sodipo. *Knowledge, Belief, and Witchcraft*. Stanford, 1997.
Harris, M. *Cows, Pigs, Wars and Witches: The Riddle of Culture*. New York, 1974.
Harrison, S. *The Mask of War*. Manchester, 1993.
Heusch, L. de. *Sacrifice in Africa*. Manchester, 1985.
———. *The Drunken King and the Origin of the State*. Bloomington, 1982.
Horton, R. *Patterns of Thought in Africa and the West*. Cambridge, 1993.
Husserl, E. *Cartesian Meditations: An Introduction to Phenomenology*. Trans. D. Cairns. Boston, 1988.
Kapferer, B. 'Sorcery and the Shape of Globalization.' *Journal of the Finnish Anthropological Society* 26, no. 1 (2001): 4–28.
———. *The Feast of the Sorcerer*. Chicago, 1997.
———. *Legends of People Myths of State*. Washington, D.C., 1988.
Kelly, R.C. *Constructing Inequality*. Ann Arbor, 1993.
Kluckhohn, C. *Navaho Witchcraft*. Boston, 1967 [1944].
Knauft, B.M. *Good Company and Violence*. Berkeley, 1985.
Kuper, H. *An African Aristocracy: Rank among the Swazi*. London, 1969.
Kuhn, T. *The Structure of Scientific Revolutions*. Chicago, 1962.
Lattas, A. *Cultures of Secrecy*. Madison, 1998.
Leach, E. *Rethinking Anthropology*. London, 1961.
Lévy-Bruhl, L. *Primitive Mentality*. Trans. L.A. Clare. London, 1923.
Lévi-Strauss, C. 'The Sorcerer and His Magic.' In *Structural Anthropology,* C. Lévi-Strauss, 167–85. London, 1968a.
———. 'The Effectiveness of Symbols,' in *Structural Anthropology,* C. Lévi-Strauss, 186–205. London, 1968b.
———. *The Savage Mind*. Chicago, 1966.
Malinowski, B. *Magic, Science, and Religion and Other Essays*. Glencoe, 1954 [1926].
———. *Argonauts of the Western Pacific*. London, 1922.
Marwick, M. *Sorcery in its Social Setting*. Manchester, 1965.
Mauss, M. *A General Theory of Magic*. Trans. R. Brain. London, 1972.
Mitchell, J.C. *The Yao Village*. Manchester, 1956.
Mudimbe, V.Y. *The Invention of Africa: Gnosis, Philosophy and the Order of Knowledge*. Bloomington, 1988.

Moore, H.L., and T. Sanders. *Magical Interpretations, Material Realities: Modernity Witchcraft and the Occult in Postcolonial Africa*. London, 2001.

Munn, N. *The Fame of Gawa*. Chicago, 1986.

Nash, J.C. *We Eat the Mines and They Eat Us: Dependency and Exploitation in Bolivian Tin Mines*. New York, 1979.

Niehaus, I., E. Mohlala and K. Shokane. *Witchcraft, Power and Politics: Exploring the Occult in the South African Lowveld*. London, 2001.

Nietzsche, F. *Thus Spoke Zarathustra*. Trans. R.J. Hollingdale. London, 1961 [1892].

———. *The Portable Nietzsche*. Ed. and trans. Walter Kaufmann. New York, 1954.

Obeyesekere, G. *The Cult of the Goddess Pattini*. Chicago, 1984.

———. *Medusa's Hair*. Chicago, 1981.

———. 'Sorcery, Premeditated Murder and the Canalization of Aggression in Sri Lanka.' *Ethnology* 14, no. 1 (1975): 1–23.

Pauw, B.A. *Christianity and Xhosa Tradition: Belief and Ritual among Xhosa-Speaking Christians*. Capetown, 1975.

Peiris, R. *Sinhalese Social Organization*. Peradeniya, 1956.

Polanyi, M. *Personal Knowledge*. London, 1998.

Redfield, R. *Folk Cultures of the Yucatan*. Chicago, 1941.

Roheim, G. *The Riddle of the Sphinx*. London, 1934.

Sartre, J.-P. *The Psychology of the Imagination*. Secaucus, N.J., 1966.

Schutz, A. *On Phenomenology and Social Relations*. Chicago, 1970.

Sodipo, J.O. 'Philosophy, Science, Technology and Traditional African Thought.' In *Philosophy and Cultures*, ed. H.O. Oruka, 36–43. Nairobi, 1983.

Spiro, M. *Burmese Supernaturalism*. Pittsburgh, 1979.

Stephen, M. 'The Mekeo Man of Sorrow: Sorcery and the Individuation of the Self.' *American Ethnologist* 23, no. 1 (1996): 83–101.

Strathern, M. *The Gender of the Gift*. Berkeley, 1990.

Taussig, M. *Defacement: Public Secrecy and the Labor of the Negative*. Stanford, 1999.

———. *The Magic of the State*. New York, 1997.

———. *Shamanism, Colonialism and the Wild Man*. Chicago, 1987.

———. *The Devil and Commodity Fetishism in South America*. Chapel Hill, 1980.

Turner, V.W. *The Ritual Process*. Harmondsworth, 1969.

———. 'Witchcraft and Sorcery: Taxonomy versus Dynamics.' *Africa* 34 (1964): 314–25.

Valeri, V. *Kingship and Sacrifice: Ritual and Society in Ancient Hawaii*. Chicago, 1985.

Van Velsen, J. *The Politics of Kinship*. Manchester, 1964.

Warner, L. *A Black Civilization*. New York, 1937.

Winch, P. *The Idea of a Social Science*. London, 1958.

Wittgenstein, L. *Remarks on Frazer's Golden Bough*. Ed. R. Rhees. Trans. A.C. Mills. Atlantic Heights, N.J., 1979.

Worsley, P. *The Trumpet Shall Sound: A Study of Cargo Cults in Melanesia*. London, 1970 [1957].

Chapter 2

BEYOND VODOU AND ANTHROPOSOPHY IN THE DOMINICAN-HAITIAN BORDERLANDS

Marit Brendbekken

This essay[1] concerns the paradoxes emerging in the dynamic space of hybridisation between vodou magic[2] and the occult science of anthroposophy. These lived imaginaries and registers of interpretation are engaged within counter-modernising environmental discourses and practices in the Dominican-Haitian borderlands. Here NGO-affiliated European anthroposophists, orientated by the work of Rudolf Steiner,[3] are organising a biodynamic programme in co-operation with marginalised Dominican and Haitian borderlands peasants who live the consequences of radical deforestation. These peasants have for long been subjugated to the often violent dictates of post-colonial ruling élites, and their world of vodou spirits is itself the creation of 'resistant accommodation' to the forces of modernity/coloniality and their post-colonial transmutations.

Central to my project is to grasp processes of organic and intentional hybridisation[4] between the counter-forces of vodou and anthroposophy as emerging within environmental discourses and practices. These are made subject to evaluations in terms of magic, religion and science, but from very different subject positions. My aim is to demonstrate how the paradoxes emerging at the interface between vodou and anthroposophy have to do with the fact that both are products of the history of modernity/coloniality, although differently positioned within its historical becoming. The separate counter-perspectives they form give rise to a mutual identification in the borderlands in that both are imposed to – and resist, but again in different ways – the scientific rationalism that legitimates Dominican state modernisation. In this respect, they mutually reinforce each other vis-à-vis state bureaucratic and other non-governmental organisations promoting modernisation on scientific and also on religious fundamentalist grounds in the borderlands. This mutual reinforcement nevertheless extends only to a certain point, as Dominican and Haitian peasants nurture ambivalent feelings about the monopoly on occult science claimed by anthroposophists. This monopoly legitimates the anthroposophists' attempts at reforming the world of the borderlands peasantry, and the peasants suspect that this also includes their vodou practices.

I argue that the paradoxes emerging at the conjuncture between vodou and anthroposophy within the borderlands situation of contesting modernising and counter-modernising discourses and practices have, among other things, to do with how differently embedded historicities are brought into play, re-created and relived. This contributes to emerging dynamic and highly volatile processes of social positioning and identity contestations in the borderlands. If writ large, the dynamic space of hybridisation between vodou and anthroposophy echoes how conceptions of magic, religion and science have served to confer true science to Westerners and magic to primitives elsewhere, which is indeed a central imagery to the historical elaboration of modernity and to anthropology's relativised Other.

The borderlands situation I address raises major issues concerning conventional anthropological perspectives towards the occult and the nature of rationality. Evans-Pritchard attempted to separate European occultist notions of the magical from the understanding of magical practice in other regions. So did Rudolf Steiner on his own occult-scientific terms.[5] The Dominican-Haitian borderlands situation permits no such exclusion, which would furthermore lead to a serious misunderstanding of the contemporary processes of hybridisation and how these are historically conditioned by the forces of modernity/coloniality and their post-colonial transmutations. Vital to the argument I develop is the importance, nonetheless, of exploring in depth these not-so-alien cosmologies and their related practices, which the borderlands situation engages both contemporarily and historically. This is crucial, if the grasp of magical practices as both world-constitutive and integral to the crises of modernism and modernisation is to advance beyond the superficial. In this respect, at the end of the essay I will be extending towards a critique of recent approaches to the study of occult practices, sorcery and magic in anthroposophy.

Montaña Antigua in the Dominican-Haitian Borderlands

European anthroposophists have for more than 20 years implemented development projects in the borderlands valley Montaña Antigua[6] in the Dominican Republic. Here they have sought to create 'an anthroposophical island within the island', modelled after anthroposophical societies in European countries such as Järna in Sweden and Dornach in Switzerland. The contemporary borderlands situation I address is one in which the anthroposophists figure among numerous other NGOs concerned with the serious issue of deforestation.[7] Many of these are aligned to religious congregations (see Fundación Agricultura y Medio Ambiente & GATE 1996). These organisations, so to say, operate within the gap between the borderlands peasants and the Dominican state, a cleavage with a long historical standing.

The borderlands, for centuries a critical site for the production of state power, have been a place of its violent contestation,[8] and Montaña Antigua is no exception. Prior to the 1937 massacre, the valley was mainly inhabited by Haitian peasants and housed a lifetime prison for Dominicans during the early days of the long Trujillato dictatorship (1930–61), due to its relative geographical isolation.[9] Those Dominicans who after 1937 were compelled or forced to settle along the border were to serve as a living shield against Haitian expansion – a major feature of Dominican statecraft during the Trujillato era (Baud 1996; Krohn Hansen 1995a, 1995b; Moya Pons 1995; Derby 1994). The demonisation campaign launched by Dominican ruling élites against the Haitians, especially after the third declaration of the Dominican Republic's independence in 1865, was sharpened and by various means institutionalised during the long Trujillo regime. Ruling élites suppressed any recognition of 'the African contribution' to Dominican societal and cultural formation. Vodou was exclusively attributed to the Haitians, who were conceptualised as evil and powerful but defeated African barbarians and sorcerers who posed a major threat to the Dominican nation, the latter being praised as civilised, Hispanic and Catholic, and born out of relatively peaceful Taíno-Spanish *mestizaje* (San Miguel 1997; Krohn Hansen 1995a, 1995b; Deive 1980).

The Haitians did not return to Montaña Antigua in any numbers before the 1970s. Since then, they have comprised a cheap labour force of illegal immigrants. Despite the overall picture of ethnic stigmatisation that legitimates economic exploitation of Haitians also in the borderlands – a colonial legacy and a product of a violent history that has been consciously and effectively utilised by Dominican nation-builders since the late nineteenth century – the borderlands formation of interethnic relationships is multifaceted and defies a clearcut binary logic[10] (Brendbekken forthcoming). As Dominican and Haitian peasants are increasingly brought together through the activities of transnational non-governmental organisations, they seem to recognise relative cultural communalities vis-à-vis both foreign developmental workers as well as Dominican bureaucrats. The latter effectuate programmes launched by Dominican governmental agencies in a clear competitive vein[11] to those of a growing number of transnational non-governmental organisations. As elsewhere in the Caribbean and Latin America, NGOs are increasingly taking over the responsibility for environmental governance and the welfare of peasants that never was really assumed by Dominican and Haitian bureaucracies. Peasants who use slash and burn farming methods are targeted as being mainly responsible for causing deforestation, whereas the overall pattern of environmental deterioration figures among the consequences of the impact of past and present globalising forces[12] (Zweifler et al. 1994, Moreno 1993, Hartshorn et al. 1981). Dominican peasants are criminalised even if utilising fallow trees, as the Dominican governments since the 1960s have employed violent measures in order to deal with deforestation.[13] Haitian peasants are doubly criminalised as illegal immigrants who carry out agricultural tasks that include the felling of trees for Dominican peasants.

The anthroposophists seek to protect the borderlands peasantry from what they conceptualise as the alienating effects of Dominican state modernisation and the global culture of consumption/'Americanisation'. The anthroposophists echo Latin American traditionalist views on culture in which 'traditional' culture is seen as threatened by 'modern' cultural substitution, a view that most of my borderlands informants do not share (see also García Canclini 1995). The anthroposophical approach is holistic: they introduce biodynamic farming techniques, Waldorf pedagogics,[14] eurhythmics,[15] anthroposophical architecture and other fine works of art,[16] anthroposophical medicine[17] and an alternative theory of social organisation ('the threefold social order', see Steiner 1920) in order to put peasants on the right track towards a sound personal, socio-cultural and environmental development. We may in this respect argue that the anthroposophists exert what Trouillot (2001: 126) terms 'state effects'. During anthroposophical meetings in Montaña Antigua in 1991, the peasants were presented with 'occult explanations' for the rise of global capitalism, the Industrial Revolution, allopathic medicine, industrial agriculture, environmental destruction, nationalism, totalitarian regimes, religious fundamentalism and ethnic mobilisation.[18]

The peasants of Montaña Antigua have been drawn into different environmentalists' force fields and vice versa, into their transnational networks of funding, credit and charitable spending, and their alternative environmental discourses and sustainable practices. Despite the anthroposophists' strong counter-modernising agenda, Montaña Antigua has during the 1990s grown into a 'modern' and socially stratified village where land and labour are increasingly commodified. Most Dominican and Haitian peasants in the borderlands are '… forced to choose from an extensive menu of symbolic goods and a very different, and much more restricted, menu where access to material goods are concerned' (Hopenhayn 2000: 143). Dominican and Haitian borderlands peasants who are brought together through NGO activities and are made subject to conflicting registers of interpretation and shifting politics at the conjuncture between NGOs and Dominican state practices increasingly engage in arguments concerning vodou and compare their vodou practices. During anthroposophical meetings in 1991, Dominican and Haitian versions of vodou were openly discussed in relation to anthroposophical conceptions, while vodou tended to go underground when both Dominican and Haitian peasants were enrolled in evangelic NGOs (Brendbekken forthcoming). Here I document how the most impoverished and marginalised Dominican and Haitian peasants are empowering themselves by exchanging vodou spirits for mutual benefit. According to these peasants, vodou spirits may be evoked in order to subvert the dictates of state rationalisation or to bring NGO programmes within their grasp.

In the following I present two empirical cases centring on encounters between the peasants' world of vodou and scientific rationalism versus the anthroposophical 'occult science'. These cases also exemplify how vodou spirits – whether Taíno, African or Creole – embody an alternative historicity to that of the élite Dominican national-historical imagery in which the Spanish-Taíno *mestizaje* has been idolised and the long gone natives sanctified and in which vodou has been attributed exclusively to the Haitians. In the first case, 'zombification' and the revenge of the long gone Taíno Indian spirits arise as major tropes when peasants address environmental deterioration and its social consequences, which again evoke historical experiences of colonial repression and slavery. In the second case, biodynamic preparations introduced by anthroposophists are likened to a powerful counter-magic to the evil machinations of the Guédé/Gède[19] spirits of life, death and humour, who bear certain resemblances to Mephisthophelean beings, accounted for by Rudolf Steiner (1969) and whom anthroposophists in the borderlands address.

Science Revisited: On Indian Spirits and Oxbow Lakes

Matías, a 70-year-old herbal healer (*curandero*), my visiting husband, who is a geologist, and myself are on our way to Matías's native mountain hamlet along the Haitian border. We cross irrigated rice fields and dried-out hillsides, and on our way we catch a glimpse of Haiti, desert-like and stripped of vegetation. Matías will show me a waterhole (*charco*) where a dangerous Taíno spirit resides. According to Matías, the destructive impact of this spirit is increasing: harvests fail, children get sick and peasants migrate in search of a better fortune elsewhere. On our way we are looking for herbs serving as medicine and protection from intruding spirits (*espíritus intrusos*). Matías has adopted me as his trainee, and over several years he has instructed me in his extensive personal repertoire of medicinal and magical plants, the spirits they are associated with, and how they are engaged within magic, sorcery and counter-sorcery.

During my time as a trainee, I have learnt to keep away from the *guárana* tree,[20] as sorcerers make use of it when preparing deadly *guangás* (signifying either sorcery or sorcerer-spirits). I have learnt that peasants treat Taíno spirits as ambiguous spirits to be cautiously dealt with in everyday life. The spirits of the borderlands are variably grouped together and termed *misterios* (mysteries), *espíritus* (spirits), *ángeles* (angels), *vientos* (winds) or *sanes* (spirit beings). Many of these have equivalents among Catholic saints, and they may prove benevolent and generous as well as greedy and revengeful if the living do not pay respect to them, allow them into their daily affairs, grant them sacrifices or enter into reciprocal compromises with them when they request it.

Spirits manifest themselves in the world of the living by various means. Some, such as Barón del Cementerio, who is the divine trickster and master of life and death, build their houses in treetops. Others, such as the Taíno Indian spirits, reside at the bottom of rivers or in caves. The Taíno spirits and the Haitians killed in 1937, who are considered to have turned into spirits, are said to fly over the land when the peasants are tilling their *conuco* plots; the spirits are vengeful as a result of having been violently driven off their land and massacred. They may enter the peasants' bodies with the breeze, their smell announcing their presence. Strong-smelling plants such as *ruda*, *albahaca*, *apasote*, *anamú* and *mataguangá*[21] are indispensable within counter-sorcery and counter-magic as their smell wards off penetrating spirits. Matías has brought with him *anamú* from his yard; he makes sure that we put it in our pockets for spiritual protection.

We finally arrive in the middle of the Alcántara field where the spiritually dangerous waterhole surrounded by *matapuercos*[22] is located. According to Matías, this waterhole has taken the lives of many people and cattle because the Taíno spirit inhabiting the place is very angry. If you approach the site and fall into the water, he will immediately grasp you and draw you under, the surface turning blood red. No one knows the depth of the waterhole, but it is endlessly deep (*sin límite*). Once a person fell in, and when they tried to recover the body by using a very long stick, no bottom was to be found. Matías explains that his deceased grandmother, a powerful woman with many spiritual allies (*misterios*), was one of the few people who could control this Taíno spirit. Since her death, the site has become more dangerous and Montaña Antigua less prosperous for the farmers. Nowadays this spirit has no one to countermatch his powers and is subsequently beginning to extend his influence beyond the waterhole to the valley at large, drying out the fertility of the earth and leaving people to suffer from poverty and illness.

We cautiously go closer, climbing into the poisonous *matapuercos* that surround the waterhole. We stand on the shores looking into the muddy waters. Then my husband explains to me in Norwegian that what we are looking at is an 'oxbow lake' formed by river sedimentation and from which iron can be extracted, as in Norwegian swamps. Matías asks me to translate, and I explain that my husband has given me a scientific explanation and present a summary of its content. I add that I was also raised thinking in scientific terms. I expand on the difficulties I encountered during the beginning of my stay in Montaña Antigua when trying to understand what indeed a Taíno spirit or a *baká* might be from the point of view of the people in Montaña Antigua, especially with regard as to whether these beings were considered to be real or not, since no person can actually see them or touch them. Matías thinks for a moment and says: 'The *baká* isn't real, because it hasn't got a body by itself, but it has a reality [El baká no es real porque no tiene cuerpo propio, sino tiene una realidad].'

Matías explains that the main difference is that all living beings have bodies (*cuerpos*) and souls (*almas*). Even plants have souls because you must talk to their souls in order to make them do magic for you. Human beings have two souls. When a spirit possesses a person, one of the souls departs and the person remembers nothing afterwards. Matías repeats that the spirits are of a reality without bodies, of something existing without a body, but with a will of its own. They can manifest themselves as bodies by taking over the bodies of others as when the spirits ride their horses (*cuando los espíritus montan sus caballos*). Alternatively, a spirit may take over the body of an animal, a dog or a mule, and that is a *baká*; it hasn't got a body but can take over a body or take on a bodily form. Matías argues that if you see a dog or a mule that behaves differently, it may be inhabited by a spirit. Or the spirit takes on an illusive bodily form and pretends to be an animal. Matías adds that he is a *científico* when it comes to these questions; he can detect if a creature isn't what it appears to be at first sight.

Biodynamic Preparations and Peasant Garden Magic

'Western magic' enters the Dominican-Haitian borderlands in small white containers with the imprints '500' and '501'. These are biodynamic preparations, the outcome of processes that do not seem to astonish Dominican peasants, while educated Dominican agronomists raise their eyebrows. I accompany Juan, a 35-year-old illiterate *campesino*,[23] as he prepares and spreads preparation 501 for the first time. Juan has joined a course in biodynamic agriculture given in the village, where peasants are educated in well-known biodynamic techniques such as rhythmic crop rotation and crop intercalation, compost preparation for soil improvement and the erection of living and dead barriers for soil conservation. They have learnt about homeopathic principles and how biodynamic preparations spread in the field strengthen the growth of plants. Within the self-contained, individual 'biodynamic farm organism', there must prevail a balance between the cycling of cosmic and terrestrial forces, growth and decay.

Juan explains that somewhere in Europe there is a crystal called *cuarzo* (quartz) that has been crushed to a fine powder between glass plates and moved in a rhythmical pattern, then put into a cow's horn and buried in the ground for a year, and later exposed to the sun. Only real scientists (*científicos verdaderos*) can undertake this preparation in Europe. Other biodynamic preparations are made out of a white flower[24] buried underground within the bladder of a large animal that does not exist in the Dominican Republic. When I ask whether he thinks these preparations will work, Juan does not affirm directly, but gives a lengthy explanation of how the peasants in Montaña Antigua have always accorded the moon great importance when sowing and harvesting, how Haitians and Dominicans in the old times used to think that crystals and stones from the river could bleed and breed children, and how Dominicans talk to plants in a special language when compelling the plant to perform magic for them. Juan agrees with anthroposophists that biodynamic farming is more sound than industrial agriculture since SEA and IAD projects[25] failed and since the biodynamic powder seems healthier than the pesticides and weedkillers supplied by Dominican state agronomists, which caused humans and animals to sicken. Juan asserts that peasants in Montaña Antigua already know a lot about the spiritual forces at work in nature. The major difference between anthroposophists and peasants is that anthroposophists are more concerned with the stars and planets, with the angels and Lucifer and Ahriman (Mephistophelean beings), while peasants are more concerned with the moon, the mysteries and the *bakás* (evil phantasms), *guangás* (deadly sorcery) and *puntos calientes* ('hot points' – spiritual powers condensed in objects and words or through acts).

I ask about Ahriman and Lucifer and what he makes of them. Juan laughs when recalling how Peter, a foreign anthroposophist, dramatised during an anthroposophical meeting how the devil Ahriman wishes to destroy the environment by capturing the souls of Dominican agronomists and by promoting the spread of weedkillers, insecticides and pesticides. Our world, says Juan, is pervaded by mysteries (*misterios*) and diabolic forces (*fuerzas diabólicas*). Juan adds that he does not care whether the evangelical pastors in the valley condemn him for committing idolatry by spreading the biodynamic preparation, since believing in Jesus is hardly sufficient to combat the environmental destruction and the *zombíes* (living dead) and *bakás* that are traversing the village nowadays, of which evangelists are just as frightened as anyone else.

Juan looks very content after having spread the preparation around the *plátano* trees. According to Juan, these are seriously affected by disease – not ordinary disease, but disease resulting from evil machinations and *mal de ojo* (the evil eye). Juan comments that the biodynamic preparation may even work against the powders (*polvos*) and poisons (*venenos*) that Haitian *bokores* and Dominican *brujos* (sorcerers) prepare with the left hand for customers.

The Counter-Forces of Vodou and Anthroposophy

In the introduction of this essay, I argued for the importance of exploring in depth the cosmologies and their related practices that the borderlands situation engages both contemporarily and historically. If we are to grasp processes of organic and intentional hybridisation (Bakhtin 1981) between vodou spirits and anthroposophical gods and demons as engaged within environmental discourse and practice, we need first to identify at the level of their cosmological design how these reflect back on the history of modernity/coloniality of which they are themselves products, and how the counter-forces of anthroposophy and vodou in this respect were elaborated from very different subject positions. The material I address is special in that two cosmological systems are brought into contact, both of which comprise hybrid constructions that historically have served to subvert authoritative discourses and practices, but in very different ways. Both vodou and anthroposophy reflect at the level of cosmological design processes of intentional hybridisation, if we with Young (1995: 26–27) understand processes of hybridisation to engage '... a breaking and joining at the same time, in the same place: difference and sameness in an apparently impossible simultaneity. Hybridity thus consists of a bizarre binate operation, in which each impulse is qualified against the other, forcing momentary forms of dislocation and displacement into complex economies of agonistic reticulation'. Authoritative voices are, according to Bakhtin, marked by their singularity or monoglossia, and post-colonial scholars argue that the intentional hybridisations of authoritative (colonial) discourses serve to subvert them (see Werbner and Modood 1997, Young 1995, Bhabha 1994). According to Ahmad (1995, in Werbner and Modood 1997: 5), there are unconscious, organic mixings and cross-fertilisations that provide the foundation from which new perspectives on the world may arise and from where vodou and anthroposophy in this case build 'aesthetic hybrids ... to shock, change, challenge, revitalize or disrupt through deliberate, intended fusions of unlike social languages and images' (Werbner and Modood 1997: 5).

In the following, I will show how the Gnostic legacy of anthroposophy, combined with elements from most world religions, philosophy and twentieth-century occultism, allowed Rudolf Steiner to establish a singular, essentialised spiritual world that revealed itself as ultimate truth, and which could be assessed only by the methods of the natural sciences. Simultaneously, he demonised the world promoted by scientific rationalism and built this vision into the cosmological design of anthroposophy. This entailed a conscious 'breaking and joining' and is indeed a prime example of intentional hybridity built into not-so-unconscious organic cross-fertilisations and cultural mixings made to constitute a powerful social imaginary (cf. Taylor 2002) with related practices.

Anthroposophy, which emerged as a counter-force within the world of scientific rationalism underpinning the twentieth-century ethos of modernist progress, has been outlined in thousands of published pages. Ebbestad Hansen (2000) characterises anthroposophy as Gnostic scientism. The father of anthroposophy, Rudolf Steiner, addressed critically – both theoretically and practically – Enlightenment reasoning, social Darwinism and the global consequences of the exports of Western civilisation (Steiner 1990, 1976, 1969, 1920). Steiner shared with many of his contemporary European intellectuals and élites a preoccupation with occultism (cf. Blavatsky, Olcott and Besant's *Theosophy*),[26] which was emerging along with the rapid proliferation and expansion of scientific knowledge.

The explanatory force of anthroposophy combined Christian mysticism with theosophical ideas about karma and reincarnation, Fichte's (1762–1814) subjectivism and Nietzsche's conception of art, and Goethe's empirical science filtered through the framework of a largely mediaeval-looking 'theory of correspondence' (cf. Taylor 2002, 1982).[27] Steiner was also very attentive to the empirical knowledge accumulated by European peasantries, especially with reference to indigenous medicinal and agricultural practices deemed backwards. Steiner claimed clairvoyant access to 'the Land of Spirits' and to spiritual beings discovered by him. He argued that ever since ca. 3000 BC, and especially after 1600 AD, Mephistophelean beings termed Luciferian and Ahrimanian[28] have promoted and inspired the ills of modernity and mechanical-material science. Ahriman is conceptualised as 'the cold breath of reason' (Löfström 1989: 18), and Ahrimanian beings fix, freeze, harden and rigidify nature and society (Löfström 1989, Koob 1985). If human beings become wholly trapped by Ahrimanian spiritual beings that bind human beings' consciousness to material concerns and earthly exploitation only, there will be no passing to new evolutionary world stages, as Ahrimanian spiritual beings oppose a good earthly and cosmic development as destined by normal gods.[29]

Steiner outlined how Ahriman wishes to arrest human consciousness within its present materialist and earthbound evolutionary stage as Ahriman opposes the normal alternations between earthly and purely spiritual incarnations that human beings are destined to pass through (Mason 2002: 6, Steiner 1969). These reincarnations were initiated by the incarnation of Christ and the Golgatha mystery. The Luciferian and Ahrimanian spiritual beings are neither wholly evil nor good. When balanced by 'the Christ impulse', by each individual and by humanity at large, these Mephistophelean beings serve humanity that will move towards spiritual completion. There is a modern idea of progress and the liberation of the individual at work in anthroposophical thinking. The liberation of the individual becomes synonymous with the recognition of the spiritual relationship between oneself and divine nature, and a full understanding of the good cosmic ordering of which one forms part and with which one must live in concordance. Human liberation implies a full recognition of each individual's sacred individuality – again, a product of Western modernity.

The anthroposophists in the Dominican-Haitian borderlands argue that Ahrimanian beings inspire and promote environmental destruction, conceptualised as 'death processes' sweeping over the borderlands. Echoing Steiner (1976, 1969), they contrast their occult or spiritual anthroposophical science underpinning biodynamic methods to the scientific rationalism underpinning industrial agriculture. Biodynamic methods and anthroposophical environmentalism have generally been elaborated so as to act upon the Ahrimanian-driven processes of secularisation and destruction of divine nature that characterise Western civilisation. It has built into its cosmological design how Ahrimanian and Luciferian beings, associated with the rise of the modern world, can be counteracted to and modified by normal gods.

In contrast, Hispaniolan slaves and peasants created vodou in 'resistant accommodation' to French and Spanish colonial and Catholic impositions (Burton 1997; Bisnauth 1996; Palmié 1995; Davis 1987; Deive 1980, 1975; Mintz and Price 1976; Mintz 1974). Spanish and French colonialism brought peoples together – both forcefully and voluntarily – from different parts of the world. The historical experiences with slavery and colonial subjugation gave rise to the volatile spirits of the world of vodou, born out of the violent encounters between, among others, the colonised Taíno Indians and mostly enslaved Africans and the mostly free Spanish and French colonists and settlers. The New World was thoroughly remade through the incorporation of the Americas into what Mignolo (2000: 721–6) terms the first global design of Christianity – the sixteenth-century incorporation of the Americas into *orbis christianum* and the making of the transatlantic commercial circuit. Catholicism served to cement the hierarchical colonial order as expressed in early slave laws based on Las Siete Partidas and in the later Código Negro Carolino of 1784 (Deive 1980: 378). In Stuart Hall's (1995: 79) words: 'It is impossible to approach Caribbean culture without understanding the way it was continually inscribed by questions of power.' And Dayan (1995: 83) argues: 'The dispossession accomplished by slavery became a model for possession in vodou, for making man not into a thing but into a spirit.' Lacking scriptures, liturgies and a source of overall authority, vodou appears in numerous practised versions among Hispaniola's contemporary, destitute peasantries and urban populations, whose central experience is that power generally tends to corrupt and that '… the power that liberates also corrupts and inevitably turns against itself' (McCarthy Brown 1997: 441).

The subversive force of vodou is recognised among both Dominican and Haitian peasants. The variegated world of vodou spirits reflects back on and addresses the troubled history of Hispaniolan slaves and peasantries as they struggled to achieve an ambiguous freedom in which leaders often turned upon their followers, and in which the deep cleavages between the reconstituted poverty-ridden peasantry and the stronghold of predominantly Catholic elites belong to the dynamics of post-colonial societal formation (Farmer 1994, Belle-garde-Smith 1990, de Heusch 1989: 290–1). Vodou has also been elaborated in response to the demonisation campaigns launched by colonial elites before the Haitian Revolution (1791–1804) and as vodou practitioners were again facing political repression by Haitian revolutionary leaders once in power. Vodou has been politically exploited by US governments also operating through evangelical missionaries after the occupation of Haiti (1915–34), and by the Duvalier regime. The 'uses of vodou' and what Paul Farmer (1994) terms 'the uses of Haiti' are intimately interconnected.

A number of researchers[30] have pinpointed how many of the basically benevolent and familiar spirits of the Rada cult, which links Haitians to an African homeland (*Gine*), can manifest themselves as tricky Creole spirits of the Petro[31] cult, composed of spirits associated with the power of colonial oppression. Haitians associate the Rada spirits with the uses of plants for healing and protective purposes. In contrast, the Petro spirits and 'bought spirits' are identified with fire, coercive power and death-bringing magic, which is the magic associated with the left hand. McCarthy Brown argues convincingly that the Petro way of spiritual being-in-the-world embodies the historicity of slave-holding and the coercive powers wielded by colonising strangers – and their contemporary transmutations. These spirits are fiercely individualistic and, like strangers, simultaneously less distinguishable from each other than the Rada spirits. They are conceptualised as man-eating spirits: 'If you feed one, you feed them all' (McCarthy Brown 1997: 438). Spirits such as *gangas* and *bakas* are considered to be dangerous magicians who manipulate animals, leaves, powders and poisons in pursuit of evil ends. The peasants call upon these spirits in order to '… expropriate the power of slaveholding and its contemporary trans-mutations – oppression, prejudice, economic discrimination – and use that power against itself' (ibid.).

Borderlands versions of vodou operate with a similar basic distinction, although I hasten to add that the Rada and Petro pantheons are not directly reflected in the borderlands among Haitians or Dominicans. They develop similar distinctions in different ways. Dominican and Haitian borderlands peasants address guardian angels (*ángeles, misterios, sanes, luases*) who are basically benevolent and friendly but also austere ancestral spirits, and who belong to personal pantheons either of a family or an individual. Among guardian angels may also figure spirits who are not ancestors and who take on many of the characteristics of the violent Congo Savannah spirits of rural Haitian vodou (cf. de Heusch 1989).[32] These dangerous spirits can be legitimately called upon to unleash powerful and sometimes deadly counter-magic. If these spirits are evoked principally in pursuit of self-interest, they will ultimately turn against those who solicit their services. The guardian angels within a personal pantheon may comprise deceased family members turned into spirits, prophets, Catholic saints and Taíno spirits without equivalents among Catholic saints,[33] as well as the Creole and African spirits variably recognised by both Haitians and Dominicans in the borderlands.

Most vodou spirits have their equivalents among Catholic saints and have been saturated by their imageries: the former were worshipped under the mask of the latter during colonial times – and under the weight of Catholic impositions (Desmangles 1992, de Heusch 1989, Deive 1980, Métraux 1972). The vacillating potential of vodou spirits, and the historicity they embody, defies nonetheless in many respects what Prakash (1995: 3) terms the colonial binary logics of coloniser/colonised, oppressor/oppressed, civilised/primitive, familiar/stranger. McCarthy Brown (1997: 456) argues: 'The transformative potential of Haitian vodou does not reside in the capacity of the spirits to model appropriate behavior, but rather in their capacity to keep the full range of possibilities latent in any way of being-in-the-world before the eyes of the believers.' Dayan (1995: 66) points at how the Haitian revolution and the spirits who are seen to have accompanied revolutionary heroes such as Dessalines in strife defy '… coercive dichotomizations as genteel and brute, master and slave, precious language and common voice'. One example offered by Dayan is that of the mulatto Jean Zombi, who accompanied Dessalines in the massacre of the French in 1801 and who became a powerful *misterio* after his death. The historical Zombi, who turned the coercive power of French slaveholding against the French themselves, is conceptualised as an evil spirit among Haitians. This is also the case of other spirits seen to have accompanied war heroes, such as the female sorceress-spirit Marinette, who lights Dessalines's canons (de Heusch 1992, Dayan 1995). Jean Zombi turned *loa* constitutes '… a terrible composite power: slave turned rebel ancestor turned Iwa, an incongruous demonic spirit recognised through dreams, divination or possession' (Dayan 1995: 84).

The Guédé/Gède family of spirits is frequently referred to in the borderlands when peasants address the social consequences of deforestation. The Cemetery Baron (Barón del Cementerio/Baron Cimetiè),[34] a powerful magician, trickster and undertaker, heads the Guédé family of spirits. These are spirits of conjunctures and transitions who in the borderlands vacillate between what McCarthy Brown terms a Rada and a Petro mode of spiritual being-in-the-world. When Barón del Cementerio acts according to a Rada option of spiritual being-in-the-world, he is seen to carry out the necessary task of guarding over dead souls and bringing the souls of the dead to their spiritual homeland. He provides a linkage between children yet to be born and deceased family members (cf. also McCarthy Brown 1997: 456). In the borderlands he is associated with sexuality as well as death – and with family matters generally. He comforts those in mourning by telling dirty jokes and acting like an impertinent child, and he appears during Haitian funerals in Montaña Antigua, laughing and making obscene bodily movements as he encourages the departing soul to rid him/herself of conflicts and feelings of anger and sadness towards those familiars and friends he/she leaves behind. In contrast, when Barón del Cementerio operates according to a Petro mode of spiritual being-in-the-world, he can set in motion zombification. The imaginary of the *zombí* among borderlands peasants echoes the Dahomeyan imagery of zombies. These were people, buried and evoked anew (Herskovitz 1937), who served as soul-less tools at the hands of sorcerers. *Zombí* among Dominican and Haitian borderlands peasants are linked to devil pacts contracted with the Guédé spirits of death, life and humour. Barón del Cementerio is seen to command over evil spirits such as the *baká* and *guangá*, spirits referred to by Juan and Matías. Barón del Cementerio zombifies in order to bestow on those entering into reciprocal relationships with him the powers floating from devil contracts (*compromisos con el Diablo*), terrifying phantasms (*bakás, baka*) and death-bringing magic (*guangá/ganga*), by way of the intermediate assistance of a sorcerer (the Haitian *bokor* or the Dominican *brujo*).[35] It is argued in narratives about devil pacts that someone offers the soul of a close relative to Barón del Cementerio in exchange for the monstrous phantasm-spirit *baká*, who guards over the property of its owner-to-be and who brings about illegitimate accumulation of wealth. The *baká* spirit can dwell condensed within any object. This object is said to have a 'hot point' (*punto caliente, pwen*) that can be transformed into a phantasm creature (*baká*) when called upon in order to serve its owner.

McCarthy Brown argues that the Gède along with the Ogu spirits (a family of warrior spirits) make up two different options for urban Haitians when confronting the modern world. The Gède family of spirits meets the sufferings of modern living with 'a raucous Gède laugh' (1997: 456), whereas Ogu spirits 'wage war in the modern world' (ibid.) against unemployment, isolation, political repression, poverty and illness. Whereas the Ogu family of spirits is little evoked in the borderlands, the peasants address Guédé spirits in times of rapid social change. Barón del Cementerio is increasingly conceptualised as a spirit who splits family and friends and who promotes individualism, self-interest and impersonal relationships. According to both Dominican and Haitian informants, those who call upon Barón del Cementerio in order to set a *guangá* 'expedition' in motion or bring a *zombí* or *baká* into existence will themselves eventually be 'eaten' by the spirit they get at their disposal, as they become entrapped in the escalating sacrificial demands of these insatiable spirits.

Such imaginaries address simultaneously (1) the frailty of social relations in times of extreme competition for scarce resources whereby intimacy and trust easily flip into intimidation (the person sold to a sorcerer must be a close relative), (2) the ambiguity of power as sorcerers both cause and heal zombification, (3) the limits to the abuse of power as a *baká* finally eats its owner, (4) the immorality of becoming zombified and (5) the terror of being a zombified, powerless and despised loner. Vodou addresses how intimacy can be intimidating, how those fighting against oppression can easily turn into oppressors themselves and that there are limits to power abuse, as power can turn against the powerful, be they Dominicans, Haitians or gringos (white foreigners, Americans). This may represent what Kapferer (1997) terms the dynamics of sorcery[36] as filtered through the historical experiences of modernity/coloniality among Dominican and Haitian borderlands peasants. The basic cosmological outline of vodou and the historical experiences that vodou spirits embody are first and foremost made accessible to interpretation in the borderlands through everyday magical practices, through interpretations of dreams, through spirit possession and in stories that tell how spirits act through the world of the living.

Vodou Spirits and the Withering Environment

According to McCarthy Brown (1997: 437): 'One of the most significant changes to take place in African religions as a result of the slave experience was what I call the socialisation of cosmos. For example, natural powers such as those of storm, drought and disease paled before social powers such as those of the slaveholder.' One may speculate whether these social powers are now paling before those of environmental deterioration in the borderlands, or rather if the withering environment is becoming a privileged site through which past and present disembedding effects of modernity/coloniality can be addressed and acted upon. Vodou spirits are evoked as peasants grapple with the social consequences of deforestation, soil erosion, collapsing modernisation and counter-modernisation agendas,[37] population pressure, and governmental control and restrictions. The situation I address is also one in which conflicting systems of landholding prevail[38] and in which the peasants' definition of land ownership is losing hold as Dominican bureaucratic rationalisation and jurisdiction increasingly define ownership. The festive agricultural work parties (*combite*), which in former days brought neighbours, relatives and friends together in collective agricultural undertakings, wither, and with them a number of sacrificial practices, such as ritual offerings to the Taíno Indians.

Within a modern, secularised context, we may argue with Weber that anthroposophical environmentalism implies a re-enchantment of a disenchanted nature. When introduced in the Dominican-Haitian borderlands, it implies a re-enchantment of an already enchanted but withering nature that, from the peasants' viewpoint, increasingly bears the marks of the auto-destructiveness and barrenness associated with spirits such as Barón del Cementerio, *guangá*, *baká* and Taíno. When the anthroposophical biodynamic project boomed in Montaña Antigua during the early 1990s, and the anthroposophists nurtured peasant visions of enchanted nature vis-à-vis the scientific rationalism of Dominican bureaucrats, I experienced that a number of Dominican and Haitian borderlands peasants stressed positive aspects of how stones, plants, animals and human beings may serve as vessels for spiritual powers, and that certain plants and animals are themselves spiritually powerful due to their possession of souls. There were informants who explained that the Taíno spirits and African ancestral spirits live below the sea, and that all spirits have favourite residing places and move around in the world among the living. Youngsters asked me whether I believed that stones could bleed and whether I anticipated that spirits rest in treetops, inhabit caves, fly through the air or prefer to stay at crossroads. I experienced that sorcerers along with herbal healers (*curanderos/curanderas*) and midwives (*parteras*) figure among those specialists who obtain knowledge about the relationship between nature and the world of spirits through spiritual possession.

Such knowledge can be equally obtained by anyone during *rondas*, that is, spiritual revelations in dreams when one of the souls of a human being (*el gran buen ángel*) is seen to depart from the human body and encounters ancestral souls, spirits and the wandering souls of others who are asleep. Spirits manifest themselves during funerary rites (*velas*) or Catholic feasts when peasants dance to the drums (*bailes de palo*) beaten in honour of the dead and the Catholic saints. Here they show themselves by entering the bodies of particular participants who serve them. They may 'ride their horses' at unexpected moments, which can be potentially dangerous. The sudden possession by a Taíno spirit of a woman washing clothes in the river or the possession of a man resting below a guano tree where the spirit Ganga is said to reside may cause death and illness. The Taínos sometimes demand that even small children who have been seriously ill enter into spiritual reciprocal relationships with them. Children who grow matted hair locks are said to be protected by Taíno spirits, a protection that will prevail as long as the children abstain from cutting their hair until they reach the age of seven. Spirits are also recognised through their practical accomplishments among the living, such as in failing or abounding harvests, miscarriages or success in acquiring land, a car or a visa.

During fieldwork periods from 1990–8, I observed a shift among borderlands peasants from emphasising the manifold ways that vodou spirits engage the natural environment to stressing the destructive potential of vacillating vodou spirits, such as Barón del Cementerio and the Taínos. The former became increasingly associated with bad spirits such as *baká* and *guangá* during the 1990s as Dominican and Haitian borderlands peasants engaged the borderlands vodou spirits when addressing escalating deforestation and loss of agricultural productivity in times of strong competition over scarce resources, under conditions of increased state repression accompanying the governments' forestry management politics, and as processes of commodification of land and labour increasingly extended into the social space of close relatives and family. Recall how Matías addressed the negative influence of Taíno spirits now extending to include the entire valley. The imagery of vengeful Taíno spirits evoked by Matías bespeaks the loss of appropriate knowledge to deal with spiritual beings as the scientific rationalism accompanying state modernisation and rationalisation[39] makes its impact on coming generations of Montaña Antigua peasants, together with evangelical missionaries' doctrines. Matías argues that the vacillating powers of Taíno spirits are out of control as these have none to counter-match their powers and as they are no longer treated with appropriate sacrifices. We may say that peasants such as Matías and Juan raise a moral critique when they address modernity with disembedding effects through the world of vodou, especially with respect to the increasing stronghold of malevolent spirits (the Petro spiritual mode of being-in-the-world). Although these spirits are thought to be auto-destructive, they nevertheless tear social relationships apart, turn friends and familiars into enemies, and promote impersonal relationships even inside the family.

The world of vodou spirits and related magical practices are not manipulated by peasants simply for utilitarian ends or to serve as a moral critique, but are world-constitutive imageries that bring to mind what Gil (1998: 126–7) terms the 'exfoliation' of the body: 'Relations to a tree, a prey, a star, an enemy, a loved object, desired nourishment, set in train certain privileged organs inducing precise places of the body. Exfoliation is the essential way the body "turns onto" things, onto objective space, onto living things. Here there is a type of communication which is always present, but only makes itself really visible in pathological or magical experiences. Nevertheless the ordinary experience of relations to things also implies this mode of communication.... The body is a foundation for metaphorization; because a "petrified space", for example, speaks of nothing but the quality between the body and the objective space – something of the order of "petrification" coming from things effecting the body: and something of the order of the body ... comes to effect things.' I will provide a brief glimpse into how, in this respect, forms of protective magic among borderlands peasants bring together human beings and social relationships, the world of plants and animals, and contribute to the construction of social space.

Peasants counteract the potential destructiveness of intrusive spirits by preparing protective magic,[40] termed *despojos*, *sahumeras* and *resguardos*. These magical preparations mark off and secure boundaries between Self and Other in a situation in which such boundaries are becoming blurred. Protective magic is performed in order to ward off dreaded Petro-like spirits set in motion by Barón del Cementerio, and this magic operates according to a distinction drawn between spirits who figure within the personal pantheon of a person, as against those of others (outsiders, strangers, co-villagers, even family members) who can be potentially dangerous and intrusive. These distinctions are also laid out spatially: the magical protection of interior and exterior bodily spaces, clothes, houses and yards represents everyday life concerns among peasants through which the maintenance of autonomy, viability and bodily identity is addressed and through which social relationships are partly shaped and expressed. Plants figure prominently within protective magic, and powerful plants utilised in protective magic, such as *anamú*, *ruda* and *apasote*, are posited at the 'corners' (*las esquinas*) and at the 'entrance' (*la puerta*) of houses, yards and even agricultural fields (*conucos*). In the last case, these demarcations are largely invisible to those who are not familiar with the spatial outlay of slash and burn farming and protective garden magic. Such plants are also the symbolic markers separating 'inside' from 'outside' of a yard or a *conuco*, and the spirits that are seen to engage with the plants prevent 'magical' transfers of harvest and wealth from one agricultural field to another: thorny shrubs planted within and around an agricultural field 'pinch' intruding spirits, plants with a caustic content 'burn' the spirits, and the rotten stench of a plant such as *mataguangá* (*guangá*-plant) is as unbearable for evil spirits as it is for human beings. Olfactory substances crossing into and floating from the bodies of plants, animals and human beings are major elements in rites of healing and harm across the world (cf. Classen et al. 1994), and the borderlands are no exception (cf. Brendbekken 1998): Such plants ward off intrusive spirits. However, the spirits within a personal pantheon that operate according to a Petro mode of spiritual being-in-the-world are indispensable in that they can unleash counter-magic as the powers of Barón del Cementerio can be turned against Barón del Cementerio himself. From Petro spirits peasants learn tricks to fool Petro spirits.[41]

Magic preparations such as *despojos* are often conceptualised as a means of cleansing spiritually polluted bodily and social spaces. To stay clean (*limpio*) may also signify to stay morally clean. Persons who are considered 'without shame' (*sinvergüenzas*, that is, egoistic, breaking social rules, being merciless or sinful) are talked about as having dirty blood. Central to these imaginaries and practices is a conceptualisation of relative elasticity and vulnerability of boundaries. To be strong means to withstand spiritual intrusion, and women and children are in this respect conceptualised as vulnerable and in need of protection by men with 'stable' boundaries. To be powerful also implies to expand beyond ones' normal boundaries at one's own wish and intrude into 'the identitary space' of others at their expense. In this respect, protective magic is a way of strengthening one's own boundaries against the magical intrusion of others who seek to empower themselves. Needless to say, this is a highly gendered imagery that partakes in the structuring of gender relationships and authority structures, and in the disciplining of social bodies.

The World Proposed by Anthroposophical Environmentalism

The European anthroposophists' introduction of biodynamics implies a whole new conceptual apparatus outlining the interdependencies between all living beings in a great chain of being, bringing new imageries and governing practices into play with the peasants' governance of bodily and spiritual interrelations between spirits, humans, animals and plants. The complexity of biodynamics is beyond of the scope of this essay, but I will briefly exemplify it by touching on the relevant case of the anthroposophical conceptualisation of quartz utilised within biodynamic preparations.

Taking their lead from Rudolf Steiner's biodynamic lectures given in Köberwitz in 1924 and Kjell Arman's *La Dinámica de lo Vivo* (1986), the anthroposophists in the borderlands contend that there is a spiritual world of beings behind every worldly being and existence down to quartz, plants, manure, cow horns, earthworms and oxbow lakes. The same principles are operating at different levels of a great chain of being from archangels down to minerals. The anthroposophists assert that all things – from the growth of a plant to human warfare – represent reflections from the cosmos and simultaneously have cosmic repercussions in the sense that what happens on earth has consequences for future generations, as well as for the stages of the macrocosmic world evolution. Biodynamic preparations echo complex relationships seen to exist between spiritual-cosmic beings permeating and irradiating upon earthly beings, with the mineral kingdom as the mediator between cosmic beings and plants, animals and human beings. The anthroposophists conceptualise different regions of 'Spirit-Land',[42] with equivalents among earthly domains of nature. The distinct regions of 'the Land of Spirits' have a relationship to nature. Steiner argued that cosmic influences irradiating from spiritual beings (angels, archangels, *archai, exusiai, dynamis, kyriotetes*, thrones, cherubim and seraphim) having to do with the planets and the solar system operate through mediating physical substances and phenomena on earth, such as silica, carbon, sulphur, nitrogen, oxygen, hydrogen, iron and so on. Equally, the physical bodies made up of mineral and metallic substances on earth have as their counterpoint archetypical, spiritual beings within what is conceptualised as 'the first realm of Spirit-Land' (Steiner 1969). For example, the quartz (silicium dioxide) within the biodynamic preparation 501 has been prepared so as to condense so-called 'life-etheric'[43] forces that plants need in order to grow. In a lengthy argument, outlined in a very simplified form in borderlands lectures, Steiner argued that what makes siliceous substances on earth operative within the formation of plants, animals and human beings does not originate on the earth itself, but on Mars, Jupiter and Saturn and the spiritual beings associated with these planets positioned far off the sun.[44] Steiner argued that whereas we can observe on earth crystallisation processes and the manifest form of a crystal such as quartz, in the Spirit-Land '... the rocky substance of the crystal manifests itself as a hollow or vacuum, while around the hollow can be observed the forces building the crystal.... Even as stones, rocks and geological formations constitute the solid land – the continental region – of the world of nature, so do the entities we have been describing constitute the solid land of the spiritual world' (Steiner 1969: 84).

Biodynamics promises to restore the cosmic ordering of all living beings that has been disturbed in the borderlands, and anthroposophy presents itself as the only conscious science that accurately describes the spiritual reality of nature and cosmos by the methods of natural science. Biodynamics thinking also flows from the Land of Spirits: 'All that can come to life in the soul of man so that he becomes creative, acting on his environment in such a way as to transform and fertilize it, is manifested in its archetypal being in the fourth region of the spiritual world' (Steiner 1969: 86). The fourth region is likened to how warmth permeates all living beings and things on earth as comparable in the land of spirits to all-pervading thought-beings: 'The thoughts man apprehends within the manifest world are but a shadow of the real thought-being, living in the Land of Spirits' (ibid.: 85). In the borderlands, this was reflected in statements concerning how human beings 'receive' objectively existing archetypical thought-beings, such as those underpinning biodynamic thinking. Given that human beings have partly emancipated themselves from the great cosmic ordering, they also produce thought-beings on their own that gain access to others, for better or for worse. These are seen to have macrocosmic repercussions observable in the Land of Spirits.

The Potential of Organic Hybridisation

Can the variegated 'Creole *olymp*' of vodou spirits (Deive 1975) possibly share anything in common with the Gnostic scientism (Ebbestad Hansen 2000) of anthroposophy and the Spirit-Land to which Steiner claimed to have clairvoyant access? Does the ambivalence of vodou spirits share anything in common with the amoral spiritual beings that Steiner described in great detail at the turn of the twentieth century as he sought to combat the evils of Western modernity and the '*psychopathia professoralis*' (Steiner 1976: 156) of the academy? At a high level of abstraction, the anthroposophists' and borderlands peasants' conceptualisation of a spiritual world operating upon and through earthly beings opted for cross-fertilisation. Both anthroposophists and peasants posit a spiritual world moving and intervening in empirical processes. While Steiner argued 'It is a characteristic of everything that we have on earth that the spiritual must always have physical carriers' (ibid.: 45, my trans.), Matías outlines that spiritual beings are without bodies and must take on bodily form. Both hold that spiritual beings and spiritual thought-beings have a reality and a will of their own. Anthroposophists would deny the possibility of human beings gaining insight into the spiritual world by way of spirit possession,[45] whereas many borderlands peasants showed a keen interest in Steiner's methods of gaining insight into the spiritual world (cf. Steiner 1984), as presented in simplified form during lectures given in the borderlands.

When the anthroposophists brought up the subject of Ahriman and Lucifer during anthroposophical meetings and biodynamic study groups, the peasants explicitly related Ahriman to San Elías as visually represented on Catholic chromolithographs. Borderlands peasants view San Elías as the Catholic counterpart to the vodou spirit Barón del Cementerio. We have seen that both Barón del Cementerio and Ahriman are conceptualised as amoral spiritual beings associated with earthly greed and with death, and both are evoked when borderlands peasants and anthroposophists address the consequences of environmental deterioration.

The peasants associate biodynamic preparations with protective garden magic or a powerful counter-magic. We have seen that references to *baká*, *zombí* and *guangá* abounded whenever Dominican and Haitian peasants linked Barón del Cementerio to environmental deterioration and loss of livelihood. In this context, borderlands peasants viewed biodynamic preparations as powerful counter-enactments to the magic associated with Barón del Cementerio/Ahrimanian spiritual beings. From this perspective, the anthroposophical spiritual beings associated with nature, who counteract Ahrimanian death processes, come to the rescue of Rada-like spirits operating through nature, who are losing hold before the social power associated with Petro-like spirits and their clients. As a result, biodynamic preparations entered the world of peasants without much friction. According to Juan, these could even work against the poison and powders that sorcerers make with their left hand.

This was also reflected in the distinction that peasants drew between 'natural yields' achieved through the good magic of biodynamic methods and 'unnatural yields' springing from contracts with Barón del Cementerio. These distinctions bring to mind Colombian peasants' and other South and Central American peasantries' conceptualisations of the unnatural yields and the barrenness associated with the income that springs from pacts with the devil (cf. Edelman 1994, Taussig 1980, Nash 1979), but I hasten to add that neither anthroposophists nor borderlands peasants see monetary transactions and commodity production and exchange as inherently evil.[46] Although devil imaginaries lend themselves to address and act upon a wide variety of social conflicts, I argue that the empirical materials I present concerning the articulation between anthroposophy and vodou, between the devil Ahriman and Barón del Cementerio, between peasant garden magic and biodynamic preparations, defy unidimensional functionalist explications for the social existence of these imaginaries and related practices, whether cast in terms of a moral critique of modernity and capitalist transformation and transition, as a metaphor for class and sexual oppression (Edelman 1994), or as underpinning Dominican nationalism among the peasantry (Krohn Hansen 1995a, 1995b; Derby 1994). Rather, the devil imaginaries and 'the language of correspondence' within vodou and anthroposophy expose, reflect back on and address those colonial discourses and practices that they have been shaped through and against and their ongoing transmutations. The historicity of vodou and anthroposophy as counterforces is reflected at the level of their cosmological design as well as in how they are contemporarily articulated in the borderlands. Although vodou and anthroposophy establish profoundly different perspectives of the world, born out of very differently located subject positions, it is striking how in both cases Mephistophelean beings are conceptualised as 'divine tricksters'. Where Steiner used the Faustus myth in order to demonise modernity and scientific rationalism, the devil became an ambivalent ally of demonised Africans in the New World (Taussig 1980). While Steiner explicitly links the Ahrimanian-promoted Enlightenment knowledge to Goethe's *Faust* (in Steiner 1969), which was again based on certain sixteenth-century myths, the devil imageries within borderlands' vodou have been saturated with notions about devil pacts, *magia* and *superstitio* that the French and Spanish brought with them and which have ancient roots (Kieckhefer 1994; see also Macfarlane 1995, Edelman 1994: 60).[47]

The anthroposophists' and borderlands peasants' enchantments of stones and plants, and their considerations of planetary influences on agriculture, enabled organic cross-fertilisation. Both anthroposophists and vodou-practising peasants considered spiritual beings to operate through many of the same material objects and earthly bodies and argued that complex relationships exist between spirits, plants, animals and human beings. The crushed quartz within the biodynamic preparations makes sense to Juan in that notions about spiritual forces operating through – or condensed in – objects such as crystals and other stones are not foreign to peasants. Juan refers to peasants who in the old days believed that stones could bleed and breed children. Courlander (1944: 342) outlined how Haitians worshipped old Indian celts found in the soil: 'These *loa*-stones are identified by their clearly defined form, and by [their] ability to perspire, whistle, and talk.' Such stones, as well as Indian figurines crafted in stone, still figure among Dominican sorcerers' ritual objects: Taíno spirits are called upon as Dominican sorcerers deposit '*zemis*' stones at the bottom of glasses and fill them with water from the river. The sacredness of stones may have different origins. In ritual healing ceremonies among various *nkita* cults in Kongo, stones were used as props for *nkita* spirits, which were seen to dwell in stones gathered from the river (de Heusch 1989: 295–6). (The Kongo influence in the borderlands is evident in that the twin spirits Marassa (from the Congolese *mapasa*) as well as Ganga and Baká figure within borderlands vodou.) The so-called Piedra Imán (with a biblical origin and much utilised by mediaeval alchemists) is used as an amulet against evil in contemporary Dominican Republic as well as Cuba and Mexico, and thunderbolts are equally worshipped throughout formerly British and French Caribbean islands (Deive 1975: 284–5).

I personally experienced that stones could be considered spiritually powerful. When a Dominican man offered me a beautiful crystal as a gift, I was told by my landlady not to accept it since it probably was a magic crystal with a *punto caliente* – a spiritual power condensed within it. Although it is evident that the macrocosmological orientation underpinning the anthroposophical utilisation of quartz within biodynamic preparations differs profoundly from the 'this-worldly' cosmological reasoning underlying the peasants' utilisation of stones and crystals, the anthroposophists' preparations became added to vodou-ist practices and were absorbed into the life-world of peasants.

Both peasants and anthroposophists concern themselves with the relationship between plants, spirits and human beings. During meetings, the anthroposophists outlined how the 'building' power that floats from cosmic-planetary beings and terrestrial 'nature spirits' permeates plants. One example is the flower *achillea millefolium* – the white flower Juan referred to – that is utilised within biodynamic preparations. It is held to be a wonderful plant due to its special relationship to 'nature spirits', also termed 'elementary beings' (Steiner 1976: 94–95). These are said to operate through the sulphuric content of the flower, sulphur being conceptualised by Steiner as a carrier of archetypes from Spirit-Land and as a carrier of light. On their side, peasants such as Juan and Matías endow plants with healing and harming potentials that render them suitable for magical-protective, healing and harming purposes, among other things due to their relationships to particular spirits. The peasants, so to say, confirmed Herskovitz's (1937: 195) statement: 'If you knew all the stories of the leaves in the forest, you would know all there is to be known about the gods of Dahomey (in Simpson 1965: 104). Matías outlined how *anamú* serves to withstand intruding spirits due to its smell, while leaves and stems from the tree *guárana* (*satanyen*), where Barón del Cementerio builds his house, are indispensable for sorcerers when crafting death-bringing magic, termed *guangá*, as well as counter-magic.

Likewise, the anthroposophists operate with spiritual irradiations flowing from cosmic-planetary beings that enable the growth and life cycle of plants as well as animals and human beings. Recall how Juan on the other side likens the anthroposophists' preoccupation with planetary positions within biodynamics to Dominican and Haitian peasants' own preoccupation with moon phases in relation to slash and burn farming. Anthroposophists and Dominican and Haitian peasants argue that the moon enables human, animal and plant reproduction.[48] The borderlands peasants tended to regard Maria and Matthias K. Thun's (1990) 'Calendario de agricultura biodinámica' (anthroposophical astrological-agricultural calendar) to be a variation on their own way of considering moon phases and their *cabañuela*. The latter is an agricultural calendar, possibly of Spanish origin (Deive 1975: 293), based on divinations during the first 12 days of January that is granted importance among many peasants in Montaña Antigua.

Addressing Anthroposophy through the Ambivalence of Vodou Spirits

The potential of organic hybridisation (Bakhtin 1981) was differently appreciated among anthroposophists and peasants. Anthroposophical environmentalism as elaborated in the borderlands tends towards a 'civilising mission', and any civilising mission rests on presuppositions about a given cleavage of alterity between Self and Other that is to be transcended by peaceful persuasion, or by forcing the Other into the Self (Larsen 1999). When anthroposophy became filtered through the world of vodou spirits, the Janus face of the anthroposophical mission revealed itself.

Among those spirits seen to empower anthroposophists as well as other gringos (white foreigners, Americans) was La Reina de España (the Queen of Spain). She was possibly a recently invented spirit who had no spiritual equivalent among Catholic saints. The Queen of Spain was a fearful, violent, red-eyed and dominating spirit operating in a Petro mode. In this respect she bore certain resemblances to Marinette, who is seen to accompany the historical Dessalines turned spirit in his struggle against the French.[49] She never took no for an answer from her servants, she was pale as death, and she prepared to launch terrible assaults upon those who were reluctant to recognise her power and obey her commands. When possessed with La Reina, Rafaelito, a young sorcerer, powdered himself with a mixture of chalk, ashes and crushed bones, and perfumed himself with original Opium perfume from abroad. La Reina demanded sacrifices of gringos in order to 'open the road' (*abrir el camino*) to their spiritual empowerment. When Rafaelito became possessed with La Reina in my presence, she demanded that I, together with all gringos ('all strangers'), enter into a spiritual compromise with her. By offering her perfumes, silk clothes and gold jewellery, she would bestow upon me, anthroposophists and all gringos great power over borderlands peasants so that they irresistibly conformed to 'our gringo plans', because she realised herself among the living by making us more powerful. Needless to say, her violent way of spiritual being-in-the-world also implied that if we unleashed her power, which we were more or less forced to do – if not, we would be severely sanctioned by La Reina – this power would ultimately turn against ourselves. The catcher was caught in the rye.

The agenda of anthroposophy in no way intends a colonial or imperial expansion. Nonetheless, borderlands peasants, while recognising the benefits of the anthroposophical project, compared its 'civilising mission' with European colonialism and later-twentieth-century American imperial expansion. These dynamics, needless to say, reflect historical experiences of slavery, Catholic impositions and colonial rule, as well as post-colonial regimes of oppression, and reinforce how slaves and peasants have maintained a sense of dignity by building cultures in 'resistant accommodation' to that of the power-holders. Vodou exposes the ambiguities of peasants' reactions to the world of the anthroposophists. When anthroposophists, who depended on the co-operation of peasants in order to succeed in their project implementation and maintain their NGO vis-à-vis various transnational sponsors, were caught up in this colonial dynamics of expectations and peasant subversions, they were exposed to the paradoxes of their own agenda.

The Universality of Rationalisation Procedures

Anthroposophists live by powerful metaphors that contrast themselves to the rest of the Western world, which they view as gone astray (see Kimpfler 1989; Steiner 1976, 1969; Sahlberg 1972). Recall how Ahrimanian beings fix, freeze, rigidify and kill that which is living, and how the good cosmic order as destined by normal gods implies a constant, harmonious, balanced flow of cosmic and etheric forces and the cycling of reincarnations (Mason 2002: 6). The significance of metaphors of flow and flexibility versus the faulty fixation and rigidity of modern Western civilisation evaporates under the Caribbean sun – at what Trouillot (1992) has termed the open Caribbean frontier – where boundaries corrode and 'everything fleets to the extreme'. In order to gain control and command over the unruly and 'overflowing' spatial and bodily spaces of borderlands peasants, the anthroposophists, along with other NGOs, introduce a number of rationalising measures in order to live up to the expectations of fund-raisers and also to discipline unruly peasants. Among other things, they introduce account keeping, compost measurements by the use of liners, clock time, impersonal economic relationships (friendship-family versus business relationships), map drawing, neat separation of work and leisure, wage work and so on. In other words, 'The spatial inscription of practices and power involves ... exchanges which connect, separate, distance, and hierarchize one space in relation to others. The command of space involves the setting up of novel codifying apparatuses such as the reorganisation of the senses, mental maps, topographic origin myths, norms of spatial competence, and rules of spatial performances' (Feldman 1991: 9). The anthroposophists' regime of discipline and governance of social and natural space in the borderlands is suspiciously reminiscent of rationalisation procedures associated with the Western modernity they seek to combat; in the borderlands they seem to become trapped by Ahriman.

The anthroposophists introduce the concept of the autonomous individual (with rights and duties), which, according to Larsen (1999: 111), forms part of 'a modern abstraction package' within which is included ideas about abstract value, abstract labour (work/leisure) and abstract space (ibid.: 101). When filtered through the anthroposophical conception of divine individuality, the anthroposophists expose the metaphysical underpinnings of the individual in modernity – 'the phantom objectivity' of modern rationalism itself. However, this modern abstraction packet has in certain respects a long historical standing in New World societies that were strangely 'modern-looking' long before the Industrial Revolution in Europe (cf. Mintz and Price 1976; Mintz 1996, 1974). If by modernity we mean 'that historically unprecedented amalgam of new practices and institutional forms (science, technology, industrial production, urbanisation), of new ways of living (individualism, secularisation, instrumental rationality) and of new forms of malaise (alienation, meaninglessness, a sense of impending social dissolution)' (Taylor 2002: 91), then many of these phenomena formed part of the experiences of New World populations subjugated to slavery and colonial rule. New World 'modernity' emerged in rudimentary form during the Spaniards' experimentation with sugar cane plantations in the early sixteenth century (Deive 1980), to become fully developed on sugar plantations of eighteenth-century Saint Domingue (Haiti) and Jamaica.

In Blackburn's (1997: 4) words: 'Slavery in the Americas ... was associated with certain processes that are thought of in connection with the definition of modernity: the growth of instrumental rationality; the rise of national sentiment and the nation-state; rationalized perceptions of identity; the expansion of commercial (market) relations and wage labor; the development of administrative bureaucracies and modern systems of taxation; the growing sophistication of trade and communication; the birth of consumer culture; the beginnings of new industries; action at a distance, and the individual sensibility.' In Prakash's (1995: 3) words: 'The writ of rationality and order was always overwritten by its denial in the colonies, the pieties of progress always violated irreverently in practice, the assertion of the universality of Western ideals always qualified drastically.' In this respect, modernity – with the disembedding effects and the self-reflexivity that goes with it – represents more of a 'tradition' than a recent phenomenon in the borderlands. The historical circumstances that conditioned the emergence of vodou and of anthroposophy

– and how this is reflected at the level of their cosmological design – fire back on metaphors of pre-modern, local closures as against contemporary, open, global modernity, which is, according to Amselle, but a rephrasing and temporalisation of the older civilisation/primitivism divide (Amselle 2002: 214). Moreover, the intentional hybridisation of occult science by vodou magic in the borderlands rather serves to expose how modernist notions concerning an all-inclusive humanity were themselves the products of historical interweaving between the West and the relativised Other[50] (see also Taylor 2002, Mignolo 2000, Larsen 1999).

Vodou, Anthroposophy and Claims to Scientificity

The case materials I have presented expose how claims to scientificity operate within processes of social positioning in the borderlands. The evaluations of biodynamics products echoed by Juan illustrate that anthroposophists argue for the true scientificity of their biodynamic preparations versus the faulty science engaged in the production of agro-chemical preparations. Evangelists condemn anthroposophists for their idolatry, while their biodynamic preparations – which natural scientists such as Dominican agronomists might view as magic dressed up in scientific garb – have entered with little friction the life-world of Dominican and Haitian peasants, who tend to view them as good garden magic.

'True spiritual science against Ahrimanian science!' argue anthroposophists. 'Idolatry! False religion!' argue evangelists. 'Magic! False science!' argue Dominican agronomists. 'Good magic that may work against bad magic!' argue Dominican and Haitian peasants, who add: 'But our magic is as scientific as theirs!' These conflicting evocations and evaluations trigger numerous questions, one of which looms large: Can the anthropological categories of magic, sorcery, religion and science be applied for cross-cultural comparison when analysing these encounters and articulations? Do anthroposophical and vodouist practices conform to these categories as constructed by nineteenth-century anthropologists such as Morgan, Tyler and Frazer?

I am concerned with how the encounter and articulation between the anthroposophical counter-modernising force and the vodou-ist counter-colonial force push anthropology in the direction of addressing its own inevitable historical embeddedness and modernity-coloniality legacy. The ways that vodou and anthroposophy historically have emerged as counter-forces to New World colonialism and Enlightenment reasoning, both of which have had a major bearing on the emergence of anthropology as a discipline, explode the emic/ethic distinction of anthropological translations. The case of anthroposophy brings this problem particularly clearly into the open. Anthroposophists engage critically with Western philosophical and modernist assumptions. The anthroposophical assumption that Ahrimanian beings promote semi-conscious Enlightenment reasoning – from which anthropology was born, and from which delineations of conceptions of sorcery, magic, religion and science have been nurtured – raises several intriguing questions: How am I to understand anthroposophists on their own premises when anthropology as a discipline, and Western science generally, became the alterity by which the anthroposophical alternative spiritual science nourished itself? Can I possibly apply my own conceptions in order to understand their conceptions of my conceptions, which form part of theirs? In what way can the emergence of anthroposophical and anthropological universes of discourse be said to be interdependent? How do we depict relevant contexts for interpretation when seeking to grasp how vodou and anthroposophy interrelate contemporarily in the borderlands?

The articulations between vodou and anthroposophy refute the temporal and spatial boundaries drawn around 'Western civilisation' and its relativised Other. In Mignolo's (2000: 722) terms, modernity has always had coloniality as its darker edge and condition of possibility, and Chakrabarty (1994: 364, in Larsen 1999: 107) attacks the notion of Western societies '… as if they were self-contained histories complete in themselves, as if the self-fashioning of the West were something that occurred only within its self-assigned geographical boundaries'.[51] The ongoing conjunctions between vodou and anthroposophy are a local manifestation of the larger historical interrelations that Chakrabarty and Mignolo address, along with other scholars[52] who are preoccupied with post-colonialism and early globalisation. Amselle (2002: 228) argues that notions about cultural boundedness made such inventions possible: 'Let us not forget that this discipline was from its very beginning an arm of knowledge-as-power whose mission was to infiltrate and study the "savage", both home and abroad. This project … was … exported to the colonies where it served as an analytical model.'

Such a legacy is evident in Horton's (1970: 153) comparison between African thought and Western science, in which he argues in a Frazerian tone that the key difference is that 'traditional' cultures have not developed awareness of alternatives to an established body of theoretical considerations, while scientifically orientated cultures can be characterised by the reverse; the latter are 'open', while traditional cultures are 'closed'. Horton's argument may be turned against itself when considering the openness of vodou towards new practices, its bridging capabilities, as against the inability of the positivism that Horton celebrates to make sense of the world-constitutive force of anthroposophy and vodou on their own terms. Vodou sees no principal contradiction between the conceptualisation of a waterhole as an oxbow lake versus a site where Indian spirits regularly claim victims. Recall how Matías, who at the outset was not concerned with the truth-value of the existence of Taíno spirits and *bakás*, took my husband's perspective and provided a bridge over troubled waters by grasping – almost in a Strawsonian (1964) sense – the importance of being (and having) a body as 'a basic particular' within our thinking. From there he sought to explain in what sense Taíno spirits and *bakás* may be said to have a reality according to the kind of assumptions he was presented with by me and my geologist husband. I argue that the cosmological openness of vodou and the attitude of additivity among its adherents (Mintz and Price 1976, Mintz 1974) make the bridging over to science possible, while Western material-mechanical science is incapable of crossing the bridge due to its cosmological close-mindedness. When Dominican and Haitian borderlands peasants were introduced to anthroposophy as well as mainstream Western scientific reasoning, they showed great ease in dealing with incommensurable systems of thought by way of appropriation, mimesis, blending and translations. In Bourguignon's (1985: 292–3) words: 'An interest in new elements is made possible, I should like to argue, by the underlying assumption that, though there are many variants of vodoun rites, no ritual practice or beliefs are truly outside of the scope of this folk religion. The actions of others, including strangers, are rendered intelligible by its adherents in terms of the basic tenets of the vodoun-based world view.... In this world view every creature, spirit, human or animal, has potentially a multitude of identities.' Dayan (1995: 83) similarly expresses that '[t]he history told by vodou defies our notions of identity and contradiction. A thing can be two or more things simultaneously'. This implies that Dominican and Haitian peasants may view Western scientific explanations, anthroposophical explanations and vodou-ist explanations as valid, though in different ways.

There is simultaneously an edge to the openness of vodou. Case materials show that Dominican and Haitian peasants appropriate the anthroposophical conception of occult science for themselves and argue for the scientificity of their vodou-ist magical practices (that is, practices that they themselves term magical) vis-à-vis anthroposophists and others claiming a monopoly on science and truth. They turn the logic whereby anthroposophists have conferred true occult scientificity to themselves in opposition to the Ahrimanian-driven Western scientists (again a reversal of Western scientific rationalism vis-à-vis its occult Other) against the anthroposophists themselves. Juan argues that Dominican peasants already know the spiritual forces at work in nature and that their knowledge is as good as the anthroposophical occult science. Matías states even more clearly that he is a scientist when it comes to detecting whether an animal is not what it seems to be at first sight. Simultaneously, vodou practices and imageries threaten to absorb anthroposophical beliefs and practices as anthroposophical biodynamic preparations easily slip into vodou garden magic among peasants. Dominican and Haitian peasants corrode certain distances between Self and Other that, I argue, any civilising mission (whether modernising or counter-modernising) rests on. The combination of organic and intentional hybridisation (Bakhtin 1981) of anthroposophical cosmological thinking and practices by vodou-practising peasants exposes and subverts what the peasants see as 'the colonising potential' of the counter-modernising force of anthroposophy as elaborated in the borderlands. Dominican and Haitian peasants may render foreign practices reasonable or unreasonable according to the central tenets of vodou, or they may blur those Self-Other distinctions that any civilising mission depends on by absorbing foreign imageries and practices into vodou-ist imageries and practices without profoundly altering the latter. Alternatively, they may continue to practise vodou under the image of, and as they praise, evangelism and anthroposophy.

Beyond the Dominican-Haitian Borderlands

The slippery quality of the empirical materials I have addressed begs for a reformulation of both modernist and postmodernist perspectives upon so-called occult practices and demands a processual approach. The concern with hybridity among anthropologists is itself integral to the shift from modernist to postmodernist theory as Werbner (Werbner and Modood 1997: 1) points out. The transgressive potential ascribed to hybridisation necessarily presupposes systems and categories to be subverted, that is, presupposes modernist notions of order. Simultaneously, postmodern and post-colonial scholars celebrate hybridity as routine and normal and as integral to all historical language- and culture-building, which defies modernist notions of cultural boundedness in terms of 'purity' and 'authenticity'. There never was such a thing as bounded cultures, the post-modernists argue, a claim to which the historical elaboration of vodou and anthroposophy in many ways testifies. This point has, however, been made for a long time by scholars from Lévi-Strauss and de Heusch to Kapferer, Mintz, Thomas (1991) and Amselle, who nevertheless abstain from adopting postmodernist notions of a fragmented world without boundaries. Werbner (Werbner and Modood 1997: 1) asks: 'How is postmodernist theory to make sense, at once, of both sides, both routine hybridization and transgressive power?'

Currently, a number of anthropologists who address contemporary occultic practices across the world argue that these are integral to recent modernity, or rather 'multiple modernities'. It has become almost obligatory to seek to dissolve those 'distances' that the telos of modernity presupposed between Us and Them by proposing an almost universal 'irrational rationality' coming to expression through contemporary witchcraft and sorcery beliefs and practices (cf. Moore and Sanders 2000: 4). Within the recent anthropological engagement with occult practices, there is a tendency to lump together anything from devil pacts in Latin America, witchcraft accusations in Africa and New Age occultism as expressive of the same contemporary global dynamics, thereby reducing these phenomena to alleged 'rational' responses to the irrational overall 'casino culture' of millennium global capitalism among those suffering its consequences (Comaroff and Comaroff 2000). Magical practices figure principally as ways in which individuals address and hook on to global capitalism or as a means to manipulate state and anti-state power. Under the heading 'Occult Economies and New Religious Movements: Privatizing the Millennium', the Comaroffs (2000: 310) argue: 'These economies have two dimensions: a material aspect founded on the effort to conjure wealth – or to account for its accumulation – by appeal to techniques that defy explanation in the conventional terms of practical reason: and an ethical aspect grounded in the moral discourses and (re)actions sparked by the (real or imaginary) production of value through such "magical" means.' I have argued that the articulations occurring in the borderlands take us beyond a contemporary functionalist interpretation of so-called occult practices as social diagnosis (Moore and Sanders 2000) and resist what may be termed the surface-instrumentality view of magic that prevails within the growing literature on 'proliferating occult economies'. The celebration of a globalised world without boundaries – where all systems have withered into free-floating fragments brought forwards by and manipulated by the dynamics of global capitalism and where individuals are left on their own to map together cultural fragments into multiple modern identities – is based on the imaginary of the autonomous individual with an encapsulated inner as against an exteriority of cultural constructedness. This seems to be a central imagery to the anthropology of the occult among scholars who elsewhere express their disdain with the modernist notions of former generations of anthropologists, and who express their sympathy with those suffering the consequences of ongoing globalisation. As Trouillot (2001: 128) argues, the notion of globalisation and a global world without boundaries was first promoted by the advertising industry. The concept of naked individuality consuming its way to identity by bricolage-like dressing up in ad hoc cultural garb is a central metaphor underpinning millennium capitalism itself.

Simultaneously, postmodern scholars addressing occult practices seem to reinvent a strong rationalist-scientific, intellectualist position for themselves, despite their self-conscious and self-reflexive attempts to overcome such presuppositions inherent to the telos of modernist progress.[53] The postmodern engagement with occult beliefs and practices on the African continent and beyond continues to rest on certain distances between Self and Other, Us and Them, foreign and familiar, here and there, then and now, irrational and rational, tradition and modernity. Geschiere (1997: 19), in his study of the modern politics of *sorcellerie* in Cameroon, struggles with 'the thorny question of truth' related to sorcery and magic accusations. He holds that Western anthropologists cannot escape entirely the question of whether such representations correspond to reality. In order to avoid an evaluation of his informants in terms of their rationality/irrationality, Geschiere will not emphasise 'too strongly the reality of these beliefs' (ibid.). In contrast, Evans-Pritchard situated magic, witchcraft and sorcery practices at the centre of social realities and in the richness of lived life. Geschiere echoes the problems involved in contemporary anthropological analyses of sorcery, magic and witchcraft as the malcontents of modernity in Africa (see Comaroff and Comaroff 2000, 1993) and Central and Latin America (see Edelman 1994 for a critical overview). He acknowledges along with Shweder (1991) that anthropology still has a troubled relationship to magic, although he simultaneously points out how different universes of discourse are to a certain point world-constitutive by themselves, as Lévy-Bruhl argued and as post-empiricists from Kuhn to Feuerabend and Goodman have insisted. Although anthropologists pay lip service to post-empiricists, the abstractions of logical positivism and 'reality in itself/reality as perceived' still linger in the background when anthropologists account for strange beliefs and practices among their relativised Other whereby they reanimate, under a different guise, the strong rationalist claim of their forefathers such as Tyler, Morgan and Frazer. What seems to be happening is that anthropologists reinvent a solid, rationalist Self – a safe harbour of singularity in 'an ocean of heteroglossia', ruined modernisms and fragmented multiple modernities, which they themselves are partly inventing.

Do anthropologists include themselves within the framework of multiple modernities? Or do they claim for themselves a privileged position, an omniscient rational eye, a historically neutral and context-free location from which to judge the mystifying theories of the founders of social science as well as the irrationality of contemporary practitioners of the occult across the globe? Such a claim is echoed in Moore and Sanders's editorial introduction (2000: 19) in which they ask suggestively: '[A]re western teleological beliefs about progress, development, rationality and modernity – those ready-made explanations for social change that provide answers to the Big Questions in life – really so different from the idea that occult forces move the world?' At first glance, one may afford Moore and Sanders a generous kind of levelling-out relativism, an exemplary of the postmodern and post-colonial self-reflexive attitude, in which anthropology is offered no privileged place in the world of enquiry. On the other hand, philosophically inclined anthropologists would probably argue that there are many reasons for eschewing such a comparison, particularly with respect to questions concerning the incommensurability of theoretical social canons and occult explanatory provisions. A foundational metatheory about the world is mistakenly being compared to something else, to another way of being and making sense of the world than one based on theoretical contemplation, combined with worries concerning that which accompanies modernity as in Marx, Weber, Durkheim and Tönnies. Winch (1979) would perhaps argue that Moore and Sanders are erroneously comparing very different language games. However, Moore and Sanders's rhetorical question seems first and foremost to testify to Wagner's (1975) claim that relativity has always been of vital importance to anthropologists in the sense that Western anthropologists have invented and justified themselves (and their society) as more rational, more highly developed, scientific and civilised against the background of the otherness of 'primitive' societies in which superstition and primitive thought and forms of life prevail. The difference is that within the category of primitives are included mistaken foundationals mystifying social theorists with their 'invisible hands', disenchantments, dialectical drives, fetishisations and social anomies, along with all those irrational human beings spread across the earth's surface who (still) believe in occult forces moving the world, against whom Moore and Sanders, along with others, invent and justify themselves.

European anthroposophists in the borderlands and beyond reverse this construction and justify themselves by arguing that Western scientific thinking is semi-conscious, and that the Enlightenment-derived delineations of magic, sorcery, religion and science are products of the alienating machinations of

Mephistophelean Ahrimanian beings who promote scientific rationalism. I have a certain feeling that Moore and Sanders, along with other scholars addressing occult practices, would judge anthroposophy from another viewpoint than that of 'postmodern rational irrationalism' when confronted with the suggestion that they themselves are 'puppets in the hands of Ahriman' and as such are engaging in occult practices (e.g. science) without being aware of it – since their 'scientific consciousness' is only semi-conscious. Recall Charles Taylor's (1982: 91) argument about how we tend to judge as irrational '[s]omeone who flagrantly violates the canons of theoretical discourse, while claiming to talk about things and describe how things are.... Of course, if the agent is a member of our culture, we can interpret this as contradictory behavior.... But the judgment of irrationality, or at least of lesser rationality, doesn't depend on contradiction. For we are tempted to judge as less rational members of other cultures who plainly don't accept our canons.'

Whatever disturbances anthroposophy and vodou caused my scientific self – that is, whether my informants tentatively conceptualised me as 'a puppet in the hands of Ahriman' or as 'a puppet in the hands of the colonial spirit La Reina', and whether I engage in judgements concerning the potential rationality/irrationality of anthroposophical and vodou-practising informants – they create an alternative universe of discourse and practice to that of scientific rationalism and global capitalism that simply cannot be explained away as functional responses to recent modernity fragmented by globalising trends. Neither can the impact of an anthroposophical version of world-making in the borderlands be fully assumed by way of symbolic analysis that renders anthroposophical cosmological thought as expressive of something else than itself. Nothing is said about Goethe's scientific approach underpinning biodynamic methods, if discounted as German idealism and romanticism, as Horton (1970: 140) argues while idealising true scientific thinking devoid of magic.

Anthroposophy, vodou, and their amalgamations and recrystallisations make up versions of 'world-making' in their own right. Anthroposophical practices as much as vodou practices and their cross-fertilisations and 'intentional hybridisations' accomplish things in the world and partake in the ongoing reality-constitution down to the existence of forests and micro-organisms. Although I have not intended a thorough phenomenal analysis in this essay, I argue that phenomenological perspectives on 'world-making' (cf. Gil 1998, Kapferer 1997, Goodman 1985) serve to locate various contestations, delineations and hybridisations of magic, sorcery, religion, and scientific and commonsensical beliefs and practices within the realm of the historically conditioned fabric of reality and weaving of identity among practitioners. Rather than engage with magic and science as neutral categories of comparison, I argue that we should focus on practices whereby magical, scientific and commonsensical inscriptions into spatial and bodily domains announce themselves as part of phenomenal world-making in which power is always a crucial dimension. These versions of world-making are historically embedded and continually in the making. Variably conditioned by the modernity-coloniality dynamics of global designs, they nevertheless form genuine perspectives upon the world; people live by them, and they take on world-constitutive forces. I am therefore prepared to modify Mignolo's (2000: 741) claim that '[t]he notion of cultural relativism transformed coloniality of power into a semantic problem. If we accept that actions, objects, beliefs, and so on are culture-relative, we hide the coloniality of power from which different cultures came into being in the first place'. Rather, I emphasise that any cultural formation or any religious phenomenon represents a structured hybridisation of something being always already hybridised, and that we should investigate the forces impinging upon the structuring of hybridisation – including the anti-hybrid, essentialising forces born out of past hybridisations – in the course of history, among which also figure foundational social science and anthropological conceptions of magic, sorcery and science.

NOTES

1. I owe special thanks to Bruce Kapferer for comments on, and suggestions about, this essay. I also thank Hilde Nielssen, Kari Telle, Cecilie Ødegaard and Lars Gjelstad for valuable comments and encouragements.
2. The citations in this essay show variations in the spelling of the word 'vodou'. Deive (1980, 1975) and Davis (1987), who have published fine studies of Dominican versions of vodou, spell it 'vodú'. For the sake of simplicity, I label the variegated borderlands versions 'vodou' rather than making distinctions throughout the text between 'vodú'/'vodou', although I acknowledge that this is indeed problematic. On the one hand, my informants, whether Dominican or Haitian, do not speak of their practices in terms of either vodú or vodou, but conceptualise themselves as 'persons who serve mysteries' (*servidores de misterio*). On the other hand, both Dominican vodú and Haitian vodou may differ from person to person, regionally and according to gross urban/rural distinctions, but Dominican vodú is generally less elaborated and more 'privatised'. It is, however, beyond the scope of this essay to deal with the patterns of similarities and differences between Dominican and Haitian forms of vodú/vodou and their amalgamations in the borderlands, or to address the debates concerning whether these different versions have emerged out of a partly shared colonial history and/or as a result of diffusion. I refer the reader to Davis (1987: 55–75) and Deive (1980, 1975) for comparisons between Dominican vodú and Haitian vodou and their historical foundations. I follow Dayan (1995), McCarthy Brown (1997), Desmangles (1992) and Wexler (1997), who use the spelling 'vodou' rather than 'voodoo', 'voudo', 'vodoun', and so forth.
3. Steiner (1861–1925) was an Austrian philosopher, scientist, artist and social reformer renowned as the father of the anthroposophical movement. He was of humble origin, the son of a poor railway worker. He studied mathematics, physics, chemistry and biology in Vienna. Here he came into contact with the famous theosophist Friedrich Eckstein, but did not join the Theosophical Society in Germany before the turn of the twentieth century, and was in early years highly critical of theosophical doctrines. He spent seven years in Weimar editing and publishing Goethe's scientific works. Steiner was inspired by Johann Gottlieb Fichte's (1762–1814) subjectivism, and his doctoral degree in philosophy

submitted at the University of Rostock in 1891 concerned an alternative theory of knowledge inspired by Fichte's theory of science. Steiner also devoted his life to social reforms, and concerned himself particularly with folk-educational matters. He was inspired by anarchists and feminists such as John Henry Mackay and Rosa Mayreder. Steiner was attentive to the sufferings of Europe's working classes, the disabled and the peasantry deemed backwards, but he found no solution in Marxism. Equally critical of the spread of capitalism and the global design of the nation-state, he worried about the violent implications of nationalism based on ethnic mobilisation and exclusion, and in this respect the atrocities of the Second World War attest to the relevance of his perspectives. He also devoted himself to artwork and became a famous architect. Steiner developed a holistic vision of human development based on his anthroposophical 'occult science' and his alternative social theory, termed 'the threefold social order', in which artistic activities are ascribed a major role. From 1913 onwards, he sought to realise his vision by building an alternative anthroposophical society in Dornach, Switzerland, because a conflict between the German and British theosophical societies had led to fission. Most of the German theosophists broke with the theosophical movement and joined Steiner's anthroposophical movement. The anthroposophical movement proliferated rapidly within European countries, but came under increasing attack during the rise of the Nazi movement. The Goetheanum building in Dornach was set on fire on New Year's Eve in 1922. Steiner died in 1925 (Waage and Schiøtz 2000, Blomquist 1990, Carlgren 1985, Sheperd 1983).

4. By organic and intentional hybridisation, I refer to Bakhtin's (1981) distinction in his 'dialogic imagination'. When applied to cultural processes, the notion of organic hybridisation serves to identify how cultural exchanges, appropriations, mimesis and blending historically form part of culture and language-building across the world. Such non-disruptive fertilisations may nevertheless give rise to new visions and perspectives on the world (cf. Werbner and Modood 1997: 5). Werbner argues that 'organic hybridity creates the historical foundation on which aesthetic hybrids build to shock, change, challenge, revitalise or disrupt through deliberate, intended fusions of unlike social languages and images. Intentional hybrids create an ironic double consciousness'(ibid.: 5). The relationship between forms of organic hybridisations and intentional subversions and their historical foundations is a central concern in this essay, and I address these processes at the level of agency among borderlands peasants.

5. Steiner drew a distinction between Western and Eastern satanic brotherhoods: The Western satanic brotherhoods promote the spread of materialism, and seek to trap the souls of the dead on earth by preventing them from passing through cycles of spiritual and earthly reincarnations. Such reincarnations, according to Steiner, promote sound micro- and macrocosmic development. The Eastern satanic brotherhoods, on the other hand, permit demonic beings to dress up as ancestors, as the so-called etheric bodies (cf. note 44) that ancestors leave behind them on earth after death that are taken over by demonic beings. Spirit possession is thus conceptualised as demonic (Steiner 1966: 21–22, cited in Blomquist 1990: 23).

6. All names of Dominican and Haitian people and places as well as foreigners have been changed.

7. The deforestation rates of Hispaniola, along with other Caribbean and Central American countries, are alarming. By 1996, an estimated 90 per cent of the Dominican forest reserves had vanished (García and Roersch 1996), and according to a statement made by the Minister of Agriculture in 1995, only 3 per cent of Haiti's surface was by then covered with trees (see Guenther et al. 1995).

8. We know that the Haitian revolution (1791–1804), followed by the Haitian occupation of Santo Domingo (1822–44), was welcomed by Dominicans along the border (cf. Franco Pichardo 1997, Moya Pons 1995, Deive 1980). Peasant guerilla groups (*cacos*) fighting the American occupation (cf. Bellegarde-Smith 1990) and subversive millennium movements such as *Liborismo* (cf. Lundius 1995), incorporating both Dominicans and Haitians, thrived in this area during the early twentieth century.

9. During the early days of project implementation in the early 1980s, one could reach the village only by travelling a strenuous one-day's ride on mule. For centuries, this part of Cordillera Central has been largely isolated from urban Dominican centres because of high mountains, dense forests and deep rivers.

10. There are many Dominican peasants who have established life-long friendships with Haitians. They tell of social relationships and contraband trade that cross-cut the border even during the Trujillato period. Among my informants, figure old vodou-practising Dominican peasants who fled to Haiti during the 1940s because of the violent persecution of any practice deemed 'Haitian'. Many Dominican borderlands peasants acknowledge a mixed ancestry. During my meetings with Haitian refugees in Montaña Antigua in 1991, I was given many accounts of how Dominican peasants have protected Haitians from political persecution. To mention an outstanding example, a Haitian woman who had recently given birth to twins was helped by a Dominican neighbour woman during one of many expulsion campaigns launched by Dominican governments. The Dominican woman, who also had recently given birth, breastfed the Haitian woman's twins until she could safely return to retrieve her babies. However, the Haitians also told of mistreatment and economic exploitation on the part of Dominican peasants.

11. During the period of the intense implementation of development programmes during the late 1980s and early 1990s by transnational NGOs, the Balaguer government launched a number of 'counter-programmes'. One example is that the anthroposophists engaged the peasant population in a housing project, in which building material was fabricated out of local resources. Balaguer personally launched a 'counter-programme' whereby the village homesteads were razed by bulldozers, houses for free were granted to a number of selected peasants and half of the population was subsequently left without housing facilities.

12. With the agro-industrial modernisation from the 1960s onwards and the export-led industrialisation from the 1980s, the national economy was ever more firmly drawn into the world market through the export of primary products. In the course of the twentieth century to the present, the peasants have been driven off the fertile lands and serve as a reservoir of cheap labour. There is an ongoing pauperisation, marginalisation and criminalisation of peasants. Accounts of the grim fate of these countries' peasantries, who are carving out a meager living on steep hillsides that are eroding at dangerous rates, mostly reach us as dry statistics. Haitian and Dominican peasants figure among the 200 million Latin Americans and Caribbeans living under conditions of extreme poverty, population pressure and political repression (Hopenhayn 2000, Krohn Hansen 1996, Safa 1995, Sagawe 1991, Vargas-Lundius 1988).

13. This is according to National Law 5856, which prohibits the felling of trees, placing the government of the forest reserves in the hands of the Forestry Office led by the military (see Moreno 1993).

14. The Waldorf School was initiated in 1919 in Stuttgart at the Waldorf Astoria cigarette factory. Workers at the factory asked Steiner, who was renowned for his activities in folk-educational matters, to create a school for their children. The factory owner also gave his consent. This gave rise to the first school in Germany that incorporated pupils from different social classes. Since that time, Waldorf pedagogics has developed into a method in which drama, music, play, story telling, painting and other arts are integrated into subjects such as physics, biology, history and language. The method builds on a particular vision of human development from childhood to adulthood (cf. Carlgren 1985).

15. Eurhythmy represents an art of movement originally developed by Steiner, from 1911 onwards. Steiner claimed that eurhythmic movements could reflect the supersensible realm of human ways of being-in-the-world. Eurhythmics works from the assumption that words largely based on vowels express inner feelings and experiences, while words dominated by consonants reflect happenings in an individual's outer world. Each vowel or consonant has its own pattern of sound that is reflected in movement patterns; in this way, one can 'dance' a poem or one's name (Carlgren 1985: 31).

16. Steiner, who also was an artist and architect, argued that architecture and all art forms talk to human beings' emotional lives. When engraved into one's character, art forms cause a positive transformation in the direction of bringing individuals into contact with their divine nature and the cosmic ordering to which they belong.

17. Anthroposophical medicine is based on a particular tripartite conceptualisation of the basic processes of the human body and seeks to restore their balance. Practising doctors prescribe homeopathic as well as pharmaceutical allopathic preparations to patients (Wolff 1977).

18. In anthroposophical thinking, there is a tension between interpreting Steiner literally or symbolically, and the philosopher Trond Berg Eriksen (2000: 222) has argued that the esoteric visions of Steiner as expressed in his many lectures and books may represent more of a technology of speech, whereby his listeners were torn from the modernist hypnosis and compelled to raise questions concerning notions of progress. My fieldwork experiences both confirm and run counter to Berg Eriksen's interpretation. The world of spiritual beings that Steiner described is taken both concretely and metaphorically by anthroposophists. We may add that such variations are also found among Dominican and Haitian peasants with respect to both anthroposophy and vodou.

19. Guédé and Gède are respectively Dominican and Haitian names for the same family of spirits.

20. *Cupania Americana L.* All Latin names of plants have been determined by botanists at the Botanical Department, Jardín Botánico Dr. Rafael M. Moscoso, Santo Domingo. In Brendbekken (1998) I describe peasant usages of some 250 plants.

21. *Ruta chalepensis L., Ocimum campechianum P. Miller, Chenopodium ambrosioides L., Petiveria alliaceae L., Narvalina dominguensis Cass.*

22. Literally, the name means 'killing-pork'. *Matapuerco* is a poisonous plant (*Dieffenbachia seguina (L.) Schott*). It is planted outside of people's houses to chase away evil spirits.

23. Juan is one of 10 landless peasants enrolled in the anthroposophical biodynamic Pilote Project in Montaña Antigua, where I carried out a substantial portion of my fieldwork.

24. He refers to the flowers of *achillea millefolium* put in the bladder of a hart. According to Steiner, the bladder of this animal 'is almost a representation of the cosmos' (1976: 97, my translation).

25. The Dominican Secretariat (Ministry) of Agriculture (SEA) and the Dominican Land Reform Institute (IAD) have made various attempts to increase agricultural productivity by distributing titles to land on a usufruct basis to peasants selected on unclear premises, and by introducing industrial agricultural programmes to the title-holders.

26. The Anthroposophical Society came into being in Germany in 1913 as the British theosophists excommunicated Steiner and the German Theosophical Society due to a controversy regarding the leadership of Annie Besant and her promotion of Jiddu Krishnamurti as the reincarnation of Christ (Blomquist 1990).

27. In Taylor's (1982: 94) terms, this is a system in which 'elements in different domains of being could be thought to correspond to each other in virtue of embodying the same principle'. Again, in Taylor (2002: 94): 'The other type of premodern moral order is organized around a notion of a hierarchy in society that expresses and corresponds to a hierarchy in the cosmos. These were often theorized in language drawn from the Platonic-Aristotelian concept of Form, but the underlying notion also emerges strongly in theories of correspondence (e.g. the king is in his kingdom, as the lion among animals, the eagle among birds, and so forth). Thus, the idea emerges that disorders in the human realm will resonate in nature, because the very order of things is threatened.'

28. There are other demonic beings dealt with in the writings of Steiner (1969) such as Asuras, but I abstain from including these as they were not evoked in anthroposophical lectures given in the borderlands.

29. It is beyond of the scope of this essay to present the complex cosmology that anthroposophy rests upon. I refer the reader to Carlgren (1985), Mason (2002) and Sheperd (1983) for simplified accounts. Lucifer and Ahriman were lectured about in the borderlands to

project-enrolled peasants, where Steiner's (1969) visions were presented in a very simplified form. According to Steiner, there are seven great ages of world development. We have
behind us the great cosmic ages called Saturn, Sun and Moon, and the coming ages are
Jupiter, Venus and Vulcan. We find ourselves currently in the fourth stage, also termed
'Consciousness Soul Epoch' or 'Great Earth Age'. This is the period in which Ahrimanian
beings and the power they exert over human consciousness and social developments are
reaching their climax. The spiritual beings are grouped in nine hierarchies, with Ahriman
(a name that was revealed to Steiner by Zarathustra) operating as an *Arche* (singular for
Archaie). Angel and supra-angel beings are seen to pervade the world, but are invisible to
the majority of human beings. Mephistophelean beings oppose human evolution as destined by normal gods. Steiner briefly indicated that Lucifer incarnated in a human body
in the third millennium BC (Mason 2002: 6). Lucifer's specific role was to inspire a revolution of human consciousness. This revolution implied a transfer from an instinctual
childhood stage of humanity to the development of human speech and thought and
human self-consciousness. Luciferian beings promoted pagan cultures of nature-wisdom.
The rise of Christianity and the incarnation of Christ were interpreted by Steiner as a fulfilment of pagan wisdom, having been prepared by Hebraic culture with its moral
impulses and its separation of human beings from nature. Lucifer has been preparing the
ground for the coming of Ahriman since the sixteenth century. According to Steiner
(1969), both Ahriman and Lucifer oppose the spiritual development towards 'the tenth
hierarchy', where human beings have become independent and unique individuals, with
true clairvoyant insights into the good, cosmic ordering of the universe, and where they
are themselves creators of their own deeds. This kind of individualism is not to be con-
flated with Luciferian individualism. Anthroposophists associate Lucifer with 'pride, ego-
tism, disinterest in one's fellow humans, fiery emotionalism, subjectivity, fantasy, and
hallucination' (Mason 2002: 6) where the 'essential Ahrimanic tendency is to materialize;
to crystallize; to darken; to silence; to bring living, mobile forces into fixed form – in other
words, to kill that which is living. Within proper bounds, this tendency, in itself, is not
evil; the dead, material world is necessary for God's plan of regular human and cosmic
development' (ibid.).

30. Cf. Courlander (1960), Dayan (1995), Deren (1970), Desmangles (1992), Herskovitz
(1937), Janzen (1982), McCarthy Brown (1997), Métraux (1972) and Thompson (1984).
31. Luc de Heusch (1989: 293) has convincingly argued that the Petro name of this spiritual
division has to do with four Petro kings ruling in Kongo from the mid sixteenth to late
eighteenth centuries: 'Don and Dona were honorary titles used by the Kongo in imitation
of the Portuguese.'
32. Luc de Heusch (1989) has elaborated upon how sacred, monstrous, nature spirits associated with magic and sorcery among Kongo and Angola peoples of the Old World were
transformed into the violent *kita*, *baka*, *bumba* and *ganga* spirits when socialised by
New World experiences. These spirits acquired their violent nature when slaves, who
arrived late to colonial Saint Domingue and Santo Domingo, brought them to Hispaniola
from Kongo and Angola. *Baká* is possibly derived from *mbaka*, which in Kongo traditional beliefs referred to dwarfs and sacred monsters associated with wild nature, magic
and sorcery: 'In the traditional Kongo religion, *mbaka* refers to dwarfs.... Dwarfs and the
lame have the important ritual role of nature spirits in the *kimpasi* initiation ceremony....
Dwarfs and the lame, the family of Ti Jean Petro and the *baka* are ... symbolically equivalent' (ibid.: 294). Dwarfs are also central to the devil lore of Central and South American peasantries, and in this respect, there may be organic hybridisations involved in the
borderlands. We might suspect a certain overlap between the *mbaka* of traditional Kongo
religion, who were conceptualised as dwarfs, and the devil lore reported from different
Central American countries, in which the seven hard-working dwarfs of European fairy
tales were to be associated with the hard-working Africans, presented as the devil's offspring. The seven dwarfs became associated with the seven working days of the Africans

(cf. Edelman 1994: 74–75). My Haitian informants referred to *ganga* and Dominican informants to *guangá* either as wicked *luases* (spirits) or as the products of the illegitimate interaction between human beings and bad *luases*. *Ganga* was associated with paralysis in the legs or gangrene caused by magical poisoning. Luc de Heusch's informant Simon Hèrard conceptualises Ganga as a great magician who practised sorcery and for that reason had to be chained up by his father. Simon Hèrard belongs to a Maroon family that once established an independent Kongo kingdom in Nansoukry in Haiti. The *ganga* spirits of Haiti bring to mind the Bantu word *nganga*, meaning diviner or conjurer (see Courlander 1944: 340). According to a Haitian borderlands informant suffering from paralysis of the leg, the major spirits of the Petro division cause paralysis or gangrene. These spirits are said to be *guangá* or to unleash the powers of *guangá*. According to Luc de Heusch, the Petro division bears a remarkable continuity to the Congolean sacred monsters conceptualised as the maimed, the lame, the blind, dwarfs and twins. The Kongo *mahassa* was transformed into *marassá* among Haitians. Among my Dominican and Haitian borderlands informants, *marassá* denotes a twin spirit, and twins are seen to be spiritually powerful beings. The next-born after twins, termed *dosú* and *dosa*, are even more powerful.

33. Borderlands peasants distinguish between Catholic saints and African/Creole/ Taíno spirits, and borderlands vodou differs from Davis's (1987: 55–66) outline of Dominican vodou in that my informants to only a small degree regard vodou spirits to be the servants, handmaidens or slaves of the Catholic saints, as outlined by Davis. Some informants viewed the spirit and a corresponding saint – when such a correspondence was recognised – as two different manifestations of the same spirit-being, the Catholic chromolithographic representation figuring as the 'official' imagery. However, my informants do not agree upon how to conceptualise the relationship between saints and vodou spirits. Certain borderlands *servidores de misterio* expressed that spirits were called upon under the guise of Catholic saints. Others argued that the Catholic saints were called upon in order for a spirit to perform white magic, while their African/Creole counterparts were called upon in order to perform magic 'with both hands', implying also sorcery. Again, others drew distinctions between God's black and white angels, the former being spirits recognised as African, Creole, Haitian or Taíno, whereas the latter were basically recognised as Catholic and 'white'. Within borderlands versions of vodou figure also a number of spirits without equivalents among Catholic saints.

34. I will basically use the Dominican Barón del Cementerio in the following. Baron Cimetiè is the Haitian counterpart within Haitian vodou.

35. According to Courlander (1944: 340), *bokor* or *bocö* is derived from the Dahomeyan word *bocono* meaning diviner.

36. Kapferer engages a phenomenological concept of sorcery that corresponds well with Dominican and Haitian peasants' understanding of their practices, 'those practices, often described as magical, that are concerned to harness and manipulate those energies and forces which are centered in human beings and which extend from them to intervene – heal, harm, or protect – in the action and circumstance of other human beings'. Sorcery can dispose 'the irrationality of the rational, the terrible absurdities and uncertainties in experience of worlds commanded by the most rational and technically efficient values and systems of organization'. The symbolic power of sorcery rests in its potency to address and act on 'the tragedies in experience flowing within worlds overridingly committed to forms of contemporary rationalism; economic, political and technological' (Kapferer 1997: 15).

37. The state-directed agricultural modernisation programmes have failed either by reason of bad planning or by corruption, leaving a number of overall illiterate peasants seriously indebted to the Dominican Agricultural Bank (BancoAgrícola). Equally, the anthroposophical NGO's counter-modernising biodynamic programme has failed – especially with respect to a system of circulating microcredits granted to peasants who agreed to convert

their slash and burn agricultural plots (*conucos*) to 'biodynamic farm organisms'. There are examples of seriously indebted peasants enrolled in the anthroposophical NGO who have turned their land over to the local anthroposophical board (the local NGO that receives grants from the NGO in Europe), due to their inability to repay their debts to the programme. I hasten to add that the mother organisation in Europe was unaware of this, and that these developments were absolutely not intended on its part. Nevertheless, these processes – combined with a sharp demographic increase, accelerating deforestation and fluctuating prices on the world market for cash crops such as coffee – make the peasants' situation increasingly unpredictable.

38. All land is officially owned by the state, and SEA (the Dominican Secretariat (Ministry) of Agriculture) and IAD (the Dominican Land Reform Institute – an SEA subdivision) redistribute titles in usufruct land (Gutiérrez-St. Martín 1988). There exists an unofficial parallel system based on *terreno comunero* (common land) whereby those who occupy a portion of the territory are regarded as owners of *la mejora*, meaning 'improvements of the land' such as fences, coffee and orange trees, etc. Montaña Antigua peasants recognise both systems, and plots of land may be sold, although the transaction is officially illegal.

39. I am referring to state rationalisation in terms of how land recognised as *terreno comunero* has been divided haphazardly and distributed to selected peasants in terms of titles to usufruct land owned by the state.

40. The peasants prepare *despojos*, which are herbal infusions utilised as magical protection. *Despojos* are sprinkled inside and outside the house, on animals, on human bodies and at the conjuncture between an agricultural field and a neighbouring agricultural field. These preparations drive off intrusive spirits. *Sahumeras* (*sahumerios*) are fumigations, burned in order to ward off intrusive spirits. Composed of olfactory herbs combined with feathers and pieces of rubber from a car wheel, they are basically modelled on the incense burned during Catholic ceremonies. *Resguardos* are amulets that often contain a biblical prayer and a protective herb such as *anamú*.

41. One example is this: due to the association between sour lemon and the Guédés, the sour lemons are placed on sticks and planted in the field in order to ward off the female witch (*la bruja*) who has empowered herself by entering a compromise with Barón del Cementerio. Depositing multiple seeds of the plant *ajonjolí* (*Sesum indicum L.*) at certain places within the garden makes the female witch and the *galipote* and *zángano* (sorcerers who transform themselves into animals or invisibles, due to their illegitimate interaction with spirits of the left hand) change course so as not to fly over the land. The seeds distract them from destroying the harvest by compelling them to count all of the seeds.

42. The first three regions of the land of spirit are comparable to the earthly regions of nature: (1) the solid land, (2) rivers and oceans, and (3) the airy atmosphere. The solid land of the first region of the spiritual world is the archetypical beings standing behind physical forms on earth. The rivers and oceans of the second region of the Land of Spirit have, as their earthly counterpart, the flowing life-etheric essence that permeates every living being on earth, and gives these a definite form of life. The airy element of the third region of the Land of Spirit has as its earthly equivalent all that is feeling and sensation. Apart from the fifth region of the beings of wisdom that is compared to the light of the physical world, there are yet higher regions of Spirit-Land (Steiner 1969: 82–108).

43. During lectures given in the borderlands, the anthroposophists outlined the relationship between what they term the physical, etheric and astral body. They argued that when we observe life processes on earth, we are confronted with the fact of death, which the lifeless kingdom of minerals carries within it (see Steiner 1969: 39). The same substances and forces are at work in the physical body of humans, animals, plants and minerals; plants, animals and human beings all share in common a physical body that, after death, is of like nature with the minerals. The physical body of all living beings is kept together and endowed with life and reproductive capabilities due to 'etheric' form-giving and life-sustaining forces. There is an etheric body that permeates the physical body of plants,

animals and human beings in order for these to become alive. The etheric corresponds to the life-essence of the second realm of the Spirit-Land, likened to the rivers and oceans on earth: 'Life is a flowing essence, like sea and river pervading the Spirit Land' (Steiner 1969: 85). Whereas plants are in a perpetual state of sleep, animals and human beings have an inner conscious experience of pain and pleasure, thirst and hunger. Their etheric body is awake and conscious due to the 'astral body' that illuminates it. Animals and human beings share in common a consciousness of their bodily state of being. However, the human soul is separated from that of the animals in that human desires, wishes and thoughts transcend the outer-worldly experiences and are not contingent upon these alone. The home of the astral body is the Land of Spirits, to which it returns in sleep and after death. This is where it works upon earthly experiences before incarnating anew. The 'I' of human beings is distinct from the kingdom of animals, in that human beings have an inner consciousness about the permanence of its being across shifting sensory and inner experiences. The human 'I' is conscious about its own possibility to be aware of itself as a knowing entity, is capable of judgements, can reflect upon its own being, can master its bodily desires and can will impulses. This is the human 'I' that works upon the astral, etheric and physical body, and transforms these at a 'lower' spiritual level into the sentient soul, the intellectual soul and the spiritual soul, and at a 'higher' spiritual level into Spirit-Self, Life-Spirit and Spirit-Man. Through the influence of the 'I' upon the astral, etheric and finally the physical body, it will become united with the same spiritual forces that bring about the physical processes of its body and the hidden, spiritual world underlying these, thereby turning into a completed Spirit-Man: 'These are the invisible forces to which the coming-into-being and also the decay of the physical body are due' (Steiner 1969: 57). These forces are also those that biodynamic preparations are made to act upon. The nature of human beings stands in a variegated relationship to the whole universe, as the universe, so to say, evolves out of the archetypical Spirit-Man.

44. The cosmic-planetary beings operating through silica as earthly mediator are contrasted to the cosmic-planetary beings associated with the moon, Mercury and Venus operating through calcium (and calcium carbonate). The latter function above the earth's surface and enable plants, animals and human beings to reproduce (Steiner 1976). The anthroposophists argue that the biodynamic preparation 501 strengthens the 'life-building' capability of plants as the crushed silica is prepared in a way that condenses planetary influences irradiating from spiritual beings far away.

45. The anthroposophical conception of how human beings may gain insight into the interrelationship between the Spirit-Land and nature contrasts significantly to that of peasants. Dominican and Haitian peasants' conception of spirit possession was not what the anthroposophists had in mind when speaking about clairvoyant insights into the spiritual reality behind every manifest phenomenon, given that spirit possession, as conceptualised by peasants, implies a loss of consciousness which guarantees that it was indeed the spirit, and not the person, speaking. In contrast, the anthroposophists put great stress on the human Self, or 'Yo' (the divine 'I'), which enables human beings to know nature consciously. Spirit possession was seen to give rise to distorted insight into the Spirit-Land in that Mephistophelean beings interfere. The anthroposophists argue that the interrelationships between the world of spirits and that of earthly existence are not accessible to us without proper, conscious, supersensible training, implying a moral discipline of the human body and soul.

46. Among Colombian peasants, certain pacts with the devil are undertaken in order to increase plantation agricultural production beyond what is considered natural by peasants, orientated towards household subsistence production. However, neither Dominican nor Haitian peasants – nor anthroposophists – view money or money transactions to be inherently evil: there is no idyllic past of natural Aristotelian-use value and pre-capitalist mysticism in the Dominican-Haitian borderlands. Devil pact imageries have a long historical standing among Hispaniolan slave populations, who have been accustomed to

market transactions since the early days of colonisation. Money transactions implied the commercialisation of the slaves' bodies and the means by which a limited number of slaves managed to buy their freedom, and by which many more sustained their lives as they developed 'black markets'. See Batista (1993) and Deive (1980) concerning the *jornalero/a* marketing slaves of colonial Santo Domingo. See Edelman (1994) for an overview of Taussig's critics among Latin American scholars.

47. Kieckhefer (1994: 816) argues: 'The notion of demonic intervention in the natural order on behalf of those who invoked demons was deeply rooted in the religious and theological literature of Christianity; the idea of occult powers and processes within the natural order was firmly established and variously developed in philosophical and scientific writings from antiquity through the early modern era.'

48. Dominican and Haitian peasants ascribe a female principle to the operation of the moon upon earthly beings and a masculine principle to that of the sun. The rhythmic cycle of the moon is of paramount importance, in that peasants do not cut trees, prepare the soil, sow or harvest without taking into consideration the moon phases in relation to particular plants conceptualised as either 'female' or 'male'. These are, respectively, those that yield beneath the soil (tubers) versus those that yield above (beans, *maíz*, rice and so on). The days of the week are similarly conceptualised as either female or male and are also taken into consideration.

49. La Reina de España, who is seen to empower gringos in their struggle to make peasants comply to their demands and expectations, takes on many of the characteristics of the female vodou spirit, Marinette, who is seen to have accompanied the historical Dessalines in his struggle against the French. Dayan reports that the historical Dessalines, who became the spirit Ogou Desalins, is accompanied by a sorceress-devil by the name of Marinette-Bwa-Chèche (Marinette Dry Bones), who is a man-eating spirit (*Kita denanbre*), originally of Kongo origin (*Nkita*), also recognised by the name Marinette-Limen-dife (Marinette Light the Fire) (Dayan 1995: 83). According to Luc de Heusch (1989: 294), Marinette bears the imprints of the awesome and ugly Kimpasi mother who guarded over the *nkita* initiation ritual, where novices 'died' ritually at her hands. The red-eyed Marinette, who eats bones and lights fire, is so frightful to most Haitians that she is tied up with ropes or nailed to trees in the forest due to the terrible destructive powers associated with the *Kitas* of Haitian vodou (de Heusch 1989). My informant, Rafaelito, similarly conceptualised La Reina as a red-eyed spirit. She was served crushed bones and associated with the auto-destructive power of the Petro way of spiritual being-in-the-world.

50. Colonial encounters also inspired the emergence of foundational social science. One example is the debates following the Sepúlveda/Las Casas controversy of the sixteenth century (Mignolo 2000, Jahoda 1999, Larsen 1999) concerning the nature of Indians and their rights to their land. Another example is how Marx developed his conceptions of commodity fetishism after having become familiar with the worship of gold among Caribbean Indians, following their encounter with the Spaniards whom they understood to be gold worshippers, as described in Herrera's (1730) *History of the West Indies* (Krohn Hansen 1995, McNeill 1988). Herrera tells a story about the Cuban *Cacique* Hatuey who, when hearing about the coming of the Spaniards in 1511, warned his followers about the great sufferings that the Taíno Indians had experienced on Hispaniola, and that these sufferings were all due to a great lord which was gold: '[A]nd then taking some Gold out of a little Palm-tree basket, added "therefore let us ... dance to him, to the end that when they come he may order them not to do us harm"' (Herrera 1730: 10, in McNeill 1988: 12; quoted by Krohn Hansen 1995: 143).

BIBLIOGRAPHY

Amselle, J.L. 'Globalization and the Future of Anthropology.' *African Affairs* 101 (2002): 213–29.

Arman, K. *La Dinámica de lo Vivo.* Trans. Equipo de Agricultores de Canarias. Madrid, 1986 [1976].

Bakhtin, M. *The Dialogical Imagination.* Ed. M. Holquist. Trans. C. Emerson and M. Holquist. Austin, 1981.

Batista, C.A. *Mujer y Esclavitud en Santo Domingo.* Santo Domingo, 1993.

Baud, M. 'Constitutionally White? The Forging of Dominican National Identity.' In *Ethnicity in the Caribbean: Essays in Honor of Harry Hoetink,* ed. G. Oostindie 121–52. London, 1996.

Bellegarde-Smith, P. *Haiti: The Breached Citadel.* Boulder, 1990.

Bhabha, H. *The Location of Culture.* London, 1994.

Bisnauth, D. *History of Religions in the Caribbean.* Eritrea, 1996.

Blackburn, R. *The Making of New World Slavery from the Baroque to the Modern, 1492–1800.* London, 1997.

Blomquist, H. 'Antroposofi. Okkultismen som ble stueren.' *Humanist* 1 (1990).

Bourguignon, E. 'Religion and Justice in Haitian Vodoun.' *Phylon* 46, no. 4. (1985): 292–5.

Brendbekken, M. Forthcoming. 'Historicities and Local-Global Articulations in the Weaving of Identity among Peasants of the Dominican-Haitian Borderlands.' Ph.D diss., University of Bergen, 2003.

———. *Hablando con la Mata. Las Plantas y la Identidad Campesina.* Santo Domingo, 1998.

Burton, R.D. *Afrocreole: Power, Opposition and Play in the Caribbean.* Ithaca, 1997.

Carlgren, F. *Den Antroposofiske Rörelsen.* Järna, 1985.

Classen, C., D. Howes and A. Synnott. *Aroma: The Cultural History of Smell.* London, 1994.

Comaroff, J., and J.L. Comaroff. 'Millennial Capitalism: First Thoughts on a Second Coming.' *Public Culture* 12, no. 2 (2000): 291–343.

———, eds. *Modernity and Its Malcontents: Ritual and Power in Postcolonial Africa.* Chicago, 1993.

Courlander, H. *The Drum and the Hoe: Life and Lore of the Haitian People.* Berkeley, 1960.

———. 'Gods of the Haitian Mountains.' *Journal of Negro History* 29, no. 3 (1944): 339–72.

Davis, M.E. *La Otra Sciencia.* Santo Domingo, 1987.

Dayan, J. 'Haiti, History and the Gods.' In *After Colonialism,* ed. G. Prakash, 66–97. Princeton, 1995.

Deive, C.E. *La esclavitud del Negro en Santo Domingo (1492–1844), Tomo I & II.* Santo Domingo, 1980.

———. *Vodú y Magia en Santo Domingo.* Santo Domingo, 1975.

Derby, L. 'Haitians, Magic and Money: Raza and Society in the Dominican-Haitian Borderlands, 1900 to 1937.' *Comparative Studies in Society and History* 36 (1994): 488–526.

Deren, M. *Divine Horsemen: The Voodoo Gods of Haiti.* New York, 1970.

Desmangles, L.G. *The Faces of the Gods: Vodou and Roman Catholicism in Haiti.* London, 1992.

Ebbestad Hansen, J. 'Autoritetens Filosofi.' In *Fascinasjon og Forargelse. Steiner og Antroposofien sett Utenifra,* ed. N. Waage, P. Schiøtz and C. Schiøtz, 119–33. Oslo, 2000.

Edelman, M. 'Landlords and the Devil: Class, Ethnic, and Gender Dimensions of Central American Peasant Narratives.' *Cultural Anthropology* 9, no. 1 (1994): 58–93.

Eriksen, T.B. 'Steiner for brød?' In *Fascinasjon og Forargelse. Steiner og Antroposofien sett Utenifra,* ed. N. Waage, P. Schiøtz and C. Schiøtz, 217–23. Oslo, 2000.

Evans-Pritchard, E.E. *Witchcraft, Magic and Oracles among the Azande.* Oxford, 1985 [1937].

Farmer, P. *The Uses of Haiti.* Monroe, Me., 1994.

Feldman, A. *Formations of Violence: The Narrative of the Body and Political Terror in Ireland.* Chicago, 1991.

Franco Pichardo, F. *Sobre Racismo y Antihaitianismo (y otros ensayos).* Santo Domingo, 1997.

Fundación Agricultura y Medio Ambiente & GATE. *Directorio de organizaciones no gubernamentales en la República Dominicana.* Santo Domingo, 1996.

García, R., and C. Roersch. 'Politica de Manejo y Utilización de los Recursos Floristicos en la República Dominicana.' *Journal of Ethnopharmacology* 51 (1996): 147–60.

García Canclini, N. *Hybrid Cultures: Strategies for Entering and Leaving Modernity.* Trans. C.L. Chiappari and S.L. Lopez. Minneapolis, 1995.

Geschiere, P. *The Modernity of Witchcraft: Politics and the Occult in Postcolonial Africa.* Charlottesville, 1997.

Gil, J. *Metamorphosis of the Body.* Trans. S. Muecke. Minneapolis, 1998.

Goodman, N. *Languages of Art: An Approach to a Theory of Symbols.* Indianapolis, 1985 [1976].

Guenther, D.W., et al. *Proyectos de Desarrollo Agroecológico en la República de Haiti. Informe Sobre una Mision de Intercambio.* Santo Domingo, 1995.

Gutiérrez-St. Martín, A.T. *Agrarian Reform Policy in the Dominican Republic: Local Organization and Beneficiary Investment Strategies.* New York, 1988.

Hall, S. 'Negotiating Caribbean Identities.' *New Left Review* 20 (1995): 3–14.

Hartshorn, G.G., et al. *Country Environmental Profile: A Field Study.* McLean, Va., 1981.

Herskovitz, M. *Life in a Haitian Valley.* New York, 1937.

Heusch, L. de. 'Kongo in Haiti: A New Approach to Religious Syncretism.' *Man (N.S.)* 24 (1989): 290–302.

Hopenhayn, M. 'Globalization and Culture: Five Approaches to a Single Text.' In *Cultural Politics in Latin America,* ed. B. Jones, A. Munck and R. Munck, 142–57. London, 2000.

Horton, R. 'African Traditional Thought and Western Science.' In *Rationality,* ed. B.A. Wilson, 131–72. Oxford, 1970.

Jahoda, G. *Images of Savages. Ancient Roots of Modern Prejudice in Western Culture.* London, 1999.

Janzen, J.M. *Lemba, 1650–1930: A Drum of Affliction in Africa and the New World.* New York, 1982.

Kapferer, B. *The Feast of the Sorcerer: Practices of Consciousness and Power.* Chicago, 1997.

Kieckhefer, R. 'The Specific Rationality of Medieval Magic.' *The American Historical Review* 99, no. 3 (1994): 813–36.

Kimpfler, A. 'Kulturgestaltning ur Människans Väsen.' In *Maria Magdalena* 4 (1989): 4–9.

Koob, O. 'Kunskapen om det Onda.' In *Nutidsfrågor. Falk Järna* (1985): 18–35.

Krohn Hansen, C. *The Social and Political Roots of Deforestation in Central America and the Caribbean.* Oslo, 1996.

———. 'Magic, Money and Alterity among Dominicans.' *Social Anthropology* 3, no. 2 (1995a): 129–46.

———. 'From Violence to Boundaries: The Production of the Dominican Republic in the Dominican-Haitian Borderlands.' Ph.D. diss., University of Oslo, 1995b.

Larsen T. 'Den Globale Samtalen. Modernisering, Representasjon og Subjektkonstruksjon.' In *Ambivalens og Fundamentalisme. Seks Essays om Kulturens Globalisering,* ed. T.H. Eriksen and O. Hemer, 91–112. Oslo, 1999.

Löfström, B. *Fragment af en Världsbild.* Sweden, 1989.

Lundius, J. *The Great Power of God in San Juan Valley: Syncretism and Messianism in the Dominican Republic.* Lund Studies in History of Religions 4. Lund, 1995

Macfarlaine, A. 'The Root of All Evil.' In *The Anthropology of Evil,* ed. D. Parkin, 57–76. Oxford, 1995.

Mason, R.S. 'The Advent of Ahriman: An Essay on the Deep Forces behind the World Crisis', www.geocities.com/Athens/Sparta/1105/ahriman.htm, 1997/2002.

McCarthy Brown, K. 'Systematic Remembering, Systematic Forgetting: Ogou in Haiti.' In *Afro-American Religion: Interpretative Essays in Culture and History,* ed. T.E. Fulop and A. Raboteau, 433–62. London, 1997.

McNeill, D.J. 'Fetishism and the Value Form: Towards a General Theory of Value.' Ph.D. diss., University of London, 1988.

Métraux, A. *Voodoo in Haiti.* New York, 1972.

Mignolo, W. 'The Many Faces of Cosmopolis.' *Public Culture* 12, no. 3 (2000): 721–48.

Ministère de l'Agriculture des Ressources Naturelles et du Développement Rural. *MARNDR.* Port-au-Prince, 1995.

Mintz, S.W. 'Enduring Substances, Trying Theories: The Caribbean as Global Oikomenê.' *Journal of the Royal Anthropological Institute of Great Britain and Ireland* 2, no. 2 (1996): 289–311.

———. *Caribbean Transformations.* Chicago, 1974.

Mintz, S.W., and R. Price. *An Anthropological Approach to the Afro-American Past: A Caribbean Perspective.* Philadelphia, 1976.

Moore, H., and T. Sanders, eds. *Magical Interpretations, Material Realities: Modernity, Witchcraft and the Occult in Postcolonial Africa.* London, 2000.

Moreno, S. *La Deforestación en República Dominicana y sus Consecuencias Juridicales.* Santo Domingo, 1993.

Moya Pons, F. *The Dominican Republic: A National History.* New York, 1995.

Nash, J. *We Eat the Mines and the Mines Eat Us: Dependency and Exploitation in Bolivian Tin Mines.* New York, 1979.

Palmié, S., ed. *Slave Cultures and Cultures of Slavery.* Knoxville, 1995.

Prakash, G. 'Introduction: After Colonialism.' In *After Colonialism*, ed. G. Prakash, 3–17. Princeton, 1995.

Safa, H.I. *The Myth of the Male Breadwinner: Women and Industrialization in the Caribbean.* Boulder, 1995.

Sagawe, T. 'Deforestation and the Behavior of Households in the Dominican Republic.' *Geography* 76, no. 4 (1991): 304–14.

Sahlberg, I. 'Rudolf Steiner och Världen av i Dag.' *Antropos* 18, no. 6 (1972): 51–55.

San Miguel, P.L. *La Isla Imaginada: Historia, Identidad y Utopia en La Española.* Ed. I. Negra. Santo Domingo, 1997.

Sheperd, A.P. *Scientist of the Invisible.* New York, 1983.

Shweder, R. *Thinking Through Cultures: Expeditions in Cultural Psychology.* Cambridge, Mass., 1991.

Simpson, G. *The Shango Cult in Trinidad.* Caribbean Monograph Series no. 2. Río Piedras, 1965.

Steiner, R. *Frihetens Filosofi. Grunddrag av en Modern Världsådskådning.* Stockholm, 1990 [1918].

———. *Hur Uppnår man Kunskap om de Högre Världarna?* Stockholm, 1984 [1931].

———. *Bidrag til en Fornyelse af Landbruget på Åndsvidenskabeligt Grundlag.* Trans. Henning Anthon. København, 1976 [1924].

———. *Occult Science.* Trans. G. Adams and M. Adams. London, 1969 [1925].

———. *Kärnpunkterna i den Sociala Frågan.* Trans. J.Wolontis. Norrköping, 1920.

Strawson, P.F. *Individuals: An Essay in Descriptive Metaphysics.* London, 1964.

Taussig, M. *The Devil and Commodity Fetishism in South America.* Chapel Hill, 1980.

Taylor, C. 'Modern Social Imaginaries.' *Public Culture* 14, no. 1 (2002): 91–124.

———. 'Rationality.' In *Rationality and Relativism*, ed. M. Hollies and S. Lukes, 87–105. Cambridge, Mass., 1982.

Thomas, N. *Entangled Objects: Exchange, Material Culture and Colonialism in the Pacific.* Cambridge, Mass., 1991.

Thompson, R.F. *Flash of the Spirit: African and Afro-American Art and Philosophy.* New York, 1984.

Thun, M., and M.K. Thun. *Så och Skördekalender 1990.* Järna, 1990.

Trouillot, R. 'The Anthropology of the State in the Age of Globalization: Close Encounters of the Deceptive Kind.' *Current Anthropology* 42, no. 1 (2001): 125–38.

———. 'The Caribbean Region: An Open Frontier in Anthropological Theory.' *Annual Review of Anthropology* 21 (1992): 19–42.

Vargas-Lundius, R. *Peasants in Distress: Poverty and Unemployment in the Dominican Republic*. Lund, 1988.

Waage, P.N., and C. Schiøtz, eds. *Til Fascinasjon og Forargelse. Rudolf Steiner og Antroposofien sett Utenfra*. Oslo, 2000.

Wagner, R. *The Invention of Culture*. Chicago, 1975.

Werbner, P., and T. Modood, eds. *Debating Cultural Hybridity: Multicultural Identities and the Politics of Anti-Racism*. London, 1997.

Wexler, A. '"I am going to see where my Ougan is": The Artistry of a Haitian Vodou Flagmaker.' In *Sacred Possessions: Vodou, Santería, Obeah, and the Caribbean*, ed. M. Fernández Olmos, and L. Paravisini-Gebert, 59–79. New Brunswick, N.J., 1997.

Winch, P. 'Understanding a Primitive Society.' In *Rationality*, ed. B.R. Wilson, 78–111. Oxford, 1979.

Wolff, O. *Den Antroposofisk Orienterade Medicinen och dess Läkemedel*. Trans. K. Almquist. Järna, 1977.

Young, R.J.C. *Colonial Desire: Hybridity in Theory, Culture and Race*. London, 1995.

Zweifler, M.O., M.A. Gold and R.N. Thomas. 'Land Use Evolution in Hill Regions of the Dominican Republic.' *Professional Geographer* 46, no. 1 (1994): 39–53.

Chapter 3

THE SMELL OF DEATH
Theft, Disgust and Ritual Practice in Central Lombok, Indonesia

Kari G. Telle

> Every secret is explosive, expanding with its own inner heat.
>
> – Elias Canetti, *Crowds and Power*

Introduction

In this essay I examine a form of stealing that people in rural Sasak communities on the island of Lombok find deeply problematic because of its intimate nature: theft of which they suspect that someone in their own hamlet or village is culpable. In the large village in central Lombok where I have carried out fieldwork, theft that is attributed to a so-called 'neighbourhood thief' is said to produce a foul smell (*bais*) that begins to ooze out from where the theft occurred, enveloping the neighbourhood in a putrid stench.[1] This smell is particularly intense when the thief is not caught in the act of stealing, but manages to slip away. In connection with a theft of two heirloom daggers and several pieces of old cloth that occurred one Saturday night in June 2001 and of which a close neighbour soon emerged as a suspect, Bapen Seni, a man who lives nearby, commented in disgust: 'Now this neighbourhood really stinks [*bais gubuk*]! The stench is smelled even far away, it cannot be sealed off.'

That foul smell becomes a problem in connection with theft points to a concern with boundaries and to the sensuous and symbolic efficacy of odour, which I explore by focusing on the meaning of 'bad' smell and the disgust it provokes. Much as theft entails a violation of symbolic and spatial boundaries, smell – whether foul or fragrant – is characteristically unbound and wafts through space in a manner that resists containment. Drawing on phenomenological approaches to sensory perception (Bubandt 1998, Gell 1977), I will suggest that the border-transcending quality of smell is both a resource and a problem for the Sasak, who accord odour considerable importance in sensing, and making sense of, the world.

The Sasak, who form the dominant ethnic group on Lombok, which is located between the islands of Bali and Sumbawa in the Indonesian archipelago, often express moral indignation through olfactory metaphors. Various practices that are symptomatic of disorder are said to 'stink' and to be almost impossible to keep secret because they reek. But malodour is not merely a conventional linguistic trope; odour is also a substance-like phenomenon in itself. Of all the senses that orient and connect people to the world, the Sasak give smelling a central place since odour is perceived to give access to what is inner and intrinsic, yet hidden from view. Whereas sight gives access to surfaces, smell puts people in sensuous contact with interiors. Involved here is a notion of odour as 'essence', containing as well as communicating the intrinsic identity of its source of origin (Classen 1992: 155). What makes the smell that escapes after theft so unsettling is that it indexes decay. As the 'foul' scent exudes evidence of transgression, prompt efforts are taken to identify the source of the malodour and to stem the contagion.

One such measure is a public ordeal called Garap, whose twin purpose is to disclose the thief and to 'cleanse the neighbourhood' (*bisoq gubuk*). The practice of Garap, a highly institutionalised ritual that is performed at the request of victims of theft, is a major focus in this essay. Garap entails swearing an oath of innocence and drinking water mixed with soil that is taken from the tomb of a Muslim saint, which is located in the Rembitan area of southern Lombok. Steeped in the symbolism of death, Garap is built around a demonised 'Other' – the thief who epitomises the enemy within – who must be revealed and rendered harmless in order for the victims and the moral community to thrive. No one is ever named or accused in the course of Garap, however. The refusal to identify suspects is critical to the dynamics of this ritual, which is directed towards bringing the negativity of theft to a conclusive end by swearing innocence. In my discussion of Garap, I will emphasise how themes of healing and destruction are thoroughly interrelated in this ritual that promises to 'cool' those who are afflicted by theft and to inflict a devastating curse on those who commit perjury. The most powerful linguistic resources that the Sasak command, that is, prayer and oath, are mobilised to overcome the harmful forces unleashed by theft and to revivify those who take part in Garap, whether in person or by proxy. Operating directly on the bodies of those who participate, Garap also serves to reconstitute the social body, reaffirming distinctions that are vital to its reproduction.

Following the trail of 'foul' scent that a local thief provokes leads me to consider affinities between thieving, witchcraft (*ilmu selaq*) and sorcery (*ilmu seher*), and to draw out some of their connections. So many symbolic linkages are made between these covert acts that they cannot properly be treated apart from each other, for instance by regarding the illicit appropriation of objects (theft) as a more self-evident or 'natural' kind of offence than sorcery or witchcraft, which have often been deemed 'supernatural' offences (see Heald 1999, 1998). While anthropologists have long insisted that such distinctions make little sense outside their socio-cultural milieu, Suzette Heald (1999: 73) has recently argued that anthropologists, by and large, have treated theft as 'a self-evident category of offence, with a direct relationship between delict and accusation'. This assumption, she maintains, implies that anthropologists have neglected the implications of calling someone a thief and why thieves may be regarded as more of a problem in some societies than in others – why one might have 'thief-crazes' as well as 'witch-crazes' (1999: 73–4).

Among the Sasak, notions of witchcraft or sorcery cannot be analysed as self-contained explanatory systems or as discrete phenomena, and my analysis implies that they should not be treated in isolation from other sources of trouble and misfortune, including thieves.[2] To depict sorcery in purely negative terms is not consistent with Sasak opinion on this subject – a subject that it is difficult, if not impossible, to delimit as sorcery is patently not a thing in itself. Narrowly conceived, sorcery (*ilmu seher*) connotes secret and purposefully executed acts that aim to exert control over other people in the most direct manner possible and requires specialised knowledge, often in the form of spells. But this narrow view fails to capture how people quite unintentionally may affect others because the sentiments they harbour are not limited to the body but transcend it. Given that the malevolent sensibility of other people can cause serious afflictions, much effort goes into fortifying the boundaries of the body so as to make them less permeable.

Pervasive and invisible, scents spill across boundaries and are notoriously difficult to avoid because distancing is 'annulled with nasal perception' (Taussig 1999: 4). Odours, as Bauman (1993: 24) observes, 'cannot remain unnoticed, however hard one tries; one cannot isolate oneself from their presence the way one isolates oneself from sights by closing eyes or decreeing that eyes should be kept closed'. For these reasons, pleasant odours are often harnessed for seductive purposes and used to facilitate propitious communication with unseen forces (see Gell 1977).[3]

In this essay, I consider the perception and symbolic significance of 'foul' odour, focusing to a lesser extent on pleasing scents. Specifically, I will show how the idiom of 'foul' odour meaningfully connects a series of deeply problematic interpersonal relations and moments in which people fear that they will be consumed, hence destroyed, by forces beyond their control. The intensely loathed 'neighbourhood thief' – a label that is applied only to men – is in some ways conceived as a witch, a figure of radical evil who saps people of their vitality and blood. Unlike witches, whose nefarious acts do not prompt collective efforts at redress, thieves are improper accumulators whose anti-social acts demand a communal response. Thieving, as any other social practice, has its own standards of propriety, and I will suggest that thieves who traverse the boundaries between different communities embody qualities of maleness that are highly prized among the Sasak. The loathing provoked by men who steal close to home is thus in my view tinged with contempt that is informed by notions of morality and appropriate gender behaviour.

A key point to emerge from this material is that notions of sorcery and witchcraft are integral to an ontological orientation to the world, a world in which 'foul' smells are both constitutive of and active in the destruction of social order. Inherently ambiguous, 'foul' odour attests to the fragility of social order that constantly wages a war against the destructive potential of smell. Although Garap is considered to be the most refined and powerful way of dealing with intimate theft and combating stench, it is also surrounded with ambivalence. That ambivalence relates to the ambiguity of 'foul' smell that must be banished if social life is to be maintained, yet is fundamental to human existence.

Introducing Garap: 'To Search for Something That is Hidden'

Cast as a rite of purification, Garap is designed to expose and punish a local thief whose act of trespass has caused anger, mistrust and a menacing stench. Garap is widely considered to be the most refined (*alus*) way of addressing and resolving theft, but it is not a practice that is undertaken lightly. Garap entails pledging an oath of innocence and drinking water mixed with soil that is taken from the grave of Wali Nyato', a saint who is reputed to have brought Islam to southern Lombok and whose tomb, located atop a hill close to the village of Rembitan, is a popular pilgrimage site. Although this site resembles a grave, with stones marking the saint's head and feet, it is not properly a grave. Legend has it that those who carried the corpse felt the bier turn lighter and lighter, and by the time they reached the intended burial place, only the funeral shroud was left. As he was no ordinary mortal but a 'friend of Allah', he simply vanished and moved on into the invisible realm, just as the earliest ancestors, ancient Sasak kings and other Islamic mystics are alleged to have done.[4] That his body did not succumb to the ravages of putrefaction, and hence never exuded the acrid scent of decomposing flesh (*bais*), attests to his abundant spiritual potency (*sakti*). The site that marks his entry into the invisible world is a juncture where different realms interpenetrate. Such a place of power (*keramat*) is to be approached with respect for the appropriate times of visit and mode of conduct. Wali Nyato' is assumed to reside in Mecca, the spiritual centre of all Muslims, but to return to Lombok on Wednesdays and Saturdays, when the site is packed with hundreds of people from all over the island who come to pay a devotional visit, to pray, to picnic, or to make and fulfil vows. Soil to be used for the purpose of curing or swearing is removed only when the site is 'filled' with invisible presence. Likewise, Garap may take place only on Wednesdays or Saturdays. In this way, a temporal link to the figure who many regard as having instituted Garap just before his ascent is established.

For people in Bon Raja and neighbouring communities whose forebears migrated from the hot and arid south to the lush and densely populated central plain that is ideally suited for wet-rice cultivation, Garap also reaffirms a connection to their place of origin. Garap is mainly performed in southern Lombok and in communities where the majority of the population trace their origins to the Pujut, Kuta and Rembitan areas. Over the past two to three decades, this practice has also become incorporated into the ritual repertoire of several villages in central Lombok that formerly had no such tradition.

No one could offer the etymology for the name Garap, but a number of people explained that it means 'to search for something that is hidden' or 'to grope for something in the dark'.[5] The image of searching for something 'in the dark' suggests that the endeavour is difficult and that it may fail, but Garap is carried out with great certitude. People are adamant that if the thief, who invariably is assumed to be a man, or any of his male or female collaborators participate in the ordeal, they will be struck (*kena'*) by the curse of Garap. That is, sooner or later, those who commit perjury will begin to exhibit bodily signs that reveal their true identity. The onset of and the symptoms themselves are quite varied, but by far the most commonly cited sign is that the abdomen begins to swell, becoming big and bloated. 'It's almost like being pregnant [*maraq betian*]', a young mother of three explained, folding her hands together as if she were cradling an almost full-term belly. It is not only the distended belly that attracts attention, but also the putrid scent (*bais*) that seeps out from the body. I shall have more to say about this bodily imagery later; the point to note here is that both the malodour and the swelling belly indicate that an advanced and irreversible process of putrefaction has been set in motion. For the thief and his accomplices, concealment yields to disclosure in a visual as well as an olfactory mode – they are quite literally pregnant with death. The curse is said to be so potent (*mandi'*) that it relentlessly will pursue their offspring for no less than seven generations.

These olfactory signs of dissolution and rot – a standardised Sasak nightmare – suggest that a strong element of vengeance is contained within this practice of communal oath-taking, which serves to 'cleanse the neighbourhood' or an entire village, as the case may be. As such, they intimate something of how serious an offence theft is deemed to be. Equally, statements regarding the inexorable consequences of taking a false oath affirm the constitutive power of this form of speech. On Lombok, the swearing of an oath (*besumpa'*) is associated with intense feelings that arise out of troubled interpersonal relations. The swearing of an oath between two parties, when one has accused the other who denies the charge, is a discursive device that people may resort to in order to settle conflicts. Because the swearing of an oath is regarded as such a potent speech act, challenging someone to take an oath or threatening to swear one can be an effective strategy for accomplishing a variety of goals, though such rhetorical ploys tend to be frowned upon as unseemly and irresponsible.[6] On numerous occasions I heard people say how afraid they are of swearing (*takut sumpa'*) or that they are not brave enough (*nden bani*) to do so. In fact, many Sasak friends and acquaintances explicitly stated that it is forbidden or even taboo (*maliq*) to swear. In Garap it is authority figures who voice the oath, and their work is geared towards appeasing victims of theft and rejuvenating the broader moral community. Garap exploits the transgressive power of the oath and revels in imagery of death. Objects, substances and images that are associated with death dominate this ritual, which is modelled upon the burial ceremony. Herein lies much of the compelling and transformative power of this practice; it fascinates but also seems to elicit a sense of disgust among those who participate. In Bon Raja, Garap often takes place in the cemetery, and many people noted that the severity of the ordeal is most intensely felt amidst the ancestral graves.[7]

Before discussing the Garap that was staged after Amaq Inang, an older man, discovered that two of his most treasured heirloom daggers and several pieces of old cloth had been stolen while he played flute in a night-time shadow play performance in a nearby town, I will introduce the two men who figure prominently in all Garap performances and briefly discuss on what basis people are made to participate. If those who have been visited by a thief want to call for Garap, the first step is to contact the *klian*, who is sometimes referred to as the 'father of the community' (*aman kanoman*). This respectful designation is a remnant from when the *klian*-ship was a traditional *adat*-office associated with governance and worldly affairs. Under the New Order regime (1965–May 1998), this office was incorporated into the bureaucratic structure with the *klian* becoming responsible for registering marriages and land transactions at the sub-village level. The *klian* is supposed to act as a conduit facilitating communication between village administrators and local residents, but rather than benefiting from a closer affiliation with the state apparatus, the status of this symbolically 'male' office has been compromised. Nonetheless, the *klian* plays a central role in Garap where he is complemented by a *kiyai*, also known as the 'mother of the community' (*inan kanoman*). As the holder of a feminised ritual office that is strongly associated with Islam, the *kiyai* is steeped in 'spiritual' affairs. A *kiyai*'s primary responsibility is to care for the recently deceased and to aid their passage into the invisible realm. The practices in which *kiyai* engage have been modified as the boundaries between 'tradition' and 'religion' have been debated and redrawn over the past few decades, under pressure from state officials who push for modernisation and standardisation in the domain of religion.[8] But the careful manner in which *kiyai* perform ritual services in conjunction with death and other critical moments of the life cycle earns them great respect. The office is no longer strictly passed down in the male line, but it remains a lifetime appointment and candidates who are chosen by villagers to serve the community may not refuse. When these two figures are called upon to deal with theft, the *kiyai* embodies feminine 'inner' spiritual power while the *klian* embodies masculine 'outer' worldly power.[9] As 'mother' and 'father', they convey an image of completion and unity – a unity that is strong and authoritative because it draws on different sources of power.

At no point in the meeting between the injured party and the *klian* should suspects be identified by name; only the hamlets where they live will be indicated. This indirect quality is a mark of refinement as it protects those who are involved from making an accusation. The number of suspects and their place of residence determine the spatial scope of Garap. The farther apart victims and suspects live from each other, the wider the circle of people who are drawn in. The best way to ensure that no one feels accused is by casting a wide net around those who are to be included, for example by involving an entire village subsection (*dusun*) which may range anywhere from 120 to 460 households. Garap may also be organised on a smaller scale, and by using well-established territorial markers, such as roads and irrigation channels, the chance of someone feeling stigmatised is reduced. Though it is conventionally said that Garap serves to 'cleanse the neighbourhood', the notion of neighbourhood (*gubuk*) is elastic, and an entire village may potentially need to be rid of a 'foul' smell.[10]

There is one exception to the basic principle that at least one member from every domestic unit is obligated to take part in Garap, with the husband typically acting on behalf of his wife and dependants. Those of noble status (*raden*), who make up about 5 per cent of the village population numbering approximately 7,000 people, have so far avoided participating in Garap because there is a hint of accusation in the mere fact of having to take part. Since participating would be tantamount to publicly admitting that nobles may be guilty of stealing, most members of the nobility are adamant that they should continue to stay aloof. Given that the nobles are painfully aware that many of their privileges have been eroded over the past few decades, it is understandable that they find it important to symbolically declare themselves above and immune to the 'stench' that engulfs everyone else. After the 'era of reformation' was ushered in when President Suharto was forced to resign in May 1998, some commoners have felt emboldened to challenge this noble privilege as a vestige of the past that is contrary to the spirit of democracy and Islam that is associated with equality. But there has not been any concerted effort to force the nobility to take part. Although a few men of noble status have lately opted to take part when Garap is arranged in their neighbourhoods, my hunch is that the nobility will continue to avoid Garap because it is a key arena where their physical absence affirms their distinction. Given that the right to stay away solely belongs to those of noble status, this is a privilege they will not easily give up.

Swearing Innocence and Drinking Soil in 'the Space of Death'

Close to 200 men from the hamlet of Sukadane, with the exception of several prominent nobles, were crammed together in the compound outside the communal prayer house and prepared to pledge their innocence by 'drinking soil' (*ngenem tanah*) one Wednesday afternoon in July 2001. Seated up on the porch, the man who had called for Garap appeared tired and withdrawn. According to one of his close companions, the loss of the two heirloom daggers (*keris*) had been especially distressing to Amaq Inang, who felt listless, had lost his appetite and alternated between sleeplessness and excessive oversleeping since the break-in two weeks earlier. These symptoms of withdrawal were worrisome because a person who is 'startled' (*tenjot*) is vulnerable to visitations by harmful spirits and disease. Family members had therefore sent him to a traditional healer, who prepared medicine (*sembeq tenjot*) to make him regain his composure and protect against the potentially very serious conditions that can occur when the soul is dislodged from the body.[11] Garap was on the verge of being postponed for a week when it became apparent that one man, a well-known troublemaker with a violent demeanour, was conspicuously absent. This absence did not come as a total surprise. At a social gathering some days earlier, he had announced that he would move out of the neighbourhood if Garap were to be carried out. When the *klian* asked if people were willing to proceed despite this absence, a handful of men shouted that the man was 'welcome to leave, but should drink first'. There may have been other opinions, but since no one objected, this loud response appeared to express shared sentiments. The two men who were despatched to convey this collective opinion did not find the man at home, but his wife was prepared to take part and 'brave enough to guarantee' (*bani tang-gung*) that her spouse was innocent. As she made her way into the crowded compound, looking down and covering her mouth, people muttered that she was giggling because she was shamed by her husband's 'dirty' work. The man next to me whispered: 'I pity her. If only she knew how she will suffer by drinking on his behalf and feigning ignorance, she would not have come.' Whatever her motivations for participating were, her presence meant that Garap could be carried out.

By this time, a man designated by the *kiyai* had already brought the covered basket with soil into the prayer house in a sling made from a white funeral shroud (*leang putiq*), carefully shielding the bundle with an umbrella. Babies are carried to the cemetery in this manner. The first glimpse that those who are present get of the concealed substance is apt to prompt memories of premature deaths, and such memories are likely to be relatively personal as infant mortality has been and remains high on Lombok.[12] The babies who are buried so soon after they are born epitomise the frailty of life. It is this frailty – how easily the life force pales and then leaves the body cold and perfectly still – that is evoked by the soil that is carried in a white sling. The tools that are used for digging a grave, such as a long rod, a couple of shovels and a bucket made from buffalo hide, are also basic Garap paraphernalia. Here these grimy tools do not serve to dig a pit, but rather to prepare an emotional space within the participants. Such a space may be cleared because it is filled with prior experience: these are the tools that open and close graves. When I asked why these tools were present, people would answer that they are there in case someone collapses and 'dies immediately' (*mate terus*) after taking the oath. Such remarks are made with a keen awareness of the importance of selecting props that are likely to make an impact. The ubiquitous presence of cloth and tools associated with corpses and burials does indeed create a sombre and tense atmosphere. The sense that people may be brought to death as a function of pledging the oath is conveyed through material objects and reinforced in speech.

That the act of drinking the soil may be tantamount to ingesting death is explicitly stated in the brief speech that always precedes the oath. But before the *klian* began to speak, he ordered two men to find a couple of branches from a banyan tree and a twig of *kelor* leaves. These two types of leaves are integral elements in Garap. Leaves from the tall and impressive banyan tree, which is associated with strength and traditional leadership, are folded into simple spoons. To appreciate the significance of the *kelor* leaves in this context, it is important to note that these tiny leaves are instrumental in marking the transition from life (*urip*) to death (*mate*). Specifically, a twig of *kelor* leaves is used to splash water that has been blessed and spoken into by a *kiyai* onto the body of a person who has ceased breathing to inform her that she is now dead. Until this act has been carried out, the person is merely 'sleeping'; it is the sprinkling of water that makes the person truly dead. Another function of this so-called 'naming water' (*aiq pemaran*) is to postpone the onset of putrefaction and thereby prevent the smell of decomposing flesh from spreading before burial. The importance of exercising such olfactory control will be discussed later. *Kelor* leaves wilt soon after they are picked, and this phenomenal property informs their usage in Garap; they are iconic of the swift demise that awaits those who take a false oath.

Now that all of the required items had been fetched and placed on top a raised tray where the soil and water jar were placed, the *klian* grabbed a microphone and said: 'Anyone who has seen, heard or has any knowledge of the theft may still step forth and report. But once I open this basket with soil and mix these two substances in this earthenware bowl, then it is too late.' Noting that he himself and another *kiyai* had travelled to Rembitan earlier that day to fetch the soil, he observed that the soil's effects (*pemuru' tanah*) would be particularly potent since it was fresh from the source. 'This soil', he continued, 'is not just like any other piece of dirt but a very special substance [*barang mulia*] whose qualities are such that those who are guilty, or implicated in the theft, will surely suffer [*kena sangsara*]. Not everyone who is "struck" by Garap will "die at once" [*mate terus*]. Rather, the person may suffer one mishap after the other, lose his sense of direction, never find well-being or feel pleasantly 'cool' [*embel bau*] and healthy. In fact, the effects of swearing falsely may be felt for as long as seven generations. But those of you who do not know anything about the theft should not be afraid to drink this substance, because it will enhance and heal you [*eat kerisa'm*]. You will be healed of all kinds of ills. The soil truly becomes a medicine that cures [*jari oat*].'

He then asked if everyone wanted him to 'open the soil'. Many of the men, who were growing restless, replied: 'Open!' Now the *kiyai*, who until this moment had been almost completely passive, began to pray (*bedoa*). After a brief invocation and another prayer using Arabic, he carefully removed the shroud from the soil while two men lifted it up so it formed a canopy. Taking the dry clump out of the basket, he put it into an earthenware bowl and poured water over it, stirring with a branch. Thereafter, the *klian* stated the name of the person who had wanted to arrange the ordeal and enumerated the missing items: two heirloom daggers and ten pieces of antique cloth. Grabbing the twig of *kelor* leaves and waving it in the air, he swore: 'If there are people among those who drink this water who have stolen these things, or who know about the theft, may they wither and shrivel up [*raraq*] like these *kelor* leaves.'

Beckoning to Amaq Inang to come forth to drink first, since he was the one who had called for Garap, he then fed the *kiyai* and thereafter himself. This order of drinking suggests that those who arrange Garap should also be the first to suffer the consequences if they are implicated or duplicitous. One by one, the men stepped up into the prayer house, bowed and gulped down the potion, most of them muttering a prayer as they did so. Towards the very end, the woman who represented her husband also got up to be fed. After all of those who were obligated to take part had their turn and their names were ticked off on lists that had been compiled by representatives from each neighbourhood association, quite a few children and dozens of women and men from other parts of the village surged forward, requesting to be fed. They used the opportunity to ingest this potent substance, hoping that it would cure them of their physical ailments and other afflictions. The crowd quickly disbanded while the two men who led Garap accompanied Amaq Inang to his house where they shared a ceremonial meal accompanied by prayers.

Disgust and the Force of the Oath in 'the Space of Death'

Going through Garap, participants are shown objects that are used in the context of funerals and are made to swallow a substance from a grave, thereby coming perilously close to the situation of the deceased. This is not a far-fetched claim on my part. Everyone who takes part in Garap knows that at the moment when they take the oath, they are positioned like the deceased who is being lowered into the ground, never to be seen again. This is effectively conveyed through the white funeral shroud, which forms a canopy – literally, a sky or heaven (*langgit*) – over the scene of the burial and the moment of drinking the oath, and thereby makes a symbolic bridge between these two moments. Whenever a funeral procession enters the cemetery, the corpse is held high until it is gently lowered into the grave. At this time, the shroud that has been draped over the body is lifted up to form a protective enclosure until the grave is completed; it is thereafter folded up, taken home and stored until death claims another life. In Garap, the bundle of soil is similarly held, or rather lovingly cradled like a dead baby, until it is placed on a tall tray that honoured guests eat from on ceremonial occasions. It is only when the feeding is about to begin that the shroud is removed and lifted up, forming a canopy over the person who is fed by the 'father', who administers the oath, and watched by the 'mother'. Thus suspended, the shroud envelops both moments and reveals that they are one. In short, the message that is displayed before the eyes, spoken into the ears and forced down the throat of those who take part is that the consequences of taking the oath may be no less than a death sentence. When Garap takes place amidst the graves, where the white flowers on the strangely twisted Cambodia trees give off their overwhelming, sweet fragrance, this frightful prospect takes on even more sensuous immediacy.[13] It is thus not solely a figure of speech to say that people are plunged into the space of death.

The 'space of death' that Taussig (1987) depicts is an emotional space that emerges from the experience of dying, in which established meanings fall apart. This hallucinatory void on the edge of non-existence is, according to Taussig, 'preeminently a space of transformation: through the experience of coming close to death there well may be a more vivid sense of life; through fear there can come not only a growth in self-consciousness but also fragmentation …' (1987: 7). New meanings and cultural syntheses can potentially be forged in this space where 'reality is up for grabs', but what is compelling about Taussig's argument is his insistence that there may not be any harmonic closure. The space I explore in Garap is quite different. What is similar and gives the performance of Garap its eerie quality is that it is carried out in order to interrupt a situation of animosity and endemic mistrust, but also sets in motion forces that are assumed to be impossible to stop. This is not a ritual that unfolds according to a Van Gennepian tripartite scheme in which a perilous state of liminality is neatly hemmed in and definitively superseded. Going through Garap, people are brought uncomfortably close to objects, images and substances associated with death, and I will argue that it is in this multi-sensorial experience of being exposed to residue and reminders of mortality that the transformative potential of this practice lies.

One may be fascinated by the stark symbolism in Garap, but what is it like being put in the position of the corpse and plunged into the space of death? Judging from my experience of watching and talking to men – and to women, albeit to a lesser extent since they rarely participate – both during Garap and in other contexts, it seems clear that most people are rather apprehensive about and feel repulsed by taking soil from a tomb into their body. The heavy presence of items associated with the burial ceremony further nurtures this aversion. One woman said that just seeing the white shroud, which reminds her of funerals, causes her to shiver in horror (*ngri'*), and she can hardly bear to watch. Numerous men told me that they felt anxious and nauseous, and were about to vomit. Others noted that they felt like spitting out the murky water. Not surprisingly, the soil is said to taste very 'cold' (*enyet*) – like death. It is relevant to note that aversion to eating is a common reaction to death. Food that is prepared in the vicinity of a corpse is usually said to taste insipid and cold. Experientially, it is as if the coldness associated with death seeps into the food, making it a vehicle of lethal consumption rather than a source of nurturing 'warm' (*angat*) sustenance.[14] In contrast to funerals where it is possible to avoid eating, people are not in a position to avoid drinking the oath, and this provokes what I will call a gut feeling of disgust.

Disgust, as Miller (1997) makes clear, is an immediate visceral emotion that simultaneously expresses condemnation. Far from being a mere instinctual reaction, disgust is a complex sentiment that conveys 'a strong sense of aversion to something perceived as dangerous because of its powers to contaminate, infect, or pollute by proximity, contact, or ingestion' (1997: 2). Miller stresses that disgust evaluates negatively that which it touches, proclaiming the meanness and inferiority of its object. By so doing, the bodily force of disgust 'presents a nervous claim of right to be free of the dangers imposed by the proximity of the inferior' (ibid.: 9). Because disgust arises from a recognition of having been in contact with something that defiles, the assertion of superiority is nervous and ambivalent. As he demarcates disgust from its neighbours, Miller stresses how the aversive style of disgust 'consistently invokes the *sensory* experience of what it feels like to be put in danger by the disgusting' (ibid.), and how that which is disgusting forces us to attend to it because it is acutely present to the senses. Kristeva (1982) does not treat disgust per se, but her notion of the abject as 'something rejected from which one does not part, from which one does not protect oneself as from an object' (1982: 4) seems to have a close affinity to the dynamics of disgust. Kristeva emphasises how the embodied subject violently pulls away from the abject in order to save herself, but also how repulsion and desire are intertwined. In spite of their different theoretical perspectives, both Kristeva and Miller point to the inherent ambivalence of disgust as based in the admission that the boundaries of the body have already been breached.

I find these analyses helpful in coming to terms with some aspects of Garap and the ambivalence that surrounds this practice. Fostering a sense of disgust, Garap creates the need for purification and provides the means whereby people may rid themselves of defiling matter that palpably threatens their integrity. The violent act of swearing separates people from the forces that threaten to engulf them and thus promises to restore a sense of bodily integrity and wholeness. Although the experience of revulsion that is fostered in the course of Garap demands, and to some extent justifies, the transgressive act of cursing, people do not seem to take much delight in this act. While people feel driven to curse, the lack of pleasure they derive from this act probably owes something to the anatomy of disgust. As Miller observes: '[D]isgust never allows us to escape clean' (1997: 204). I will further suggest that the very efficacy of the ritual – the ineluctable fate that awaits those who swear falsely – paradoxically helps to explain why no unambivalent pleasure accompanies the performance of Garap.

Garap is widely considered to be the most 'refined' (*alus*) yet powerful way of dealing with theft when the culprit is assumed to be a fellow villager, and at least three interrelated factors inform this view. For one, from the moment Garap is announced until its conclusion one week later, a predictable and ordered (*tata*) sequence of acts is likely to take place; the procedure is considered refined because it proceeds according to a conventional scheme. The possibility of surrendering stolen goods to the *kyiai* or *klian* and being guaranteed anonymity, which is built into this scheme, adds to its refinement. That this option is rarely taken advantage of nurtures the perception that although thieves are morally corrupt and perhaps incorrigible, they are nevertheless treated in a 'civilised' way. A second factor that makes Garap refined is the indirect quality of the practice; at no point in the preparation or during the ritual will suspects be named or directly accused. The identity of the suspect, unknown before Garap takes place, may well be as obscure by its conclusion. To the extent that someone does emerge as a suspect, the person appears to incriminate himself, usually by abstaining from participation or failing to get his spouse or parents to swear on his behalf. In such cases, Garap will be postponed. But if someone fails to show up by the third time, they may be forced to move out of the village. Alternatively, neighbours will take the person to the police, but this is perhaps the least desirable option, not only because the police are considered to be notoriously corrupt, but also because the legal system operates according to an entirely different logic and is unable to address the concerns that arise in the wake of theft. Thirdly, Garap is refined because there is no physical violence. Although a capacity for violence is regarded as a masculine asset, it is nevertheless considered a 'coarse' (*kasar*) mode of behaviour. Whereas physical violence is inflicted from the 'outside' (*duah*) and impacts the gross body, Garap engages subtler forms of power that work from 'inside' (*dalam*) the body. This power is assumed to have far more devastating impact on the thief than the pain and humiliation he would suffer were he caught and beaten on the spot. The power that Garap engages is deemed superior, having lethal force and simultaneously a capacity for healing and reconstruction.

A symbolic doubleness whereby themes of death and destruction are intermingled with those of cleansing and regeneration permeates this practice. The potion that participants are made to drink encapsulates the inherent doubleness of Garap: it has the capacity to infuse bodies with vigour, but it may also drain them of vitality. Garap is directed towards overcoming the rupturing effects of theft, yet it is the imagery of death that is most dominant. Far from displacing violence, violent techniques are employed in order to enable victims of theft to overcome their anger and anguish at being robbed and invaded. Garap engages a form of exemplary violence that seeks to overcome the negative forces unleashed by theft and to regenerate those who take part in the ritual either in person or by proxy. This violence can be termed exemplary in that it is deemed to have unparalleled force. At the same time, it is a practice that purports to bring the negativity occasioned by theft to a conclusive end. As such, Garap engages what Kapferer (1997: 206) terms the 'paradox of violence, that it is both a generative and destructive force in the world of human beings'. A range of discursive forms, including formal speech and prayer, is harnessed to this end, but it is above all the act of swearing accompanied by cursing that has life-giving and death-dealing potency. The oath that is voiced in Garap is formulaic and has an almost object-like fixity. Spoken in the context of rite, the oath is especially potent (*mandi'*) or efficacious in Austin's (1962) sense of the performative utterance that brings about the stated result. The term *mandi'* refers predominantly to powerful speech, but certain weapons, notably the blade of ceremonial daggers (*keris*), are also characterised as such.[15] A cognate sense of this word is 'poisonous' or 'venomous' (see Beatty 1999: 45). In Garap, the oath is spoken into water, which serves as the medium that transfers the words into the mouth of the participants. The inside of the body is thus infused with speech that may become an all-purpose medicine or could course through the body, destroying it from within. The performance of Garap promises to 'cool' those who are afflicted by theft and to inflict a terrible curse on those who swear falsely, thereby combining healing and harming in a single process. For all its indirect refinement, a strong sense of vengeance is contained in this practice of communal oath-taking. To appreciate the force of this response, it is necessary to consider some of the meanings that attach to thievery and how different categories of thieves are perceived, a subject to which I now turn.

Stealing Outside: A Reputation for Theft

A thief (*maling*) can loosely be characterised as someone who actively crosses spatial boundaries, appropriating objects of value that belong to others. Most Sasak condemn stealing as immoral behaviour, but thieves are also a source of fascination, if not admiration. In parts of Lombok, thieving has long been intimately bound up with notions of masculinity and power. Certain Sasak villages have a long-standing reputation for theft, and I happen to have worked in one of them. Mention the name Bon Raja, and people – seemingly anywhere you go on Lombok – are likely to exclaim that *that* village is full of thieves who are virtually invulnerable (*teguh*) because they possess such potent 'magic'.[16] In the 1990s, many villagers were somewhat uneasy about this reputation, and would note that stealing is contrary to the moral teachings of Islam and is rightly deemed illegal by the state. Yet many of those who condemn thieving are also likely to entertain less dogmatic views, as exemplified by an older man's comment that 'as long as those who "like to steal" [*suka maling*] do so in faraway places, they do not cause trouble to people back home'. But men who 'move about at night' (*lampa malam*), which is a euphemism for thieving, are not merely grudgingly tolerated. A certain masculine mystique surrounds men who are assumed to be operating in distant towns and communities and who are noted for their cunning (*lueq akal*) and the courage (*vanen*) to successfully pull off such risky ventures. This aura of shrewdness and bravery is particularly notable in the case of older men who have had careers as thieves when they were younger. Equipped with an arsenal of spells, protective amulets and other forms of secret knowledge, they would travel to the far-flung corners of the island and in the process bolstered the village's reputation for theft – cattle rustling, in particular. Through the daring exploits of such men, some people would proudly note, their village has acquired a name whose pleasant fragrance (*harum*) can still be smelled in distant places.

The nearly island-wide fame as a place of thieves wielding potent secret knowledge is a source of pride to many villagers, whose own sense of self is enhanced by virtue of being linked to such legendary men of prowess. Even those who distance themselves from this legacy and who deny that there is any truth in this reputation suggest that it serves to keep 'wicked' people away from the village. This widely circulating reputation is effectively imagined as an invisible layer of defence, for it is assumed that thieves and more brutal bandits (*rampok*) are reluctant to enter a village where they are bound to meet notorious thieves and ex-thieves. The reputation is a collective asset that informs people's sense that they live in a place which is unusually safe by Lombok standards. In the early months of 1998, when the repressive New Order regime came under heavy political pressure and the effects of the Asian monetary crisis began to be felt in steeply rising food and fuel prices, this reputation was often brought up amidst reassurances of safety. At that time, newspaper reports and rumours of robbers on the rampage created an impression that violent crime was on the rise.[17] In a climate in which state-level disorder and fear of break-ins generated a nagging sense of insecurity, people were comforted by the assumption that this 'sweet-smelling' fame would protect them against harmful intruders. The raids of local men were thus explicitly credited with fortifying the boundaries of their native community, making it less vulnerable to penetration.

The aura of masculine prowess that surrounds thieves on Lombok is in large part generated by the grave dangers they court by stealing, a hazardous activity that demands considerable skill and deftness. Judging from the accounts of friends and companions who have had shorter or longer stints as thieves, the prospect of being beaten to death by a crowd armed with machetes and other weapons is ever present in the minds of anyone who steals outside his own community. While men sometimes portray themselves as being driven to thievery due to circumstances of abject poverty, there is also a strong element of testing oneself (*coba diri*) associated with being able to get away with theft. By intentionally 'diverting' property away from its expected trajectories (Appadurai 1986), a man demonstrates his heightened capacity for action and is likely to be granted a measure of recognition. Thieving may confer positive appraisal from a man's most immediate circle of companions and generate value in the form of circulating fame. That thieves exert a strong hold on the Sasak collective imagination may be because they are particularly effective in putting manhood into action. The figure of the thief embodies qualities such as mobility, cunning, boundless courage and a capacity for violence. These are qualities associated with maleness that young men especially strive to possess. An accomplished thief has proven to possess these qualities in excess to most men. He is, to borrow Herzfeld's felicitous phrase, 'good at being a man' (1985: 16), commanding respect and inspiring fear.

I hasten to say that while stealing is tied to notions of masculinity and potency, with stealing being metaphorically linked to elopement and the ability to marry, this is not intended to nurture the stereotype that the Sasak are all a bunch of thieves. Sasak men often fancy themselves as being good at 'stealing women' and take endless delight in talking about the dangers of elopement. Considering that the couple usually agrees upon the time and place of elopement in advance, these risks are greatly exaggerated. A number of scholars have noted that the Sasak have a reputation for being thieves, especially among their Balinese and Javanese neighbours (Ryan 1999, Hay 1998), but bringing a bride safely back home is the closest that the vast majority of Sasak men ever get to stealing.

Some of these notions regarding the heightened agency of thieves converge in the assumption that their bodies are invulnerable to penetration (*teguh*). When such a person is stabbed, beaten or even shot, the skin will not be pierced or show any marks, and sometimes no pain will be felt. That the surface of the body is impermeable and immune to extraneous influence is a sign of being self-contained, commanding full possession of the senses. An invulnerable body, which is often likened to a container, is explicitly understood as being 'filled' (*teisi*), as opposed to being empty and weak and hence liable to invasion. This state of fullness is also associated with possessing *ilmu* or secret knowledge, which can obtained in a number of ways: by seeking out traditional healers or Islamic teachers, through asceticism and meditation, by reciting Qur'anic verses and spells, by wearing charms and objects infused with power, by visiting tombs that are 'filled' with the invisible presence of spiritual beings.[18] Apart from seeking knowledge and remedies that confer invulnerability, thieves are known to seek techniques so as to prevent dogs from barking; make targeted occupants sleep unusually deep; inspire paralysing terror, which makes their victims unable to move or scream for help; and make themselves invisible and inaudible.[19] A range of pragmatic methods that fall under the broad rubric of sorcery is seen as being vital for the thief's venture to succeed. The sorcerous techniques that thieves employ are directed towards dimming and closing off the perceptual sensitivity of their targets in order to safeguard their own perilous passage. Given that the realm of sorcery is not a delimited or fixed system, but rather a mode of practice that constantly incorporates novel and foreign elements, it is evident that no single person can have complete mastery over such potentially limitless pragmatic knowledge. I take the notion that a seemingly invulnerable body invariably has a 'weak' or 'soft' spot that can be penetrated as expressing the insight that in spite of the amazing capacity that people have for creating themselves through intentional activity, vulnerability is integral to the human condition.

The notorious fame that clings to the village of Bon Raja is paradoxically not so much generated by the thieves who ably slipped away without attracting notice as by those who failed and were promptly beaten to death. That the violence meted out to an alleged thief is likely to have a fatal outcome is readily confirmed by those who have had to bring back the bruised and sometimes badly disfigured body of a close relative who had been captured and killed (*mate maling*). Fetching the body of a slain thief is an experience that many villagers share, but the aesthetic forms that mediate such experiences have changed over the past three to four decades. The way that family and friends have acted at this moment of devastating loss has, in my opinion, been instrumental in generating the reputation for theft that still clings to the village and in nurturing the perception that the village possibly harbours thieves who truly are invulnerable. In the not so distant past, bereaved family members used to dress up in their best clothes before going in a small procession to recover the corpse. On this occasion, men would adorn themselves with 'flowers behind right and left ears' (*besumping kiri kanan*). Usually worn for joyous occasions, such bright flowers would be a jarring sight in a regular funeral procession; hence, their sweet scent and eye-catching appearance would convey a sense of pride in their kinsman's bravery. When Aman Ita, a rice farmer and shadow play puppeteer in his mid-fifties was young, such processions were still fairly common, and he recalled: 'At that time we did not feel ashamed [*nden lile*] when we went to take the corpse home. In fact, we almost felt proud [*terasa bangga*].' This remark intimates how the experience of dressing up, moving in unison and assembling into a collective subject created an enhanced sense of self. Processions are themselves 'pragmatic icons of the extension of self' (Keane 1997: 82), and as kinfolk have retraced the steps of slain thieves, the name of their natal village has been carried to the far reaches of Lombok.

As thievery has been increasingly tainted as a loathsome activity, processions that turn the thief's demise into a triumphant celebration of the masculine prowess that he embodied have disappeared. Gone from sight, the significance of such processions could more easily be reinvented. Hence, in the late 1990s, my host-father Guru Lebak, whose knowledge of 'tradition' is paired with a penchant for the interpretation of symbols, claimed that the deceased's family dressed up to show how glad (*senang dait gembira*) they were to be rid of the thief and his wicked work. The fact that the body of a murdered thief is brought straight to the cemetery, since it is taboo to bring it back into the house, was also added to bolster the claim that thievery has never enjoyed any legitimacy. What he failed to mention is that whenever a corpse is dug from a temporal burial site to be interred in the cemetery, the remains are taken straight to the grave.[20] While Guru Lebak denounced stealing as a despicable activity that goes against the teachings of the prophet Mohammad, he could also become quite absorbed in relating the daring ventures that local men, especially in his youth, would embark on to secure their livelihood and to test their mental acuity and physical strength. In those days, he observed, some men would even cross over to Sumbawa in small rafts looking for cattle – not even water was a barrier. Temporal and spatial distance clearly lends enchantment (cf. Herzfeld 1997). In spite of the ambivalence that currently surrounds the practice, thievery and processions that convert the thief's all-too-human weakness into a show of exuberant strength have been enabling elements in the reproduction of community identity and its mythology. Decades after such processions have ceased to be a feasible commemorative activity, the fame they have fostered continues to circulate through the minds and speech of others. In so far as fame is a mobile, circulating extension of a person or a collective entity, it is obviously difficult to control, being ambiguously attached to the subject to which it refers (cf. Keane 1997, Munn 1986). While many villagers continue to take pride in and feel protected by the 'fragrant smell' that has made their village widely known, they also know that this reputation could potentially be turned against them.

Stealing Inside

Having noted some of the ways in which men who steal in distant places are perceived and how fame has been generated from their nocturnal raids, I now turn to the issues that arise in the wake of intimate theft. Whereas generations of thieves are recognised as having created a protective shield around the village, men who violate the cardinal rule against stealing from kin, neighbours and co-villagers are condemned for their low and dirty (*remis*) behaviour.

While men who raid in far-off places possess a heightened form of agency that is associated with being invulnerable to penetration, so-called 'neighbourhood thieves' (*maling gubuk*) are considered to be weak and cowardly (*perot*). Given that categories are structured in relation to each other, it is not very surprising that *maling gubuk* are conceived as the inversion of thieves who operate in remote places, but this does not mean that they are considered a harmless nuisance.[21] On the contrary, apparently petty theft, as when a young man snatches a couple of chickens on the way home from a late evening out, is likely to cause considerable anger and anguish. It is the smell of flesh that rots and falls apart in an uncontrolled process of decay that escapes after an act of theft attributed to a local thief. This 'foul' smell intimates that stealing is at once a violation of particular persons and an assault on the community at large.

Villagers emphasise that it is not necessarily the loss of material objects that is most disturbing about theft, but that the illicit seizure of objects breeds suspicion and mistrust (*nden saling sadu'*). Theft thwarts the kind of relations that ought to prevail among those who share the same place and whose life-courses are therefore inextricably enmeshed. The recognition that people are fundamentally embedded in webs of affective relations makes most Sasak cognisant of the importance of managing their emotions, speech, appearance and behaviour 'so as to harmonize with others' – to borrow a phrase from Beatty's (1999: 178) account of Javanist ethics – particularly those who live within the same hamlet and wider neighbourhood. It is above all the flow of small gifts and the frequent rendering of assistance that generate the mutuality of social relations. Such gifts and supportive gestures are treated as 'outer' (*duah*) manifestations of what can only be known indirectly, that is, the other person's 'inner' (*dalam*) and ultimately unknowable being. The emphasis on intersubjective relations requiring a visible manifestation in the form of material signs is pervasive in the Sasak moral economy and may partly be a culturally elaborated response to the assumption that people are inscrutable (see also Keane 1997). Gifts and various forms of assistance that are readily forthcoming are taken as tangible evidence of trust and support. A very different process is set in motion by theft, which is a form of negative reciprocity that disrupts relations among neighbours and villagers at large.[22] The illicit appropriation of objects provokes anger and mutual suspicion, and threatens to undo the relations through which people realise themselves and create a sense of community. In so far as intimate theft undermines the basis of sociality, this implies that the same response is warranted in cases of petty pilfering as in the theft of major valuables. Whether a thief runs off with a couple of chickens that have relatively minor monetary and affectional value or absconds with a motorbike, a cow or valuable heirlooms, theft is considered an unwarranted intrusion that impairs the victim's ability to engage with others and creates barriers to social exchange.

Although some women pilfer and steal from neighbours and co-villagers, these women are not called *maling gubuk*, a characterisation that is reserved for men. When it is women who appropriate objects, their acts are usually characterised as snatching or pickpocketing (*nyopet*). In a conversation I had with

Kiyai Alim, a Muslim ritual specialist, he said: 'Surely, there are women around here who like to snatch things, such as sarongs, cloth, soap, eggs and chickens. This kind of pickpocketing is women's work [*begawean nine*]. It doesn't count as stealing [*paling*]. Women always do it during the day. If a woman is caught, she may receive a beating and she'll be gossiped about [*jari isin penginang*].'

This comment sums up widely held views regarding the gendered nature of theft: stealing is a 'male' activity, whereas pickpocketing is deemed a 'female' occupation. What then are the connotations that surround *nyopet*? This is a form of theft that is associated with congested markets and bus terminals where strangers brush against each other and a pickpocket easily disappears in the crowd. So strongly are these places of anonymity and transience associated with trickery that those who are robbed or deceived there only have their own naivety to blame. Despite the fact that such pickpocketing runs the risk of attracting a violent mob, it is considered a lowly form of theft that requires relatively little cunning since the same old tricks can be used on new targets. Moreover, pickpockets do not exert themselves in novel places as 'real' thieves are supposed to do. There is no way that women may gain symbolic capital by thieving, which is a male activity (*begawean mame*).

By characterising theft carried out by women as *nyopet* not only when it occurs in the market but also in the neighbourhood, these acts are trivialised. Such acts are trivial in that they do not require extraordinary skill; they are also trivial in the sense of being commonplace. This does not imply that women are less communal actors than men, nor that being suspected of pilfering does not disrupt a woman's relationships. Such women are stigmatised and a source of shame (*lile*) to their family members, who try to rectify their behaviour by verbal threats and various forms of punishment. Girls or women with a penchant for pilfering are sometimes said to be 'ensorcelled', which makes them lose their sense of propriety, and they may be taken to healers to be cured. In sum, while women who engage in petty theft are condemned, they are not deemed a danger to the community at large. 'Neighbourhood thieves' are by definition men, and they embody a perverted masculinity. By thieving locally, rather than exerting their masculine force outwards and against other communities, these men become an internal menace.

The Smell of Theft and Witchcraft

A notion of the community as a body, an organic whole with porous boundaries that are vulnerable to rupture, is implicit in the olfactory imagery of putrefaction that accompanies theft attributed to a local thief. The smelly spectre that theft conjures up suggests that this transgressive act not only obstructs the flow of social relations but also threatens to dissolve distinctions that are basic to social order. The 'neighbourhood thief' is an ambiguous figure who is both internal and external and thus upsets the social order that is founded on categorical distinctions, such as those between insiders and outsiders, male and female, friends and enemies. Because the thief is internal to the social body on which he preys, his acts have uncanny harmful potential. The smell he provokes is associated with death and is in itself death-like, characterised by elusiveness, intangibility, formlessness and the ambiguity of outside and inside.[23] Even though a thief goes after tangible material objects, his acts are perceived as causing far more serious 'inner' damage. Ultimately, a *maling gubuk* threatens to rob a precarious moral community of its vital spirit, leaving an assemblage of bodies in a frightful process of dissolution and disorder.

The morbid scenario of decay that accompanies intimate theft casts the *maling gubuk* as a figure of malevolent consumption who devours those with whom he comes in contact. This imagery speaks directly to a concern with agency and implies that the connection between the thief and his victims is akin to what Kapferer calls a 'demonic connection', which is characterised by a 'fusion of victim and assailant, in which the victim has no agency, no capacity for action' (1997: 201). As this monstrous connection leaves little or no scope for action on the part of the victim, it is actually 'nonrelational' (ibid.). In this case, the relation becomes a form of consumption that incorporates and eventually obliterates the victims.

The following incident can serve to illustrate that it is appropriate to speak of stealing in terms of consumption. People in Bon Raja are adamant that thieves who return to steal in the same place are the most despicable (*nista*), as thieves go. The first time I heard this expressed was one morning just before dawn when Inan Ita, in whose house I lived, discovered a notorious thief running away with four of her geese. Distressed and fuming with anger, she worried that he would return for the remaining two the next night or some days later, but a couple of neighbours reassured her that '[e]ven among animals it is only crocodiles who scavenge on prey that already stinks [*bais*]'. In other words, however debased *maling gubuk* are considered to be, few sink as low as the most beastly of animals, which eats putrid leftovers. In this remark a metaphorical equation is made between stealing and eating, in which a negative form of theft is linked to an abhorrent form of consumption – eating putrescent flesh. While some animals eat carcasses, it is above all cannibalistic witches (*tau selaq*) who are associated with this mode of consumption. The smell of rotting flesh is offensive to most people, but it serves to attract witches who feast on carcasses and human corpses. The men who reassured my friend that it was unlikely that the thief would return made no mention of witches. By downplaying the likelihood that he would return to finish off the remaining geese – leftovers from the kill – they implied that there are significant differences between thieves and witches. Nonetheless, I will argue that in order to appreciate the concern with 'foul' odour in the wake of theft and the intense loathing that neighbourhood theft provokes, it is necessary to consider witches and their nefarious activities.

In so far as a *maling gubuk* is figured as an intruder who impairs his victim's ability to act and destroys the social body from within, stealing clearly has affinities with other forms of covert malevolence. In particular, the thief appears to be symbolically linked to the witch (*tau selaq*), a figure of malevolence par excellence. The witch, whose desires are excessive and perverted, is a personified evil force who is associated with all kinds of inversions of what is properly human and moral. Overwhelmingly depicted as female, witches are reputed to have the capacity to change their form at will, fly, traverse space at great speed and penetrate physical barriers, including other persons' bodies. Their seductive appearance enables them to attract men, whom they subsequently control, torture and humiliate in the most grotesque manner, for example by urinating and defecating in their face. It is not only men who are objects of their ravenous desire to conquer and ultimately kill. Witches also go after more vulnerable targets, such as newborn babies, and they like to hang around people who are weakened by disease, eagerly anticipating their death. While witches delight in scaring and tormenting people, their ultimate desire is to cause death, which they effect by sucking (*mot*) their victims empty of blood. Mary Judd, who worked in the same area as myself in the late 1970s, noted that with each death that witches cause, their position within the hierarchy of witches is enhanced and the green light they emit from the head increases in intensity (1980: 100). So insatiable is their lust for blood that witches sometimes kill their own babies by sucking out their blood from their anus with their long pointed tongue. But at least one child will be spared so that the witch's knowledge, of which there are many levels, may be passed on to future generations. Witches possessing the highest forms of knowledge are said to live on the island of Bali, where they are reputed to be in abundance.[24]

Before going further into how witches are perceived, I should say that both their existence and destructive potential is a matter of dispute. Many of the villagers who would agree with this synoptic depiction and could supply more details about witches' modes of operation are precisely those who deny that there is any truth in these 'superstitions' (B.I. *kepercayaan*). People for whom witches are a menacing fact of life – and death – are far more reluctant to talk about their wicked work, presumably because this may attract their attention, but also in awareness that many consider belief in witches' destructive power to be a misguided remnant from the time when people were less knowledgeable of Islam. Quite a few people acknowledged that there used to be witches around, but that as people have lately become more observant Muslims, witches have moved away or disappeared. To underscore that they no longer pose a threat, several people noted that it is no longer necessary to 'guard the grave' (*jaga' kubur*) for the first seven nights after burial. One of the motivations for staying at the grave site had been to protect the body from being disinterred. Over the past thirty years, practices that acknowledge the presence of witches have been banished from the ritual repertoire of death. This move is part of a broader politics of religious reformation, but it is doubtful that the spectre of witches has thereby been vanquished. I suspect that the stark contrast between those who deny their existence and those for whom the threat of witchcraft is most real may break down in association with death, particularly deaths that are preceded by prolonged and agonising illness.

Witchcraft victims are said to suffer a drawn-out and difficult death. Since they have been more or less emptied of red blood, their skin is likely to take on a pale whitish (*pucat*) hue. In some respects these people only *appear* to be living, drained as they are of blood and vital inner organs, notably the liver, entrails and the stomach. Centrally located within the body, the liver (*ate*) is the seat of the emotions and of intentionality, being the locus of genuine emotions. The Sasak, much like people on Sumba, consider the liver to be 'the organ of sincerity, where it is not possible to dissimulate' (Hoskins 1993: 170). The other organs of the belly area regulate digestive processes and ensure that ingested substances are duly excreted. The unobstructed circulation of fluids and food in the body is regarded as essential for health and vitality.[25] By devouring these organs, the witch assaults people at the core of their embodied being, emptying them of 'inner' content. This is akin to what Bercovitch (1998: 211) terms 'dis-embodiment: the process by which people's bodies and bodily capacities are actually or imaginarily taken away from them, in part or in whole'. Although such a person still breathes and is capable of movement, the putrid scent that emanates from the body is an 'olfactory clue' (Gell 1977) signalling that the person is already dead. Such a person literally 'dies rotting' (*mate embus*), a most horrific demise which suggests the presence of witchcraft, though sorcery is not ruled out since some sorcerous spells give similar symptoms: a bloated belly and putrid scent.

Under normal circumstances, death is marked by the cessation of breath, and odour becomes a problem only after some hours. To comment that a dying person smells or that a fresh corpse smells strongly is thus to voice suspicion that the person has suffered an 'unnatural' death that reverses the 'natural' process of death and decomposition (cf. Bubandt 1998, Mimica 1996). I have not heard such comments voiced close to a dying person or during a week-long wake. They either have been whispered to me at a comfortable distance from a dying person or have been stated more openly once a greater period of time has elapsed since the death and burial. Given that witches are assumed to be most active in the transitional time before and after death, this contextual avoidance suggests that the haunting spectre of witches has not lost its hold, despite verbal assertions to the contrary.

'Foul' odour is a potential problem with every death, not only those in which witchcraft or sorcery are suspected to play a part, and several practices that routinely are carried out in connection with funerals are designed to control stench. As soon as a person has ceased breathing, a male family member approaches a *kiyai*, who will henceforth be responsible for the funeral, asking for blessed water. Apart from pronouncing the person dead, the purpose of sprinkling the body with 'naming water' (*aiq pemaran*), as indicated in the discussion of Garap, is to postpone the onset of putrefaction and to reduce the intensity of the smell. Although the explicit focus of the *kiyai*'s work is to aid the deceased's posthumous transformation into a disembodied spirit, there is a more implicit concern with protecting the living against the smell of the corpse. This kind of olfactory control aims to prevent the smell from spreading uncontrollably by ensuring that it is released only after burial. People said that they found the smell of corpses revolting, but they were less able, or willing, to articulate what they found so frightening about it. On the basis of what has been said thus far, it seems obvious that the smell announces the possibility of death being contagious, though it is not said that smelling a corpse can be deadly. Discussing images and odours in Javanese practices surrounding death, Siegel argues that Surakartans react to the smell of corpses with terror because it disrupts the idealised notion of the corpse as an unchanging image. Noting how odour appeals to the senses, triggering thoughts that threaten to break down the difference between oneself and the deceased, Siegel (1983: 9) observes: 'If there is no decisive difference between the living and the dead, death is already contagious. One could die smelling a corpse.'

The Sasak prefer to avoid the smell of putrefaction and have devised ways to prevent the death of one person from repeating itself in others, but it is an odour that accompanies the passage from life to death and that is basic to human corporeal existence. I will not go into the dangers that accompany entry into life; suffice it to say that concern with smell and witches who like to eat 'raw things' (*barang kata'*) – that is, blood – also surface in connection with birth. Numerous post-parturition practices aim to make newborns less vulnerable by transforming their (blood-)red rawness through various heating practices in which they are symbolically ripened or cooked (*mansak*). Bubandt's argument about odour in Buli, a village cluster on the island of Halmahera in Eastern Indonesia, where 'bad' smell (*pupúi*) terrorises the two life crises of birth and death, is also relevant in the Sasak case. Noting how people in Buli wage an olfactory war against the chaotic potential of bad smell, Bubandt observes that the terms of this war are unequal because malodour cannot be relegated to the margins of social order. In Buli, he notes: '[T]he smell of putrefaction threatens society not only from the outside but, more disconcertingly, also from the inside. Social order is in this sense not primordial. Order is rather a continuously negotiated outcome of controlling and transforming stench' (1998: 64). Bubandt finds ambiguity to be omnipresent in Buli and suggests that this is partly because olfactive metaphors are used to describe and understand the fundamental processes of life and death. In Buli, the smell of *pupúi* is, he argues, 'the fundamental dis-odour of life. It expresses in olfactive terms an irreconcilable tension between dis-order and order, being at the heart of both' (1998: 65). Emanating from the origins of social existence, foul smells are simultaneously a 'fog-like menace to social life itself' and function as 'double-edged facilitators' (1998: 49) of a deeply ambivalent and 'disquiet ontology'.

When the Sasak detect the smell of putrefaction after theft, they express moral indignation at behaviour that is an affront to basic values and assert their own sense of morality. Such condemnation expresses a concern with maintaining purity that is threatened by impurity, both in the sense of dirt and mixed categories (cf. Douglas 1966). Abhorrence of the foul smell that escapes after theft is a sign of moral sensitivity that produces its own form of social power (cf. Corbin 1986). Yet people know that they cannot insulate themselves against these despicable figures in their midst, and 'bad' smell recognises the problematic side of sociality in that people are existentially affected by others. People's reaction to this smell is one of disgust, understood as a visceral repulsion that also expresses moral condemnation. Being so much in the gut, the disgust idiom, as Miller writes, 'puts our body behind our words, pledges it as security to make our words something more than *mere* words' (1997: 181) and thereby fuses the sensory and the intelligible. The problem is that as soon as one feels disgusted one is already affected, hence the ambivalence associated with this emotion. In the Sasak case, disgust is largely expressed in olfactory rather gustatory terms; it is a matter of 'dis-odour' rather than distaste. When moral indignation operates within an ontology in which personal and intersubjective well-being is a matter of controlling stench, the thief becomes an internal menace, sharing commonalities with witches, who represent an inverse image of sociality premised on circulation and exchange. Unlike witches, who exercise their powers for no other reason than because they exist, 'neighbourhood thieves' are far more prosaic figures whose actions are assumed to stem from moral weakness and such sentiments as envy and spite, whose locus are in the abdominal area. Although witches, predominantly considered to be female, are feared, there is, to my knowledge, no tradition of accusing anyone of witchcraft. Apart from the general reluctance of making accusations, one reason for this may be that witches, as manifestations of radical evil, are largely beyond such human concerns as interpersonal discord, although witchcraft is a fertile source of expressive language, symbolism and allegory as in many parts of South-East Asia (cf. Watson and Ellen 1993). Stealing and witchcraft are both conceived in terms of malevolent consumption, but it is only male theft that becomes a focus of collective action.

Concluding Remarks: Garap and the Smell of Death

If I have kept returning to odour, it is because smells are pervasive and hard to avoid. Closely bound up with breath, one is filled with the presence of others by inhaling their odour. Such 'olfactory interchanges' (Classen 1992) are potentially very unsettling, for by sharing odour and breath with another person, one 'shares insides' (Krogstad 1989: 97), and the boundaries between Self and Other become blurred. Scents are arguably 'the most obstreperous, irregular, defiantly ungovernable of all impressions' (Bauman 1993: 24), and the fact that odours often emanate from unlocalisable and diffuse sources makes scent a powerful symbolic vehicle, as attested to by the recent spate of writings on smell (cf. Classen et al. 1994). On Lombok, smells are also difficult to avoid because moral repulsion is predominantly expressed in olfactory terms. Garap is a practice that deals with the problem of 'stench' which arises in the wake of theft when the culprit is assumed to belong to the village community but is not caught in the act of stealing. The ritual is carried out explicitly in order to 'cleanse' the moral community of malodour and to reconstitute the categories that have been transgressed by smell.

Plunging participants into 'the space of death', the performance of Garap produces a gut feeling of disgust, a complex emotion that harbours a range of meanings, as I have indicated. Partly because it is so unpleasant to go through this ordeal, Garap effectively fosters disgust with the thief whose act of trespass has prompted the need for the ordeal in the first place. The central act in Garap, which is modelled upon the burial ceremony, is that of drinking an oath that contains soil from a saintly tomb. Combining powerful speech with a potent substance that is incorporated into the body, Garap pivots around and articulates an existential tension between being consumed and actively consuming, between being engulfed and keeping death at bay by taking life. Swearing is a violent act of separation whereby people extricate themselves from the destructive hold of relations that threaten their being. In the case of intimate theft, this is expressed in terms of a suffocating stench that dissolves vital distinctions, enveloping victims and assailants in a deadly embrace. On Lombok, swearing is recognised as a particularly potent (*mandi'*) form of speech, though it usually arises from situations of impotence and anguish. What gives the oath that is voiced in Garap its awesome force is partly that it expresses the kinds of emotions that are lodged in the liver but rarely cross the lips in a public forum. In a culture that values circumspect speech, in which people take great pains to avoid making direct, harmful statements that penetrate to the core of a person's being, a communal oath-taking ritual – in which the desire to destroy someone and their future in the form of descendants is loudly spelled out – upsets deeply ingrained sensibilities. Shocking and repulsive as it is, the violent act of swearing is nonetheless rendered meaningful and experientially justified in the course of Garap as people are made to take residual matter from a tomb into their bodies. The act of swearing in Garap is a declaration of independence that cuts – like the lethal blade of a ceremonial dagger – a destructive relation that is perceived as a palpably invading force. This violent act of instantiation is geared towards restoring the embodied integrity of particular persons and re-creating the corporate social body; it is a matter of healing diseased relations.

The ambivalence that is associated with this practice, which is widely considered to be the most 'refined' yet powerful way of dealing with theft, is not merely that it is unpleasant to go through or that ordinarily concealed sentiments are expressed, but that the ritual is assumed to generate more stench. During Garap it is stressed that the consequences of committing perjury are devastating, but the effects are kept deliberately vague as regards their temporal onset, who will be 'struck' and what the symptoms might be. Outside the context of Garap, however, the standardised Sasak nightmare of a swelling belly, pregnant with death, is usually brought up as evidence that someone has been 'struck' by the curse of Garap. The initial embodied sign that a person is cursed is usually that he or she looks unusually 'pale', and this typically pertains to those who have actually taken part in Garap. Witchcraft and the most heinous and jealously guarded sorcery spells are known to produce very similar and often smelly symptoms of death-in-life. But whereas malevolent sorcery can always be combated by more potent sorcery so that a seemingly moribund person recuperates, this is decidedly not the case with those who are struck by Garap. Being cursed by Garap entails an irreversible descent towards death and there is no other exit. Garap is a practice in which the human capacity for creative action is conceived as being at its most powerful; this efficacy is in turn associated with the ability to condemn people to the most abominable state of abjection.

One could argue that Garap, in linking regeneration to the symbolic taking of life, operates according to a sacrificial logic. Though I have not explicitly discussed Garap in these terms, I will simply conclude by saying that Garap is a practice which enables people to overcome the negative forces that are set in motion by theft and to get on with life. The ambivalence associated with Garap, which reinscribes vital distinctions, is that it invariably will produce new dying bodies that have to be dealt with. Implicit in this practice is the recognition that one ultimately cannot get rid off the smell of death, which is simultaneously constitutive of and destructive to social life. This nasty smell is, to borrow Bubandt's terms, nothing but the 'fundamental dis-odour of life'.

ACKNOWLEDGEMENTS

I want to thank Angela Hobart and Bruce Kapferer for inviting me to the workshop titled 'Ritual and Performance', held in Ascona, Switzerland, in May 2002, where I presented an earlier version of this essay and benefited from the keen comments of the participants. In particular, I thank Bruce Kapferer, Hilde Nielssen, Marit Brendbekken and Olaf Smedal for their suggestions, criticisms and encouragement.

NOTES

1. I have carried out three periods of fieldwork for a total of 15 months between 1993 and 2001, based in a village I term Bon Raja located in the district of Jonggat, Central Lombok. Another six weeks have been spent in different parts of the island. All personal names are pseudonyms. Research was conducted under the sponsorship of the Lembaga Ilmu Pengetahuan Indonesia and Universitas Mataram. Terms in brackets are Sasak terms, except where I indicate that Indonesian (B.I.) has been used.
2. The Sasak have separate terms for witchcraft (*ilmu selaq*) and sorcery (*ilmu seher*), but in my experience, witchcraft is talked about as one manifestation of the myriad forms that sorcery (*seher*) may take, and is hence subsumed under this broad term.
3. Gell argues that the semiological status of smells is highly ambiguous because the phenomenological properties of smells are charactised by formlessness, indefinability and lack of clear articulation: 'The smell of an object always *escapes* – it is an active principle' (1977: 27). Lefebvre insists that odours 'do not signify; they *are*, and they say what they are in all its immediacy' (1991: 198).

4. Islam was probably brought to Lombok in the early part of the sixteenth century. For information on the history and dynamics of Islamisation among the Sasak, see Cederroth (1981, 1996), McVey (1995) and Ryan (1999).

5. Goris (1938) glosses *garap* (noun) and *begarap* (verb) as 'taste', meaning 'touch' or 'feel'.

6. Lambek (1993) discusses the subtleties of oath-taking involving verses from the Qur'an among Muslims on Mayotte. He observes that people not infrequently threaten to recite prayers (*dua*), but refrain from doing so because it is assumed that people bear the responsibility for setting divine punishment in motion (1993: 127–32).

7. Busy crossroads, the spacious yards in front of state buildings or neighbourhood prayer houses are also suitable locations for performing Garap, because they are public, open and visible.

8. For accounts of such processes on Lombok, see Cederroth (1981, 1996), McVey (1995) and Telle (2000). The essays in Kipp and Rodgers (1987) analyse related processes in other Indonesian societies.

9. The penchant for assigning gender connotations to ritual offices and objects is common in many Indonesian societies; see the essays in Fox (1980) and Hoskins (1998).

10. I have participated in five Garap rituals that were carried through and another two where everyone had gathered, but the ritual had to be postponed because parents or a spouse did not dare to take the oath on behalf of a missing person. In another case, a young man suspected of stealing some chickens ran away to the island of Sumbawa just after Garap was announced and has settled there.

11. In another case, a teenage boy died of typhoid fever. The shock of discovering that the money which his father, who worked as a labour migrant in Malaysia, earned had been stolen just after the son had brought it home was said to have made his condition worse, and to have precipitated this fatal outcome. Several weeks after the funeral, the father was notified that his son was slightly ill, again to spare him from shock. For a detailed account of how Senoi Temiar in Malaysia and other South-East Asian people deal with the dislocation of self that results from being 'startled', see Roseman (1990).

12. Lombok has acquired the unenviable reputation of having the highest recorded rate of infant and child mortality in Indonesia; see Rusman et al. (1999).

13. Cambodia trees (plumeria) grow in virtually every cemetery on Lombok. They are said to 'have always been there', like death, as it were. My understanding is that their intense fragrance facilitates propitious contact with invisible spirits, carrying thoughts and prayers upwards, similarly to the way incense is employed. At the same time, their intense aroma masks the foul scent that emanates from corpses, and thus exercises a form of permanent olfactory control.

14. I discuss the complex and contested role of food and a range of food-related practices in connection with death and mortuary feasts in Telle (2000).

15. If it is impossible to obtain soil from the tomb of Wali Nyato', a *kiyai* or *kliang* may remove soil from where water is first let into a rice field using the tip of a *keris*. The dagger's awesome power to kill and protect is thus exploited in this substitute option that is rarely resorted to, now that buses and motorcycles make travelling to the tomb less cumbersome than in the near past.

16. The English word 'magic' is sometimes used. This curious usage probably owes much to persistent efforts to teach Indonesian schoolchildren to distinguish religion, which has connotations of modernity and progress, from magic, animism, polytheism and other 'primitive' and 'backward' beliefs and practices; see Kipp and Rodgers (1987). In this context, the very foreignness of the term 'magic' gives such practices a certain allure.

17. It is probably the case that there was an upsurge in theft around this time, and that criminal gangs became more sophisticated and violent. The only published account to date that deals with popular vigilante activity to combat 'crime' is a brief article by Cederroth (2000), which mainly deals with the massive riot targeting Chinese and Christians that occurred in and around the provincial capital Mataram in January 2000.

18. Writing about similar notions among the Javanese, Barker (1999: 110) observes: '[W]hile the *keramat* is a territory by virtue of being occupied, the *kebal* (invulnerable) body is a territory by virtue of being protected by an *ilmu* (magical science).'

19. Divination and the discovery of auspicious times is important to thieves on Lombok, as it appears to have been among their Javanese counterparts; see Quinn (1975) on 'The Javanese Science of Burglary'.

20. A *kiyai* is supposed to be in charge of the actual work of disinterring and reburying remains. One of the arguments that Guru Lebak has used to defend the value of having this ritual office remain hereditary is that *kiyai* have learnt to overcome the fear and revulsion that decomposing bodies inspire, and can be counted on to bring back the stinking remains of a slain thief. Just because someone has good doctrinal credentials due to training in an Islamic boarding school (*pesantren*), he reasoned, it does not mean that a person can perform such a 'heavy' task – a task that even close family members may shy away from because of the stench.

21. Mary Douglas's (1966) work on purity and pollution makes this point forcefully, as do Stallybrass and White (1986) in their analysis of the symbolic extremities of the exalted and the base.

22. In his tripartite scheme of generalised, balanced and negative reciprocity, Sahlins (1972: 195) depicts the last as the unsociable extreme.

23. Devisch (1999: 68) stresses that 'sorcery is the topos of movement, entwinement and interaction', and that sorcerous imagery is at home in ambivalent zones. Likewise, Kapferer (1997: 20) insists that the symbolism of sorcery is 'frequently that of an internally unstable form'. One can therefore surmise that smell is likely to be a central aspect of sorcery, as Malinowski (1929) indeed documented as being the case in the Trobriand Islands.

24. The Balinese term for similar witches is *leak*. Wikan (1993: 86) characterises *leak* as 'females of inborn evil, with the capacity to transform themselves into any kind of shape'. She also notes that 'Lombok lurks in the minds of Balinese as the homeland of black magic' (ibid.: 6).

25. Notions of circulation and blockage are central in Sasak understandings of health; see Hay's (1998) excellent study. The ubiquitous flow/blockage symbolism is also extended to interpersonal and broader social processes.

BIBLIOGRAPHY

Appadurai, A. 'Introduction: Commodities and the Politics of Value.' In *The Social Life of Things: Commodities in Cultural Perspective*, ed. A. Appadurai, 3–63. Cambridge, 1986.

Austin, J.L. *How to Do Things with Words*. Oxford, 1962.

Barker, J. 'Surveillance and Territoriality in Bandung.' In *Figures of Criminality in Indonesia, the Philippines, and Colonial Vietnam*, ed. V.L. Rafael, 94–127. Ithaca, 1999.

Bauman, Z. 'The Sweet Scent of Decomposition.' In *Forget Baudrillard?* ed. C. Rojek and B.S. Turner, 22–46. London, 1993.

Beatty, A. *Varieties of Javanese Religion*. Cambridge, 1999.

Bercovitch, E. 'Dis-Embodiment and Concealment among the Atbalmin of Papua New Guinea.' In *Bodies and Persons: Comparative Perspectives from Africa and Melanesia*, ed. M. Lambek and A. Strathern, 210–31. Cambridge, 1998.

Bubandt, N. 'The Odour of Things: Smell and the Cultural Elaboration of Disgust in Eastern Indonesia.' *Ethnos* 63, no. 1 (1998): 48–80.

Canetti, E. *Crowds and Power*. Trans. C. Stewart. New York, 1984 [1962].

Cederroth, S. 'Patterns of Modern Islamic Fundamentalism: The Case of Lombok.' In *Political Violence: Indonesia and India in Comparative Perspectives*, ed. O. Törnquist, 33–8. Centre for Development and the Environment, University of Oslo. Sum Report no. 9, 2000.

———. 'From Ancestor Worship to Monotheism; Politics of Religion in Lombok.' *Temenos* 32 (1996): 7–36.

———. *The Spell of the Ancestors and the Power of Mekkah: A Sasak Community on Lombok*. Gothenburg, 1981.

Classen, C. 'The Odor of the Other: Olfactory Symbolism and Cultural Categories.' *Ethos* 20, no. 2 (1992): 133–66.

Classen, C., D. Howes and A. Synnott. *Aroma: The Cultural History of Smell*. London, 1994.

Douglas, M. *Purity and Danger: An Analysis of the Concepts of Pollution and Taboo*. London, 1966.

Corbin, A. *The Foul and the Fragrant: Odor and the French Social Imagination*. Cambridge, Mass., 1986.

Devisch, R., and C. Brodeur. *The Law of the Lifegivers: The Domestication of Desire*. Amsterdam, 1999.

Fox, J.J. *The Flow of Life: Essays on Eastern Indonesia*. Ed. J.J. Fox. Cambridge, 1980.

Gell, A. 'Magic, Perfume, Dream…' In *Symbols and Sentiments: Cross-Cultural Studies in Symbolism*, ed. I. Lewis, 25–38. London, 1977.

Goris, R. *Beknopt Sasaksch-Nederlandsch Woordenboek*. Singaradja, 1938.

Hay, C.M. 'Remembering to Live: Coping with Health Concerns on Lombok.' Ph.D. diss., Emory University, 1998.

Heald, S. *Manhood and Morality: Sex, Violence and Ritual in Gisu Society*. London, 1999.

———. *Controlling Anger: The Anthropology of Gisu Violence*. Oxford, 1998.

Herzfeld, M. *Cultural Poetics: Social Poetics in the Nation-State*. New York, 1997.

———. *Poetics of Manhood: Contest and Identity in a Cretan Mountain Village*. Princeton, 1985.

Hoskins, J. *Biographical Objects: How Things Tell the Stories of People's Lives*. New York, 1998.

———. 'Violence, Sacrifice and Divination: Giving and Taking Life in Eastern Indonesia.' *American Ethnologist* 20, no. 1 (1993): 159–78.

Judd, M. 'The Sociology of Rural Poverty in Lombok, Indonesia.' Ph.D. diss., University of California, Berkeley, 1980.

Kapferer, B. *The Feast of the Sorcerer: Practices of Consciousness and Power*. Chicago, 1997.

Keane, W. *Signs of Recognition: Powers and Hazards of Representation in an Indonesian Society*. Berkeley, 1997.

Kipp, R.S., and S. Rodgers. 'Introduction: Indonesian Religions in Society.' In *Indonesian Religions in Transition*, ed. R.S. Kipp and S. Rodgers, 1–31. Tucson, 1987.

Kristeva, J. *Powers of Horror: An Essay on Abjection*. New York, 1982.

Krogstad, A. 'The Treasure House of Smell: From an "Unsensing" to a "Sensual" Anthropology.' *Folk* 31 (1989): 87–103.

Lambek, M. *Knowledge and Practice in Mayotte: Local Discourses of Islam, Sorcery, and Spirit Possession*. Toronto, 1993.

Lefebvre, H. *The Production of Space*. Oxford, 1991.

McVey, R. 'Shaping the Sasak: Religion and Hierarchy on an Indonesian Island.' In *Kulturen und Raum*, ed. B. Werlen and S. Wölty, 311–31. Chur, 1995.

Miller, W.I. *The Anatomy of Disgust*. Cambridge, Mass., 1997.

Mimica, J. 'On Dying and Suffering in Iqwaye Existence.' In *Things as They Are: New Directions in Phenomenological Anthropology*, ed. Michael Jackson, 213–37. Bloomington, 1996.

Munn, N.D. *The Fame of Gawa: A Symbolic Study of Value Transformation in a Massim (Papua New Guinea) Society*. Durham, 1983.

Quinn, G. 'The Javanese Science of Burglary.' *Review of Indonesian and Malayan Affairs* 9, no. 1 (1975): 33–55.

Roseman, M. 'Head, Heart, Odor, and Shadow: The Structure of the Self, the Emotional World, and Ritual Performance among Senoi Temiar.' *Ethos* 19, no. 3 (1990): 227–50.

Rusman, R., E. Djohan and T. Hull. *They Simply Die: Searching for the Causes of High Infant Mortality in Lombok*. Jakarta, 1999.

Ryan, B.J. 'Alif Lam Mim: Reconciling Islam, Modernity, and Tradition in an Indonesian Kampung.' Ph.D. diss., Harvard University, 1999.

Sahlins, M. *Stone Age Economics*. Chicago, 1972.

Siegel, J.T. 'Images and Odors in Javanese Practices Surrounding Death.' *Indonesia* 36 (1983): 1–14.

Stallybrass, P., and A. White. *The Politics and Poetics of Transgression*. Ithaca, 1986.

Taussig, M. *Defacement: Public Secrecy and the Labor of the Negative*. Stanford, 1999.

———. *Shamanism, Colonialism, and the Wild Man: A Study in Terror and Healing*. Chicago, 1987.

Telle, K.G. 'Feeding the Dead: Reformulating Sasak Mortuary Practices.' *Bijdragen Tot de Taal, Land-en Volkenkunde* 156 (2000): 771–805.

Watson, C.W., and R. Ellen, eds. *Understanding Witchcraft and Sorcery in Southeast Asia*. Honolulu, 1993.

Wikan, U. *Managing Turbulent Hearts: A Balinese Formula for Living*. Chicago, 1993.

Chapter 4

SORCERY, MODERNITY AND THE CONSTITUTIVE IMAGINARY
Hybridising Continuities

Bruce Kapferer

I

... man is not an abstract being squatting outside the world.
– Karl Marx, *Critique of Religious Belief*[1]

The cosmologies implicated in sorcery practice are human-centric. Within them, human beings are at the heart of processes that are integral in the formation of their psychical, social and political universes. Sorcery fetishises human agency, often one which it magically enhances, as the key mediating factor affecting the course or direction of human life-chances. The fabulous character of so much sorcery practice, its transgressive and unbounded dimensions, a rich symbolism that appears to press towards and beyond the limits of the human imagination, is surely connected to the overpowering and totalising impetus that sorcery recognises in human agency and capacities. Sorcery is that magical additional force that unites with the intentional direction of human beings into their realities – a creative and destructive directionality. Such sorcery must needs affect the lives of others because of their co-presence, their ongoing involvement in each other's life circumstances.

The overriding concern of sorcery with the problematics of human agency means that it is a highly differentiated practice, produced out of a great diversity of circumstances and often taking the shape of the very situations and problematics that it addresses. Sorcery has the capacity always to be reinvented as something new. In Sri Lanka, from whence the ethnography for this essay is drawn, the most powerful destructive sorcery is not only that which is hidden, secretive, but also that which engages in highly original practices. There is a tension in sorcery towards hybridity, a mixing up of procedures often kept separate and, too, towards borrowing. The most powerful spells are often conceived to be from elsewhere. Foreign magic is particularly highly prized.

The following discussion explores some of the foregoing observations.[2] More specifically, I address the cosmology of sorcery which underpins its symbolic or, as I prefer, its imaginal density. It is this (the cosmology of its imaginary) which may go some way to explain why sorcery in numerous situations worldwide is sustained as an important mode of social and political discourse and is continually reinvented. In Sri Lanka, the cosmologies of sorcery are connected with all-embracing ontological and existential concerns that might be said to exhaust meaning, that is, they can draw within their compass a myriad of concerns and problematics. Cosmologically, sorcery is conceived to be an enduringly present potentiality integral with existence from the beginning. It becomes active through its intimate connection with the motivation of human beings to form and re-form their realities. As a consequence, any particular act or effect of action recognised as sorcery (sorcery being manifest largely as effect) can never be *mere* sorcery or, as is often claimed, mere metaphor. So vitally inherent in the scheme of things, sorcery cannot be anything but an ordinary, ever-present, commonplace, force in social existence. This does not exclude the terror of sorcery in its destructive possibility. Then it can raise its dreadful spectre as a thoroughly negative cosmology, something whose enormity is capable of tearing apart the whole pattern of life upon which existence depends. Such, of course, is how destructive sorcery is often objectified in Sri Lanka and elsewhere.

Perhaps a routine concern with sorcery (and especially sorcery as a negative effect, often of the positive) is to be expected in ideological contexts where socio-political orders of human creation are inherently faulted and where such fault is linked with sorcery as both a generative and destructive force. I note that major cosmologies associated with sorcery in Sri Lanka, which engage popular stories of state and social formation, describe fault (*dosa*) as being vital in the very ground from which social formation and de-formation spring. Further, the ordinary expectation of the presence of sorcery in social existence may be excited in contexts such as Sri Lanka where karmic ideologies, which accentuate the causative interconnection of all action (action as effect), receive considerable import.

Such orientations as the above may receive renewed relevance at moments of apparent social and political transition and transformation – in other words, at intense moments of social formation – when new patterns of social differentiation and division are in evidence. What I am saying is that the dynamics of modernity might be expected to gather impetus through the kinds of cosmological/ontological orientations to which I refer. As such, modernity acts within such orientations, bringing forth original objectifications of the sorcerous and expanding the relevance of actions and understandings connected with sorcery to an ever-diversifying range of contexts and problematics. This discussion will conclude with a brief attention to these kinds of processes.

My primary aim, however, is to explore a cosmology of sorcery in Sri Lanka that is closely tied to practices in popular Buddhism and, especially, with healing and other rites that address the ills and everyday suffering (*duka*) of ordinary life. Most illness and suffering dealt with by folk healing traditions in the villages and towns of Sri Lanka (particularly in the most densely settled parts of the country in the south and west) engage some notion that they are the effect of others' human agency. The major rites of demon exorcism (*yaktovil*) and more minor rites (*pidenna, tel matirima, kapuma*) involve practices to off-set the possibility of sorcery (see Kapferer 1991). The continuity of such prac-tices, which have long histories (many reaching back centuries), as well as the continual invention of new ones, maintains a consciousness of major cos-mologies having a bearing on sorcery practice. Much religious practice in the temples, which is not immediately linked with sorcery, rituals for the deities and also recent political nationalism, which has re-enlivened mythologies hav-ing to do with the cosmology of sorcery, continually prepare the ground, nour-ishing a consciousness of sorcerous forces and impelling people to engage with the potencies that sorcery embraces.

While social and political forces are continually at work making the 'tradi-tional' modern, often by way of reinvention, a major point that I will elaborate is that some practices connected with sorcery are inherently or enduringly modern. This is a property of cosmologies that is internal to their dynamic and largely apparent only through their practice. I stress the importance of the dynamics of sorcery practice over its representational dimensions, or those fea-tures that tie it into the historical and socio-political contexts that surround it. The symbolic force in sorcery practice is in its dynamics, and it is this which gives it durability through time and which people, acting in changing historical contexts, may pick up and intuitively develop, engaging in sorcery practice to situationally relevant effect.

Obeyesekere (1981) has brilliantly explored the value of a psychoanalytic perspective to reveal how personally unconscious factors are engaged in ritual innovation, especially in the sphere of sorcery, which is a major space of inven-tion. But I am concerned here instead with the 'unconscious' dimensions of already available practices (certainly not neglected in Obeyesekere's work) in the complex and highly diverse historical/cultural field of Sri Lanka. What I suggest is that in the ongoing creation of practices, innovators intuitively grasp the import of available dynamic structures and elaborate them. They do so by unconsciously (i.e. unreflectively) drawing out the significance of contempo-rary social and political processes through the elaborations they construct. In other words, they catch up what is already implicit in wider realities, fashion-ing to some degree original forms with innovative effects. One point I will briefly consider is how contemporary processes may reveal potentials in already tried practices. In other words, the import of dynamics is not reducible to the act of interpretation in the present but is already suggested in the practice – is a priori the interpretative act.

My discussion opens with an account of some common conceptions of sor-cery in Sri Lanka and then moves to a consideration of a cosmology that unfolds in a major rite of counter-sorcery. Widely known as the Suniyama, this ritual, connected with a sorcery god known as Suniyam, is highly significant for the development of original forms of sorcery. Suniyam and his temples have emerged in the conditions of modernity and appear to be gaining in popularity. The essay will close with a consideration of this phenomenon.

Conceptions of Sorcery and the Suniyama Anti-sorcery Rite

There are two common words, *huniyam* and *kodivina,* used in relation to a wide and ever-expanding diversity of practices and experience described as sorcery in Sri Lanka. The former, *huniyam,* indicates the highly ambivalent destructive and generative human force which is at the heart of sorcery and which is personified as both a demon (Huniyam) and a deity. The word is also applied to the mate-rialisations, objects and rites that embody the dynamics and force of sorcery. The latter, *kodivina,* refers to the activity (*vinaya*) – usually conscious, but it can cover unconscious acts as well – that brings other human beings hurt, injury and death. I should stress that sorcery terms can cover a wide variety of protec-tive devices and other practices that assist people through life, especially during what may be conceived as its dangerous passages. These are most commonly available as amulets and various kinds of charms, which are usually worn on the body but may be present at doorways or other vulnerable places. Often they are buried at the perimeter of houses (especially when newly built) to protect the inhabitants. Charms, usually those that are hidden, are considered to have sorcerous potential because the boundary that they secure is intended to prevent or hurt those that would transgress it. Such understanding encourages an alert-ness to the sorcerous effect of these things as an ordinary, sensible precaution. If a family experiences misfortune, a specialist will often be called in to look for buried charms that may have been put there by earlier house inhabitants. Sor-cerous objects and curses are quite commonly uttered against others, and spe-cialists in sorcery admit to engaging a wide range of practices to harm and even kill others.

The main word for sorcery – *huniyam* or *suniyam,* in the etymology of Sin-hala ritualists – derives from the Sanskrit *sunya* or 'void'. *Huniyam* carries a sense of barrenness, emptiness – a condition devoid of generative or regenera-tive capacity. Accounts of the experience of sorcery expand such notions. One ritual specialist in sorcery likened its experience to that of the newborn child strangled by its umbilicus as it struggles to draw its first breath. To be caught in the grip of sorcery is to be tightly bound, constricted and immobilised in bonds and tethers controlled by others. Metaphors of marriage (e.g. *hira bandana*), indicative of a virtually unbreakable, close and intimate bond, are used to con-vey ideas of the immobilising confinement of sorcery. Physical paralysis and refusal to interact are regular symptoms of sorcery. The events of sorcery that some victims report communicate a sense of a familiar and taken-for-granted world that has been transmuted into hostility and rage towards them. Stones thrown against one's house are a common indication of sorcery's onset. I have encountered a number of men and women who tell of poltergeist-like experi-ences, of useful objects for routine tasks unaccountably attacking them. One woman described how her kitchen utensils flew at her. The motivations behind sorcery, as widely reported in ethnographic studies elsewhere, are envy and jealousy (*irisiyava*). In other words, victims conceive of themselves as being at the centre of the destructive desire and interest of a malignantly oriented world that presses against them as if to exclude or reject them.

Huniyam, as sorcery's demon, is the coagulated heterogeneous formation of humanly caused distress which deprives human beings of their capacity for social action and consciousness. The representations of Huniyam, especially in Sinhalese village traditions, are extraordinarily grotesque, as if expressing the impossibility of representing the unimaginable or the impossibility of constructing the meaningful form of something which escapes or is outside of meaning. Huniyam is the figuration of the human being at risk, cast outside the bounds of meaningful social existence and threatened with the negation of existential continuity. The symbolic form of non-meaning and the loss of all life-giving potency, Huniyam condenses the significance of sorcery as it is diversely realised in Sri Lanka, and his form resonates with much of that which anthropologists describe as sorcery worldwide. It is from *huniyam* that the major ritual exorcism to overcome the effects of sorcery, the Suniyama, derives its name.[3]

As I will discuss, the Suniyama ritual is performed under the sign of Suniyam, the arch-sacrificer, the sorcerer supreme, a being of monstrous ambiguity who is both a destroyer and a (re-)creator. He is the figuration of sorcery's ambivalence, a feature that is almost universally acknowledged and which recognises the volatility of sorcery as a practice whose malign effects can turn back on those who wish to employ it. Suniyam both articulates this danger, this risk, controls it and, in effect, turns the sorcerous effects away from the victim and back towards the perpetrator.

The Suniyama, understood as the master rite in exorcism practice, is conducted in the western and southern coastal areas of Sri Lanka. It is regarded as the highest in a hierarchy of demon rites (*yak tovil*) (Wirz 1954) commanded by specialists in the *bereva* (drummer) caste who perform their ritual services for members of all other communities in the region. A common reason given by some for the pre-eminence of the Suniyama is because of its dominant Buddhist 'cooling' themes and effects (*santi karma*). It is accordingly viewed as a relatively 'pure' rite, although it is classed as belonging to that category of demon rites that is often regarded as anti-Buddhist. More importantly, in my opinion, and as asserted by the *bereva* specialists, is that it is the rite which is the knowledge source upon which the other exorcisms are based. It is the ritual invented by the original exorcist Prince Oddisa, so many say, who conferred on the *bereva* his knowledge as the arch-ritualist, the arch-sacrificer and arch-sorcerer. My brief discussions here regarding the *mythopraxis* of the ritual should further underline why it is a rite held in high regard and with a certain amount of awe.

The Suniyama is not a common ritual, although in the small region of southwestern Sri Lanka (during the 1980s and since) I was able to see two or so performances a month. It is an expensive rite that is usually performed for the wealthy since it is they, of course, who have the most to fear from the envy of others. The ritual is in many ways a magnificent display of wealth and in one key respect can be conceived as a 'destruction' of wealth, the source of the desire and envy that is conceived as producing the ground from which malign sorcery develops (see Kapferer 1997). People who have the rite performed are often returning migrants from the Middle East, who are concerned about the potential of envy from fellow villagers. A sudden downturn in business may occasion a performance. Frequently, it is held following a prolonged series of accidents and illnesses that has inexplicably befallen members of a household and which has not responded to other measures.

The rite as a whole, as with other major exorcisms, is a compound ritual form – that is, it systematically structures into its overall scheme of perfor- mance a collection of major and minor rites connected with sorcery (benefi- cent, protective and malign) that can be performed independently. The power of the rite is in this fact, for it aims to close off all possibility as to cause and seeks to negate all manner of technique that might have been used to render harm. I note one point here for future reference: although the rite itself may be relatively rarely performed, some of the differentiated practices it co-ordinates are more repeatedly practised, many appearing as elements in other rites. Therefore, parts of the rite – dimensions of the knowledge from which it is com- posed – will be in the field of cultural awareness of many. This is so even if the Suniyama rite has never been witnessed.

I will initially present some of the main ritual events and the key narrative schema of the rite. These achieve their meaning and logic through each other. Thus, the practice of ritual events achieves its import through the key myths, but what is of much import in the myths is revealed through the ritual prac- tice. My presentation will, of course, include aspects of my own interpretative understanding of the rite, based on my own experiences of this ritual and on discussions with the specialists and lay participants. No description can stand outside interpretation, and the one I start with here is necessarily restricted (see Kapferer 2000b, 1997). I will address further interpretations later, but I am conscious that numerous other understandings are possible. This aware- ness is part of my central point that sorcery, or what is reacted to as sorcery, gives rise to a huge variety of existential concerns that the cosmological imag- ination of the Suniyama encompasses. If the implications of sorcery that such a cosmology grounds are not grasped, an understanding of the anxieties and fears that the term 'sorcery' may cover, and the extraordinary assault it may imply even in the most outwardly trivial instances of hurt or upset, is likely to be greatly impoverished.

The Suniyama: An Anti Anti-anticosmological Practice

The Suniyama is usually performed over a period of 12 hours or so, starting at dusk (6:00 p.m.) and proceeding almost continually through to dawn (6:00 a.m.), but it is often not completed until after midday. At various stages in the rite, usually during the major sequences of dance and especially towards dawn when the main episodes of drama occur (including a comedy concerning some failed Brahmin healers and a sequence of considerable tension when the great sorcerer or Vasavarti Maraya, the Great World Poisoner, makes an appearance), a large crowd of spectators, often numbering more than 200, will gather. The performance is normally held in the yard in front of the sorcery victim's house. The rite begins with the ritual seating of the victim at the perimeter of a ritually demarcated space. The victim confronts a large, magnificently festooned structure, situated some 20 feet away. This is the palace of the first King Mahasammata and Queen Manikpala.

The objective of the rite is to move the victim into the palace (the victim crawling through a small doorway), where the victim will be seated in a space known as the nuptial chamber of Mahasammata and his queen. It is the most auspicious place (*atamagala*) – the world centre. The movement of the victim from the margins of the ritual space (which demarcates the space of Mahasammata's city-state) to the bedchamber traces a progress from a position poised at the dawn of being to that at the edge of non-existence, the ultimate point beyond which lies nothingness or the infinite. This space is also a site of reunification – of King Mahasammata with his Queen Manikpala, of the re-origination of body and world, of the order of the cosmic hierarchy and of much else. Most significantly, it is the space of the Buddha, a place of enlightenment, and conceptually the highest point of consciousness. Such understandings are progressively revealed in the course of the victim's movement through the various ritual events.

The victim (or patient, *aturaya*) begins the rite from the position of Queen Manikpala, the first person to be struck down by sorcery. All victims, regardless of gender, are understood to be effectively in Manikpala's situation and must wear her head shawl (*mottakkili*). One of the critical ideas of the rite that motivates its inner dynamic is that it is the 'power' of the palace that will draw the victim into it. This power is '*within*' the palace, the truth of the Buddha's teaching, the higher consciousness, the Buddha's reason. This is hidden inside (it is the *atamagala*, effectively an empty space where the victim will become seated) and is obscured by the outward glitter and splendid richness of the palace. What the palace presents is the object of desire and the source of envy, which the patient will pass through. In other words, in the progression into the *atamagala* the victim is cleansed and sheds all thought of desire and the pollution it brings. The end of the rite is marked by the destruction of this outer presentation of the palace, which symbolically is the destruction of the grounds for the production of sorcery. Significantly, this destruction is conducted by the great being of sorcery, Vasavarti Maraya (the World Poisoner), who also destroys himself against the edifice of desire.

The foregoing is the marvellous simplicity of the idea that overarches and guides an inner complexity of the ritual and its cosmologies of practice. Some sense of this complexity – what might be regarded as the machinery of the rite (ritual as a machine) – is apparent in the story of world origin, destruction and renewal (*loka upattiya*) and also, most importantly, of the events of the first attack of sorcery and their overcoming. The story is told before the victim and audience at the very start of the rite and has significant parts repeated and elaborated in poems, songs and other dramatic actions at various stages in the course of the ritual. In a structuralist sense it may be regarded as paradigmatic of the whole rite, whose full meaning is emergent in the syntagmatic process of ritual events. But in another sense it also hides, like the palace, the true paradigm, or fundamental principle, that lies within and that is disclosed climatically only in the ritual action at the conclusion of the rite. However, the narrative of world origin that I now present should indicate some of the cosmological density and existential complexity that is part of the potential of the rite and of the event of sorcery that it addresses.

Briefly, in the recitation of the *Loka Upattiya* the victim and audience are reminded that humans are emergent from the body of Maha Brahma (see Kapferer 1997, chapter 3). It is Maha Brahma who climbs down to earth via a lotus stalk following a great rain of destruction that has reduced the world to a primordial mud. Maha Brahma is an androgynous being within whom all is immanent. Eating the primeval mud, Maha Brahma begins to transmute into a human being, dividing into male and female which then multiply, the multiplication of human beings manifesting as a building of desire and greed and, therefore, of their suffering.

This suffering impels humans towards their self-realisation as human beings. This self-realisation, which is also the birth of consciousness, is founded on difference, on the recognition by human beings that they are distinct from other beings – the creatures of water, land and air. Furthermore, now, as beings of dawning consciousness, human beings reflect on their plight and observe that all the other creatures, who do not appear to suffer like human beings, have hierarchical orders headed by kings.

Human beings not only realise themselves to be different in nature from other beings but they must constitute their own hierarchical order. This is a copy of what is all around them, not a Platonic replication but an original copy. Their action also is not a reinstitution of an essential order or harmony in being from which human beings have fallen, as in the Adamic myths of Jewish and Christian traditions.

Human beings choose from within their midst King Mahasammata. He constitutes the order of the city-state and the internal hierarchical structuring of the different human estates (castes), the various duties and offices defined for the state, and the boundaries and armies of their protection. The completion of this constitutive process is marked by Mahasammata choosing his queen, the beautiful Manikpala, the sister of Vishnu. The eroticism of their relation is marked, and their love play, a feature of the poetry of the songs in the Suniyama rite, is the power of their harmony and the unifying force of the city-society which Mahasammata constitutes. Such eroticism is also a potent aspect of the aesthetics of the ritual performance as a whole (see Kapferer 2001b, 2000a, 2000b).

However, Mahasammata wishes to expand his order. He leaves Manikpala to wage war against the Asuras, breaking the powerful erotic unity that he has established with his queen. At this point, Vasavarti Maraya, the World Poisoner, espies Manikpala, lusts after her and approaches her in the form of Mahasam-mata. There is the implication that he is a double, perhaps the creation of Mahasammata, and certainly the force of illusion, the effect of desire, that ini-tially confuses Manikpala's mind. She blocks Vasavarti's approach but too late. Vasavarti, angry at her rejection, transmutes into a fire viper, a formation of his own essence, his semen, and the energy of sexual heat, and bursts through the gates and doors into the palace to lodge and grow in Manikpala's womb. Manikpala falls unconscious, covered in sores, and the distraught Mahasammata is powerless to revive her as, too, are the numerous yogins or Brahmins that are called to the queen's aid. At last, with the assistance of Vishnu, Prince Oddisa is summoned. He is described as a fearsome sorcerer and sacrificer (he has a huge mouth in which all is consumed) before whom even the gods tremble. It is Oddisa – a shamanic shape-changer who can assume the form of sorcery's destructive fury and who can enter within the body of the agent of sorcery – who devises Manikpala's cure. Thus he invents the Suniyama.

Oddisa asks Visvakarma, the Divine Architect, to build the main ritual struc-ture, the Mahasammata palace. This is the representation of the cosmic order that human beings brought into existence through the agency of King Maha-sammata, the collective representation of their conscious self-realisation. Odd-isa sets out the key events and procedures of the Suniyama whereby human beings can regain their consciousness and their capacity to form their social orders. The building work which Oddisa contracts and the ritual events he insti-tutes manifest the power of the ritualist to work with that which has already been humanly created, and to restore it.

The events of the rite are organised around 16 acts[4] of rupture, judgement and sacrifice out of which the conscious and self-recreative capacities of human beings are formed. The structural process of the rite involves a reunification of the victim as Manikpala with Mahasammata in the centre of the city-state. It is effected by means of the sacrificial dynamic of the rite that is a force propelling the victim of sorcery into the Mahasammata palace.

As a whole, Oddisa's ritual cure of Manikpala's sorcery affliction is con-ceived of as a sacrifice (*yagaya*). Its 16 key events of sacrifice involve intense acts of giving, the forming of relations between various beings (ghosts, demons, gods) in the cosmic hierarchy, and either the cutting or the affirming of relations with these beings – all hierarchising and differentiating acts; the destruction of whole fruits (often human surrogates); extended acts of dramatic comedy; the binding of the victim in the coils of sorcery and the breaking of these bonds; and the final destruction of the palace – the image of Mahasammata's cosmic totality (see Kapferer 1997: 139–84). All of these sacrificial events – of rup-ture, of making and breaking relations, and of judgement (punishment, i.e. acts of moral assertion) – are critical for the restoration of the victim to con-sciousness, and the restoration of the victim to a social world or to realities shared with other human beings. Consciousness and world emerge in con-junction. Through this process the victim is also understood to regain speech and to constitute realities through speech (*vac*), capacities that are destroyed in the actions of sorcery.[5]

It might be noted here that the line of orientation between the palace and the victim is described in the form of a snake with its head at the victim's genitals. This is the viper of sorcery, and it has marked in intervals along its body the barriers of the protective order that have been thrown up but which have been transgressively breached by the sorcerer. Paradoxically, these have now been re-realised as the blocks and obstacles of sorcery that now bar the victim, for the agent of desire and envy, Vasavarti, has effectively caused the rejection of Manikpala from the space of divine hierarchy, order and serene harmony at the centre of the city-state (the *atamagala*). The barriers (seven in all) are to be crossed by the victim in which process they are realised as the seven *cakra* points of re-origination. Vasavarti's viper is transformed as the spinal column of body and world (in one of its multiple meanings it is the lotus stalk by which Maha Brahma descends to earth).

This event of progression along the body of the snake, perhaps the key event of the whole Suniyama ritual, is known as the *hatadiya* (the rite of the seven steps).[6] It proceeds for some four hours during which the victim passes over seven lotus blooms (realising them as vital centres of re-creation in the passing) under which are inscribed on the ground the main vowels of the Sinhala alphabet, the elements for the restitution of the victim (silenced by the event of sorcery) to speech. As the victim crosses the barriers, the figure of the viper (and the barriers) are removed, and a cleared and cleaned path lies behind the victim's progress. The end of the *hatadiya* is reached when the victim crawls inside the palace and is seated within.

Here the victim is reoriented, turned around and directed back reconstitutively towards the world which the victim is at the point of leaving. Symbolically, the victim is in the space of the Buddha, at the contemplative point of enlightenment, on the brink of non-existence. Effectively, the victim is poised to repeat Mahasammata's world ordering re-creative act, which will be achieved through a series of sacrifices. However, before these are performed (acts which finally complete the Suniyama), the imprisoning coils of the sorcerer, the forces of desire and envy and of anger (placed as bonds over the body of the victim), are cut by the exorcist. The action is conceived of as being a bursting forth of the victim's own body, an act of autogenesis whereby the victims effect their own rebirth from out of their own bodies.[7]

At this world-reconstitutive moment – one in which not only the victim is restored, but also the victim's household, kin and community through the body of the victim – the great being of sorcery, Vasavarti Maraya (also conceived of as an incarnation of Devadatta, a kinsman of the Buddha who deserts the Buddha's teaching and path), makes his appearance. He destroys the palace, indeed acts as a kind of midwife to the rebirth of the victim, who emerges unscathed from the protective chrysalis that the palace has formed around the victim. Although Vasavarti hacks down the palace, he is otherwise impotent. However, his very appearance indicates an enduring immanent presence that must necessitate the repetition of the rite, if not for this victim, certainly for someone else. Vasavarti's annihilating force is a continuing lurking presence at the margins of the world order.

A general interpretive comment that can be made on the central myth of the Suniyama, and, indeed, on the ritual as a whole, is that it describes a process from a condition of non-selfrecognition to one of self-recognition (that yet is minimally assertive). The victim is passive throughout the rite, is enjoined to be so, and ideally should utter no words, which would be self-assertive (and contradict the Buddha's teaching). Nonetheless, self-assertion is evident and hence the destructive forces of existence cannot be avoided. This is recognised in the rite and is implied in Vasavarti's appearance and continuing menace.

The Mahasammata story and the narrative and practice of ritual events recognise the paradox at the heart of self-regenerative and world-reconstitutive action. In the dynamics of myth and rite, through the processes of self-recognition, humans are reinvented as human beings, and non-reductively so. That is, they become meaning-creating beings, re-founded within the hierarchical relations of a cosmic, social and political order. They become subject to the illusions of consciousness, as is explicit in Manikpala's mistake in confusing Vasavarti with Mahasammata. The orders by which human beings live – even the time and space of these orders (in the ritual songs it is told how human beings bring forth the light of the sun and the moon and also the astrological houses that govern their life-courses) – are constituted by the activity of their consciousness (prayer). Most importantly, it is their constructive action which paradoxically manifests the greatest potencies for their destruction.

The constructive acts of human beings, the orders of their self-invention that must involve exclusion, are what make the sorcerer manifest and objectify his potency. The sorcerer is as much a human creation as everything else that human beings form around themselves. Vasavarti is the anti-cosmological dynamic of human cosmological formation. He is anti-hierarchical and ultimately non-differentiating, reducing all in his way into a congealed mass, reproducing sameness out of difference. When Prince Oddisa transmogrifies as the body of sorcery, he is described as cannibalising human beings, breaking down their cities and masticating them. Sorcery thoroughly denies the human-beingness of human beings, their capacity to transcend themselves through their own meaningful and socially differentiating action. Sorcery is human-constructive and -constitutive potency turned against humanity itself. This is finally the great terror of sorcery, its critical paradox at the heart of existence, that the Suniyama articulates through its practice.

Virtuality and the Constitutive Imaginary

The Suniyama is one of many sorcery practices in contemporary Sri Lanka, one of the multiple forms of modernity. It is consciously reinvented by some as an expression of modernity. Thus, prominent members of local elites will have it performed because it represents Buddhist and mythological themes relevant to modern class and nationalist discourses. The Suniyama manifests variations in its performance according to the particular ritual tradition followed by its specialists and, more importantly here, in relation to the social position of the victim and household for whom it is performed. This has always been the case.[8] Ritual specialists willingly accede to requests from their clients regarding the style of decorative display and even how a particular ritual event might be performed. That the performance should represent worldly status is one of the thoroughgoing significances of a Suniyama performance and makes the rite continually modern. But this observation should not overlook or reduce crucial aspects of most performances.

The Suniyama is almost always held to overcome events of sorcery, an interest, of course, which is connected directly to the concern that it should represent social standing. Furthermore, the modernity of the Suniyama and the events of sorcery it addresses are centrally connected to what is already immanent and dynamic in the rite.

Sri Lanka is a modern class society, and an important feature of its class discourse (and also of caste and ethnic distinction), especially over the last century or so, is the engagement of Buddhist practice to the differentiation and production of status and class power. The Buddhist ideas and practices that were most crucial to this were those shaped through the ideological work of Buddhist revitalisation. This expressed a strong scientific rationalism influenced by the theosophists, most notably the theosophical movement of Annie Bezant and Colonel Olcott (who famously observed *sil* in a temple in the southern capital of Galle). Early Sinhala nationalists were central in the development of the modernist rationalism of the Buddhist revival of whom the most well-known was, possibly, the Anagarika Dharmapala (see Gombrich and Obeyesekere 1988, Kapferer 1983, Seneviratne 1978, Obeyesekere 1970). The movement of Buddhist revitalisation strove to discover in Buddhist thought and practice a rationality that was equivalent, even superior, to those rationalisms linked with foreign domination. Effort was put into purifying Buddhist practices of the 'irrational' elements generally identified as not being relevant to Buddhism as it was being redefined in modernity. In other words, the aim was to reverse the very hybridising processes that are at the root of Sinhala cultural practices, such as the Suniyama. Furthermore, where the Buddhism of the practice was evident, as in the Suniyama, it was made even more Buddhist.

The Suniyama has been influenced by such processes. Thus, the explicit Buddhist ideas and sentiments that are engaged in the Suniyama undoubtedly attracted a class and nationalist interest and have been further elaborated accordingly. (The ritual specialists are no less part of contemporary class and ethnic processes.)

But I stress that the Suniyama was already its possibility of modernity before its recognition as such. This is so because of processes that stand aside from contemporary discourses of modernity and its rationalities. I refer especially to the drive in modernism to demythologise, to divest practices of what appear to be their mystical and occultic dimensions. This is already, I claim, a feature of the Suniyama, one that it achieves through its hybrid formation regardless of modernist influences. As a distinct demythologising practice, however, it does have some congruity with those understandings of a rationalism born in different historical circumstances and apart from those that informed the structuration of the Suniyam's central inner dynamic.

Thus, the Suniyama explicitly recognises the paralysis of mind and body that the experience, fear and recognition of sorcery describe. Furthermore, the fabrications of the Suniyama (and the ritualists are explicit about the fabrication of their work) are directed towards breaking the hold of sorcery as a diverse existential complexity, which the cosmological dynamics of the rite opens up and incorporates. The Suniyama is, in many senses, a ritual 'anti-ritual' oriented towards enabling its participants to act ordinarily in the world, unencumbered by ritualistic fears. This is a major implication of the concluding destruction of the ritual buildings, a process whereby the rite collapses against itself (see Kapferer 1997 for a more extended discussion). I am aware that this interpretation is vulnerable to the criticism that it is already framed in rationalist terms external to the rite. There certainly is a domain of congruity or conjunction, but this is a consequence of a dynamic that is thoroughly integral to the rite and is its own raison d'être. This lends no final authority to an outside rationalist view (one that might refuse the cosmologically informed dynamics of the rite), even though it may discover its own legitimacy within the rite. The continuing modernity of the Suniyama is founded, I suggest, in an irreducible inner dynamic.

The point that I will now briefly pursue is that there are relatively enduring features of the rite as routinely performed (including its Buddhism) that are vital to the modernity of the ritual, to its being always already modern. More strongly, it is not so much the force of external social and political processes acting on the rite and changing or 'reinventing' it that is so important (every repetition of an act is a reinvention and must manifest a change or a variation). Rather, what I draw attention to is the relatively 'stable' inner ritual dynamic which, I contend, is more or less insulated from the effects of social and political changes and shifts that are the larger context of any performance. This is not to say that what I have described as the inner process of the Suniyama is a static cultural artefact, but rather that the changes that do occur are largely determined within the particular cosmological dynamic that the ritual articulates. The changes that are evident are variations within the same overarching cosmic scheme which found and orient the structuring of events. This receives impetus in the ritualists' concern to 'repeat' what they define to be Oddisa's original rite. They insist that any Suniyama must be precisely the same in the details of its practice as any other performance of the rite. This is what they mean by its being a repetition of the original rite; if there is any slip in detail, it will not work. The ritualists are emphatic on this point in a way which is not evident with regard to other rituals. The outer form of the rite may be altered (but even here there are many restrictions), but not the practices and events at the centre of its process and upon which key transitions and transformations are

dependent. The power of the ritual they announce is in the exactitude of its repetition. This commitment, I suggest, even though changes must occur, directs
the ritualists to continually re-create a rite that in key respects does not represent external realities and actively turns away from them. Its process of representation is directed into that cosmic reality which articulates its process and,
indeed, enables its repetition.

The Suniyama does not primarily represent the social and political realities
that are its broader context. Indeed, this is not the direction of the organisation
of the rite, which, if anything, is away from such a direction. It opens its own
space within the midst of external realities and in a manner that does not seek
their representation in the symbolically expressive sense still dominant in much
anthropology. I suggest that it is in the very non-externalist representational
process of the rite that the Suniyama achieves its potency in overcoming sorcery.
Furthermore, it is through such a process that the Suniyama is able to continue
to have force in modernity. This, I claim, has likely always been the case, even
for those historical contexts that might have seen its creation and whose symbolic orders might appear to be more relevant to the internal process of the rite.

There is textual evidence for performances of rites such as the Suniyama
well into pre-colonial Sri Lanka (see Nevill 1955). It is a rite which has elements
that share much in common with Sinhalese mediaeval annual rites of renewal
of kingship and the cosmically ordained social order (Seneviratne 1978). But in
such contexts, the Suniyama, if it was performed in the distant past, was similarly non-representational of external realities.

The non-externally representational form of the Suniyama (which for some
modernists might enhance its value as a 'traditional' rite) lies at the very crux
of its modernity *in the present and in the past.* This is also the force behind its
reproduction as an effective practice dealing with the problems of modernity.
The very non-representational form of the rite (what after all is immediately
apparent at the surface) should force the consideration of the potency that is
inherent in the inner dynamic of the rite *qua dynamic.* This is, as I have already
indicated, an internal discourse of representations or significations that generates meaning and import through the practice of the rite. Such meaning and
import are relative to the positioning of participants in the rite and to the experiences and memories they bring to the action and have excited and structured
through the action.

What I have presented here is what I have described (Kapferer 1999, 1997)
as aspects of a ritual virtuality.[9] This implies neither that the Suniyama is a
model *of* or *for* reality, as in a Geertzian (1973) interpretation, nor that it is an
abstract model of reality (Handelman 1990). Such perspectives always locate the
potency of rite elsewhere. I stress that the power of the Suniyama is in the reality it composes through its cosmological practice within the space of its own
performance. This is a reality that it produces and which generates its own
imaginal field. I use the term 'imaginal' to indicate that the factuality and the
lived quality of this field are generated by the activities within the rite. I posit
that they may not even require prior belief or need to be conceived as projective

fantasies of inner psychological states, although such factors would certainly intensify their potency. Indeed, as my description has already implied, the Suniyama often appears to operate as a tabula rasa, directed towards wiping the slate clean, as it were, and starting anew. This is, of course, one aspect of the comprehensive argument of the Suniyama's inner cosmological process and the dominant symbolism of rebirth (inherent in the rite's Buddhist mythology but which it otherwise might be given to invent).

The Suniyama can draw within the space of its imaginal phantasmagoric processes almost any problem grasped as sorcery in everyday reality. It is this fact that makes it always relevant to the difficulties identified with the shifting and changing contexts of ordinary existence. Within the virtuality of the rite (which in the course of its performance is no less real than the reality outside it), victims not only become reoriented and recentred (thus overcoming the marginalisation of sorcery), they also come to engage in constitutive practice. Victims are made to practise or perform acts that are the vital forces of the production and transformation of the imaginal reality that they create. They engage repeatedly in what Castoriadis (1997: 311–30, 1991) calls the constituting or 'instituting imaginary'. It is through the imaginary that reality, all reality, is created. The ritual specialists make this point by continuing to involve the victim in sacrificial constitutive practice after the Suniyama is formally completed and after all the main ritual paraphernalia have been taken away.

The project of the Suniyama is not aimed at changing the world external to the rite, but at reorientating victims into it in a way that will enable them to act within the often chaotic and uncertain motion of external realities. The Suniyama takes place within a world that is endemically uncertain and in which human beings are always in a condition of some vulnerability. This, I contend, is the circumstance of any human reality at all times. It is not the argument here that uncertainty and vulnerability are the raison d'être for the Suniyama either in the past or in the present. If there is point to such a view, it can only be a trivial observation, so true as to be banal. What I focus upon here is the potency of the rite in effecting reorientations of participants that enable them to meet the manifold contingencies of existence. The basis for the power of rites such as the Suniyama, and what I regard as their enduring modernity, is in the rites themselves and not in any essential character of the external realities for which their performance is, nonetheless, significant.

Transmutational Continuities

The Suniyama (and numerous rites connected with it) is a major reference for the emergence of a new god in Sri Lanka, known as Suniyam, who is increasingly being addressed in temples and shrines devoted to him in the major urban centres, especially Colombo. His invention is without doubt connected with the forces of modernity; he is a figure who addresses 'the malcontents of modernity' (Comaroff and Comaroff 1993). In certain respects he symbolically represents some of the key problematics of modernity. However, he is not a unique invention of modernity to the point that analysis should disregard his ritual antecedents, since much of his contemporary potency is immanent in them. Indeed, his current formation realises more evidently what was already present within the structures of practice surrounding the force of sorcery he represents but, perhaps, required recent history for its manifestation. My point is that understanding the potency of the new god must take into account the way that modernity is able to find expression through certain distinctive features of the processes attached to Suniyam in other rites, rites that are still contemporary with the new god but have a deeper lineage. Further, I suggest, that the particular force of the new, enshrined god Suniyam is in the reissuing of the logic of practice at the temples apparent in rites such as the Suniyama. Here I note that this does not imply any necessary translocation of practice (although it is likely). Rather, what is suggested is that practices such as the Suniyama may expand an understanding of the force of temple practice directed towards Suniyam, his relative distinction of other beings and his popularity. I stress that the form of temple practices before Suniyam, although frequently innovative (see Bastin 1996, and chapter 6 in this volume), are relatively distinct from other practices before the gods (with the exception of those such as Kali or Devol Deviyo, who are other major beings of sorcery and cursing). As I will indicate, the form of practice at the Suniyam shrines may be described as a compressed and reduced form not entirely dissimilar from that elaborated in rites such as the Suniyama.

I open with a consideration of some of the processes underlying this construction, the concretisation of this energy of human agency as a god. This necessarily brief discussion (see Kapferer 2001a, 1997) closes with aspects of the dynamics of practice surrounding the god Suniyam and their development or transmutation on cosmological patterns engaged in the imaginal force of the Suniyama rite.

The urban god Suniyam is, as with the rite I have been describing, a hybrid or heteronomous form, a bricolage made up from a diversity of cultural materials included in village practices, as well as practices in the formal institutions of worship in Buddhism, Hinduism and Christianity. This is greatly facilitated by the fact that Suniyam's creators and priests are not from well-established, kinship-based ritual traditions such as those which produce the Suniyama. Although nearly all Sinhala Buddhists, they come from all walks of life: teachers, civil servants, labourers and the ranks of the unemployed.

I stress that Suniyam's shrines are located in the cities, the centres of commerce, the points of entry and egress where the forces of economic and political transformation, ordering and disordering radiate through Sri Lanka. In Colombo, his more potent shrines are at the political and economic boundaries of urban space or at the social lines of neighbourhood demarcations. Powerful shrines are located in ethnically mixed areas that are inhabited by the poor and are recognised for the density of violent crime. They mark points of social and cultural crossover and fusion within the shifting orderings of the city. In certain aspects Suniyam manifests the speed of the city, an image of the labile energies of its forms of life in its changing circumstance and uncertain fortune, as human beings pass through different social contexts, engage in particular activities and shift their identities. This urban god is the radiating potency that consumes and disrupts the lives of human beings, their relations and the grounds of their sustenance, and also the dynamic of their reconstitution.

I concentrate further on some of the more specific symbolic dimensions of contemporary processes that a being such as Suniyam is likely to encompass in his form. Suniyam the god first began to appear as a separately enshrined divinity towards the end of the nineteenth century, in the capital city Colombo. It is probable that migrants from the south of the island were mainly responsible for his development. The moment of Suniyam's appearance coincides with a high point of modernising British colonial power. The increase in his popularity up to the present is associated with urban and industrial growth, particularly in the period between the world wars and especially immediately afterwards. That Suniyam's popularity is still in the ascendant could be linked to current globalising processes.

Suniyam might be conceived of as a being at the crux of the paradox of consumption, of the social divisions it exacerbates and the desire, greed, and envy it encourages. He expands what is already implicated in the rites and already projected in the ritual idea of Oddisa's enormous, all-consuming sacrificial mouth – if anything, a radical image of consumption. Such notions continue in the modern mythology of the Suniyam shrines (Gombrich and Obeyesekere 1988), in which the image of Suniyam seems to be a conflation of sorcery's ambivalent force with that of Oddisa's potency as the sacrificer supreme.

In accord with sorcery's association with rupture, there is a link between the current history of ethnic conflict and the god Suniyam. This conflict was brought to life in the context of colonial rule, its flames fanned in the circumstances of post-coloniality. Suniyam's temple of origin (established in the 1920s), the place of the root or Mulu Suniyam, is in a zone 20 kilometres from Chilaw which is a borderland between ethnic Sinhalese and Tamils. Even at his place of origin, Suniyam is dividing, rupturing and differentiating. For here there are two shrines in close proximity, each contesting the right to being recognised as the 'true' origin site.

All of the above dimensions associated with Suniyam's modern incarnation could be broadly described as implicitly marking a crisis of the state and of its force of social inclusion and exclusion. Such a crisis is evident in the colonial occupation and in the ensuing crises of the post-colonial state as reflected in deepening class, caste and ethnic alignments and growing poverty. The master narrative of the Suniyama rite, the story of Mahasammata, is centrally about the crisis of the state, which is also a feature of other myths well-known in modern Sinhala nationalism. The Vijaya/Kuveni myth tells of the founder of the ancient Sinhala state who was assisted by the sorceress Kuveni (who slaughtered her own people, the original inhabitants), whom Vijaya then deserted, bringing sorrow and suffering on his people. This story is important in the Suniyama rite and in other exorcisms and at temples where curses are routinely uttered (see Kapferer 1988).

The enshrined image of Suniyam represents him as a god of constitutive sacrifice who engages and forces the ordering and socially generating potency of the state. Amoral in himself as the sorcerer/sacrificer, Suniyam is an instrument of the inclusive/exclusive force of the state. Suniyam re-creates the state that protects and guards those who are brought into its domain. I stress the sacrificial dynamic that Suniyam embodies and its radical connection with political, social and personal reconstitution, all of which are bound together in his sacrificial action.

The image of Suniyam is represented as holding aloft the sword of judgement – in some interpretations, the sword of state (*kaduva*) – which constitutes as it cuts, divides and separates. In contemporary Sri Lanka, the word *kaduva*, is used to refer to the English language, the language of colonial authority and of colonially fomented class hierarchies, of new barriers created through a foreign language that persists in post-coloniality and has, in fact, resurged in the conditions of globalisation (see Kandiah 1984).[10] The sword, of course, is also the sacrificial instrument of Oddisa by which he regenerates human order. But, conversely, it is also Vasavarti's weapon of destruction with which he destroys the imagined totality of Mahasammata's state order in the Suniyama rite. In his left hand, the image of Suniyam carries a broken pot (*kabala*) of fire, the intense symbol of sorcery's destruction and of the suffering born of exclusion – a symbol of a broken womb of life that is halted in the midst of its fruition. He is astride a light blue (sometimes white) horse, representing the powerful generating energy of *sakti*.

People go to the sorcery shrines for every possible reason: to seek protection at dangerous moments, when the continuity of their lives is interrupted, or at times when they feel personally reduced; before a surgical operation; when travelling overseas; to get through examinations; to attack a deserting spouse; to help in business; to disrupt the success of others and perhaps to socially elevate oneself; to exact revenge for attacks on persons and family which may involve murder; to bend the will of a politician or government bureaucrat; to achieve a favourable court decision; to stop impending police arrest; to punish a landlord. The list is endless. In 1989 and 1990, at the height of Sinhala youth insurrectionist activity against the Sri Lankan government (in which, according to government estimates, approximately 60,000 youths lost their lives and thousands more were incarcerated), the shrines were crowded with anguished parents imploring Suniyam to intervene on their behalf either to kill the perpetrators of their children's death or betrayal, or to have their children released from prison.

The supplicants to Suniyam express that their lives are at risk, that they are in some way diminished, blocked in their ongoing activity, unable to pursue their normal social relations, and are in a situation of disjuncture or rupture. They express an externalisation from their social worlds by social and political forces. This is implicit, at least – and more often explicit – in their anguished pleas before the shrines (see Kapferer 1997, chapter 7). The location of the Suniyam shrines and the manner in which supplicants are oriented within them emphasise this further. The pleas and curses before Suniyam's image and the violence of the other ritual practices that centre upon him engage destruction to generation. Through the agency of the violent activity at the shrines, through the sacrificial violence of Suniyam, supplicants regenerate themselves. They bridge gaps and ruptures in their lives, break through barriers and limitations, and extend their social relations and influence into regions where they have none. Through Suniyam's punishing sacrificial power, they turn the wills of government bureaucrats or officials, individuals to whom access is socially or politically barred, making them arrive at favourable decisions.

Overall, then, the emergence of Suniyam to a degree of pre-eminence among the various Sinhala beings connected with sorcery (and his growing importance in the Sinhala pantheon) is associated with his powerful figuration as a sacrificer, especially one who is connected with the ambivalent forces of the state. Such ambivalence is born of the state in crisis and of the potencies of destruction that this releases.

While the urban shrines are no less original formations of modernity, they nonetheless extend and transmogrify processes that are present in rites such as the Suniyama. The actions at the shrines are condensations of those actions apparent in the rites. No less phantasmagoric loci than the rite, the shrines open up space in the midst of social existence, enabling people to radically reorient themselves into the world and to regain their composure.

The violence of the shrines distinguishes them from the sense of non-violence and aesthetic balance that pervades rites such as the Suniyama, no less contributing to its appeal in modernity as, perhaps, does the violent Suniyam at the shrines. But the latter can be seen, in their distinction, to expand dimensions otherwise suppressed, for example in the Suniyama, and vice versa. Thus, for all the Buddhist non-violence that is expressed in the Suniyama, its process rests on a logic of reconstitutive sacrifice that has the effect of destruction, an aporia of the rite. This is manifest in both Vasavarti's violence and, as often happens, the destruction of a straw dummy who represents the human agent sorcerer of suffering. The presence of the Buddha at such violent places as the sorcery shrines might appear to flout Buddhist values, more especially so when clients in their destructive cursing express the wish for Suniyam to be a future Buddha (see Gombrich and Obeyesekere 1988, Kapferer 1997). But I suggest that this is a continuation of an aspect of the Buddha's power in the rite. The orientation towards the Buddha assures the positive direction of Suniyam's force and controls his negative possibility. In rite as in shrine, the Buddha is functional in deciding the directionality of the force. Shrine and rite bear traces of each other, perhaps building upon and more evidently revealing the paradoxes. This underlines the fact that the logics of their dynamics share much in common, even though they are a source of their different, if contradictory, appeal.

The Fault in the State

There is one observation that will move this discussion to a conclusion. Within the Suniyama rite there is an implicit critique of the state, albeit an imaginal state. The appeal to the sorcerer and the sacrificer is to correct a fault in the state. This fault emerges in the effort of Mahasammata to totalise his power, to go beyond the limit and to encompass all in his domain. In so doing he breaks the compact of his unity with Manikpala. This is also a feature of the treatment of the sorceress Kuveni by the Sinhala hero Vijaya, who is regarded by many as the founder of the actual, empirical state of Sri Lanka (see Kapferer 1997, 1988). The result is that Manikpala is effectively flung to the margins where she assumes an identity with the destructive sorcerer, a creature of the outside. In the rite, the victim begins the ritual progress parallel to a ritual structure that is the manifestation of all destructive cosmic force. She herself is an abject being of pollution, and she embodies the force that will extinguish her and threaten others. This is a potency that impels her to be set in motion, which ends in her being recentred in the state and its social order that she reinstitutes as the imaginary of the rite. Figuratively, Manikpala, the universal victim with whom the 'ensorcelled' are made to identify, re-forms the state, re-establishing its conditionality within the moral order of the Buddha's teaching. In the course of the victim's progress, destructive forces that have fused with the victim's body are removed, to be remaindered as the fragmented and fragmenting debris that they are, while the victim regains the composure of body and mind.

Something like the above is re-created at the shrines, although more unconsciously than consciously, where it becomes a more complete expression of the body and where individual motivations, suppressed and silenced in the Suniyama, for example, can have more open voice. In the shrines, victims often approach Suniyam in a condition of dishevelled fury and engage rancid and decaying matter to their work. Their anger and their filth, their sorcerous condition, is a force of destruction, but also of regeneration. The shrines are littered with such elements which are, in effect, the sorcerous remains from which victims have become released. Amidst all the destruction and fury of the shrines there is, nonetheless, a moralising sense. Victims who mimetically engage in sacrificial action before the god Suniyam might also be said to be engaged in action corrective of the state, as is implicit in Oddisa's cure of Manikpala. As such, they also bring forth the conditionality of such a correction, the all-encompassing potency of the Buddha and his panoply of supporting divinities.

The state at fault, I suggest, is expressed in the abjection of many of the victims, in their own sense of marginalisation and suffering in the face of the rupturing force of the powers that exclude them or place them at risk. The shrines themselves appear to be in process. In continual construction, they are accreting more and more gods of the Sinhala pantheon and more magnificent images of the Buddha.

The progressive surrounding of the Suniyam shrines with increasing and more magnificent Buddha images, and also images of the major deities supportive of the Buddha's teaching, is open to many interpretations. These range from the materialistic, for they indicate the increasing wealth of the Suniyam shrines, to the idea that the process is one of making Suniyam a central Buddhist god. Such a process is seen by some as flouting the Buddhist teaching and as indicative of the secularising decline of Buddhism in the circumstances of modernity (see Gombrich and Obeyesekere 1988).

However, the supplicants before Suniyam generally view him as being extraordinarily dangerous and recognise that their practices around him are often base, disgusting and, indeed, inappropriate to Buddhist ideals. Much of Suniyam's potency continues to be valued, in part because of his capacity to threaten and even pollute the gods. In a major shrine in Colombo, the Buddha and the deities that are placed alongside him are protected in a glass case. The new god Suniyam, in my interpretation, is far more consistent with Oddisa and the Suniyam of the Suniyama rite; he has grown beyond them, but along the same trajectory. At the shrines he is expanded in his amorality and in his sacrificial potency. It is these that implicitly underlie, on the one hand, the expanding wealth of the shrines and, on the other hand, the bringing forth of the powers of the Buddha and the deities who, through Suniyam's intervention, generate the ultimate condition for the correction of the fault of the state.[11]

In this correction, in which the emergence of the Buddha and his supporting divinities must be implicated, lies Suniyam's capacity (both at the shrines and in major rites such as the Suniyama) to overcome the problems that the supplicants bring before him. Behind such problems is the fault of the state. This fault is what Suniyam corrects. It is a fault at the centre of the despair of sorcery victims and which, as with Vasavarti invading the abode of Manikpala, is at the heart of that socio-political world upon which the existence and finally the humanity of victims depends.

A Concluding Remainder

I have explored certain aspects of the modernity of sorcery in Sri Lanka. Within the broader context of scholarly discussion of the phenomenon there has been a tendency to subdue an attention to the cosmologies that are embedded in its practice, which can be consciously and unconsciously reproduced, and which direct its appeal and force. The concern with its cosmologies indicates that sorcery is not mere sorcery and drives at the heart of the human condition. I have focused on the question of the power of representations, in particular on the imaginal force of representations and their potency as not essentially or necessarily being a direct reflection of surrounding existential realities. The major argument underlying the discussion is that sorcery, or what anthropologists conceptualise as sorcery, is always already modern. It is outside, even transcendent of, those categories of an anthropology that distinguishes between tradition and modernity. Paradoxically, this distinction is implicit in the work of anthropologists who are committed to demonstrating the thoroughgoing originality of sorcery in the postmodern and post-colonial condition. This implication maintains an effect like sorcery or its sacrificial dynamic, which re-creates the very terms of the discourse it otherwise refuses. My aim here has been to step aside from the traditional-modern dichotomising that still lurks behind anthropological discussions and that may impair a more complete understanding of the phenomena it addresses.

Sorcery destroys meaning and stands before meaning. In its more positive aspects it brings human beings to that brink from which they can once more generate meaning and establish a continuity with the ongoing and shifting directions of social processes. And here is a dilemma for an anthropology still legitimately obsessed with meaning and the dynamics of its social production: the forcing of sorcery into a framework of meaning may paradoxically destroy and do violence to it as a phenomenon. It is in its very non-meaning that sorcery remains such a powerful vehicle of human anguish, in its always creative and inventive coming-to-meaning that its force resides. This may be one dimension behind the enormous all-embracing cosmologies that are implicit in the actions of sorcery or to which they can give rise.

NOTES

1. Cited in Sahlins (1976: 113).
2. The research on which this essay is based has been supported by grants from the H.F. Guggenheim Foundation and the Lauritz Meltzer Foundation.
3. In Sinhala, 's' and 'h' are transposable, 's' indicating a higher, more honorific form. In this context, the title of the rite, arguably the most magnificent in the repertoire of the ritual specialists who perform it, describes its aim, which is to reverse the destructive malevolence of sorcery attack.
4. The exorcists (*adura*) who perform the Suniyama say that there is one event for each of the 16 years that Manikapala had reached at her marriage. The number 16 is symbolic of the process of her reaching conscious maturity. The events are known collectively as the *solos tinduva*. A *tinduva* is a finishing act, a cutting act. It is also understood as an act of judgement.
5. The motioning of the victim across the *cakras* also is a crossing over and embodiment of the vowels of speech. The events of comedy follow from this. The comedy manifests the power of speech as the power of consciousness. In the comedy, the consciousness of speech is made constitutive; also, through the play of the comedy consciousness is made an object to itself. This is the pleasure of the comedy for victims and for an audience (see Kapferer 1997: 158–67).
6. In accordance, with the clear tantric influences in the rite (important in the historical formations of Sinhala Buddhism) the lotus or *cakra* points are the vital plexuses along the spinal passage (*susumna*) of the human body, the critical sense points of renewal. They are also revealed (in accompanying songs) as the first seven steps of the Buddha, of Prince Siddharta. The viper also becomes the protective shadow of Muchalinda, whose cobra hood protects the Buddha and, for the exorcist performers of the rite, is a form of Maha Kela Naga, the great snake of time. The *hatadiya* is a vital reconfiguration of space and time shattered by the sorcerer's attack.

7. A useful comparison may be made between this event and others in the Suniyama and Davis's (1991) fascinating discussion of the mediaeval Indian *saiva* ritual.

8. In the past, the structure of the palace (e.g. the number of pinnacles) was related to the caste and status of the victim and household. It was important that the appropriate rite was performed for the appropriate status. To have an inappropriate rite performed negated the efficacy of the ritual and intensified the force of sorcery. There are stories circulating to this day in southern Sri Lanka that tell of families who are still suffering the damage of an inappropriate Suniyama.

9. I develop the concept of 'virtual' largely from the usage of Deleuze and Guattari (1994). The virtual, as I use it, is not to be conceived as a representation of a reality, a reproduction of the realness of some aspects of ordinary existential reality, or as the creation of a reality so that it can feel 'as if' it is lived in. These all carry a notion of model, from which I also want to distance the concept. What I argue is that the virtual is thoroughly its own reality, its own life-world, whose structures of signification are relative to itself alone (see also Kapferer 2000a, 2000b).

10. From the late 1950s through to the late 1970s there were strong efforts by the Sri Lanka government to make Sinhala (*swabasha*) the dominant linguistic medium. The language issue was a major factor in the Sinhala nationalism of this period and part of the government's efforts to win popular approval. But from 1977, with the accession to power of the United National Party, there were shifts back to the importance of English. This was the language of elites in Sri Lanka, and the Sinhala-language movement had provided disadvantages for these elites. In fact, they saw the movement to Sinhala in education as seriously affecting their social and political reproduction. English has now reaffirmed itself more than ever as the language of the elites, and marks with some clarity major class divisions and barriers.

11. Gombrich and Obeyesekere (1988) mark Suniyam as clearly a creature of modernity. More precisely, they see him as being produced out of the disorganisations of modern life, and expressing its violence and moral decline (see also Obeyesekere 1975). In this context, they conceive of the appeal to the Buddha, in light of the violent sacrifices to Suniyam, to be a modern development associated with general contemporary devaluations of the Buddha's teaching. However, looking at such practices in the context of the Suniyama rite, which spells out such an association as being consistent with Buddhist moral values, provides a modification of the view expressed by Gombrich and Obeyesekere. I add that their approach, a universalising sociology of the dysfunction, is elsewhere balanced by Obeyesekere (1984: 64–70) in a kind of culture history. Suniyam is but a particular manifestation of a historical cycle, driven by Sinhala Buddhist culture. The apotheosis of Suniyam and his great popularity can be expected to follow the same rise and fall of a great many other gods in Sri Lankan history, whose Ozymandian remnants litter Sri Lanka's terrain. Suniyam, it is predicted, will fall foul to a similar divine rake's progress. This cultural historicism recognises a fundamental pragmatism which is Obeyesekere's key to understanding how history is likely to repeat itself. Suniyam, as Obeyesekere explains, like other erstwhile powerful gods often also connected with sorcery, is acutely pragmatic. It is this pragmatism in the cultural context of Sinhala Buddhism that is the clue to his impending downfall. Thus, the more good turns Suniyam does, the more Buddhist merit (*pin*) he acquires which, as with other gods in the past, will function to shift him up the divine hierarchy, making him more and more a remote object of piety reduced in practical mundane value, which will force a decline in his popularity. In other words, Suniyam is subject to a kind of law of diminishing returns, a universal economy of rationality that is treated as the engine of a general cultural effect.

The argument, of course, does not sufficiently allow for the very different historical formations that have emerged in the course of Sri Lanka's long history, and the quite distinct cultural structurings of power and economy that have arisen and crossed each other in the course of this history. The extraordinary profusion of gods and other kinds of beings, many of which have, indeed, fallen into disuse, is a consequence of differentiating and disjunctive processes in culture and history.

Suniyam is a being of a particular conjuncture and also of a specific form and an internal dynamic which does not permit an easy categorisation with other gods in the Sinhala pantheon, as I will show. Indeed, an attention to the nature of his specific constitution and dynamic might reverse Obeyesekere's hypothesis. Thus, rather than diminishing in appeal and perhaps potency, Suniyam might be expected to expand in power, the more he is used.

BIBLIOGRAPHY

Castoriadis, C. *World in Fragments.* Stanford, 1997.
———. *Philosophy, Politics, Autonomy.* Oxford, 1991.
Bastin, R. 'The Regenerative Power of Kali Worship in Contemporary Sri Lanka.' *Social Analysis* 40 (1996): 59–94.
Comaroff, J., and J.L. Comaroff. 'Introduction.' In *Modernity and Its Malcontents: Ritual and Power in Postcolonial Africa,* ed. J. Comaroff and J.L. Comaroff. Chicago, 1993.
Davis, R.H. *Ritual in an Oscillating Universe.* Princeton, 1991.
Deleuze, G., and F. Guattari. *What is Philosophy?* London, 1994.
Geertz, C. *The Interpretation of Cultures.* New York, 1973.
Gombrich, R., and G. Obeyesekere. *Buddhism Transformed: Religious Change in Sri Lanka.* Princeton, 1988.
Handelman, D. *Models and Mirrors.* Cambridge, 1990.
Kandiah, T. "'Kaduva': Power and the English Language Weapon in Sri Lanka.' In *Honouring E.F.C. Ludowyck: Felicitation Essays,* ed. P. Colin-Thorne and A. Halpe. Dehiwala, 1984.
Kapferer, B. 'Sorcery and the Shape of Globalization.' *Journal of the Finnish Anthropological Society* 26, no. 1 (2001a): 4–28.
———. 'Sorcery and the Beautiful: A Discourse on Aesthetics and Ritual.' Unpublished paper presented at the Conference on Ritual, Aesthetics and Performance. Ascona, 2001b.
———. 'Sexuality and the Art of Seduction in Sinhalese Exorcism.' *Ethnos* 65, no. 1 (2000a): 5–32.
———. 'The Sorcery of Consciousness: Sinhala Buddhist Ritual Discourse on the Dynamics of Consciousness.' *Communication and Cognition* 33, no. 1/2 (2000b): 97–120.
———. *The Feast of the Sorcerer.* Chicago, 1997.
———. *Legends of People, Myths of State: Violence, Intolerance and Political Culture in Sri Lanka and Australia.* Washington, D.C., 1988.
———. *A Celebration of Demons.* Bloomington, 1991 [1983].
Nevill, H. *Sinhala Verse.* Vols. 1–2. Ed. P. Deraniyagala. Colombo, 1955.
Obeyesekere, G. *The Cult of the Goddess Pattini.* Chicago, 1984.
———. *Medusa's Hair.* Chicago, 1981.
———. 'Sorcery, Premeditated Murder, and the Canalization of Aggression in Sri Lanka.' *Ethnology* 14, no. 1 (1975): 1–23.
———. 'Religious Symbolism and Political Change in Ceylon.' *Modern Ceylon Studies* 1, no. 1 (1970): 43–63.
Sahlins, M. *Culture and Practical Reason.* Chicago, 1976.
Seneviratne, H.L. *Rituals of the Kandyan State.* London, 1978.
Wirz, P. *Exorcism and the Art of Healing in Ceylon.* Leiden, 1954.

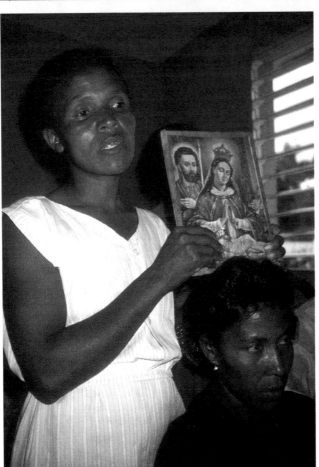

Top: Children who grow matted hair-locks are seen to have entered into a spiritual 'compromise' with vengeful Taíno Indian spirits. Montaña Antigua, 1991. Photo: Marit Brendbekken.

Left: Seeking spiritual aid and protection (see chapter 2). Montaña Antigua, 1991. Photo: Marit Brendbekken.

Top: A victim of theft (in blue shirt) talks with the two men who will lead Garap: the *kiyai* (to his right) and the *klian*, who wears a white cap (see chapter 3). The covered box contains soil from the tomb of Wali Nyato'. Central Lombok, Indonesia, 1997. Photo: Kari Telle.

Bottom: The white flowers of the Cambodia trees (plumeria) that grow on most Sasak cemeteries have an intense fragrance. A woman pours 'cooling' water on the grave of a deceased relative. Central Lombok, Indonesia, 1997. Photo: Kari Telle.

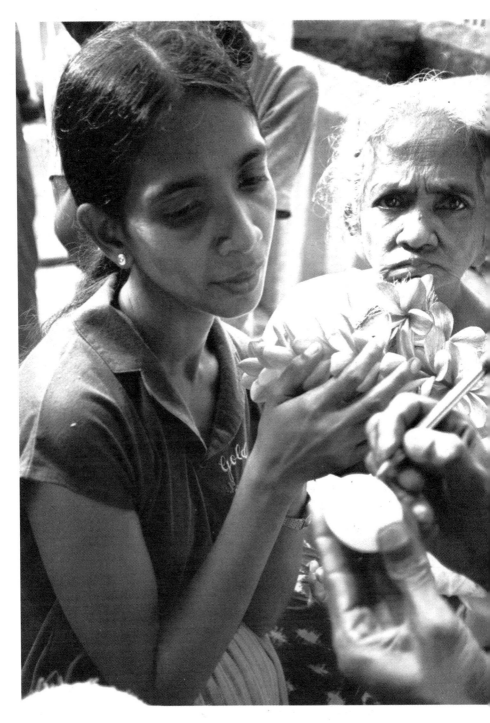

Paligahanawa. A woman curses her wayward spouse as her mother looks on. A sorcery
priest writes the husband's name on an egg, which will be destroyed (see chapters 4 and 6).
Sri Lanka, 1985. Photo: Bruce Kapferer.

Above: A sorcery victim is presented with Queen Manikpala's shawl. Articles (symbolic lotuses) for the ritual sequence known as *hatadiya* (Suniyama) are at the victim's left (see chapter 4).

Right: Becoming Animal: the leopard pot, associated with the sorceress Kuveni, is an article used in cursing.

Sri Lanka, 1993. Photos: Bruce Kapferer.

Top: Men of the village of Fanla showing off their customary dress of penis-wrappers and pig's tusks for tourists in a dance performance (see chapter 5). North Ambrym, Vanuatu 1999. Photo: Knut Rio.

Bottom: Performance of *rom* in the village of Melbulbul. The dancers are young men who have been initiated into the secrecy of the *rom* society. North Ambrym, Vanuatu, 2000. Photo: Knut Rio.

Left: The Munnesvaram Bhadrakali statue covered in sandalwood paste to control her ferocious power (see chapter 6). Sri Lanka, 1999.

Middle: A group of female trance specialists (*maniyan*) at the Munnesvaram Bhadrakali temple. Sri Lanka, 1994.

Bottom: Pile of chillies at the Sinigama Island sorcery shrine – the heaped remains of hundreds of individual acts of 'striking revenge'. Sri Lanka, 1996.

All photos this page: Rohan Bastin.

Above: A popular contemporary depiction of Kali at the end of time, dancing on the corpse of her spouse Siva.

Above: This important power object, woven as a double moebius knot, mobilises ambivalent or versatile 'forces'. It is able both to unbind forces intended to harm or bind the victim, as well as to turn the harmful forces against themselves self-destructively (see chapter 7). Malaatu village, 1974. Photo: René Devisch.

Left: Ritual weapons for defence and attack from Yikwaati village, 1991 (see chapter 7). Photo: René Devisch.

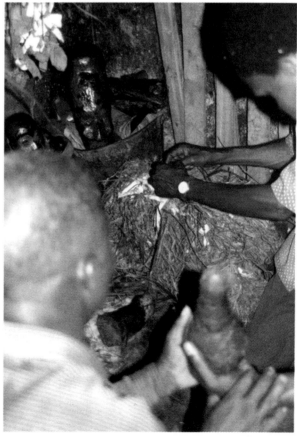

Top: Political life 'in the open': a public meeting in a Tswana *kgotla* (see chapter 9), 1985. Photo: Ørnulf Gulbrandsen.

Above: *Khosi* cult figurine, Yibwaati village, 1974 (see chapter 7). Photo: René Devisch.

Left: Shrine enclosing the paraphernalia for making *binwaanunu*. Kinshasa-Masina, 1990. Photo: René Devisch.

Chapter 5

THE SORCERER AS AN ABSENTED THIRD PERSON

Formations of Fear and Anger in Vanuatu

Knut Rio

Introduction

This essay revolves around a recent intensification of homicidal sorcery on Ambrym Island in Vanuatu, central Melanesia. During my periods of fieldwork on the island, spanning from 1995 to 2000, the situation in my region changed dramatically. Even though Ambrym social life has always been imbued with sorcery, the circumstances around the turn of the millennium represented a complete loss of control and an existential crisis.

I will explore the historical specificity of these developments and simultaneously try to situate sorcery on Ambrym in a larger comparative framework of human sociality. Like earlier writers in the tradition of British social anthropology (see Kapferer 1997), I see sorcery as fundamentally an expression of people's acknowledgement of the immanent powers of sociality itself. In the Melanesian context, sorcery must be seen to be part of the larger social networks and agency that not only cause production and reproduction, but also destruction and death. I will show how sorcery on Ambrym is fundamentally part of the interpersonal realm of reciprocity, and that it actually represents a constant 'regulation' on the changing patterns of reciprocity that take shape in the post-colonial situation.

Sorcery on Ambrym works as a cultural recognition of some principles of reciprocity, wherein the triad becomes central. I see these principles as exemplified in the abstract by Jean-Paul Sartre's theory of reciprocity outlined in his *Critique of Dialectical Reason* (see Sartre 1991). In his elementary example of how reciprocity is essentially bound up inside triadic relationships, he describes himself standing in a window, observing two workers outside. The two workers cannot see each other, and their mutual relationship as workers is constituted only through him as a third party. As a result of his totalisation, they come to stand for a unification of their mutual reciprocity as 'workers' of the same class. But this reciprocity exists only as his totalisation and in so far as they have not yet been engaged with one another. Once they meet face to face; their mutual reciprocity as in the eyes of the third is closed off, and they engage in a seemingly dyadic relation. But Sartre's point is that even though they themselves close it off through their interaction, the triadic constitution of their relationship continues to hold, and the absented mediation of the third is in fact the only way in which they can come to interact in exchange (Sartre 1991: 100–9; see also Sahlins 1972).[1]

With regard to the modern character of sorcery on Ambrym, a lot of power seems here to be invested into this dialectic, and its relational composition is set up along a similarly triadic structure as in Sartre's example. Sorcery here not only concerns the victim and the accused, but also the sorcerer himself, who is a third party to that relationship. The sorcerer is hence like Sartre's man in the window – an outsider who through his 'absented presence' constitutes other people's relationships.

By approaching sorcery in this framework of reciprocity and totalisation, I wish to avoid seeing sorcery as masked expressions of people's problems with 'reality'. Indeed, I do not address how sorcery attacks represent down-to-earth social conflicts in another, often fantastic guise (see Patterson 1974–5), or how they are an expressive 'metaphor' for the political arena (see Lattas 1993). Rather, I explore how it is the totalising perspective of the attacks that actually reveals the problematic social situations in the first place. In other words, I see sorcery itself as constitutive in the process of social relations and as a key element of their dynamic.

Kastom and 'the Great Terror'

My initial impression of North Ambrym[2] when I first arrived there in 1995 was as a place of harmony and peace. Despite the rumours in the capital of Vanuatu that Ambrym was a place ridden with sorcery – or 'poison', as it is phrased in Bislama (the pidgin-based national language of Vanuatu) – which spread anxiety throughout the archipelago, people of the island didn't seem to worry about sorcery or any form of aggression at the time. They emphasised that sorcery, warfare and rivalry belonged to the past.

In a historical survey of deserted villages that I conducted in the area, this situation of peace and tranquillity was in people's discourse strongly opposed to the historical period that I am tempted to call 'the Great Terror'. Along with many other Melanesian islands, Ambrym was heavily depopulated between 1910 and 1940 . In the area concerned in my survey, a population of about 3,000 people, spread out over 30 villages, was seriously decimated by these developments, and in 1940 only five villages remained, with a population of only 300 to 400 people. From one perspective, we can account for this radical disruption by referring to the new diseases, rifles and alcohol that were introduced to the island by missionaries, traders and colonial personnel (see Rivers 1922). But according to North Ambrym people themselves, the many deaths were considered unanimously to be caused by *kastom*.

In many respects, the concept of *kastom*, the Bislama term and pan-Melanesian idiom for a pre-colonial realm of 'customary' practices (see Lindstrom and White 1993), can today be used synonymously with sorcery. Even though *kastom* refers to ceremonies of food exchange, men's cults and 'the indigenous way' in general, it now also carries with it a conception of evil, of malevolent and uncontrollable forces dwelling inside these powerful practices. This concept of evil has arisen out of an indigenous churchly[3] discourse that has been preoccupied mainly with opposing these destructive forces at the core of *kastom*. In North Ambrym, the current stories surrounding the period of the Great Terror generally reference the crisis in terms of rivalry between neighbouring men's lodges. It was inside the customary cult-house that the secret remedies for *abio* (the North Ambrym term for poisoning, magic, sorcery and witchcraft) were kept, and here the men exchanged secret knowledge and planned schemes for murdering their rivals.[4] During this historical epoch, the rivalry of open warfare, fought with both rifles and homicidal sorcery, so intensified that very few people survived.

In the period that followed the Great Terror, the church was set up as a sanctuary from these lethal forces that were hiding inside the darkness and secrecy of the ceremonial ground, and by 1950 most people in North Ambrym had abandoned their sorcery-ridden home-places to the advantage of a centralised church-community. Here, the people in exile submitted to the assumed peace and friendliness that the church villages promised. People now considered the prospect of the future as one of love, friendship and co-operation, in direct opposition to the fatal rivalries and hostilities of the past.

I will describe how this prospect is constantly being threatened by the ever-returning theme of sorcery. When I returned to North Ambrym in 1999, the village of Ranon was completely devastated by a wave of deaths which were attributed to *abio,* acts of sorcery. A whole new reality was opened up to me, a kind of terror that was reminiscent of the Great Terror that I had become aware of in my historical survey. People were now afraid that this would mean an end to the villages as they knew them. Some were sleeping with shotguns beside their beds out of fear of nightly attacks. My family and I were warned not to go outside our house after dark, and our friends in the village told us that they heard strange noises at night-time. Strangers were walking around in the village knocking on people's house walls, and dogs were barking all night against some unknown creature in the dark. People were terrified that there were *abio* in the village. One man, who had been afflicted by a giant sore on his buttocks, was told by a diviner that there were at least five people in Ranon who were playing with sorcery. Then, in June of 1999, a large meeting was held in Ranon over these issues. The assembly was triggered by a diviner from a neighbouring village, who came down to announce that a Ranon man had approached him to purchase lethal sorcery. He also claimed that someone had planted in Ranon a *werefil,* a decorated stone or piece of wood that works as a curse. He believed this passed a death sentence on the whole Ranon population.

For weeks after this meeting, people in Ranon were going around in amazement. What had, since the Great Terror, been a sanctuary and a refugee camp for people who had escaped from other places torn apart by sorcery and warfare had now itself turned into the centre of these malevolent forces. Ranon – the first mission station and the only colonial plantation centre in North Ambrym, the place where people believed they would meet the future with open arms – turned out to be haunted by the past. People were now confused about this paradox, that sorcery had again caught up with them, even though they themselves had abandoned *kastom* and secrecy in order to rid themselves of these things. It was as if the past had played a trick on them and now returned in a disguise.

I here choose to see these developments as a local commentary on historical circumstances, instead of seeing them merely as irrational or 'creative' responses to diseases or other 'natural causes'. I now follow the local viewpoint on the processes involved, extending on Taussig's insistence that such apparently irrational beliefs can be 'intricate manifestations that are permeated with historical meaning and that register in the symbols of that history' (Taussig 1980: 17). I think that these recent events of sorcery on Ambrym also manifest a certain loss of control that is due to the Western presence (impregnated with the cosmologies of Christianity, colonialism and capitalism), akin to that experienced by Taussig's South American workers in relation to capitalist alienation of their labour. It is, however, not first and foremost a question of an invading 'mode of production', as in South America, and wage labour and cash-cropping are, again, rather peripheral to the Ambrym subsistence economy 20 years after independence. Instead, I will suggest that these incidents on Ambrym represent a reaction to other historical circumstances tied to the post-colonial situation. They take place in an era when much of the colonial history has to be reframed with regard to local idioms such as rights, ownership and belonging, and it is within this nostalgic climate that the *abio* reappears. It is now manifested as a destructive force that in a sense reinforces the communal moral of giving and sharing as against the modern tendency to claim rights and keep to oneself, which comes with money and the commodity market.

Differentiation and Conflicts in the Colonial Era

The issues of sorcery and witchcraft have, of course, a significant history in the region of Melanesia. Malinowski's work on the Trobriands especially made manifest the overall importance of magic, sorcery and witchcraft in all domains of social life in the Massim (Fortune 1932, Malinowski 1926; see also Tambiah 1985). Not yet being set up as something evil by the church discourse, sorcery represented a legitimate use of power by influential men, and was in fact a necessary prerequisite for the functioning of the *kula* trade (see also Munn 1986). This perspective has also been upheld in the more recent contributions to

Melanesian sorcery. These studies mostly concern themselves with the political role of the sorcerer and the structural functioning of warfare, sorcery and witchcraft (see Mosko 1994, Stephen 1987, Godelier 1986). Few of these approaches, though, have managed to realise the full ethnographic potential of these practices of terror (see, however, Kelly 1993, Knauft 1985), and in a volume dedicated to sorcery and witchcraft in Melanesia, Michelle Stephen (1987) has pointed out the great difficulty anthropologists have had in trying to understand these phenomena in the region. Like Malinowski, she emphasises that such practices are considered to be not just evil, but also often in the interest of the social good, as legitimate sorcery is common throughout the region. However, she fails to emphasise that it was often the ideology of Christianity and colonialism that cast sorcery as unambiguously 'evil' in some places, thus forcing the practice to become an issue of morality as well.

In a more recent article on sorcery among the Mekeo of coastal Papua New Guinea, Stephen (1996) relates the practice of sorcery to the 'relational paradigm' of Melanesian anthropology (cf. Strathern 1988). A crucial point in Stephen's argument is that the Mekeo have institutionalised the role of the sorcerer for 'the invasion of other selves'. In relation to Strathern's idea of Melanesian personhood – the idea being that Melanesian selves are partially and 'dividually' distributed in relationships – Stephen claims that 'this very embeddedness of person and self in social relationships makes the differentiation of self a source of acute anxiety and concern for Melanesians' (Stephen 1996: 98). In a region where the flow of objects, food and people is crucial to the conception of 'society', and where giving is crucial to all constructions of sociability, the differentiation of Self and acts of keeping things to oneself are bound up with tensions (see also Weiner 1992, Munn 1986). In Stephen's view, the sorcerer among the Mekeo is the negative counter-force to this paradigm of relatedness, enduring a lifestyle of taboos, seclusion and 'individuation' in order to 'invade' other people and thus break up and in fact *destroy* relationships.

I think this point about sorcery's ability to open up relationships to external agency is crucial to recognise, especially with regard to the post-colonial situation. In my view, it is not necessary to refer these tendencies to strictly 'Melanesian' contexts, since the same tendencies can be found in other areas of the world (see Kapferer 1997, Boddy 1989), and since sorcery can thus be seen to manifest the *human* capacity for articulating the world in social terms. Therefore, Ambrym sorcery, which manifests one specific instance of this capacity, might just as well communicate with Sartre's theories as with Strathern's.

What we do have to pay attention to is how the history of the region has brought about certain ideologies, discourses and parameters that people engage in their daily interaction. On Ambrym, the colonial presence represented an external judgement on local relationships through the court system, taxation and the church's moral order. But while the colonial agents believed themselves capable of resolving local conflicts through Western standards of court cases and imprisonment, they could not mediate in the real arena of conflict on Ambrym, the field of sorcery and witchcraft. The sorcerer's work was unintelligible to the colonial agents, since the cause and effect involved in the local view of sorcery agency could not be made to converge with Western views on individual agency and the principle of the unity and coherence of the 'act of crime'. In local explanations of how people died, the agent of the murder was not at all clear, but the colonial officials had to make hasty and random arrests in order to uproot the 'evil' forces at work. In the Ambrym understanding of these actions, the colonial police were thus seen as using their mediating role to act like sorcerers themselves by abducting people and taking them away to imprisonment. Interpreting events in a simplified 'sociology of conflict', the colonialists believed sorcery was simply a tool that could be the weapon of one man against another; they failed to realise the complexity of the agency involved. Anthropologists have, of course, been guilty of making the same mistake, interpreting sorcery as disguised expressions of conflicts arising from structural circumstances, such as marriage and settlement organisation (e.g. see Patterson 1974–5).

In North Ambrym the centralisation of plantation work and mission stations had certainly created a demographic situation full of potential conflict. The colonial villages were created under the era of the Great Terror, as people moved away from their home villages and formed new villages around the church and the plantation. These composite settlements brought together people from widely different and often rivalling places under the unified banner of Christianity and plantation work. A wide variety of conflicts were thus built into the very history of these places – conflicts over positioning as labour on the plantations and over positioning in the churchly hierarchy, as well as disruptions and issues of pollution with regard to the male hierarchy and principles of avoidance. Relatives who would previously have been highly taboo to one another (especially in-laws) now came together in the same hamlet, and men belonging to different 'sacred fires'[5] of the men's lodges came together to sleep and eat in the same barracks. People who previously had fought each other with muskets and sorcery were now supposed to engage peacefully and forget all the conflicts of their past. Through their riddance of *kastom* as terror, they supposedly could now enjoy the love of Christianity and see the Other as a friend.

On top of these sociologically given conflicts of the colonial village, another overt theme of conflicts has been the presence of money. Ever since the plantation was set up in the village of Ranon around 1860, money has been a motivating factor in village life. Gold sovereigns and silver sterling figured in the prestige economy of the male hierarchy at an early stage and, for a period, almost replaced the valuable tusked pigs in the ceremonial economy, as pigs were forbidden by the churches. People, however, learnt that money – in North Ambrym called *buwir* (literally, 'lumpy stones') – was very different from pigs. Money represented a more solid, material presence that was problematic to people on Ambrym because it, in a sense, resisted transformation. I would suggest that money is by its very material stability and durability antithetical to the paradigm of the local ceremonial economy of flow and transformative gifts (see also Rio 2002). Money is seen to produce jealousy (*brire*) and anger (*lolfrifri*), since it has a potential for being kept to oneself and apart from social engagement. It does not deteriorate, cannot be eaten or replanted, and thus represents an enduring and coagulated presence in social life. People always tend to imagine that their relatives are holding back money from them, and when there is a question of money changing hands, the demand for sharing and 'borrowing' always comes up. We can then understand why the generation of men who worked for the 'Master' at the Ranon plantation put the gold and silver coins they earned in jars and buried them in the ground when they were full. Even though this 'planting' of the money could not produce increments, like the food they planted, at least it was invested into the soil of the place.

The specific history of Ranon hence leads people of other villages to think that money is indeed captured in this village, both under and above ground. Ranon village has, even after the plantation era, continued to attract money. Following independence, certain entrepreneurs have benefited from a veritable industry of wood carvings that are being sold to the commercial markets in the capital, as well as in New Caledonia, Australia and the United States (see Rio 1997, Patterson 1996). In addition, the village attracts tourists, who come to see both the active volcano of the island and the performance of *kastom* dances and magic.

The imagery of accumulated and coagulated money was again evoked when the issue of the destructive curse of the *werefil*, which had allegedly been planted in Ranon village, came up in 1999. The *werefil* was said to have been planted in the village by outsiders who were jealous of the Ranon riches and who wanted to take part in the wealth. Even if the money was out of sight and hidden away, it still posed a threat to relationships, since everyone knew that it was there as a historical fact. As we shall see, it is as if the containment of money itself – and the jealousy and anger that comes with it – attracts *abio* to relationships.

Lattas (1993) comments that in Melanesia there is a greater tendency for sorcery to pop up in places where there is an accumulation of money (see also Chowning 1987, Lederman 1981, Zelenietz 1981). Among the Kaliai of West New Britain, Lattas also observes how sorcery accusations are directed towards the new elites created by the colonial situation: priests, government officials and businessmen. These new forms of sorcery are in Kaliai called 'the sorcery of whites' (Lattas 1993: 59), not because the white people perform it, but because the whites control the spaces where it is bought and sold and seen to grow out of – the markets, the plantations, the church. Lattas (ibid.: 53) comments: 'Sorcery here is not a continuation of tradition, an archaic superstition or falsehood which stubbornly clings on and which is destined to disappear with the growth of knowledge and development. Rather development itself spawns new forms of sorcery, new narratives of evil. Instead of treating development as antithetical to sorcery, as being the bearer of that modernity which eradicates superstition, it is possible to see development as consolidating the powers of sorcery.'

Hence, I believe that the *abio* dwelling around colonial spaces such as Ranon village is also very much related to the processes of modernity that have been in motion. By taking on disguises of past historical connections, the recent and strong sorcery tendencies may be seen as a 'backlash' at the disruptions caused by the colonial and post-colonial situation. But unlike earlier writers of the conflict framework, I would insist that these more recent attacks of *abio* concern much more than tense relationships. Even though the relationships themselves, the rivalries and disagreements implicit in the colonial village history, figure as the settings for the sorcery attacks, we must also pay attention to the changing character of the socio-cultural stage that the sorcery attacks create (see also Knauft 1985). Like Lattas, I also maintain that there is a radical break here between sorcery before (as in the rivalries of the Great Terror) and sorcery now, even though they appear to be the same.

North Ambrym *Abio*

The first effort to describe Ambrym sorcery is an account from the Catholic mission in Olal village, North Ambrym. It is part of the memoirs of Père Suas, who established the mission there in 1893, and Père Jamond, who accompanied him: 'The individual who is *hableou* has the power to do whatever he wants – to change himself into a chicken, a dog, a bird, a snake, etc. – to go, without physically going, wherever he wants – to make people die, by removing their heart or intestines or other organs – to play tricks on people, such as forcing someone to climb a coconut palm and leaving him up there so that he cannot move' (my translation, Jamond 1949).

This is a description of the Ambrym sorcerer or witch.[6] To avoid the many dangers inherent in translating such a concept into 'sorcery', laden as it is with Western exoticism and orientalism (see Kapferer 1997), I will carefully try to follow the manifestations of the indigenous term. I understand *abio* as sorcery since it is about interfering in other people's lives through what is indigenously recognised as a special kind of agency. *Abio* is used to stand for all kinds of agency involved in meddling with other people's *hal* (road), the course of their acts and conditions, mostly to hurt or kill them, but also to make them act in certain ways. *Abio* can make people give away their possessions. It can involve so-called 'parcel magic', which hurts people by treating some of their intimate belongings in certain ways, and it can result in the straightforward abduction and murder of people. To avoid confusion I must also point out that the term *abio* covers acts and remedies of sorcery, as well as the sorcerer himself. I will here be mostly interested in this last concept of *abio* as a person who takes up a specific place in social interaction.

Writing about the decades before 1900, Jamond describes this personage, the *hableou*, as part of a 'secret society' in which men had to sacrifice pigs to other sorcerers in order to become sorcerers themselves. After the payment in pigs, the apprentice would be let into a 'sacred ground' at the cemetery, where the initiator said spells over him and rubbed him with magical leaves in the presence of the ancestors. The apprentice would then be ready for the transformation that made him into a *hableou*. According to the story Jamond had been told, the initiator would now cut off the candidate's head and limbs with a knife. He would say spells over the body parts before he refitted the body of the candidate, who would now come back into life as a man transformed into a sorcerer. When re-created, the man was called by his new title, *Hableou* (Jamond 1949). Many similarly fantastic stories about Ambrym sorcery continue to circulate today on Vanuatu, as Ambrym is characterised as the 'Mother of Darkness' and the centre of sorcery practices in the archipelago. These beliefs are, however, the view of sorcery as seen from the outside, as the practice of the Other. But also on Ambrym such horrific ideas figure as theories about what hides inside the darkness of other villages. The prototypical act of the murderer *abio* is to ambush someone who is out in the forest by himself. The victim is blinded by spells and magical remedies and made unconscious. The *abio* then cuts open his belly, removes his intestines, replaces them with magical herbs, patches up the open wound and then brings him back to consciousness. The victim will then continue on his path, not knowing that anything has happened to him. When he returns to his house, he will later die a sudden death. Thus, when someone dies unexpectedly, people are immediately suspicious about the cause of death: a sudden demise without warning is a sure sign of *abio*.

Diviners of *abio* affliction are in North Ambrym called *vanten ne hal* (man of the road). One says that *vanten ngea vanten hanglam rolhe* (lit., this man is a taboo man who can see). Such people, who are called 'clever' in Bislama, can 'see' the cause of problems and provide cures (see also Tonkinson 1979). If people suspect that someone is after them, they can visit a *vanten ne hal* and pay him to 'see the road', that is, the past and future course of actions and relationships. This role of diviner is something that people might choose to take on if they feel that they are capable of seeing things. It takes a lot of courage (*helhel*), since looking into these things constantly must necessarily be both frightening and dangerous. Such men must therefore go though fasting and other strong taboos that affect their lifestyle before they can engage in this type of work. They must be afraid (*lummørmør*) all of the time, since they especially are open to attacks.

The Colonial Overturning of the Sorcerer

This story about sorcery initiation opens up the question as to how sorcery was, and is, institutionalised on Ambrym. From many places in Melanesia we hear that the role of sorcerer is itself an acknowledged position, a kind of 'office'. As in Mekeo on the southern coast of Papua New Guinea, we have learnt that the 'war sorcerer' and 'peace sorcerer' are concrete positions held alongside the 'war chief' and 'peace chief' (see Mosko 1994). Likewise, among the Garia of the central Papuan Coast, the sorcerer was an acknowledged ritual expert (see Lawrence 1987). In this more 'egalitarian' society, all boys, even as children, entered into a 'series of initiatory ceremonies' in which they were initiated into the secrets of the Garia cosmos and were fed secret remedies to make them mature as men. The most dedicated in this learning would become acknowledged sorcerers.

As I have pointed out above, sorcery on Ambrym was also closely related to the 'secret societies'. We here recognise both Stephen's and Lawrence's material as also relevant to North Ambrym sorcery, as something that was taught to people through their career of secret initiations that involved transfers of secret knowledge. In the *mage* hierarchy of sacred fires, the life of the highest man, the *mal*, was led in isolation because of the strong power that he embodied. Through many grade initiations and pig sacrifices and his ascetic lifestyle, he had embodied so much secret knowledge and manly power that he in many instances now represented the very principle of *abio*, having power and influence over all people and creations within his district. These men, who embodied extraordinary capacities through their initiations and their lifestyle of taboos and avoidance of contact with female substances, were considered so dangerous to other people that they spent their days in permanent seclusion, in fact, sleeping and cooking inside their own graveyard, a circular stone fence. As the motors of all ceremonial exchange, they were acquainted with other people, but their social interaction was always imbued with a certain danger.

The high men who turned into sorcerers were referred to as *vanten hanglam* (a term for a man who is taboo but implicitly also an *abio*). They were known for their magical capabilities and their ability to make things happen to both people and things. Villagers I talked to commented that these sorcerers 'were almost like spirits' (*temær*), referring to their ability to travel through the air and to do incomprehensible things. A man from West Ambrym is today known to have been such a man. He had gone through all of the grades in the male hierarchy, even starting over again when he had reached the highest step and made multiple 'rounds' of the twelve steps of the *mage* hierarchy, and had in addition undergone a whole series of other spectacular ceremonies to achieve this spirit-like power. When his father had died, he had for 100 days washed only in the water of the decaying corpse that he had kept under the ceiling of his *imkon* taboo-house. After this and other similarly symbolic rituals of regeneration, he had at the peak of his career the power to do anything he liked. He travelled to places without actually leaving, and he killed hundreds of people by sorcery without even going near them. The power of these high men was based on an acknowledged and legitimate use of sorcery and magic. In a sense, they incorporated principles of state-like formations in their person, creating an imagery of a personified totalisation that was in fact present behind every social scene and inside all relationships.

An important idiom for male power is *meje fofo*, which means literally to 'open eyes turning around', implying one's capacity to see things from all sides, to see and understand everything. Like the Big Brother of George Orwell's *1984*, this character both embraced the totality of the community, by standing on top of the male hierarchy and overseeing all ceremonial activity, and represented the instrument of further totalisation and control as the *abio*. The *vanten hanglam* of West Ambrym referred to above in 1913 allegedly brought about a volcanic eruption in order to wipe out most of his rival villages in West Ambrym, even succeeding in devastating the biggest mission hospital in the New Hebrides at the time. Like generals in totalitarian states, these men were imagined capable of controlling all social interaction. Speaking about the early colonial period in South East Ambrym, Tonkinson (1981: 79) writes: 'A vital element in the power of chiefs was their monopoly over sorcery, which was allegedly used to maintain the loyalty of their followers (by threatening persistent offenders) and to combat the power of outside enemies, real or imagined. Sorcery was considered a legitimate institution, which kept people in line in an otherwise somewhat anarchic society.' Tonkinson, however, goes on to point out that after a period of pacification and the fall of the institution of the male hierarchy, sorcery radically changed its character on Ambrym. In what he calls 'a democratisation of sorcery', the practice became available to all people through inter-island exchange. In the highly mobile era of colonialism, people brought back sorcery from plantations on other islands and from the urban cultural conglomerate. Sorcery became the tool of everyone and everybody. Those who had purchased sorcery could now pose a threat to others without being legitimately known as *vanten hanglam* (high men).

Another factor in this change was, of course, the church discourse, which through its moral of equality, love for the next man and individual freedom had managed to break down the legitimacy of the former *vanten hanglam*. In fact, both the church and the colonial government set forth to strike down every incident of alleged sorcery on the part of the high men. In 1964, the British District Agent of the Ambrym district wrote in his quarterly report:

> North Ambrym: A number of visits were paid to north Ambrym to investigate allegations of murders in that region. Preliminary investigations revealed an extraordinary series of murders as far back as 1930 that had not been reported, and that witchcraft was still being extensively practised. One murder was reported to the Resident Presbyterian Missionary at that time, who agreed to overlook it provided the offender agreed to join his Mission! Two other murders were reported to the French District Agent who took no action on the report. The Commandant of police Mr. Walford and the Officer-in-charge of Police, Santo, Mr. Dumper visited the region on several occasions. It was decided not to prosecute in those cases which occurred many years ago; in the more recent cases it has not yet been possible to obtain sufficient evidence to common proceedings. One of the most feared of the pagan chiefs, Tofort, the son of the highest grade chief in the region, Tainmal, was sentenced to one year's imprisonment for witchcraft and generally with Tofort's absence from the island the position seem to be much improved. (British District Agent 1964)

Within these developments, the powerful men of the male hierarchy lost much of their power.

Tonkinson remarks that in the 1970s people's characteristics of sorcerers were completely altered. People now conceived of them as degraded and immoral, instead of powerful, recognisable by their 'sickly looks, poor hygiene, absenteeism from church, night prowling, a propensity for making veiled threats when angered' (1981: 81). As sorcery was now freed from the male hierarchy and let loose among men of less regard, it became a question of moral authority instead of power:

A major reason [for the change] is that it has become identified with secrecy, death and evil powers and in the view of the Ambrymese must be condemned because it breeds fear, tension and hostility. Villages are no longer at war, and sorcery no longer has an acceptable place in the inter-village quarrels when they occur. The trouble with sorcery is that too many innocent people of all ages are thought to be its victims. There are too many motiveless deaths; accidental, experimental mistaken identity-killings. This suggests to people an essential lack of control, a disorderliness which convinces beyond a doubt that reckless and inexperienced men are not in full command of the dangerous powers they are manipulating. (Tonkinson 1981: 84)

The situation was hence out of control because people could no longer appreciate the agency of the sorcery act as an expression of power, since it was no longer seen as the tool of the socially constitutive high men of the hierarchy. These men had now been struck down by this new moral authority, and, in the Bislama terminology, ancestor spirits (*temœr*) and the powerful men who were 'almost like spirits' came to be called 'devil'. This went hand in hand with the Christian overturning or uprising against the influence of the *vanten hanglam* and against *kastom*, setting up this practice as one of darkness, evil and destruction.[7]

Sorcery without Sorcerers

If we now return to Ambrym around the turn of the millennium, the effects of these historical shifts are still clear. There has been a complete figure-ground reversal of the relation between sorcery and *kastom*. Previously, sorcery was taught to apprentices in initiation ceremonies and inside the secrecy of men's lodges, and hence represented forms of knowledge transferred as part of the initiation package. If a man was a good apprentice in sorcery, he also became a man of *kastom*. Today, a man who merely expresses an interest in *kastom* practices is liable to raise suspicions of also trying to bring back sorcery. People who have engaged themselves in the recent reappraisal and reappearance of *kastom* are likely to be automatically blamed for 'pulling in' sorcery, even though the men's lodges are practically extinct. This process involves a certain degree of 'fantasising' about people of other villages and how they are hiding schemes of sorcery attacks inside imagined new secret lodges. It is therefore a common statement in Ranon that there is no sorcery in Ranon, only in the uphill *kastom* villages that Ranon people rarely frequent. This reflects that sorcery is mostly feared from the outside; when I talked to men in the uphill villages about this, they on their side actually feared the Ranon people for their sorcery more than anything else. According to them, *abio* has all the time been in the possession of the Ranon people, even though they have officially abandoned *kastom* (as grade-taking). Sorcery is hence viewed always the practice of Others, outsiders who then try to plant their 'seeds' in one's own village.

The ethnographic reality of sorcery today in North Ambrym is not seen as sorcery practice, but is instead found in the realm of sorcery effects, of the everyday aching bodies, of things that go wrong in the garden, and of sudden and unexplainable deaths. It is as if the sorcerer has been absented from the scene of sorcery, hiding somewhere in the background of the relationships in which people take part. The acts of sorcery have in a sense been obviated, made unnecessary by the self-evident signs of sorcery that come up all the time in relationships. In this situation, we must then approach sorcery as a field of relationships stretching between the victim, the 'diviner', who can talk about the reasons for the attack, and the man who is the alleged cause of the attack. Behind this triadic field of concrete relations lurks the *abio* himself.

The Mediating Appearance of *Abio*

One of the victims of the terror that swept over Ranon in 1999 was an old man who had originally come from a neighbouring village to work at the plantation in Ranon. He had married a woman and stayed on even after the plantation was overtaken by the independence movement in 1980. One day as he came back from the garden, carrying some firewood that he had collected on his way down, he fell to the ground outside his house. He was already dead when his wife found him. People suspected that this was an act of *abio*, and on closer inspection of the corpse they found that the neck was twisted off angle and therefore assumed that someone had broken his neck. Looking for further evidence of this, they found that the dead man's toilet had an opening on the back wall, an opening that they had not seen there before. The dead man's son consulted a diviner who could 'see' that the man had actually been killed in the morning by an *abio*, who had grabbed him through this hole in the toilet wall and broken his neck. Then the attackers had restored him to life again with herbs and spells so that he could go to the garden as usual. He only died when he came back, the guilty men having disappeared from the scene of the crime in the meantime.

In the proceedings that followed, the dead man's 'brother', his close neighbour and friend, was charged with the murder. He allegedly had an accomplice, a man from the same village, the dead man's son's wife's brother (his classificatory 'mother's brother') and an elder of the Presbyterian Church. During the court that was held against these two men, it came out that they had been observed one morning as they were walking together close to the dead man's house. They had allegedly put something there that attracted the *abio*. Another important issue that came up was that the cousin-brother had had an argument with the deceased over a recent 'project' that they had going. They had been initiated together into a special kind of *rom* ceremonial[8] that they had imported from West Ambrym. The dead man had later initiated other men into this ceremonial without letting his 'brother' take part in the profit, and several men during the court witnessed that he had reason to be discontent with his 'brother' over this. The court ended with a decision that the accused should pay a penalty to the dead man's son. The two men did not object to the verdict, and people commented that they were 'completely silenced' by the sentence.

They hence accepted it, not because they admitted to having done the deed, but because it stood as the community opinion, a 'social fact' that they had to agree with after hearing the arguments brought forward.

The fine was merely symbolic, but the worst thing about the sentence was that they now had to fear the revenge of the dead man's son and other relatives. Under this threat of becoming victim to another sorcery attack, the elder immediately took off for the regional town centre and worked on a kava plantation for six months. Shortly after the incident , the 'brother' became seriously ill – from tuberculosis, according to the doctors – and spent several months in a town hospital. When he came back, he had quit smoking and kava drinking, the main activities for socialising among the men in Ranon. People saw his physical weakness and his retreat from the social scene as clear evidence that he was admittedly corrupted by the sorcery presence and now feared that revenge and *abio* would strike him if he associated frequently with the men of the village.

When I later discussed the court decision with another Ranon man and expressed my surprise and disbelief in the verdict, he tried to explain to me the logic of the outcome. The point was not that the 'brother' and mother's brother had necessarily actually killed the victim themselves; we all knew that they could not have done it. But it could be that they had expressed themselves in a manner which indicated that they *wanted* him dead. If you sit in your kitchen and talk to your wife about someone in an angry manner and say in anger that 'this man might as well be dead', an *abio* might actually hear you and commit the murder on your behalf. Hence, by expressing the will to do other people harm, you are liable to attract *abio* who want to harm them. Bad feelings and anger directed towards others make those people vulnerable to acts of sorcery and witchcraft. The *abio* is in a way equivalent to the 'diviner' in his position as a mediator between the two parties in the relationship, but his is a force that mediates only the negative side of the relationship. It is a totalising force that can 'see' the true character of relationships when there is disruption and destroy them, just as the 'diviner' can see the same disruption and try to mend it.

So the sorcerer is still around on Ambrym. He has changed from being a concrete, legitimate, known person to becoming an absented principle that is attracted to tense personal conflicts. This is then no longer a matter of anyone and anybody performing sorcery, as Tonkinson earlier maintained was the case with the 'democratisation' of sorcery. At this point, nobody performs sorcery, but it is as if the image of the *vanten hanglam* has returned.

Solitary Anger and Communal Fear

In Vanuatu there is, as among the Gebusi (see Knauft 1985) and in many other places in Melanesia, a clear ideology of 'good company'. On Ambrym, friendship (*bulbulan*, a word also used for the white 'glue' of the breadfruit) is the overall frame of social interaction, and all face-to-face interaction goes on with an open smile. Even when facing their sworn enemies, people act in a mild and open manner. Anger and aggression do sometimes occur as loud swearing and outright fighting in rare cases when the steam of anger (*lolfeangfeang*, lit., inside is burning) gets too high. But it is when people do not openly display their anger that the *abio* sets in. The incident of the two 'brothers' who co-operated over the *rom* project was hence typical. The man who had been accused had kept the anger to himself, and my friend who commented on his sentence said that he had expressed his anger only inside his house in front of his fire. This solitary emotion of anger and grudges is seen to attract *abio*. It is often from the interpretation of 'qualisigns' (see Munn 1986: 16–18) that villagers on Ambrym realise that people among them conceal grudges and that something is wrong. It shows on their faces, in their general bodily disposition and in their absence from social interaction. When I discussed the concept of anger with a friend of mine in Ranon, I asked him how he would know that a man was angry. He explained it in an example: if he was in a meeting with another man and he told him off about something or if he strongly disagreed with him, and at the next meeting the other man did not show up, it meant that he was now angry. His inside was so hot that he could not show himself, and he now only wanted to fight. He would then keep to himself until the thing passed over, so that people could not see his face deformed by this anger. This form of concealed anger is considered dangerous because it threatens to bring *abio* into the relationship. The evidence of this is brought only after the fact, since the anger is always concealed. This was also probably why the 'brother' of the dead man was accused – because he had kept to himself after his 'brother' had sold the *rom* rights, and had not said anything about it.

Abio is linked to this emotion of solitary anger, anger that is concealed and enclosed in the individual. This is illustrated by another incident that took place during this traumatic time in Ranon. A man who had spent almost his entire life away from Ranon, living in the capital, suddenly came back to Ambrym and set up his house in Ranon. It then became known that he had for a long time planned on claiming the entire ground of Ranon village as his own land. Through his genealogical tracings before the Island Council of Ambrym he had even managed to get the court's support for his claims. He now began to demand money from people. He claimed that all the people in Ranon who had made money in the tourist traffic and wood carving sales owed him a percentage of their income and that the villagers owed him more than 10 million vatu (the equivalent of US$100,000) altogether. These were absurd amounts of money to the villagers, who did not have any money at all, at least not for open display. The intruder was seen to walk around the village with an angry grin on his face, never engaging in friendly interaction with anybody. He instead hastily walked around to other villages, visiting the feared uphill villages to seek support for his land claims, promising them money and land if they helped him.

As I was observing the completely improper behaviour of this man, I became worried that he would be killed or at least beaten up. But the villagers, on the contrary, treated him in a friendly manner, and supplied him and his family with food, seemingly taking no notice of his aggressive desire for money.

People shrugged their shoulders, saying, 'We'll see what happens' or 'Let him carry on'. When people are in conflict, they are expected to stay quiet, to let the village court or Island Council settle the matter and to see if 'something' happens. One should not walk around too much when embroiled in a conflict, since this is a sure sign that one is looking for sorcery. Accordingly, there is also an unspoken rule that one should not stay overnight in another village if a member of one's own village is sick. If one happens to be away while another man gets sick, one should stay put until he recovers. This clearly has to do with the agency of sorcery and malevolent powers, which are seen to come from outside of villages while being mediated by inside people to afflict their co-residents. This intruder in Ranon, who was constantly observed walking around to other places, became more and more associated with sorcery.

One day, a diviner from a neighbouring village came down to Ranon and claimed that this man had approached him to buy sorcery that he would use to kill the three most prominent men in Ranon. A village court was organised for the next day. The accused man sat down in the middle of a circle, surrounded by the district population. People then threw out accusations towards him,[9] claiming that he had tried to purchase sorcery. There was, however, no hard evidence, and the court decided that he should get away with a slight fine. After all, he could not be charged with any murders, and no one believed him really capable of causing sorcery either. The man he had approached about buying sorcery was, for that matter, now a member of the church, and despite what the urban dweller had believed, he was not involved in sorcery either. The accused had to pay a small amount of money to the three men whose names had figured on a list that he had made, showing the order of the men he was going to kill. These men, however, also had to give him some money in return, to release the tension of the accusations brought forward during the court. After this, people were satisfied, since the accused, now considered to be 'finished', had been spotted as a man looking for sorcery remedies. With the urban dweller's dispositions having been revealed, and thus no longer hidden, the people would no longer fear his anger. The to and fro of the payments appeared to settle the tension. This, then, was regarded as a happy ending, since the man had been brought forward, taken out from the secrecy of the *kastom* people he was allegedly seeing, before anyone had been killed.

Even though the claims of the man, his greed, his clearly displayed anger and his lust for money were not mentioned during the court, this behaviour had clearly triggered the accusations levelled at him. By giving him food and trying to accommodate him in the village, people had sought to deal with his desires. In the court he was now compensated with return payments so that he should let his demands on his rivals drop. The accused claimed he was completely ignorant about these things, and that he knew nothing about sorcery. He had merely come up from the capital to claim what he saw as his rights, and was surprised and frightened by these massive charges against him. The following night he boarded a ship headed for the capital, and he did not return to Ambrym, dying the year after (allegedly a victim of Ambrym sorcery).

In most of the cases of sorcery that I have encountered, the setting of the relationship between the accused and the victim is rather straightforward. The accused had motives for being angry or jealous, due to disagreements over land, money, rights or women. These motives are enough for people to suspect that the accused has worked as a channel for sorcerers, either explicitly through seeking remedies from sorcerers or unknowingly by merely holding grudges. If people have reason to be angry or jealous of someone, this is enough reason for the sorcerer to mediate their anger and kill the person. Hence, there is a clear moral issue at work here. People believe that if they have done anyone an injustice, by holding back something from him, this can make them victims of sorcery.

Interestingly, another emotion that comes up in this regard is fear. When discussing the concept of fear with my informants, it was often in relation to sorcery. When a person feels that he is being afflicted with some sort of sorcery, he goes to see a diviner and pays him to express his opinion. The diviner tries to 'see the road' of the victim – the state of his relationships and whether someone is after him. Often, he will see that someone is actually trying to hurt the victim, and the prophylactic is that 'he must be afraid'. This concept of fear (*oulmørmør*) literally means 'the breakdown of the skin'.

The concept of the skin, as a covering or a wrapping that is both symbolically and pragmatically related to the constitution of communality, is well known in the Pacific (see Gell 1993). On Ambrym, *lu-* (the suffix-taking form of general *oul*) refers to human skin, to tree bark, to clothes and to leaf coverings. But this word also comes up in economical usages. The word *lumlum* (skinskin) is used for compensation for work or favours, such as midwifery and personal care that have to be appreciated through return gifts of food. A word for bride price is *wulum vehen* (lit., return on the skin of the woman), a term that refers to the payment and overtaking of the plaited 'cover' that the bride has over her head when she enters her new household.

These usages are tied up with the idea that the skin or the 'cover' of a person is a matter of communal input. The fear – when 'the skin breaks' – is an expression of a need for further interpersonal care. When the diviner tells a man to be fearful, it is not only a warning that he should watch out, but implicitly also an expression of his need for communal engagement, both by opening himself up and giving and by seeking help from others in nursing his relationships. The emotion itself creates a need to engage socially, and in practice this means to initiate some way of giving to specific relatives. Significantly, fear is thus an emotion of the surface, while anger is an emotion of the inside (*lol*, inside). Fear opens a person up, while anger is enclosed within him. The prophylactic against *abio* is hence fundamentally to engage in mending one's surface. As a case in point, a businessman in Ranon tried to deal with the threat of sorcery caused by people's jealousy towards him. He was known to have a lot of money, and he felt the grudges against him very strongly. At one point he staged a ceremony wherein he paid his wife's relatives, as well as some known *kastom* performers, with gifts of expensive pigs. Through several similarly costly ceremonies, he in fact gave away everything he had, causing his entire business to collapse. Giving and fear are hence two aspects of the same pratico-symbolic principle of avoiding the emotion of anger and thus the involvement of *abio*. In a rather simplified manner, we could display the social dynamics and logic of the Ambrym sorcery arena as in figure 1.

By being fearful and mindful of their communal engagement, victims of sorcery will then also ideally take away the reason for the attack, admitting that he or she is withholding something from the social flow. Another version of this principle often takes place during ceremonies when people are not satisfied with what they are given to eat. In one case, I attended a small ceremony for the birth of a child at his father's hamlet. The agnates of the baby's mother came to receive the tokens of their important relationship to the child. During this small ceremony, the baby's mother's brother openly expressed his dissatisfaction with the food presented to him and stated that he wanted to eat 'food that tastes', implying that he wanted pig meat. The father of the child had to bring forward a pig, which he immediately killed and gave to his wife's brother. This desire for meat, for an opening up of the man's store of food, could easily have transformed into anger and then to sorcery, as an alternative way of 'eating' the man's substance.

As we see in figure 1, the assumed negative relationship brought into question by the sorcery attack does not exist before the misdeed of sorcery is a fact. The anger of the accused is concealed inside him and is not made manifest on the level of everyday relationships, and the fear of the victim is experienced not in a relationship to anyone in particular. It is a matter of following the moral obligation of the community and of trying to maintain all relationships in general. The relationship to the accused only comes up in the meeting with a third party, the diviner, and then the character of the relationship turns out to be determined by another third party, the *abio*. It is hence the *abio* who first brings the accused and the victim together in concrete reciprocity, a relationship marked by 'negative reciprocity', so to say, and it is the 'clever' who again 'sees' this reciprocity and tries to turn it into a 'positive reciprocity' through gifts and communal engagement.

Sorcery and Agency

Like Sartre's man in the window, the *abio* is here constituted at the very same time that the relationship between the victim and the accused is constituted. Like Sartre says, it is not *for* the third party that the two people have a relationship, it is *through* him. Their reciprocity is in fact constituted though their 'mutual ignorance' of each other, but this ignorance presupposes a knowing third party. Sartre's two workers each know of the *possibility* of other workers, but this is only possible if they construct a subjectivity outside of this ignorance, a knowing subject. Sartre (1991: 103) speaks of himself standing in the window: 'Even my subjectivity is objectively designated by them as Other (another class, another profession, etc.) and in interiorising this designation, I become the objective milieu in which these two people realise their mutual dependence *outside* me.'

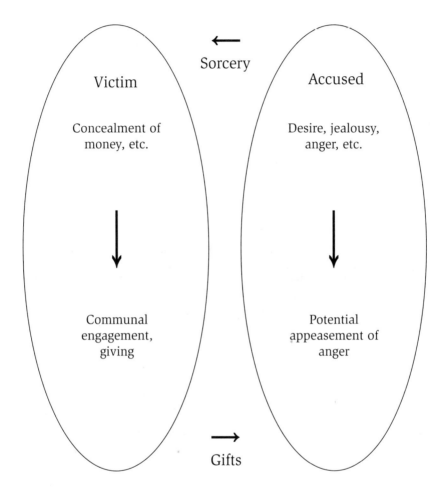

Figure 1 The logic of the assumed relationship between the victim and the accused in sorcery trials

It is exactly in this way that I think the dialectics of sorcery works on Ambrym. The *abio*'s subjectivity is 'objectively designated' by the situation when the victim and accused become aware of each other. But at the same time it becomes clear that it is he who has made the linkage between them, in this socially 'objective milieu', and forced them to engage with each other. If they are lucky, if the act of sorcery is discovered before someone is killed, they can engage in exchange and make the *abio* disappear, just as Sartre's man in the window would disappear out of focus if the two workers saw each other and started to interact.

There is, of course, a difference here between the two cases, between French workers and Ambrym villagers, the difference being that people on Ambrym realise that this constitution of reciprocity is immensely powerful. Granting that the third party can constitute relationships, it is understood that he can also destroy them, and people therefore do not look lightly on the issue of reciprocity. Hence, as a slightly different version from what Stephen calls 'individuation', we see here that the emotion of anger is logically bound up with sorcery as part of an 'economics of communal substance'. Sorcery is working as a moral sanction against differentiation, and is therefore also seen almost as a necessary outcome of immoral behaviour that people themselves have no control over. If people keep their riches to themselves, they are liable to become victims of sorcery, and they therefore become afraid and have to engage in giving and reciprocity. On one level, this is a concern of the relationship that is afflicted by sorcery – between the victim and the man accused of having caused it – but the agency of the sorcery act places this relationship in the grasp of an outsider.

In recent cases on Ambrym, one form of sorcery has been especially prevalent. The man accused of sorcery is believed to dig up the grave of a mother who has died in childbirth in order to take a bone from the corpse of the baby who is buried with her. He touches the head of the victim with this bone, and the victim then loses his mind, walking around in a haze. The purpose of this is to make him drop his defences against the *abio*, the personified sorcerer or witch. When *abio* arrives, the victim will 'only wish him welcome', and the *abio* is free to do what he pleases with the victim, in the end killing him and stealing his inner organs. We here realise how the structure of sorcery on Ambrym is fundamentally grounded in the relationship between the man assumed to be using sorcery and his victim, with the murder itself being committed by a third party. As we have seen, people can commit murders through these outside agencies both knowingly and unknowingly, but the triadic relationship works on the premise that the character of the relationship is dealt with from the outside. The third party hence represents both a principle of justice and social regulation and an absolute dispossession of control. In these cases it is hard to believe that anyone would have actually dug up the graves of dead women; at least in the cases that I have taken part in, I know that the accused would not have done it. That they are being accused comes as a shock to them, and they are forced into an awareness of their relationship with the victim. They are thus being compelled to look at themselves through the eyes of the totaliser, the third party, who can see that things have gone wrong between them. The judgement of this triad is then also simultaneously the totalising view of the community, and it is of course this fact that forces the accused to take the charges seriously and to leave the community.

There are thus two opposite totalising forces at play here. One is the third person, the *abio*, who in the first place opens up the relationship between two persons by using one of them to gain an entry into killing the other, because he has been keeping things to himself and caused jealousy and desire. The other is the judgement of the community on the accused in the court, which 'sees' how the accused has been guilty of keeping his anger and desire to himself. Both of these acts of totalisation represent moralities, and we could say that while the *abio* is a negative force with a positive morality, the communal judgement is a positive force that removes solitary anger and desire from community, but which at this point in history has been deprived of its absolute moral force, which was earlier represented by the high men of the hierarchy.

What we see here is a change in the concrete pattern of agency in the sociality of the sorcery field. Without people figuring as concrete and proclaimed *abio*, the sorcery has instead been internalised into the quality of relationships themselves. The *abio* has become a diffuse being, a monster-like creature that can appear anytime and anywhere, popping up with its superhuman qualities. Just like the malaria mosquito, this bloodthirsty creature lurks near human habitations, seeking a way to kill people. But also like the malaria parasite, it needs the mediation of other people to be able to dwell there. This is hence a special version of Stephen's 'invasion of other selves' that must be seen to come out of specific historical circumstances.

Sorcery and a Celebration of History

At this time, around the turn of the millennium, when the many sorcery attacks occurred, Ranon and the surrounding villages were in a phase of a growing collective consciousness of the history of the place. In 1997 there had been a big national celebration in Vanuatu, and also in Ranon, of what was called the 'Golden Jubilee'. This was a celebration of the anniversary of the Presbyterian Church, and there were great festivities and feasts all over Vanuatu. In Ranon, the day was celebrated by a performance of theatre, enacting the landing of Reverend Murray, the first missionary on Ambrym, on the beach of Ranon. A Ranon man dressed as Murray came ashore on the beach and was immediately attacked by other actors dressed as 'cannibals'. However, he managed to talk them into a peaceful arrangement and was led over to the ground where Murray's house had been set up in 1886. When the drama ended, Murray was celebrated as a hero, and a cement monument was erected with his name on it.

In another similarly historically laden event, a cruise ship visited Ranon in 1998. As the tourists walked ashore on the Ranon beach, a similar drama was acted out before them. This time the hero of the story was Captain Cook, who, according to people on Ambrym, landed on the Ranon beach and gave Ambrym its name. After an attack on the tourists by Ranon men dressed as savages, the ship's captain was implicitly made to act as Captain Cook, exchanging presents with the village landowner.

Together with these events, there had been a massive mobilisation of history in Ranon over the last years to celebrate its moments of success. The history of the plantation, the recent yachting business and the success in producing wood carvings for the larger markets only complemented this imagery. During the very formation of this image of Ranon, during this very process of claiming origins, Ranon village was also suddenly torn apart by conflict. In the 'essentialisation' of belonging that occurred, the place was riven with disagreements over who owned the land and who should profit from all of the money coming into the village. In the process, people had to account for their origins, their belonging, and this brought into focus names of ancestors, the history of places, narratives of past ceremonies and rituals, and possessions of rights in customary emblems.

The past then stood to represent what was right, and the men who knew the stories of the past would also claim a right to ownership. In this way, the past had been drawn into the present as an ideal, and it was through the importation of this ideal into the present that they wanted to construct the future. It then seemed as if this focus on the past simultaneously brought back an unwanted remnant of the past, notably *abio*. This was of course not intended by anyone, but in the act of 'pulling back' secret *kastom* ceremonies, such as the *rom*, and by evoking past conflicts and rights, the larger imagery of the past was also reignited.

It was in the middle of this period of historical consciousness that the *abio* started to turn up. In most cases it killed people and stole their intestines, but sometimes it also turned up without killing them. In one case, a married man had for some time been having an affair with a girl from the neighbouring village. He had managed to hide this from people in his village for some time, but in the end his wife had suspected him and people had seen him walking with the girl. One night he woke up in his house in Ranon, his bed surrounded by men dressed in *kastom* outfit, penis-wrappers and face paint. He could not recognise them, but he knew they were *abio*. They did not speak, but he understood that they had come to kill him. He however managed to get out of his house and fled to another village. He stopped seeing his mistress and paid pigs in compensation to his mistress's agnatic kin. In another similar case, a man knew that people in his village had for a long time held grudges against him because he had negotiated several big sales of wood carvings without sharing the money with his brothers. One night *abio* men walked up to his house and knocked on the door. They were dressed in penis-wrappers and face paint, and clearly intended to abduct him. He had a cunning wife, however, and she went in between them, holding out her Bible in front of her. This made the *abio* retire, and her husband managed to escape. He had to move to another village after the attack.

This view that *abio* now appeared before people in the disguise of the *kastom* outfit of penis-wrapper and face paint became an accepted idea among villagers.

When picturing the *abio* to themselves, they now imagined a fierce man dressed up in a disguise from the past. Of course, most old men do still have complete *kastom* equipment, concealed from rats and decay above the fire in their houses. There the bark belt; the dyed, plaited wrapper; the bow and arrow and clubs hang under the ceiling, sometimes taken out for dances or to show off for tourists. But for most of these men it is unthinkable that they should put on the outfit and walk around to other villages to kill people. No one believes that they do this either.

It was clear that during these sorcery attacks, the *abio* was believed to be a spirit-like creature. Significantly, the *abio* did not figure as anyone in particular, and their faces were not known to the victim, since they were in disguise. It sometimes seemed to me that they were seen as revelations of ancestral creatures, but in other cases they were described to me as if the sorcerers were actually village people, only transformed into a double self who committed the murder in the disguise of *kastom* without knowing it. In the disguise, they in a sense personified *kastom*; they became manifestations of the *kastom* 'machine', which stands for communal justice, for social control and for the bitterness of the past over the colonial influence.

Harrison (1993) in this regard makes an interesting point about the effects of masks and disguises in Papua New Guinea warfare. In Mount Hagen feuds, men must mask themselves in collective identities, disguising themselves with paint that takes away their personal appearance and that indicates 'the presence of ancestral ghosts on the men's faces' (Harrison 1993: 114). I believe that this same effect is suggested by the *kastom* disguise of the *abio*, the difference being that this is *not* a disguise, but a revelation of the past *vanten hanglam* in the present. We must remember that these men had something of a 'universal presence' and a power to mingle with the dreams and actions of anyone. Even though the people holding this power are now gone, the power itself remains in society. Their presence is hence a matter of a collective memory, projecting these powers into the matters that have become pressing in the post-colonial scene.

Conclusion: History Coming Back

We thus realise that *abio* today actually represents an absolute loss of agency. The principle of mediation, the very fundament of reciprocity, kinship and production on Ambrym, was now transformed into a monster-like figure who turned up and killed people. With the *abio* as an abstracted but present third party, we realise that sorcery represents a key factor in the maintenance and persistence of the principle of totalisation, despite colonialism's effort to wipe out totalising agency on the part of the high men. The *abio* forces people to act in a Sartrean dialectical intentionality, moving the focus between singular acts and relations and the totalising potential of their acts.

Abio hence places conflicts into a perspective of history and future socialisation, working as a commentary on the larger framework of people's lives, as a view from the past. The *abio*, in his disguise from the past, takes in all perspectives in his overtaking of people's relationships and passes total judgements on them. It is as if the community's historical 'in-itself' suddenly is exteriorised and set to pass judgement from the outside. What then becomes clear is that this ideal morality of the past has actually never gone away. Even though the colonialists did their best to destroy the totalitarian and hierarchical agency of the *vanten hanglam*, their morality, surveillance and control is still functioning underneath the new Christian morality that denies their presence. Therefore, people immediately also recognised *abio* when it struck in Ranon, understanding perfectly well that this was a reaction on the part of a morality that had come into the background of people's dealings with money and property. With the history of Ranon in mind, we must then also acknowledge how the sorcery trial is an institution that passes through the moral discourses of Christianity and colonialism on its way to its collective judgement in accusations and courts. The whole situation hence represents a moral with a twist, expressing itself against the growing tendency amongst people of 'keeping instead of giving', yet simultaneously taking up the tenet from the Bible that one should not desire other men's possessions or women. I think that this battle between the communal judgement on desire and the *abio*'s judgement on selfishness today represents a highly potent tension in the Ambrym community, a constant re-evaluation of what has been gained and what has been lost during its specific history.

In practice, however, actual events of sorcery do much more damage than what these moral tenets would suggest to us, and it is really the community's admonition against desire that causes people worry. If the victim is dead, the accused is confronted with an unbearable social pressure, and people go out of their way not to reveal their desire for other people's things. The force of *abio* accusations is very strong, and in most cases the accused also feel that they *are* guilty, admitting that they *did* hold grudges against the dead and that they *did* turn away from the relationship in question – they *did* conspire with the 'devils', so to say. Most people cannot bear these charges, and instead of trying to mend the damage, they leave. In many instances they have never come back, instead spending the rest of their lives away from their closest relatives, outside the Ambrym universe of sharing and jealousy.

NOTES

1. The same point has been raised by Sahlins (1972). In his re-evaluation of Mauss's Maori material, he finds that a concept of the third party is crucial to the concept of the Maori *hau*.
2. This discussion in this chapter specifically concerns the area of North Ambrym, a linguistically distinct region with about 30 larger villages, and around 5,000 inhabitants.
3. Missionisation gained a foothold on Ambrym Island around 1870, but because of the harsh environment, Western missionaries did not stay on the island for long. Early on,

Christianity took a strongly indigenous character, being mediated by indigenous 'teachers' who had been baptised either during their Australian plantation work or in the central mission stations in Vanuatu.

4. This tendency of secrecy involved in Vanuatu customs has historically given rise to the conception that customs always and everywhere wrap up malevolent agencies inside the seemingly harmless visible display of dance, music and magic. Therefore, it is a commonly held idea in Vanuatu that the big arts festival that was held in the capital in 1980 to celebrate independence after almost 80 years of a colonial regime caused many deaths because of the release of the power of *kastom* from different islands. The presence of Ambrym *kastom* during the festival especially caused a lot of anxiety, and the casualties were numerous.

5. The *mage* hierarchy consisted of 10 to 12 different fires in the men's house, where men belonging to the different ranks would cook their food. The fires of higher grades were considered dangerous to the lower initiates, and the food of the higher grades could itself be poisonous to men of lower ranks.

6. In many parts of Melanesia, it is difficult to distinguish between sorcery and witchcraft, and the *abio* has something of both these Eurocentric concepts (see also Knauft 1985, Stephen 1987). The missionary Paton translates *able* in West Ambrym as 'witchcraft', 'poison', this being the general term covering many items 'also used of the person'(Paton 1971: 1). When one talks about *abio* in Bislama, the pidgin-based national language of Vanuatu, it is framed as *posen*, indicating that it refers to using poisonous substances or practices to inflict disease and death upon others.

7. A very similar situation is reported by Williams (1976).

8. *Rom* is a general term for a secret ceremonial cycle that revolves around the making of a dance costume and the transferring of the costume's secret knowledge. The initiation culminates in a public display of the costumes and a dance in which the individual dancers are believed to be overtaken by the spirits of the *rom* costumes. The dance itself has a violent appearance, as the dancers strike the audience with their sticks when they come running into the dance field. The masks are either hidden or burnt after the ceremonial and must never be seen by uninitiated people, except during performances. Sometimes the dancers reappear in other villages to haunt the inhabitants and beat them with their sticks. During the period of revival of *kastom,* starting in the 1990s, the *rom* has become popular among young men because it gives them the right to carve the design of the *rom* mask in wood. Such design carving is popular with the tourists. The young boys have to pay men who have been previously initiated for their own initiation.

9. Someone had seen him carrying octopus tentacles, a well-known mystical substance used for poisoning fruit trees, into the village. Six months before this court, a man had died, supposedly from this form of poison, and another man claimed that the accused had been responsible for this death. He had even overheard him saying that the dead man's son should also 'die by eating fruit from the same tree as his father'. Other people also testified to having seen him in distant villages, asking around for sorcery remedies.

BIBLIOGRAPHY

Boddy, J. *Wombs and Alien Spirits.* Madison, 1989.

British District Agent. 'Quarterly Report of Central District 2 of New Hebrides.' Manuscript. Vanuatu National Archives, 1964.

Chowning, A. 'Sorcery and Social Order in Kove.' In *Sorcerer and Witch in Melanesia,* ed. M. Stephen, 149–83. New Brunswick, N.J., 1987.

Fortune, R.F. *Sorceress of Dobu*. London, 1932.

Gell, A. *Wrapping in Images: Tattooing in Polynesia*. Oxford, 1993.

Godelier, M. *The Making of Great Men*. Cambridge, 1986.

Harrison, S. *The Mask of War: Violence, Ritual and the Self in Melanesia*. Manchester, 1993.

Jamond, P. 'Ambrym Hableo.' Unpublished manuscript. Noumea, 1949.

Kapferer, B. *The Feast of the Sorcerer: Practices of Consciousness and Power*. Chicago, 1997.

Kelly, R. *Constructing Inequality: The Fabrication of a Hierarchy of Virtue among the Etoro*. Ann Arbor, 1993.

Knauft, B. *Good Company and Violence: Sorcery and Social Action in a Lowland New Guinea Society*. Berkeley, 1985.

Lattas, A. 'Sorcery and Colonialism: Illness, Dreams and Death as Political Languages in West New Britain.' *Man* 28 (1993): 51–77.

Lawrence, P. '*De Rerum Natura:* The Garia View of Sorcery.' In *Sorcerer and Witch in Melanesia*, ed. M. Stephen, 17–41. New Brunswick, N.J., 1987.

Lederman, R. 'Sorcery and Social Change in Mendi.' *Social Analysis* 8 (1981): 15–27.

Lindstrom L., and G. White, eds. *Custom Today: Anthropological Forum*, special issue 6, no. 4 (1993).

Malinowski, B. *Crime and Custom in Primitive Society*. London, 1926.

Mosko, M. 'Junior Chiefs and Senior Sorcerers: The Contradictions and Inversions of Mekeo "Hierarchy."' In *Transformations of Hierarchy*, ed. M. Mosko and M. Jolly, 195–222. Canberra, 1994.

Munn, N. *The Fame of Gawa*. Durham, 1986.

Paton, W.P. *Ambrym (Lonwolwol) Dictionary*. Pacific Linguistics Series C, no. 21. Canberra, 1971.

Patterson, M. 'Mastering the Arts: An Examination of the Context of the Production of Art in Ambrym.' In *Arts of Vanuatu*, ed. J. Bonnemaison, C. Kaufman, K. Huffman, D. Tryon, 254–62. Bathurst, 1996.

———. 'Sorcery and Witchcraft in Melanesia.' *Oceania* 454 (1974–5): 132–60, 212–34.

Rio, K. 'The Third Man: Manifestations of Agency on Ambrym Island, Vanuatu.' Ph.D. diss., University of Bergen, 2002.

———. 'Standing Drums in Vanuatu: The Cultural Biography of a National Symbol.' Unpublished *hovedfag* thesis, University of Bergen, 1997.

Rivers, W.H.R, ed. *Essays on the Depopulation of Melanesia*. Cambridge, 1922.

Sahlins, M. *Stone Age Economics*. London, 1972.

Sartre, J.-P. *Critique of Dialectical Reason*. Vol. 1: *Theory of Practical Ensembles*. Trans. A. Sheridan-Smith. London, 1991 [1985].

Stephen, M. 'The Mekeo "Man of Sorrow": Sorcery and the Individuation of the Self.' *American Ethnologist* 23, no. 1 (1996): 83–101.

———, ed. *Sorcerer and Witch in Melanesia*. New Brunswick, N.J., 1987.

Strathern, M. *The Gender of the Gift*. Berkeley, 1988.

Tambiah, S. *Culture, Thought and Social Action: An Anthropological Perspective*. Cambridge, 1985.

Taussig, M. *The Devil and Commodity Fetishism in South America*. Chapel Hill, 1980.

Tonkinson, R. 'Sorcery and Social Change in South East Ambrym, Vanuatu.' *Social Analysis* 8 (1981): 77–88.

———. 'Divination, Replication and Reversal in Two New Hebridean Societies.' *Canberra Anthropology* 2, no. 2 (1979): 57–74.

Weiner, A. *Inalienable Possessions: The Paradox of Keeping-While-Giving*. Berkeley, 1992.

Williams, E.F. *The Vailala Madness and Other Essays*. London, 1976.

Zelenietz, M. 'Sorcery and Social Change: An Introduction.' In *Sorcery and Social Change in Melanesia*. Special issue. *Social Analysis* 8 (1981): 3–14.

Chapter 6

SORCEROUS TECHNOLOGIES AND RELIGIOUS INNOVATION IN SRI LANKA

Rohan Bastin

This essay examines the importance of sorcery in the dynamics of religious innovation in contemporary Hindu and Buddhist Sri Lanka.[1] My interest stems from two observations. First, in almost stark contrast to other Hindu ritual forms that emphasise unchanging text-based rites, the sorcery practices I describe display an almost modernist preoccupation with innovation. Second, much of this innovation originates, or is seen to originate, from outside the cosmic order both of the pantheon and of society. Consequently, sorcery practices manifest a dynamism that often results in the appearance of sorcery having sprung up from nowhere or of being on the sharp increase. However, such an appearance of growth is less of an increase by degree than a shift in visibility. Moreover, it is a characteristic Sri Lankan sorcery practices share with practices elsewhere. When social scientists whose gaze has been primed for spotting anomalies light upon these shifts in visibility, the reaction is usually one of alarm. Scholars whose basic orientation is to the problem of social order and stability tend to judge these apparent aberrations in terms of social breakdown and anomie. Instead of considering what sorcery reveals anthropologically, they instead analyse sorcery as a symptom of a social pathology. The restless dynamism of sorcery and its role in religious innovation remain unaddressed, and this contributes to a conservative view of both the phenomenon of sorcery and the study of religion in general.

I commence my discussion with the Tamil Hindu Bhadrakali temple at Munnesvaram on the north-west coast of Sri Lanka in order to introduce a major site for sorcery practice in present-day Sinhala Buddhism. Having situated the Hindu goddess Bhadrakali (or more simply Kali) in the contemporary pantheon and introduced some of the sorcery practices associated with her, I turn to an analysis of a special ritual event held near the west-coast town of Kalutara and sponsored by a female trance specialist, or *maniyo*, who is a devotee of Kali. Sorcery is a practice that looms large in this *maniyo*'s world, but so too is the pursuit of new sorcerous technologies. Followers of the *maniyo* include a significant number of women who are returned labour migrants to

the Persian Gulf. Their presence raises issues about gender relations in contemporary Sri Lanka and suggests arguments about sorcery as a practice on the
rise in relation to social change and what Gombrich and Obeyesekere (1988)
call 'urban anomie'. However, we must be careful when performing this kind of
analysis, because it presumes that sorcery is a form of deviant behaviour that
must be explained in terms of its pathology.

Striking Revenge at the Bhadrakali Temple

The Hindu goddess Bhadrakali, or Kali, is worshipped in Sinhala Buddhism as
a fierce demoness who has been tamed by the goddess Pattini. Kali's temple at
Munnesvaram on the north-west coast is believed by Sinhala Buddhists to be
her original temple in Sri Lanka, the place where Pattini subdued and thereby
encompassed Kali within the Buddhist pantheon (Bastin 2002, 1996). As such
an original site, the Bhadrakali temple (with 'Bhadra' – Auspicious – as the honorific title) is understood to command a tremendous religious potency (*haskam*,
in Sinhala). This attracts large crowds of Sinhala Buddhists to Munnesvaram,
where they make extensive offerings to Kali, particularly while requesting the
goddess's intervention in personal crises. Such intervention can range from simply providing protection to her devotee to acts of *paligahanava* (striking revenge,
or simply glossed as *pali* – revenge)[2] on behalf of a devotee. The latter action is
sorcery in the sense that it involves the recognition of another human agent with
the desire to modify that agent's reality. It takes several forms, including the sacrifice of a chicken (to simply harm an enemy) or a goat (to cause death).[3] The
principal form consists of an act of submission to the goddess in which devotees
rub the ends of their hair (if female) or their foreheads (if male or a short-haired
female) three times in a paste of fresh cow dung while uttering the name of the
accursed. Other forms include breaking a coconut (which is a standard offering
at Hindu temples regardless of sorcerous intentions), breaking an egg, burning
an egg in oil in a papaya fruit vessel, boiling milk rice (which may also have no
sorcerous involvement), and having Indian coins cut by a priest inside the temple's inner sanctum.

Munnesvaram's cow dung revenge rite is done at a special stone on the
ground in front of the Bhadrakali temple at which a metal trident is fixed. The
trident (*trisula*) is an icon of the main deity of the Sri Lankan Hindu pantheon,
the god Siva. It is his weapon, and when it is presented alone, it represents his
demon-like guardian form Bhairavar. The trident also represents the demon-like
goddess Kali, who stands in a close relationship to Bhairavar, having forms
associated with ambiguous locations such as crossroads, temporal junctures,
cemeteries and cremation grounds. Bhairavar and Kali are thus deities of the
margins and ambiguous spaces who share characteristics in common with both
deities and demons. In the logic of Tamil Hindu (or Saivite) belief, they occupy
significant junctures in cosmic processes that involve the double movement of
creation and destruction or, more accurately, emission and reabsorption (Davis

1991). These junctures are extreme points of active manifestation at which the cosmos returns to a more passive and quiescent condition of possibility. Elsewhere (Bastin 2002), I describe this process in terms of the symbolism and meaning of the Tamil Saivite temple, whose architecture and ritual describe cosmogony as an unfolding differentiation of form. Critically, identified at the limits of differentiation are the points of return to the undifferentiated state. It is this potential of the goddess Kali to originate and re-originate the cosmic order that makes her especially powerful in sorcery.

Sinhala Buddhists distinguish the practice of striking revenge from acts of sorcery (*kodivina, vina*) that are regarded as far more heinous and secretive. *Vina* takes several forms, including the manufacture of special spells inscribed on a thin copper sheet in a geometrical *yantra* pattern that is then secreted in the victim's house compound.[4] One may well react to the knowledge of a *vina* by performing a *pali*. It is a retaliatory action involving justice meted out by the deity as the champion of the plaintiffs who request violent punishment for the wrongs done against them. For this reason, the plaints often conclude with the hope that the deity will soon become a Buddha, and thus that the requested act of justice will only contribute positively to such a quest. Such morality also attends *vina*, but this action relies more on the abstract manipulation of cosmic forces than on the support of a deity. The sponsors of the act are usually seeking retribution for some kind of wrong done against them. In this way, the process of sorcery can be likened to the movement of a feud (Kapferer 1997: 41) – an endless oscillation of violent acts of transgressive retribution in which both sides claim the moral high ground.

While performing *vina* is more secretive than performing *pali*, temples for *pali* are usually remote from the everyday worlds of people and are travelled to without fuss or fanfare in something of an obverse manner to the pilgrimages made to important Buddhist and Hindu/Buddhist sites. There is no merit to be made from performing sorcery, although there is arguably merit to be made for the deity who assists in it, because the deity's assistance is a charitable act. However, more important than this issue of merit is that of surprise. Sorcery involves a technology of cosmic manipulation, and with that, of manipulation of consciousness (of both victim and perpetrator) (Kapferer 1997). However, its technology can be dulled by counteractive means whereby the intended victim asserts his or her conscious mastery over the situation more successfully than the perpetrator. It is thus far better to catch one's enemy unaware and also vitally important that people who suspect sorcery take precautions.

Closely tied with sorcery beliefs and practices, therefore, is protective practice. At Munnesvaram, the main form of protection, apart from a straightforward entreaty with an offering, is a protective ritual for malevolent planetary influence. Importantly, if close kin such as children have a bad planetary configuration and there is a fear of sorcery, there is greater impulse to have the planetary rites performed, as the power of sorcery will extend to the child even though the child is not the one named by the sorcerer. The child's horoscope may well suggest the need for the protective rites as a general measure, but sorcery fears provide an important incentive, because malevolent sorcery does not attack simply the body and mind of the victim. It attacks the victim's life-world, which includes significant others. A core theme of protective ritual, therefore, is the development of a full awareness of the nature of this life-world. I recorded several instances of planetary rites performed for entire families when the Sinhala Buddhist father suspected sorcery.

In addition to precautions, it is important that people learn as much as they can about what their enemy is doing. Closely associated with sorcery, therefore, is divinatory trance and spirit-mediumship. Trance is a common feature of Kali worship in Tamil Hinduism in Sri Lanka and south India, with trance possession desired quite simply as an expression of devotion (*bhakti*) (Caldwell 1999). Kali possesses devotees in one or several of her forms, or through a member of her demonic retinue. Very often, an individual's power of trance derives from a dead relative who shared a deep attachment to both the individual and to the goddess. Possession occurs most commonly in the context of temple ritual, especially the Tuesday and Friday morning *puja* to the goddess when Kali and all of the other deities in the temple are propitiated. The priests accept large offerings of fruit, flowers and money from devotees during this morning rite, with many devotees offering chickens and, more rarely, goats as live offerings that may or may not require sacrifice. In addition, several devotees, roughly 65 per week, perform the cow-dung curse as soon as the rite is completed (and the presence of Kali thereby strongest). Temple musicians playing the *tabla* drum and *nagasvaram* reed instrument, accompanied by the incessant ringing of the temple bell, lift the tempo among the devotees with aggressive rhythms through which many begin to tremble, dance and fall into trance. The music, itself an offering to the goddess, is also an expression of the goddess embodied now by the devotee.[5]

In association with sorcery practices, trance relates specifically to knowledge and control. Devotees gain knowledge as to the true nature of their crises, including knowledge about the identity of their enemies and the appropriate form of action to take. Specialist consultants (*sastra karaya*) do most of this trance work. They are people who, upon first experiencing trance, seek to develop their skills through extensive worship whereby they gain a mandate (*varam*) from Kali, and with that an ability to control their trance and to speak lucidly and knowledgeably while in trance rather than mutter gibberish. Mainly women, who are known as *maniyan* (plural of *maniyo* – mother), they go into trance in the context of worship of several popular deities in contemporary Sinhala Buddhism, but particularly in relation to Kali (Bastin 2002, Kapferer 1997, Obeyesekere 1981).

Sorcery Deities in the Cosmic Hierarchy

Other deities important to the *maniyan* are Dädi Munda, Devol Deviyo and Suniyam. Like Kali, each of these deities has a special shrine in the country associated with the origin of the deity in the hierarchy of the Sinhala Buddhist pantheon. For Suniyam, the shrine is at Kabalava, roughly 30 kilometres south-east of Munnesvaram, where, according to some, Pattini tamed the deity in his unruly demonic form.[6] For Devol Deviyo, the shrine is at Sinigama to the south, where Devol arrived from overseas and passed over the seven mountains of fire that Pattini erected to stop him. For Dädi Munda, the shrine is at Alutnuwara and appears to be closely associated with Visnu and Suniyam. Critical, there-fore, to the shrines, which are all major sorcery shrines in Sinhala Buddhism (Obeyesekere 1975), is the association between their potency and their location in the social and mythical landscape.

The shrines are situated on the margins of Sinhala Buddhist society, away from the major ritual centres such as the Temple of the Buddha's Tooth Relic in Kandy. More than this, the shrines also exist at important junctures in the mythical past of the cosmic hierarchy, when, as expressions of wild unruly forces attempting to disrupt the social and cosmic order, the major sorcery fig-ures were encompassed by the moral order of the pantheon, usually in the form of the goddess Pattini who somehow tamed them. Thus, the point about the shrines and the origin of the deities associated with them is that the shrines mark not so much the birthplace of the deity, but rather the entry of the deity into the cosmic order. The condition they attain is thus analogous to the con-dition of a person who obtains a trance warrant (*varam*). Wildness gives way to lucidity without the disappearance of destructive potential.

It is striking, moreover, that the four major sorcery shrines are for four lower order deities/demons (Kali, Suniyam, Devol Deviyo and Dädi Munda) who cor-respond to the four principal gods of Sinhala Buddhism (Pattini, Visnu, Natha and Kataragama). Temples for each of these high gods stand adjacent to the central Temple of the Buddha's Tooth Relic in the old Sri Lankan capital of Kandy. The scheme thus elaborates a *mandala*-like pattern (with Buddha at the centre) through which the sorcery shrines have a marginal yet originating power. The principles of this '*mandala*', as expressive of cosmic manifestation, relate very closely to the Hindu ideas that place deities like Kali and Bhairavar at the emission/reabsorption juncture.

The Devol Deviyo shrine at Sinigama illustrates these relations most clearly. It was here that Devol arrived from overseas and climbed the seven mountains of fire erected by Pattini to stop him. He succeeded because he and Pattini were siblings in a previous existence, but his passage through fire transformed him from a demon (*yakku*) to a god (*deviyo*). On the seashore stands the temple to the god, while on a small rock outcrop 150 metres offshore stands the shrine for the demon. Devotees pay local fishermen to be rowed over to the little island, where striking revenge rites are performed that involve chillies and ginger being ground together at the base of a tree. Thus, Devol retains an ambiguous deity/demon status that is most powerful at the site of his entry to the Sinhala Buddhist pantheon. The same holds for Kali. Munnesvaram is the site where Kali arrived from India aboard a stone raft, whereupon she attempted to kill and eat Pattini. However, Pattini subdued Kali, stopped her from eating humans and allowed her to receive animal sacrifice.

Cosmic Empowerment through Religious Revitalisation

Kali is, however, the only one of the Sinhala Buddhist sorcery deities who is seen as thoroughly outside the Buddhist pantheon. Gombrich and Obeyesekere (1988: 134) explain that she is 'too ghoulish' to be admitted and popular because of 'Hinduizing trends' in contemporary popular religion (Gombrich 1988: 208). In my view, Kali's modern 'Hinduisation' is a result of religious revitalisation, both Buddhist and Hindu, which has separated many aspects of popular religion as belonging exclusively to one or the other of the two religions (Bastin 1997, 1996). In both cases, revitalisation developed in the nineteenth century, and the separate fields of activity share several elements.[7] These include direct confrontation with colonial missionaries, a changing social formation consisting in large measure of mercantile capitalism and rapid growth in formal education.

Central to Buddhist revitalisation is a style of fundamentalism that seeks a pure Buddhism uncorrupted by 'non-Buddhist' elements. In the course of the nineteenth and twentieth centuries, champions of revitalisation also construed these elements, and the people most closely associated with them, as 'non-Sinhalese' as well as 'non-Buddhist'. Thus, religious revitalisation was woven together with ethnic politics, both informing and being informed by the consolidation of ethnic groups in the framework of the emerging bureaucratic nation-state. As the Sinhalese ethnic group was consolidated vis-à-vis Tamils, Europeans, Burghers and Muslims, certain religious practices – including deity and planetary worship, as well as sorcery – were marginalised as non-Buddhist and thus non-Sinhalese.[8] Such a marginalising discourse serves mainly to redescribe the cosmic hierarchy. Deities like Kali, instead of being excluded, are remarginalised and effectively re-empowered in the cosmic hierarchy.

A similar process occurred in the Hindu revival with its emphasis on the reconstruction and renovation of ancient temples such as Munnesvaram, which was destroyed by Belgian Jesuits in the early seventeenth century.[9] The revitalised Hindu temple of Munnesvaram influenced the growth of Kali worship in the nearby Bhadrakali temple, marking both temples as distinctly Tamil Hindu and thus marginal to the Sinhala Buddhist scheme. The popularity of the Munnesvaram Kali temple thus grew in the circumstances of religious revitalisation quite contrary to the wishes of the various protagonists of that revitalisation.

Of great significance to these developments in religious practice was the influx of Indian Tamil labour to the plantation sector, which boomed throughout the central hill country and south-west quadrant of the island from the second half of the nineteenth century until the 1960s. The rapid expansion of tea plantations in the hills and, to a lesser extent, rubber plantations closer to the western littoral resulted in an influx of Indian Tamil families. Predominantly Hindu, these generally poor Tamils began to influence the popularity and wealth of a number of Hindu temple complexes, their festivals and their interconnection.[10] Forms of worship, glossed by Obeyesekere (1978) as 'Bhakti religiosity', grew in popularity for many Sinhalese also. These included fire-walking, hook-swinging, *kavadi* dancing, the Kataragama pilgrimage and divine possession. Reconstructed and newly built Hindu temples provided a focus for new forms of old worship, such as Sinhala Buddhist planetary worship (de Silva 2000). Instead of traditional *bali* rites performed in house compounds by traditional specialists (*aduras*), people with bad horoscopes attended Hindu temples and made offerings to the planets' shrine or had special rites performed by the temple priests. Thus, it was not a simple matter of old beliefs and practices dying out, but a transmutation of the religious field in which the beliefs and practices occurred (ibid.). Critically, the new sites were public places – shrines and temples – which intensified the sense of novelty over that of reproduction and change. Kapferer (1997) describes a similar and closely related process for sorcery tied to the emergence of sorcery shrines.

Kali in Kalutara

Two Sinhala Buddhist Kali temples near the west-coast town of Kalutara over 40 kilometres south of Colombo illustrate these points about religious innovation in the late colonial and post-colonial eras. A male Sinhala Buddhist priest (*kapurala*), with a family history of Buddhism and Catholicism, runs the older temple, which was established in the 1940s.[11] The temple is a few kilometres inland and once would have attracted the Tamil labourers working on the rubber plantations nearby. The priest never goes to Munnesvaram and barely maintains his rarely open temple. The newer temple, established in the 1980s, is very different. It was established by a *maniyo* in her house compound in a relatively well-to-do suburban area near the coast. The temple draws a largely Sinhala Buddhist clientele from the surrounding coastal area. Following the decline in the numbers of Tamil plantation workers, particularly after anti-Tamil riots in 1977 and 1983, the popularity of the older temple has waned considerably.[12] The *maniyo*'s temple is thriving. As often as she can and both with and without clients, the *maniyo* travels the 120-odd kilometres north to attend the Munnesvaram Bhadrakali temple. Like many others in her profession, the *maniyo* regards the originary nature of Kali at Munnesvaram as filling the site with religious potency. She periodically draws upon this potency (*haskam*) to reinvigorate her special powers.

To summarise, the popularity of Munnesvaram Kali worship in Sinhala Buddhism is entwined with the colonial history of ethnic relations, religious revitalisation and the changing social form of a society enmeshed in colonial mercantile capitalism. At the same time, this popularity asserts an original and originating relationship between the goddess Kali and Sri Lankan religion and society, as well as their spatial arrangement. It does so particularly through the connection between Kali worship and sorcery practice.

Religious Innovation in the Kalutara *Maniyo's* Festival

Every year the Kalutara *maniyo* sponsors an all-night event, known as a *devol maduwa*, at the shrine. The chief celebrant is a male deity priest (*kapurala*) of the *goyigama* caste, accompanied by *berava* caste dancers and musicians.[13] The priest, dressed as Pattini, undertakes the rite, which principally re-enacts the arrival to Sri Lanka and incorporation into the Buddhist pantheon of the over-seas god Devol Deviyo.[14] In accordance with such conventional rites, the *devol maduwa* was a largely male affair. The *maniyo* remained virtually out of sight inside the house while her male partner took the role of the ritual sponsor who interacts with the priest, the dancers and drummers. The traditional patron of such Pattini rites is a man who additionally should be a local political leader and high caste. That is not the case here, but it is noteworthy that the *maniyo* drew the line at fully assuming the patron's role. Part of the opening cere-monies included lighting the electric lamps in all the shrines in the house com-pound. Due to my status as a foreign scholar, but especially because of my close links with the Munnesvaram Bhadrakali temple, I was invited to switch on the lamp for Bhadrakali, after which the *devol maduwa* could proceed.

While the *maniyo* was absent during the performance, the audience stayed well away from the performance area, watching from the garden and inside the house. At 11.30 p.m. the Pattini priest and other performers retired to eat and rest. The ritual arena then filled with people, mostly women who were dressed mainly in red. They gathered for the *maniyo's* performance, which involved her entering trance and the piercing of her left breast to draw blood that was offered to Kali, but offered inside the shrine room containing Pattini, the main focus of the *devol maduwa* rite. When she did so, many of the women who had crowded into the tiny shrine with her offered coins wrapped in red cloth, which were tied around Kali's trident weapon. The *maniyo* then came out of the shrine and danced around the ritual enclosure before entering her house and sprinkling rit-ually blessed water. The crowd heaped garlands of red frangipani flowers around her neck, frequently covering her head in a mass of red petals. In contrast to the studied movement of the dancers and priest in the preceding events in the ritual enclosure, with worshippers observing from a distance, the *maniyo's* perfor-mance was chaotic, and the enclosure was filled with people, mostly women and mostly wearing the colour red. Music, supplied by a group of young Tamil men from Indian estate backgrounds, largely consisted of raucous saxophone-domi-nated popular Tamil movie songs, such as are played for *kavadi* dancing at Murugan temple festivals, notably the very popular festival at Kataragama.[15]

When the *maniyo's* performance ended at about 12.30 a.m., the *kapurala* returned and the *devol maduwa* continued until 8.30 a.m. Having enjoyed a rest (while her partner quietly complained about having to sit up and act as sponsor), the *maniyo* made a second appearance, again with a large (albeit reduced) crowd and the Tamil musicians. As in the midnight performance, gen-eral pandemonium was the dominant feature. Instead of offering red frangipani garlands, the remaining crowd covered the *maniyo's* head in red cloths. The *maniyo* began speaking in trance. She answered several questions put to her by the devotees concerning their personal lives. In the manner of *maniyo* consultations at the major sorcery shrines, such as Munnesvaram's Bhadrakali temple, devotees were anxious to learn the truth about their personal situations and future prospects.

Like the pierced breast, the red cloths piled onto the *maniyo*'s head could also bear an association with Pattini, for whom a white veil is an important iconographic element incorporated into such Sinhala Buddhist rites as the Suniyama, in which it is worn by the anti-sorcery patient (Kapferer 1997: 116). However, whereas the *maniyo* and her devotees were specific about the link between the breast and Pattini, there was less clarity on the subject of the cloths, and other associations are more likely. The cloths are individual offerings in the manner of the bunting flags Sinhala Buddhists hang from sacred *bo* trees and the votive flags Sinhala Catholics tie to church festival flagpoles. In the area of the Western Province, where the *maniyo* lives and works, these different traditions have interacted, often aggressively. The pure Sinhala Buddhist rite of the *devol maduwa*, itself far from uniform across the country, confronts other traditions in dynamic interplay, including Tamil Hindu (Sri Lankan and Indian) as well as Roman Catholic. In other words, the religious field is one of intense interaction between religious traditions. The *maniyo*'s *devol maduwa* establishes a powerful interface for religious innovations that are themselves emergent from previous instances of interaction, such as the incorporation of flagpoles in Catholic church festivals (Bastin 2002: 170, 180n8). Drawing directly from the use of flagpoles in both Tamil Hindu and Sinhala Buddhist temple festivals, Catholic church festivals (and even a number of mosque festivals) commence with the installation of a flagpole. Individual offerings of flags tied to the guy ropes are thought to remove sin from the donor. Red, the predominant Hindu colour, also features prominently with the church festivals for the popular Saint Sebastian, who is associated with healing and, along with Saint Anthony, with sorcery and anti-sorcery.[16] Seen in these terms, the red cloth offerings suggest cathartic votive offerings by individuals as the culminating act of the *maniyo*'s annual event.

Kapferer (1997: 117) describes the white veil used in the anti-sorcery rite as 'filled with the sense of the immanent dangers, transformation, conscious awakening, and repotentiation of the victim it protectively enshrouds'. The individual offerings of red cloth probably share a closer provenance with the flag offerings on Catholic church festival poles and probably a closer meaning. The white veil is a protective shroud whereas the red cloth bears away the person's sin. It piles up on the head of the *maniyo*, like detritus, immediately prior to her mediumship when the truth about social relationships comes out.[17] Thus, just as the *maniyo* establishes an iconicity with Pattini and becomes the site and source of repotentiation, she also acquires the detritus of human relationships and becomes, in effect, the pole (*kapa*) – the site of origination. This is the essence of the *maniyo*'s relationship with the goddess Kali. She occupies a marginal location in Sinhala Buddhist society through which she effects originary transformation in the cosmic hierarchy of deities and humans. She repotentiates her clients, and closely connected to this repotentiation is the mediation of sorcery.

The *maniyo*'s *devol maduwa* began in 1989 and steadily attracted popular participation. As with many Sinhala Buddhist rituals, especially those traditionally performed by the *berava* caste and, in the case of Pattini worship, by the *berava* and others, there has been a growth in non-specialist participation as well as in the formation of new performance contexts, such as the *maniyo*'s event. It reflects the broader process of religious innovation in contemporary Sri Lanka – innovation in which traditional priests and specialists take part rather than against which they represent the 'old religion'.[18] The *maniyo* had inserted herself into the Pattini rite, recognising the religious supremacy of Pattini and symbolically emulating the goddess through the self-inflicted wound on her left breast. This recalls the moment in the main myth of Pattini when, in her fury at the Madurai king's execution of her husband, she tears off her left breast and casts it at the city, causing it to burn. The *maniyo*'s action was, however, a blood offering to Kali that is also iconic with Pattini, and thereby redolent of meanings associated with Pattini's act of striking revenge. These involve the interplay between life and nurturance (the breast) and righteous destruction as the fire Pattini causes when, with her breast, she curses the city of Madurai.[19] Connected to it are the various curses and requests for aid made by worshippers to the goddess Kali in the form of the coins wrapped in red cloth and tied to the trident. This form of offering is common in Hindu temples. It can be about sorcery or, like other sorcerous technologies described above, more simply a request for benevolent protection.

Gender Relations and Social Change in Contemporary Sri Lanka

As I noted, the official patron of the *maniyo*'s *devol maduwa* is her partner, a young man with whom she developed a relationship following the growth of her religious activities. The *maniyo*, like most women in her profession, is separated from her first husband, and like many others, she has a younger partner whom she maintains through her good income.[20] This economic independence is matched somewhat by the economic independence of a very large number of the women who attended the rite. Many were returned labour migrants to the Middle East, and many of them were widowed or separated from their husbands. They constituted a significant number who attended the rite and became active during the two events centring on the *maniyo*. Many of them were friends who had worked in the Middle East at the same time. Their presence during the *maniyo*'s performance highlighted the contrast to the *devol maduwa*. Studied performance gave way to chaos, Pattini gave way to Kali, white gave way to red and men gave way to women.

The changing forms of labour associated with Persian Gulf oil economies and the rise of manufacturing industries in underdeveloped countries have profoundly affected Sri Lankan society, especially in the urbanised areas of the

Western Province. Between 1985 and 1995, the rush of mainly unskilled labour to the Persian Gulf grew considerably, but then slowed, principally in the area of male employment. The emphasis on employing housemaids remained fairly constant, and, although there has been a growing preference for employing Muslim women over Sinhalese women, many Sinhalese women have had the opportunity for re-employment at the end of their contracts. Such women tend to be older and married. In many instances, their work has become the major income for a household while the husband's opportunities for labour migration have diminished. As Gamburd (2000) shows, this change in a woman's earning power puts stress on the family. Not only does the woman go away for one or two years, leaving children in the care of the husband or parents, the man may find regular work difficult to secure either at home or abroad.

In the same period of the 1980s and 1990s, garment exports eclipsed tea as the country's single largest export earner. The plantation sector, established in the conditions of the bureaucratic colonial state and nationalised after independence in 1948, has gone into decline. Urbanisation, principally focusing on Colombo and its surroundings, has intensified. The manufacturing industries attract large numbers of workers, particularly young unmarried women. While primarily located in the free trade zone near the international airport north of Colombo, the factories have also sprung up in smaller versions throughout the Western Province, with a few not far from Kalutara.

Both young and older working-class women have thus gained access to limited forms of economic autonomy through labour migration, either to the growing industrial belt around Colombo or to the Middle East. Such women are rarely well educated, although they are literate, and this is striking for a society that traditionally valued education and identified education as fundamental to social and economic development. In respect to Middle East labour migration, the consequences for traditional households have frequently been intense, with increased alcoholism and gambling among men, domestic violence and marriage breakdown resulting (Gamburd 2000). Many women who work in the Persian Gulf do not become affluent, for often their savings are swallowed by the creditors who lend the large sums needed to get the job (paying agents' fees, air fares, etc.). A second stint may be the solution, but this raises the risk of the earnings being squandered by wayward husbands.

In a way, the men are not unlike Pattini's husband in her myth (Kovalan, in the textual version). Enchanted by the charms of a courtesan, Kovalan steadily wastes all of his money and then sells all of Pattini's jewellery, save her anklets. Kovalan later repents and is reunited with his wife, but this seems to be rare for contemporary Sinhalese men, at least the men whose wives have become significant contributors to the household through labour migration.

On top of this, Sri Lanka's civil war – combining both the Sinhalese/Tamil ethnic conflict, war between the Sri Lankan military and Tamil militants, and the 1989–91 conflict between the Sri Lankan government and forces aligned to the Sinhalese People's Front (JVP), has drawn the entire population into cycles of violence and loss. While young women can seek work in factories, young men can receive good salaries as soldiers. However, the risk of serious injury or death is enormous and many families have suffered. Others have suffered because their sons became embroiled in the politics of the JVP struggle and simply disappeared.

Specific features of innovation in ritual practices are a result of the changing social situation. Commenting on one new form practised at both the Munnesvaram and Bhadrakali temples, a couple of priests from each temple separately opined that labour migration and interaction between labour migrants from different parts of South Asia was giving the process of innovation a new dynamic. Women, they added, were very important to this development because with so many young men killed or missing, young women's marriage prospects had altered.[21] The rite in question involved making nine oil lamp wicks from the fibres of the lotus root and burning them in separate clay pots also containing limes. The purpose of the rite is to request the goddess's help in a woman's marriage. In such 'love magic' the lotus root bears potent symbolic associations with cosmogony and rebirth (Bosch 1960), while the lime is particularly important in the alleviation of sorcery with a similar theme of regeneration.[22] This is not to suggest that the rite is a sorcery rite in the manner of the *pali* rites. However, it can carry all of the meanings associated with sorcery in the sense of desiring to influence another's life-world and, with that, to alter one's own. It expresses a profound wish by young women to change their situation in the circumstances of some adversity and thus shares with the sorcery rites the theme of the sponsor's regeneration in the cosmos (Bastin 1996). For the priests, the rite probably originated in Kerala, and its growing popularity stemmed from Sri Lankan and Keralan women working and/or living together in the Persian Gulf. Knowledge is passed down from the elder to the younger, and then the rite takes on its own dynamic as other devotees observe the rite and replicate it.

The growing popularity of the *maniyo*'s *devol maduwa* rite also reflects these changes, but it would be as much of an overstatement to suggest that these changes can be attributed to the social situation as it would be to suggest that the social situation has no bearing at all. Sorcery and its associated practices, such as the few I have described here, are always concerned with the vital relation between self and society. The question is whether sorcery waxes and wanes as a human practice or simply modifies in its expressive content. In the final section of this essay I describe two typical approaches to the phenomenon that err in their efforts to explain sorcery as a form of deviance by seeing sorcery as on the rise.

Before I consider these arguments, let me stress that the west coast of Sri Lanka has been subject to major change from well before the Portuguese arrival in Colombo in 1510. The rise of the spice trade, the influx of social groups such as the *karava* fisher caste to which the *maniyo* belongs, the shifting centres of political and economic dominance, the conflicts and the imposition of nearly 450 years of European colonial rule, all have placed the western littoral and entire country in considerable (albeit periodic) turmoil for a very long time. Kalutara, where the *maniyo* lives, was a major centre for the spice trade and a major access point to the interior through the Kalu River. It was also an important area for religious interaction between Buddhism, Hinduism, Islam, Catholicism and Protestantism. The proliferation of Buddhist temples under different orders of monks reveals the importance of Buddhist revitalisation in the region's colonial struggle as well as the dynamics of social change and caste politics that accompanied these historical processes. Shifting gender relations have been critical to all of these moments.

Existing Accounts of Sorcery as Social Pathology

What I am describing, therefore, is a labile social situation in which caste, ethnic and gender relations are in flux as a consequence of globalised economies in the colonial and post-colonial eras as well as a history of violence. In this situation, the temple complex at Munnesvaram emerges as a Tamil Saivite centre of great significance to Sinhala Buddhists. Specialist female spirit-mediums, deriving their powers from their association with the fierce goddess Kali, grow in number and popularity among Sinhala Buddhists. Traditional rites such as the *devol maduwa* are reworked in certain new contexts combining Hindu, Buddhist and Catholic elements. Finally, sorcery appears to be a fundamental element and concern informing all of the changes. This seems to indicate a rise in sorcery acts as a function of modernity (and postmodernity) – an argument made over many years by Gananath Obeyesekere, both alone and in association with Richard Gombrich. Sorcery is on the rise (Obeyesekere 1975), 'Bhakti religiosity' is more popular (Obeyesekere 1981, 1978, 1977, 1975), sexually repressed women worshipping the virile god Kataragama grow more numerous (Gombrich and Obeyesekere 1988), and Kali is replacing Pattini as the main goddess of Sinhala Buddhism (ibid., Obeyesekere 1984a). The key to all of these developments is 'urbanisation', consisting primarily of a 'breakdown of traditional structures of authority and meaning' (Gombrich and Obeyesekere 1988: 53). Whereas before 1960 there were no Sinhala Buddhist Kali shrines, there are now dozens and sorcery features at all of them (ibid.: 139). The reason for the rise is 'urban anomie' (ibid.: 130).

Durkheim's concept of anomie describes the condition of uncertainty that derives from rapid change – for both the better and (more commonly) the worse – in complex societies. In connection to the incidence of suicide (Durkheim 1951), anomie reflects the failure of social groups to adjust positively to social change, thereby placing their individual members at risk. Like most social scientists applying Durkheim's concept, Gombrich and Obeyesekere's urban anomie is largely of the 'change-for-the-worse' variety. Slums, shanties, underemployment, domestic violence, affray and crime all contribute to a profound dislocation in the Sinhalese psyche. This leads both to an increased attention to negative mother images projected into the pantheon in the form of Kali (Obeyesekere 1984a) and to ethnic nationalism and communal violence (Obeyesekere 1984b). Increased aggression in increasingly fraught social relationships are channelled (or 'canalised') into sorcery (Gombrich and Obeyesekere 1988:

130–1; Obeyesekere 1984b, 1975). In general terms, the analysis of the Sri Lankan social situation is an explanatory one. It seeks to explain the nature of social practice in terms of the causes for behavioural modification among Sinhala Buddhists. It is a pathological analysis that treats contemporary Sri Lanka as a sick society in which sorcery and other practices are symptoms of a malaise grounded in the nature of social change. A form of historicism is a necessary concomitant to such a pathology. As Sri Lanka's current plight is rendered analogous to a diseased patient, its 'healthy state' must be postulated.

The pathological approach to the phenomenon of sorcery is very similar to arguments that are more recent. Jean and John Comaroff (2001, 1999), for example, associate the rise of witchcraft in post-apartheid South Africa with the situation more generally in Africa, as well as in the areas peripheral to the centres of wealth and power in globalising capitalism. Pyramid financial schemes in countries of the old Eastern European bloc, zombie beliefs in Cameroon, a veritable 'witch craze' in South Africa, all are manifestations of 'millennial capitalism' and, in particular, the despair with which so many have experienced the failure to deliver on the promises associated with freedom from the tyranny of previous (racist and Stalinist) regimes, such as apartheid South Africa or communist Albania. Importantly, this failure has been for only a majority of people, not the totality. The 'revolution' *did* deliver, but for only a small number. The striking feature of globalisation is that, as a result, we can no longer speak of the First World and the Third World, but of a global context in which the two interpenetrate (Hardt and Negri 2000). This is especially evident in and through the activities of a transnational bourgeoisie whose numbers and background can be held up as proof positive of the 'new world order' and the moral imperatives of global development. For the others – the majority, in fact – the utopian imaginings engendered by the collapse of the old regime have proven to be failed prophecies. The term 'millennial capitalism' is thus intended to convey a double sense of capitalism at the end of the second millennium and capitalism replete with the contradictions of failed expectations in the face of a world economic system that continues to produce and concentrate wealth in the hands of a few.

The Comaroffs differ from Obeyesekere (and Gombrich) in the characterisation of the recent past as reflecting the traditional society. Whereas Gombrich and Obeyesekere's analysis of social change fits the old-style developmental model, whereby a traditional rural society transforms into a modern, urban nation-state via the agency of colonialism, the Comaroffs' argument in no way suggests that apartheid South Africa or communist Albania constituted ideal traditional worlds. Instead, they emphasise the failure of utopian expectations spawned in far from ideal worlds and not in the breakdown of an idyllic past. Where one pair sees modernity and colonialism, the other sees postmodernity and post-colonial globalisation. Nevertheless, both parties postulate a prior moment that was better, at least relatively, to what we have now. For the Comaroffs, this moment was fleeting. At the point when people had reason to be optimistic – because, so to speak, the 'wicked witch' of oppression was teetering and about to die – the promise of a better future began to erode, and the 'witch' was reinvented as the magic of millennial capitalism.

Common to both arguments, therefore, is the sense that the current situation is one of deterioration from the past. While Gombrich and Obeyesekere's past ('tradition') seems to be more durable, the Comaroffs' immediate and fleeting past of a kind of revolutionary 'collective effervescence' seems to be more realistic. What they share in common, though, is a view of sorcery (or witchcraft) as similar to a disease for which they can provide the pathology: sorcery and witchcraft are symptoms of a broader socio-economic malaise that can be glossed as 'urbanisation' or 'globalisation'. One of the problems of such a degenerationist approach to cultural phenomena is that it often obscures their nature.

Kapferer (2001) describes the arguments of the Comaroffs and others as like 'old wine [that] is being poured into new bottles', and my comparison to Gombrich and Obeyesekere's analysis bears this out. Importantly, this does not constitute the grounds for disparagement (ibid.) because the insights of the old functionalist approach to sorcery highlight the undeniable impact of social change and political and economic inequality. Moreover, they reveal the common thread that runs between colonial exploitation and contemporary global economies. The difficulty stems from the reiteration of the traditional rationalist paradigm that casts sorcery and witchcraft as fundamentally being an irrational response to the world by the impotent. The new arguments differ from the old functionalism in their ascription of the irrationalities of sorcery to a world that has itself become irrational. The antics of the fringe-dwellers of millennial capitalism in Eastern Europe and Africa resemble the practices of the Hauka documented by Jean Rouch in the 1954 ethnographic film *Les Maîtres Fous*. The magic of global capitalism may be figuratively frothing at the mouth, but, hey, that's the way of the world!

Returning to the field of sorcery in Sri Lanka and the rise of Kali worship at Munnesvaram, as well as the rise of the *maniyo* as a ritual specialist and sorcery adept, I am suggesting that it is necessary to avoid casting the phenomenon as a symptom of social breakdown or failed expectations. This is not because social breakdown or failed expectations do not occur, but because they do not adequately address sorcery as a phenomenon rather than as a symptom. My inspiration is Evans-Pritchard's account of the new Zande magical associations, such as the Mani, that were gaining popularity during his research in the late 1920s (Evans-Pritchard 1937: 511–25).[23] He shows how the associations relate to social change for the Zande, but he does not attribute the movements simply to the effects of anomie or the like. Zande witchcraft beliefs and practices are analysed in terms of cosmology, not in terms of social change and social rupture. It is an attempt to understand rather than to explain.

Where sorcery does rupture is in the control over knowledge, particularly the knowledge of social relations. It is always active, but at different moments. Its insatiable appetite for new technologies renders it more or less visible to the gaze of certain types of technicians of practical knowledge. These technicians include priests and trance specialists, but also social scientists, journalists, lawyers and state functionaries. Driven by a rational emphasis on explanation over interpretation, they may conclude that sorcery is on the rise when really the new technologies of sorcery have simply made it more visible or visible in a different way.

The Sri Lankan president from 1989 to 1993, Ranasinghe Premadasa, was frequently described by his political enemies as a man who routinely made use of sorcerous technologies that he obtained from Kerala, a traditional source of such technologies, according to both Sinhalese and Tamil traditions. Accusations about Premadasa even ran to the ritual sacrifice of babies as well as large numbers of goats and chickens. Accusers even included rivals in his own political party (prior to their assassination). As Kapferer (1997: 294f.) describes, Premadasa's government was at this time engaged in the brutal suppression of the JVP. The JVP acted on the margins of the state and, in Kapferer's terms, displayed the characteristics of Deleuze and Guattari's 'war machine' (ibid.: 274–6, 292–4). The war machine is the counterpoint to the state (but not its opposite) wherein each aspect or modality represents the dynamics of power and their mutual interpenetration. Where the state displays both 'formal organisation of government' and the exercise of brutal destructive force, so it reveals the dynamic of this far from simple dualism. Kapferer illustrates the relation by examining both the JVP's push for power and the Sri Lankan government's bloody response. It also bears extension to Sri Lanka's ethnic conflict and the place of the LTTE (Liberation Tigers of Tamil Eelam) in the popular imagination. A cartoon by the Sinhalese satirist Wijesoma that appeared in 1984 in both the Sinhala and English language newspapers (*Divayana* and *The Island*) depicts an ugly-faced Tamil militant sitting astride a tiger. Like the goddess Kali, whose animal vehicle can be a tiger, the militant has several arms. Again like Kali, there is a weapon in each hand, but now the weapons are grenades and machine guns whereas Kali's weapons are swords, tridents and nooses. The 'Tigers' were thus the war machine demonstrating the ferocious power of the quintessential Tamil goddess Kali, whose worship by Sinhala Buddhists has continued to grow.

Kapferer argues that there is 'a sorcery in the processes of power' and means by this 'that we can understand power and the processes of power better by taking sorcery seriously' (Kapferer 1997: 287). His application of Deleuze and Guattari's concept of war machine and state to both Sinhalese sorcery and the circumstances of the JVP insurgency, as well as the Sri Lankan ethnic conflict (Kapferer 1988), is not meant to reduce these phenomena to an irrationality or the perseverance of a primitive mentality in the conditions of social breakdown, but rather to elicit from sorcery the nature of its insights into human practice. In no way does this deny the impact of the radical social change occurring in Sri Lanka in recent decades, nor does it deny the relation between this social change and innovative religious practices. It simply suggests that there are anthropological insights to be gleaned from these practices that go beyond simple explanatory models.

In this essay I have focused on the way in which Sri Lankan sorcery practices continually seek new technologies that inform the dynamic of religious innovation. Like the goddess Kali in Sinhala Buddhism and other sorcery deities, the new technologies of sorcery emanate most powerfully from the margins. Thus, their users capture, or strive to capture, the dynamics of Sri Lankan society, particularly its ethnic and gender relations, and in doing so give these relations their shape and reproductive potential.

NOTES

1. Fieldwork was undertaken in 1994 and 1995 while I was an Australian Research Council postdoctoral fellow and visiting fellow in the Department of Sociology, University of Colombo. Due to production constraints, diacritical marks have not been added to the Sinhala, Tamil and Sanskrit terms in this text. Purists may like to consult the glossary in Bastin (2002). Lastly, I would like to acknowledge a continuing intellectual debt to Bruce Kapferer for his important criticisms and suggestions.

2. The equivalent Tamil term is *paliyidukkurudu*, from *palivangku* – to avenge.

3. The chicken and goat sorcery at Munnesvaram is also described by Obeyesekere (1975). It is not the most common form of striking revenge, and an offering of a chicken or a goat is not necessarily an act of sorcery, in the sense of requesting the modification of the life-world of another.

4. The use of spells is more precisely *anavina*. For the different forms of *kodivina*, see Kapferer (1997: 36–39). Tamil Hindus have a very similar practice and identify eight formal types: *vasiya* (Sanskrit, influencing), *mohana* (bewildering), *sthambana* (paralysing), *utsadana* (overturning), *akarsana* (enticing), *vidvesana* (exciting hatred), *bhedana* (breaking alliances) and *marana* (killing).

5. This double movement of the offering, as both gift to the deity and expression of the deity, underlies the logic of Hindu temple worship (*puja*). It indicates how the offerings are not merely transactional goods creating a contract, but pure gifts that re-state divinity as an expression of divine consciousness (Bastin 2002: 125).

6. See Kapferer (2001, 1997) for a discussion of Suniyam.

7. The Buddhist revival has roots earlier than this and relates most profoundly to relations between the king and the order of Buddhist monks (Blackburn 2001, Holt 1996, Malalgoda 1976).

8. These processes of ethnic inscription are extensively documented. See, for example, Tambiah (1986). The Burghers are Eurasians specifically of Dutch-Sri Lankan descent, but also include people of Portuguese-Sri Lankan descent (Roberts et al. 1989).

9. The Portuguese divided their colony among different Catholic orders in 1602 and granted the lands surrounding Munnesvaram to the Jesuits. When the first missionaries destroyed the main temple image with iron bars in 1606, they described their deed in the terms of an exorcism. The devil had been presiding over the area from this shrine causing all manner of 'freaks'. Their destruction of the image and subsequent erection of a church, which was later destroyed, ensured an ordered divine presence (Bastin 2002). This evidence of Munnesvaram's long association with chaotic forces must obviously be treated with caution. At the very least, it indicates how the marginal and disruptive status of Munnesvaram was reproduced via the active participation of European missionaries in the seventeenth century.

10. For example, the Sea St. Murugan temple in the heart of Colombo's old commercial district schedules its festival around the conclusion of the Kataragama festival, when water from the latter's final bathing (or water cutting) rite is brought to the Colombo temple.

11. This is older than Gombrich and Obeyesekere state for Sinhala Buddhist-run Kali shrines, which they say do not pre-date 1960 (Gombrich and Obeyesekere 1988: 139). Actually, Munnesvaram shows such an assertion to be problematic because its priests were Sinhala Brahmins up to 1830 (Bastin 2002: 35), and its temple had an active Sinhalese partici- pation as early as 1834 (Casie Chitty 1989: 165). What is reasonable to say, *pace* Gom- brich and Obeyesekere, is that in the era of ethnic division and consolidation, there was an initial distancing between Sinhala Buddhists and Kali worship that, over the twenti- eth century, has dramatically lessened.

12. The decline is also due to the programme of Indian Tamil repatriation established between the governments of India and Sri Lanka in the 1960s.

13. The *goyigama* are traditionally landowners and farmers and occupy a superior position in the caste hierarchy. The *berava* are low caste ritual specialists, best known for their planetary rites (de Silva 2000), rites for demonic affliction (Kapferer 1983) and the anti- sorcery rite (Kapferer 1997).

14. Generally, the rite is a smaller-scale version of the *Gammaduva* rite described in detail by Obeyesekere (1984a: 71–224).

15. The red costumes and Tamil music are prolific at the annual Kataragama festival, as is the devotional dance known as *kavadi*. Indeed, Kataragama and Munnesvaram are the two important sources for the embellishments found in this rite. For Gombrich and Obeye- sekere (1988), they are the sites for the rise of 'Bhakti religiosity' and 'Hinduising trends'.

16. Stirrat (1981) describes an important Saint Sebastian shrine north of Colombo.

17. Darlene McNaughton (personal communication) has pointed out parallels between the *maniyo*'s practice and Kali worship and mediumship among itinerant traders based in Gujarat. Caste and lineage temple priests wear a red cloth prior to entering trance and answering questions.

18. 'Devil dance' performances in tourist hotels are a notable example, especially for the affluence derived from them by a number of younger ritual specialists, as well as for the number of non-specialists drawn to a traditionally low caste occupation.

19. For more information on the Pattini myth, see Obeyesekere (1984a) and for the textual version, see Alain Daniélou (1965).

20. Many *maniyan* have neither husbands nor lovers, their solitary life imitating that of the god- dess who contrasts with her more benign counterpart, the spouse of the god. At Munnes- varam, this spouse is Ambal (Parvati). She is also known as Pattini to some devotees.

21. Officially, the disappeared number just over 30,000. Roughly the same number were killed, and their bodies have been identified. The blood-letting was at its zenith between 1987 and 1989 (Chandraprema 1991).

22. I have seen lime cutting (*dehi kapima*) in the Sinhala Buddhist Suniyama rite done in conjunction with the *valvalalu tinduva* segment when the bonds of sorcery are cut in the form of vine hoops that bind the body of the patient (Kapferer 1997: 167–71). The rite is also performed by *maniyan* and other *sastra karaya* at the Bhadrakali temple (Bastin 2002: 68). Many shops and houses hang a series of three limes interspersed with red chillies above their doorways to ward off malevolence. One can even purchase plastic replicas for a more lasting effect. The lime has a powerful symbolism. It originates in the subterranean Naga (cobra) kingdom (Nevill 1955: 343), and thus bears a striking relation to the hoops described by Kapferer as linked to the Naga king's crown (Kapferer 1997: 167). The Naga kingdom replicates human society in the underworld. The cobra, cred- ited with both intelligence and vengefulness, is a creature enlisted in both Tamil and Sin- halese sorcery traditions to carry out sorcerous attacks.

23. Members of the Mani demanded technological innovation in the form of new charms and herbs, and emphasised the distribution networks of witch doctors, through which these new technologies gained in potency. Critically, the networks consisted of equal numbers of men and women, and cut across the normal lines of cleavage in Zande society. They thereby challenged the traditional power/knowledge structure ultimately controlled by

the Avongara aristocracy, and the Zande state. Mani relied heavily on money 'because unless the medicines see that they have been bought they will lose their power' (Evans-Pritchard 1937: 518). High payment to a figure of renown for his or her new knowledge thus intensified the potency of that knowledge. Hence, symbolic capital and inflation lay at the heart of the subversion of the existing structures of power and authority that was evident in a movement that had grown considerably in the circumstances of the breaking of the traditional Zande state by the British. I am struck by the parallels between this movement and the emergence of female spirit-mediums among the Sinhalese, as well as the requirement for the social networks through which religious potentiality is seen to grow.

BIBLIOGRAPHY

Bastin, R. *The Domain of Constant Excess: Religious Pluralism at the Munnesvaram Temples, Sri Lanka.* New York, 2002.
———. 'The Authentic Inner Life: Complicity and Resistance in the Tamil Hindu Revival.' In *Sri Lanka: Collective Identities Revisited.* Vol. 1. Ed. M. Roberts, 385–438. Colombo, 1997.
———. 'The Regenerative Power of Kali Worship in Contemporary Sinhala Buddhism.' *Social Analysis* 40 (1996): 59–94.
Blackburn, A.M. *Buddhist Learning and Textual Practice in Eighteenth-Century Lankan Monastic Culture.* Princeton, 2001.
Bosch, F.D.K. *The Golden Germ: An Introduction to Indian Symbolism.* 'S-Gravenhage, 1960.
Caldwell, S. *Oh Terrifying Mother: Sexuality, Violence and Worship of the Goddess Kali.* New Delhi, 1999.
Casie Chitty, S. *The Ceylon Gazetteer.* Colombo, 1989 [1834].
Chandraprema, C.A. *Sri Lanka: The Years of Terror, the JVP Insurrection, 1987–1989.* Colombo, 1991.
Comaroff, J., and J.L. Comaroff. 'Millennial Capitalism: First Thoughts on a Second Coming.' In *Millennial Capitalism and the Culture of Neoliberalism,* ed. J. Comaroff and J.L. Comaroff, 1–56. Durham, 2001.
———. 'Occult Economies and the Violence of Abstraction: Notes from the South African Postcolony.' *American Ethnologist* 26 (1999): 279–301.
Daniélou, A. *Silappadikaram.* New York, 1965
Davis, R.H. *Ritual in an Oscillating Universe: Worshipping Siva in Medieval India.* Princeton, 1991.
de Silva, P. 'Sri Lankan Culture under the Impact of Globalisation: Homogenisation or Revitalisation?' In *Sri Lanka at Crossroads: Dilemmas and Prospects after 50 Years of Independence,* ed. S.T. Hettige and M. Mayer, 206–23. Delhi, 2000.
Evans-Pritchard, E.E. *Witchcraft, Oracles and Magic among the Azande.* Oxford, 1937.
Gamburd, M.R. *The Kitchen Spoon's Handle: Transnationalism and Sri Lanka's Migrant Housemaids.* Ithaca, 2000.
Gombrich, R. *Theravada Buddhism: A Social History from Ancient Benares to Modern Colombo.* London, 1988.
Gombrich, R., and G. Obeyesekere. *Buddhism Transformed: Religious Change in Sri Lanka.* Princeton, 1988.
Hardt, M., and A. Negri. *Empire.* Cambridge, Mass., 2000.
Holt, J.C. *The Religious World of Kirti Sri: Buddhism, Art, and Politics in Late Medieval Sri Lanka.* Oxford, 1996.
Kapferer, B. 'Sorcery and the Shape of Globalization.' *Journal of the Finnish Anthropological Society* 26, no. 1 (2001): 4–28.

———. *The Feast of the Sorcerer: Practices of Consciousness and Power.* Chicago 1997.

———. *Legends of People, Myths of State: Violence, Intolerance and Political Culture in Sri Lanka and Australia.* Washington, D.C., 1988.

———. *A Celebration of Demons: Exorcism and the Aesthetics of Healing in Sri Lanka.* Bloomington, 1983.

Malalgoda, K. *Buddhism in Sinhalese Society, 1750–1900: A Study of Religious Revival and Change.* Berkeley, 1976.

Nevill, H. *Sinhala Verse (Kavi).* Colombo, 1955.

Obeyesekere, G. *The Cult of the Goddess Pattini.* Chicago, 1984a

———. 'The Origins and Institutionalization of Political Violence.' In *Sri Lanka in Change and Crisis,* ed. J. Manor, 159–69. London, 1984b.

———. *Medusa's Hair: An Essay on Personal Symbols and Religious Experience.* Chicago, 1981.

———. 'The Firewalkers of Kataragama: The Rise of Bhakti Religiosity in Buddhist Sri Lanka.' *Journal of Asian Studies* 37 (1978): 457–76.

———. 'Social Change and the Deities: Rise of the Kataragama Cult in Modern Sri Lanka.' *Man* 12 (1977): 377–96.

———. 'Sorcery, Premeditated Murder, and the Canalization of Aggression in Sri Lanka.' *Ethnology* 14 (1975): 1–23.

Roberts, M., I. Raheem and P. Colin-Thomé. *People in Between: The Burghers and the Middle Class in the Transformations within Sri Lanka, 1790s–1960s.* Ratmalana, Sri Lanka, 1989.

Stirrat, R. 'The Shrine of St Sebastian at Mirisgama: An Aspect of the Cult of the Saints in Catholic Sri Lanka.' *Man* 16 (1981): 183–200.

Tambiah, S.J. *Sri Lanka: Ethnic Fratricide and the Dismantling of Democracy.* Chicago, 1986.

Chapter 7

MALEFICENT FETISHES AND THE SENSUAL ORDER OF THE UNCANNY IN SOUTH-WEST CONGO

René Devisch

Diversely echoing Gail Weiss (1999) and Paul Stoller and Cheryll Olkes (1987), I hold that maleficent fetishes that sustain lethal sorcery shape and enact, yet pervert, their proper contours of embodied interactions and transactions. These interactions are being absorbed and consumed, if not devoured, by the sensual order of the uncanny and by forces of abjection. From my immersion in the life of the Yaka people in Kinshasa and south-west Congo, I am aiming at some endogenous understanding of how interacting bodies – or more precisely, intercorporeal awareness – can conform to (attune to) and become subordinated to (and implicated by) the frenzy of the transgressive and annihilating 'forces' mobilised by maleficent fetishes and lethal sorcerous violence. I contend that the mysterious field of sorcery and maleficent fetishes among the Yaka seems to foster among complicitous pairs some pre-reflective and interpersonal awareness of their body in the fold of (embracing) images, fantasies, experiential gestalts and desire of sorts. This primary entwinement of (inter)corporeal capacities, 'forces', cultural expectations and horizons of significance may help us to comprehend innovatively the sensual articulation of a genuine epistemology and a groping for moral economy in the very mood of transgression and perversion. This merging of desire, intercorporeality and sensing out of things paradoxically ties in with the pursuit as well as the obliteration of ethics. Such intermingling shows up in people's manifold search to tame or, for other purposes, to stir up forms of unsettling, rupture, paradoxes, indeterminacy, categorial and ontological aporias, perversion or even destructive violence.

This essay is concerned primarily with a number of epistemological and metaphysical questions regarding both desire and perversion in sorcery, as well as the sensual order of the uncanny among the Yaka. The questions about the enchanting, messy and oppressive worlds of sorcery echo my baffling exposure to, as well as my commitment to achieve some inner understanding of, the shattered existence and runaway life conditions on the neighbourhood level of suburban Kinois people. In the capital city of Kinshasa, I was witness to the widespread riots in September 1991 and January 1993, and to the fatal deterioration of the public institutions and the rampant violence in the suburbs since then. As regards the anthropologist's public role, I see my task as one of understanding local realities, such as frenzy in people spilling over into, and taken over by, the animating social and cosmological orders in their very transformations, as well as the endemic and rampant violence. To avoid ethnocentric and moralising recasting, the understanding should start endogenously from the embodied knowledge and local meanings, and not primarily from the overarching logic of violence intrinsic to the state, the post-colony or the globalising, criminalising economies.

According to the metaphysical views of Yaka society in both Kinshasa and south-west Congo, maleficent fetishes – the only type I am examining here – are designed to attack, if not to kill, one's aggressor. In a masked or blind way, they unleash sheer destructive violence directed at the 'evil-doer' by way of 'magical' ambush. What does this mean? These maleficent fetishes channel phantasmagoric 'forces' from macrocosm to microcosm, and yet operate mainly from the human body to the victim's body-self. The fetishes are the prototype of indeterminacy, malignancy and annihilation steered at victims beyond or disconnected from any social or existential dialectics of redemption, redress or regeneration. They develop an obscene, atopian, unlocalisable space-time where fear is vanquished and terror is mocked. According to a renowned master-specialist, the ritual fire-arm(*buta bwa mboomba*), which he makes at his client's demand to trap any potential evil-doer, contains cannon powder, a mixture of ash (*loombi*) and other unrecognisable, awful depositories (*pfula*) of very intimate but degraded body parts. In the master-specialist's own words, these depositories might include

> glass shards collected from a tomb, earth surreptitiously taken from below the bed of an old widow suffering from rectal piles and who cannot control her urination, a piece of cloth or leaves which have been used by a girl at the time of her first menstruation that I secretly steal from her, a madman's saliva, a rooster's heart, the 'sperm of lightning' [that is, vitrified sand, or latex exuded from a tree mutilated by lightning], the blood of murder victims, and other residual substances whose usage is revealed to me in dreams. Sometimes I add the shadows [*biniinga*, namely, nail clippings, hair, spit and other excreta] of my client. A not yet nubile child puts all of these substances into a cartouche that I seal shut with a resin. This is the spell that I whisper in different, partly inaudible tunes while my wife holds the cartouche in her left hand: 'If he (that is, the aggressor) chooses to come as an ant, bee or beetle, strike him. If he prepares to come on the ground, strike him, You (that is, my Ancestors) who live in the earth. If he moves by air, stop him.' The cartouche is deposited on the tomb of an irascible ancestor. On the evening of the third day, I treat the cartouche with a mixture of toxic plants and waste material while turning my back to the object. I carry it home, tying it against my rectum with a loincloth knotted between my legs.

I contend that maleficent fetishes are transpersonal, imaginary,[1] passionate and disruptive props and plots of 'raw experience' (Feldman 1997, 1991) engrafted in, and emerging from, the speechless body itself. They are as indistinguishably entrenched in the intricate processes of both ingestion and excretion and the mutually contaminating mysteries of life-transmission as they are enmeshed with death and decay. The intimate human body, in particular its orificial acts, is a theatre for establishing the parameters of exclusion versus purification, criminalisation versus normalisation, abuse versus loyalty (Appadurai 1998). Fetishes act beyond the discursive or cognitive order embedded in words and paradoxically exploit and pervert society's order of law and reciprocity as internalised in the members' habitus or bodily dispositions (Bourdieu 1980). Fetishes excite, in their victims and protégés, whirligig fates of cruelty and licentiousness, unbridled energies and affects, beyond any possible rebalancing. Sorcerous fetishes substantiate a 'counterpoint of culture' (Daniel 1996) that resists (re-)incorporation into the harmony of a still higher order of balanced connectedness, meaningfulness or society. They destabilise culturally and ethically established categories and norms, vitiating society's normalised clustering of, or resonance between, the physical, social and cosmological bodies, that is, between the individuals' bodies, the group and the law of society. They transfer an uncontrollably versatile amalgamation of mainly invisible life- and death-forces (including protective and hostile spirits) onto one's emotions, senses and habitual life-scenes. These fetishes thereby deliriously and indeterminately intermingle fantasies of aggression, persecution, death anxiety and defence, as well as rescue, sexual frenzy and hunting surplus life.

What is the efficacy of this attack on sight, that is, on people's habitual ways of seeing? As 'representational pathos' (Taussig 1998) in the grip of the versatile assemblage of substances entailing these delirious manifestations of vacillating categorial divisions, the fetish leaks its whirligig semantic and ethical turbulence and mess into its victims. The substances come from people's various sensuous and practical scenes of life. These manipulations deconstruct the group's ethical norms, aetiological views and culture-specific orders of speech. The fetish is the weird prop whereby meaning as determinate order collapses (Kristeva 1980). The poisonous substances, the hideous scenes replete with delirious signifiers of uncanny luck, unbalancing, encroachment, death wishes, hatred, envy, vengeance and entanglement, all amalgamated in the fetish, virtually overturn and empty out any ethical foundation for human dignity and sense of belonging, authority and political institutionality (Baudrillard 1990, Parkin 1985, Ricoeur 1967). Or should one argue that fetishes rather innocently operate at the pre-ethical level of the individual and group fantasies of good and ill fate? And thus, if their field is mainly imaginary and as such pre-ethical – yet therefore no less embodied and experiential (Kacem 2000, Lingis 2000, Kapferer 1997, Stoller 1997, Jackson 1996, Laderman and Roseman 1996, Csordas 1994, Butler 1993) – what is then the effect, in the body of the victim and the social body, of their attack on the balance of the life-world? In particular, how do the fetishes have any grip on the cultural-cosmological order of meaningfulness and values as they become congruent with the social and physical bodies? In line with Veena Das (1997a, 1997b), one may venture to postulate that the imaginary, ritual and institutional means that a society develops to channel lethal violence may pre-empt the emergence of more repressive forms of control or terror.

The term 'fetish', as the foregoing suggests, entails a polymorphic field. The word itself first appeared at the end of the fifteenth century as a derivative of the Portuguese terms *fazer* (to make), *feitiço* (the thing made, effect and, by extension, instrumentality) and *feiticeiro* (the expert). The present-day understanding of fetishism was forged in the modernist civilising and missionising enterprise, which transformed the negative racial difference of blackness, precluding assimilation, into the quest for the radical transformation of conversion (Conrad 1965, Fanon 1952). Christianity and the Enlightenment view of reason have assigned to the concepts of fetish, sorcery and bewitchment the characteristics of irrationality, superstition, occultism and pure phantasmagoric nothingness (Pieterse and Parekh 1995, Corbey 1989, Mudimbe 1988). As for the many anthropologists who have studied sorcery and power objects in African settings, until the 1980s most had done so in mere functionalist terms of their stigmatising and persecutory, as opposed to integrative, effects on social relations.

In this essay, I seek to adopt the point of view of the Yaka for whom a power object or fetish is a device, an agency charged with energies, capable of influencing someone or something. In the popular imagination of the Yaka, events or objects generically referred to as *buloki* (both benign and maleficent sorcery), *n-kisi*[2] (fetish, charm, medicine, potion, power object) or *yiteki* (fetish, wooden sculpture or figurine loaded with power) most commonly evoke an imaginary realm of energies or forces (see note 1). Fetish primarily refers to the activity of the *ngaanga* (the expert). This last term is the nominal form of *-vanga, -panga, -haanga* (to make, produce, create). In current usage, the root *-ang-* bears the connotation of a consecrated object or mastery over chance and evil (de Surgy 1994: 7). The powers attributed to fetishes 'both to protect and to attack or avenge' are as complex, diversified and versatile as the vicissitudes of human desire or the rapaciousness of certain animals. Because of my evident interest in studying the social impact of this imaginary order of forces, impulses and primal fantasies, I found myself a confidant of individuals embroiled in human passions, enigmas and paradoxes which they recounted in family sagas and personal anecdotes. I hasten to add that every paramount or family chief – or for that matter, any individual afflicted by some hardship – eventually suspects close relatives as potential sorcerers. Because their membership in a Christian or healing church forbids the use of fetishes, or at least any public reference to them, many converts turn to prayer, benedictions and offerings as an alternative recourse for protection from persecution and the whims of life (Devisch 1996).

I will draw primarily on what commoners, healers and mediumistic diviners tell about fetishes, leaving for the last section an analysis of similar discourse in the healing churches. I will not consider here the highly moralising, if not derisive, opinions regarding beliefs in bewitchment, fetishes and sorcerous practices as expressed by journalists, government officials and the established Christian churches. Venturing to analyse how power objects are made and work, my aim is to lay bare the epistemology and the mutual constructs in the imaginary and symbolic realms implicit in the discourses, practices and 'force fields' involved in Yaka sorcery. The approach will be developed to some extent within the larger framework of the ideals of the hunter and the Yaka ritual, whose aims are to unravel and domesticate the imaginary realm and the 'dually charged' forces (that is, both rescuing and destructive affects, and devastating and rehabilitating appetites and impulses) inhabiting it (Devisch and Brodeur 1999; Devisch 1998, 1995, 1993; De Beir 1975; Huber 1956).

From early colonial times to the present, the paradoxical interplay between a deep-seated fascination for, and at the same time a diabolisation of, fetishism and sorcery by the colonisers, the missionaries, the so-called *évolués* and their heirs has sustained very ambiguous interactions among their various civilisational imaginaries. The colonial and missionary rhetoric and practices were a crusade against the backwardness, heathenism and fetishism of village people 'in the bush', to be overcome by cleansing, 'whitening', schooling and development. I contend that these colonial politics were somehow set up, and caught up themselves, in a dynamic of the fetish. The *évolués*, the colony's so-called elites, were summoned to outgrow the 'village' condition and climb the evolutionary and social Darwinist ladder of hygiene, education, self-control, order and production. In the 1950s, the first suburbs and downtown for the *évolués* – also called the 'cités' (as distinct from the colonial 'white' establishment in what was called 'la ville') – harboured the nightclubs where the coloniser mixed with the local *évolués* to taste the erotic deliriums of the 'Dark Continent'. In the 1970s and 1980s, a new generation of Congolese artists and customers in the discos energised Zaire's authenticity movement: in a transgressive mood of frenzy, they celebrated freeing themselves from paternalist colonisation and moralising missionary school education. However, in the 1990s the townships increasingly became realms of poverty and exclusion, doom and depression, wrecked as they were by the nation's welfare parasites allegedly linked up with the so-called global neo-liberal capitalist forces. In previous studies (Devisch 1998, 1995), I have argued that the frenzy of the bars spilling out into the streets in Kinshasa in the 1990s, the money schemes in 1990–1 and the Luddite uprisings in 1991 and 1993 can all be seen as the convulsive attempts of the masses to come to terms with their sense of crisis. I would suggest that the riots enact the dynamics of berserk daring as entailed in the imaginaries of the fetish.

Ritual Weapons to Trap and Besiege the Evil-Doer

Successful game hunting anticipates commensality, which as a form of bodily boundary transgression in the conjugal house may for the Yaka evoke other body boundary transgressions such as conjugal communion. These connotations inspire many of the practices used in trapping evil or its doer. In Yaka society, the hunter is the supreme social player, operating 'on the edge' of life and the social order in a mixture of commitment and daring, mastery and excess, eagerness and fear. The hunter is the epitome of both the devoted/feeding husband and the seducer or wild intruder. Ritual preparations or arrangements for the hunt, as for counter-attacking bewitchment, associate the house as well as the body of a protected individual with a hunting ground, a subsocial space situated in the forest or bush. In the ritual or cultic context, a person undergoing initiatory or therapeutic seclusion calls on the therapist, who then fences off (-siinda, tsiinda) the house or ritual area. More generally, any family which feels particularly vulnerable or threatened may have a specialist install various defences around the family home. Means of fencing off or protecting against predatory sorcerers and other maleficent forces include snares, weapons or barriers placed at entryways, on walls, on the roof of the house and beneath the beds. These traps and weapons serve to hide (sweekomu) the client and attack the evil-doer or any maleficent object menacing the home or beneficiary.

The ritual weapon may be designated by any of several names: mateenda (lit., something that cuts to pieces), yingundu (lit., something which discharges or explodes), buta (gun or rifle), n-taambu (trap or snare), yinwaanunu (instrument for fighting). The weapon is attached to the middle of the ridge pole of the house or ritual dwelling, at a point where the lianas cross. When protection is needed, these n-phemba vines (Adenia cissameloides, Passifloraceae) are woven perpendicularly around the house as if to transform it into a mortuary envelope, for that is the way in which a corpse is swathed in many layers of mortuary cloth and wrapped with lianas.

During the installation, an incantation by the specialist calls the ritual weapon to counter-attack and kill the intruder, as if the aggressor were a dangerous beast – 'ndzwaandi yaamba, n-singaandi n-phemba' (may the house of the offender be transformed into a death-chamber and the n-phemba liana bind him up) – thus preparing him to be carried to the burial place. A fang of a venomous snake is often placed on the portion of this vine found above the doorway, as if to give the whole house the readiness to attack, like a viper raised on its tail. A weapon is variously slipped into a horn, shell, nut, twig, piece of pipe or even a small bottle or can, and is meant to function as either a trap or a weapon of assault. In the latter case, the object is compared to a cartouche and filled with ingredients which are thought to be explosive (khawa). The whole of the cartouche is often wrapped in leaves of the lunwaani tree (unidentified) – which by homonymy evokes struggle (-nwaana, lunwaani) – and hidden in a small blackish termite mound (yikhuku). The cartouche is prepared by the ritual specialist at midnight at a place well outside the village or at the tomb of a powerful chief. While stuffing (-koma) the cartouche, the specialist is naked and avoids touching the volatile components with his hands for fear that his immediate kin would become victims of the labile (bivalent, uncontrollable) and lethal forces he is manipulating. The cartouche is filled with the aid of a knife blade – its contents being carefully compressed – and capped with a resin-coated plug. The whole of this tense operation is also called 'loading the rifle' (*-soma buta*).

As a rule, a maleficent fetish seeks to connect with the awful characteristics of its ingredients. These evoke boundaries and boundary-violations, liminal phenomena, oddities and extreme affects that blatantly pertain to diverse, if not antagonistic, worlds and that suggest collapse and rule-breaking or daring and success, in one or the other sense. Such ingredients can include the following:

1. *Phiku*: fingernails, hair, spittle or shadow of the client, items that refer to the boundaries of the client's body-self. They signify the concealment of the body-self and thus preserve the client from sorcerers who could attack and make away with him.

2. *Mbakunumbakunu*: an assortment of trampled leaves believed to represent both the totality of the life-milieu and its degradation. It is usually composed of young shoots, cut to pieces, of different plant species of both the forest and savanna, specifically gathered at different heights from the ground both in the early morning, at noon and/or at sunset, if not at midnight. This plant collection evokes the many ways in which afflictions, ailments, pain or effects of bewitchment manifest themselves. It is used to uncover the presence of the malefactor or to thwart in advance any maleficent effect which one of these plants could channel or mediate.

3. *Khawa*: the aggressive ingredients, associated with detonation, comprise blackish cinders (*loombi*), evocative of annihilation or delusive form. They are obtained by burning small particles of a variety of toxic animals, insects and plants, or also amphibious or trickster animals, or animals that attack humans, bury their dung or eat carrion. One essential element is some ash from a dung beetle (*kokotu*). This insect enters human faeces or bores through the ground to reach buried corpses and therefore represents the sorcerer who 'restores the remains of a man to the earth'. These ingredients also comprise segments of animals which are associated with sorcery, such as the toad (*kyuula*) and frog (*soti*), by virtue of their amphibian nature; the chameleon (*lungweenya*), because of its ability to adapt chromatically to its surroundings; and the long grey lizard (*kalanga*), with mottled lips, which can disappear at a blink (*-vuulumuna*, a term which also designates how the sorcerer can move about without being seen), or its substitute, the blue-headed agama lizard (*yihala*). Because of their toxic nature, various other animals or substances may evoke, and seek to trap, the evil before it can occur: the venomous serpents; the large light-coloured centipede (*kapfiinda*); a large green, poisonous, but dried grasshopper (*dikhookwa difuula mun-zaanga*); as well as a piece of bark from the tree *phutu* (*Erythrophleum guineense, Caesalpiniaceae*), an element formerly used in ordeals by poison (because of this usage, the tree has been called 'the tree that kills sorcerers' – *yibala khasa ni-ti wudya baloki*).

4. There are also the intrinsically poisonous as well as disordering substances and parts of animals that live in more than one habitat (such as

birds living on the ground) or that have mixed attributes (of bird and mammal, or of mammal and fish). Such substances evoke, for instance, the ability to function in a different element. Other ingredients derive from surly or aggressive animals (*mbisyakhemena*), carrion-eaters and those who bury their dung, carnivores and animals with claws (*mbisya-kaandzu*), or animals with skins of opposing colour, which are considered to be belligerent. The weapon must not only acquire the force of the cruellest animals, but it must also have the ability to metamorphose into an animal such as the leopard, civet or shrew-mouse, whose saliva is deadly to the rats it attacks. The owl, a nocturnal predatory bird, is assimilated with its diurnal cousins such as the hawks, eagles and vultures so feared in the plains and forests. Certain fetishes are thought to enslave these animals, or, according to the popular imagination, the sorcerers transform themselves into such beasts. The individual characteristics of each (diet, nocturnal activities, coats or ability to climb or dig) create a force field that the fetish seeks to ally itself with.

5. The aggressive or explosive ingredient of *khawa* comprises fragments of bone, hair or scales (sometimes brought from distant areas) taken from animals, birds, snakes, plants and other dangerous substances thought to have a great ability to attack or protect. These might include: gunpowder (*thuya tsaandzi*); gunpowder extracted from unspent cartridges (*thuya mboombi*); matches, serving as a detonator (*kafofolu*); and lightning (*ndzasi*) in the form of vitrified sand or resin from a tree struck by lightning. To increase the lethal force of the ritual weapon, glass splinters (*biteenga byambwaata*) or a viper's fang may also be added.

6. *Yalwa*: a unique content that each specialist tries to give the ritual weapon, such as an arrowhead that has killed a person, the end of a vine with which someone has hanged himself, the urine or blood of a blind or dying person, or even a part lifted from a wrecked car.

If predatory sorcery or fatal bewitchment is likened to the nocturnal hunt, anti-sorcerous activities and those destined to combat annihilation use the same idiom of the hunt. Thus, the collection of plant matter ensures the protection and healing of the client by ensnaring the forces of destruction and trapping them by means of their own artifices. In sum, the intention is to reverse the harm onto itself self-destructively (called -*kaya*). For gathering an assortment of plants, the ritual specialist leaves the village at the first cock's crow; as night gives way to day, he is likely to cross paths with sorcerers who at this moment are leaving the forest or bush to rejoin their bodily sheathes still lying in bed. Contrary to the sorcerer who 'eats' the life-forces of his or her descendants, thus undermining the family life-tree he or she is a member of, the therapist collects shoots (*baana ban-ti*, literally, the vegetal descendants) by means of a trap. He thus harvests shoots growing at the cyme or the lower branches of bushes and trees (*mbakunumbakunu*), always using a crook-like stick known as *yikho*. This same term is given to the hook serving as a trigger in a spring trap. The use of the *yikho* in gathering these plant samples, even if they could easily be picked by hand, no doubt denotes and evokes the plants' capacity to entrap (*-kaya*). In order to detach a piece of the bark, the specialist knocks it off the tree trunk by hitting it with a larger rod called *yikhookolu*. Having the same root as *yikho*, this word also designates the club used to kill game trapped in a snare or in nets. Finally, *yikhookolu* is the name the collective imagination reserves for the bludgeon with which sorcerers would beat their victims to death at what is coined the sorcerers' marketplace. By striking off the bark of the tree trunk with this club and later pulverising these plant substances, after having burned them, the specialist 'cools' the agent of evil and inflicts a mortal blow on it.

In order to thwart any disorder or to prevent the malevolent use of toxic plants or rapacious birds or animals, the ritual weapon might contain fragments of charred bark of giant forest trees, some of which are toxic.

1. *M-mwayi* is a forest tree (unidentified) with a toxic bark; it is said that the area immediately around this tree becomes sterile. This characteristic is transferred to the ritual barrier invoked to contain the evil, as expressed in the phrase 'M-mwayi mbuta n-ti kamwaanga bungaanga' (Just as *m-mwayi* is a dominating tree, may the therapist's action assert itself).

2. Fragments of the *n-honu* tree (*Salacia pallescens, Hippocrateae*), found in the forest glades, are also employed in the preparation of the ritual weapon. Popular commentaries see a homonymy with the term *-honuka*, used to describe a goat struggling to free itself of the tether, and offer the following explanation: 'Mbeefu kahonuka yibeefu kyan-tabula' (The sick person fights so that the illness may release him).

3. *N-kukubuundu* (*Pachystela sp., Sapotaceae*) is another forest tree with a toxic bark; it tends to bring down many other trees when it is felled. About this tree it is said: 'N-kukubuundu, n-ti wudya makasa wasi-masana' (The *n-kukubuundu* tree is poison to the squirrel and a menace to the wild cat). The use of the bark of this tree allows the ritual specialist to mobilise its venomous force against his client's attackers.

The Fetish Bears Monstrous and Delirious Traits

Amalgamating residue, mixture and floating signifiers (see below), the fetish resonates with imaginary appetites and exploits in a no-man's-land of vertigo and fascination. Residue (such as imprints, crushed leaves, ash, traces of blood) is the privileged site of indeterminating contamination or unstoppable reversal between attack and inertness, between the voluptuousness of engendering life and the inebriation in the face of death and corruption. Thus, for example, in a sorcerous *do ut des* transactional logic, the father-accomplice claims his rights to the booty of the next sorcerous transaction – or nowadays to unexpected economic gain or political power – the very moment he delivers his son or daughter to the sorcerers' marketplace where he or she is destined to death or to a reduced existence as a mindless zombie engaged in nocturnal meetings of mixing and licence. Marketplace, rather than designating here a physical space, is rather a way of figuring the insolent conduct and logic of wicked transactions associated with lethal sorcery.

At the edge of cognitive or moral control, the fetish, like any fatal ensorcell-ment, perverts every code or possible order of things so as to free and extract life's more formidable forces and stratagems (*pfula*) that feed on life's regen-erative capabilities to the point of emptying these out. Certain forms of mur-derous sorcery spells that go with the fatal manipulation of fetishes are conceived along the lines of a process of birth in reverse, or of a kind of death-giving birth or 'anal birth-giving' entrenched in decay. The victim passes through a state of perverted sacrificial death or quasi-death to be reborn as a phantom (*tebu*) or zombie (*n-saki, suta*, derived from the French *soldat* – sol-dier) whose 'life-force or breath of life' (*mooyi*) – namely, his or her vitality, consciousness and will power – is greatly diminished and totally at the service of the master who has taken his or her life-force. Phantoms and zombies are monstrous, animal- and slave-like – living deads who have been sacrificed in payment of a nocturnal debt (*kabu dyakun-kolu*). Other such phantoms are a metamorphosis of a childless person, a perpetrator of incest, a deformed per-son, or someone injured in a hunt, wounded in warfare or killed by the very sorcerous weapons he or she had prepared. These victims join the fantasised, mythical-like, remote ecology of the small, mindless and silent anthropomor-phic beings with large heads and long hair that inhabit the deep forest or bush; some may take on the form of a hunting dog, or successful sellers of lot-tery tickets. Dwarfs are also considered to have no temporal or spatial origin and to be incapable of transmitting any form of life. These hybrid zombies impersonating radical alterity are referred to by a variety of terms: *tebu, yikuku, yikhuungi, yivwuiti, yisiimbi, yitsuutsu*. They bear the characteristics of a sub- or pre-social world whose significance is ambiguous, if not negative. It is believed that the phantom or zombie is called upon by its master to enact any crude and obsessive rule-breaking that the latter craves, be it in the domain of heroic competition, ruthless killing in hunting or war, protection of one's new and contested property, erotic adventures or sorcerous affairs of the night (*-huungula*). In sum, the phantom or zombie is a living fetish manipu-lated only by its master. Sooner or later, the zombie ends by taking the life of its owner. It can also be seen as figuring the extreme, yet temporal, subjuga-tion of the servant or the political subject, being the very inversion of the coloniser or the capitalist patron inasmuch as they are destroyers of the local communitarian moral world. The (post-)colony includes power and labour in a market system of growing economic strength, felt by the Yaka as a 'super-natural' framework.

Another term used of these beings, *sataani* – the local term for the Christ-ian-imported notion of Satan, denoting in Yaka land the demonic, the West or 'white world' of mainly commoditised relationships – refers to the subsocial universe of ambivalent and self-steering forces that may help to protect oneself or to accumulate consumer goods at the expense of the life of close kin. Under the influence of Christianity, their maleficent connotation has become predominant, for these forces, believed to stem from a contract with *sataani*, are extremely difficult to subdue or domesticate. The contract means that the devotee of *sataani* accumulates wealth or power in return for handing over the life of kinsfolk (see Krohn-Hansen 1995). In other words, any attempt at a capitalist-individualist destruction of the local communitarian moral world is considered to have its roots elsewhere.

The fetish is as bivalent and versatile as sorcery itself and encapsulates both life-bearing and harmful potencies, greed for life and the lust of predation of the hunter-intruder. Investing desire or libidinal energy in a sculpture or pouch filled with sorcerous ingredients, the fetish acts as a phantasmatic support to sorcerous actions and is capable of bearing and transmitting a series of imagoes of group energies that are death-dealing as opposed to vitalising, that excite fears rather than calm them. The fetish is bivalent and versatile in that it is – in some instances, indiscriminately – as capable of injuring, weakening or even killing as it is of protecting or endowing health and success. The fetish is a point of delirious and grotesque contamination, so to speak, between death and life, or between violation and restitution of the social code. In order to capture the forces of the fetish, to absorb them into himself and erase every trace of his use of it, and to stir up these annihilatory forces beyond any homeopathic logic of reversal and redress, the sorcerer licks the fetish and then applies it to his rectum for a period of time. The fetish captures and enacts just this sort of delirious impulse, reversing the order of body and things in what amounts to a catastrophic retroflexion (*pli-catastrophe*, Kristeva 1980: 226).

By incorporating the undifferentiation between opposites (such as life and death, alimentation and excretion), the fetish proffers itself as a paradoxical crucible of antithetic forces from which Logos and madness may indiscriminately originate. The fetish pushes the amalgamation of these opposite forces to the untameable point where symbolism itself is diverted or twisted (*-niika*), where reality seems to tip over into surreality. Weapons or fetishes charged with potent forces are no more than ashes (*loombi*), a mixture of charred remains ground into powder (also called *pfula*). The mixture resembles nothing in particular, and offers no visible signs whatsoever that permit it to be read or decoded; this sort of magma does violence to conventional frames of encoding. As an untraceable play of signs, the mixture dissolves difference. Its modes of preparation conflate origin and violence, sense and nonsense, attraction and repulsion. Displaying rootlessness and the untraceable or undirected force of nomadic contagion, the fetish thereby substantiates the forces of the uncanny, and may suck the patient into a dead end.

Floating Signifier and Cross-breeding

The fetish develops at the behavioural and semiological boundaries that define the relevant culture and its possibilities.[3] Effecting a kind of cross-breeding on that very fringe, the fetish is constituted of 'floating signifiers' – hollowed of their conventional meaning (*yibalu, khituka*) – that incessantly traverse the boundaries between the determinate and the indeterminate, the Self and the Other, the point of origin and that of disintegration. The floating signifier (*signifiant flottant*, Gil 1985: 24ff.) often bonds itself to a type of residue, to a hollow or bivalent sign (*-balula*), drained or voided (*-kituka*) of its load or symbolic valence, and charged by the collective imaginary with impulses and psychic forces. Such an object is utilised differently from the way it would normally be used in its habitual context. The floating signifier is severed from its conventional – possibly binary and reversible – meaning load, potentiated, for example, by categories such as colour, role and cosmological order. As such, it wrecks or impairs the conventional principles of categorial identification and semantic articulation.

An individual's double or shadow (*yiniinga*) is a typical example of floating signifier. Etymologically speaking, *yiniinga* refers to something that constantly swings from one side to another: it is an object which is forever seeking attachment to something new while simultaneously seeking detachment from another object (an example being the shadow of a leaf blown about in the wind). The verb *-niinga* designates the capacity to carry or balance an object on the head without having to steady it with the hand, but also designates the movement of an object, such as a log, rolling on the ground. The term *yiniinga* therefore denotes a transitional quality, with reference in the first instance to the 'shadow' or 'double' of an individual or his body, and by extension to the secretions and excretions of the body (saliva, sweat, nail clippings, head or pubic hair, urine, excrement, or blood from menstruation, haemorrhage or rectal piles) or such things as a pulled tooth, a bit of old clothing, imprints or even the warmth left by a person sitting on the ground. In so far as they are secretions and excretions, such remnants or liminal objects are bivalent. Residue carries traces of its origin, of the body from which it detaches itself with the ensuing loss of its original form. Residue is a volatile sign that materialises both the point of origin and of disintegration, meaning and phantasmagoria.

The floating signifier is a parodying of the binary ordering of signs and of any binarism of symbolic functioning operating along polarised terms such as master/slave, winner/loser, or polar opposites such as before/after, top/bottom, left/right, human/non-human, origin/copy, essence/accident, truth/falsity. It overturns the culture-specific structure of binary and hierarchical oppositions that for the given group or subjects regulates textuality, truth or conscience. It suggests that no difference, social or semiological, is immune to its subversions and overturnings. Yet in the junction and disjunction of symbolic domains, their ever-vanishing traces of irrecuperable/unrestorable differentiation may bear the imprint of desire and nostalgia regarding another social formation, topography, body symbolism or subject identity (Stallybrass and White 1986).

Residue

The Yaka thus ascribe a substantial reality to remains, residue or debris –
namely, to whatever carries traces of vitiation, decomposition or extinction.
This testifies to the architecture of a non-totalising, rhizomatic (Deleuze and
Guattari 1987) form of thinking which concurrently allows a space for the
object and its inverse. The imaginary excursion into the sorcerous indicates an
acceptance of the existence of fissures or gaps in the cognitive and moral systems which the Yaka feel compelled neither to fill in nor to negate. The excursion affords a capacity for 'understanding' the extent to which life and death,
exaltation (exuberance, excess) and violence, peace and coercion, protection
and vice, benign sorcery and unsettling sorcery (which, for example, overturns
domestic boundaries) must be seen on a par with each other. The imaginary
displayed in the fetish and sorcery puts the religious and moral economy's call
for righteousness, accountability and honour on a par with explosive impul-
siveness, vindictiveness and frenzy.

Residue erodes any foundational function associated with origin and reproduction. Like madness, exhibiting a mix of emotional numbness and hyper-
arousal, residue witnesses to a world order in which violence and origin,
destruction and beginning both simultaneously and untraceably co-originate
and dissolve their differences. Like irony, residue does not erase either the
unending and maddening quest or the negation of meaningfulness beyond the
given forms and formations of sense-making.

Residue in the fetish stirs up fantasies of total confusion. The fetish inte-
grates residue and hiatus, and accelerates the annihilatory transmutation of its
original characteristics through a violence or transgression that resists any
regenerative access: this dynamic beyond regeneration is an essential characteristic. The fetish is composed of particles obtained by sharp blows, by intrusion or thievery, and/or by violent transmutation through incineration,
pulverisation and brusque insertion into a cartouche. It is a sheer abjection or
distortion. An integral element of this process here is that the resulting debris
or compound fosters discord and abjection. The conventional given signification of the ingredients is, in fact, deflected or distorted: redness is apprehended
according to its appearance in blackish or whitish forms (the former through
incineration, the latter in the dung of hyenas, the sole predatory animal whose
excrement remains whitish, for example). Innocence is exploited inasmuch as
it serves to conceal evil. At night or outside of the village, so-called innocent
girls or boys (those who have not yet worn clothes, who are not yet nubile) are
made to charge the fatal fetishes and ritual weapons. (It seems that this is the
moment when the child is trained to perceive the meaning of the fetish by a
bodily practice, that is, when the meaning gets sedimented into the body so
that it can be excavated later.) Likewise, menarcheal menstrual blood or mati-
nal urine of a pregnant woman mixed with her vaginal secretion is deposited
in the weapons. Generally, it might be said that whatever can be stirred up, or
whatever belongs to the category of refuse and excretion, carries within itself

powers that are equivocal in that they pertain to bifaceted points or moments of disjunction which waver on the threshold between inside and outside, hot and cold, vitality and corruption, lust and languor. At one moment the fragment or residue is a symbol for the whole or the remnant of someone, while at another it represents only a single potentially discordant part of that person or thing, and at still yet another moment it may refer to several entities at the same time. It denotes both an end or absence *and* a power or (new) beginning. Through these residual elements, fetishes appropriate energies of breeding or propagation as well as transformative potencies, all the while subjugating them to bivalent and versatile intention.

Residue allows the fetish to represent and effect the paradoxical integration of antithetic elements into one another, such as violence concealing marvel, and vice versa. The preparation of the fetish demonstrates that the efficacy of something sacrificial or life-giving is in certain respects guaranteed by something harmful, and that at the highest degree of knowledge of initiatory and esoteric powers, one discovers only residue, imposture, the distorted and the versatile – in other words, a deception or void (like the eye of a deceased blind man). Fetish derives from a conception of the world that is determined yet manipulable or counterfeit. It actualises a logic of contradictions expressed in antitheses: the colour red conceals a power to release black, which is capable of generating white, and vice versa; the fetish can both kill and rescue; the excitable hides a power to obstruct and inhibit the life-flow and life-force; horror and the abominable contain the virtue of regeneration. The fetish surpasses the conventional time-space divisions, and may carry the user to virtual destinations.[4]

Other residues embody a parallel form of paradoxical logic and function, as do some of the most feared fetishes: hair stolen from an irritable (*ngaandzi*) white man, or the butt of a cigarette he has smoked; saliva from a lunatic or psychotic (which exemplifies perverted speech); the eye of a deceased blind person. The menstrual blood from twin married sisters is the very figure of violent abolishment of difference, of mimetic conflict, that is, of desymbolisation. It is also said that pieces that a relative has been able to cut off through sorcery from the clitoris of a marriageable daughter or deceased relative, or from the penis of a deceased impotent relative, may be employed. Such residues, loaded with the shocking effect of extreme intrusive daring and boundary-crossing, energise the type of fetish called *phiibita*, which is capable of making someone invisible or 'giving someone clairvoyance' (*-teemwasa*) for the hunt or sorcery. In other words, the fetish is nourished as much by the passion for life as it is by abomination and wickedness. Equally, the fetish mobilises the dynamic of transgression, with its mirror effects, as it does the art of the marvellous. The latter is exploited, for example, in allowing a dream to reveal how a fetish is fabricated, or by attributing to the fetish the characteristics of an aeroplane or electric current by inserting pieces of a motor, drops of fuel or the imprints of a white man 'who was only passing through'.

Like the imagery and practices belonging to the world of sorcery, fetishes exploit to the full the pervasive resources of the imaginary register, which are taken as more real than the tangible. This imaginary load constitutes a stock of floating forces that convey bodily affects, imagoes and vital contacts of all sorts in a terrifying sphere of secrecy and the unspeakable. Fetishism and ensorcellment fully exploit the fusion and continual passage between pleasure and torment, life and death, hate and love, to the point where a grasp of the symbolic is inadequate to distinguish between such antitheses. Like the sorcerer, the fetish plays with bodily affects and sensations in a most disordered manner.

Residue resists regeneration or recovery out of its indeterminacy. The words spoken by the ritual specialist while he 'loads' the most powerful fetishes often are barely audible or seem distorted when compared with conventional speech. This incantatory discourse conceals more than it reveals. Incantations are often accompanied by rhythmic sounds produced by artless devices such as fruits, gourds and shells. It is as if these percussive sounds and the discordant rhythms they produce clear a path towards the force field that the accompanying blood sacrifice or sorcerous act seeks to unbind and let loose. The shockingly violent sacrifice of an animal, which is a substitute for a human victim, aims at radically transforming the relation of the victim with his spirit-aggressor or tutelary. By killing the sacrificial hen with his teeth, the ritual specialist re-enacts the meeting between the aggressor and victim. He makes this relation into something versatile, so as to overturn it into a protective association of hunting with reproductive sexuality.

In loading the fetish with residue or signs deprived of their symbolic properties, the ritual specialist attests in a circuitous way to the effectiveness of the ritual object. These remains, witnessing to some meaning from which they are now cut off or of which they have been drained, serve to break open the circle of forces. Properly speaking, the ingredients of a ritual weapon, such as the claw of a predatory animal or a segment of a venomous plant, do not designate either the cause of the affliction (which is always a spirit or ensorcellment) or the illness or misfortune itself (being the result of the action of the spirit or sorcerer on the patient). Nor do they refer to their object (the body of the victim). Rather, the ritual weapon or fetish symbolises the interrelation between cause (aggressiveness, ensorcellment, forgetfulness, transgression) and effect. Thus, residue brings bivalent forces into play which allow themselves to be appropriated and recycled, all the while escaping any domestication and semiological orientation (through the use of signs, speech and tradition).

It appears thus that the more an object belongs to the order of residue, the more its symbolic function becomes blurred and nebulous, and the more it becomes lost in a search for a totality that eludes it. Oscillating between an illusion of being and a sense of nothingness or loss, sorcerous compounds open up to the annihilatory yet fascinating power of the void. Although it is not a thing, a signifier or an agent, residue may be one of the three or even all of them, in so far as it functions as a hinge between signs and forces. As a sign, residue obeys a rather ambiguous order of things in that it connotes precisely those objects that estrange themselves from everything else or from a given field. Because the floating signifier ruptures its ties with the habitual code or field, the material traces of this link give the residue an ambiguous status, that of something which seeks to sever and fragment as well as to create bonds or reconstitute a whole. Residue denotes a symbolic function in the process of disintegrating, and as such unbinds a force field to which it attests and of which it is a principal manifestation.

The Law of Retaliation

When does violence become harm and evil, and what triggers the dividing line between the fetish's regenerative and destructive violence? A crucial dimension of the harmful fetish is its subjugation to the rationale of the *lex talionis*, or law of retaliation, which turns wrongdoing against itself, homeopathically, self-destructively.[5] But the nefarious use of the fetish may reach a point beyond the homeopathic when it is sucked into the logic of treacherous immoderation and unaccountability. And the compromising exposure to the transgression of this rule of moderation and social accountability exerts a tremendous annihilatory force through its menace of defiance, anarchy, terror. The insane-like flight into acts of selfish immoderation (such as sexual depravity, lethal sorcery and denial of kinship), rather than unacceptable harm beyond the limits of explicable behaviour, is the epitome of harm, going beyond physical regeneration and social restoration. This logic of the negative adds aggressive force or destructive enchantment to the fetish. The imagery of the vindictive and destructive powers of the fetish, which may turn against the abusive or wicked user, offers for the collective representations a staging ground merging the lethal forces of the fetish, the user's treacherous intention and transgression by excess, and the harm intended by the abuser. While placing the aggressor at the receiving end of his aggressive act, the fantasies mobilised by the fetish enhance its destructive potential in line with the self-evident cycle of explosive harm, stemming from the transgression of the taboo on immoderation and treachery.

Through the discharging circuit of taboo and transgression effected by treacherous selfishness in the deceitful abuser of kin relations, the fetish does not define harm in its own right, nor does it stand for a quasi-moral statement about a wrong. The metaphysical implication is that the destructive agencies and the harm of the fetish are transacted in line with the law of retaliation for excessive self-serving malevolence; yet they refer to a self-annihilating transgression that moves the victim beyond the homeopathic logic. This deviousness is itself dependent on the context in which the malevolent action was being performed. The homeopathic logic uses the very same means for harming as for stopping and healing. According to Yaka metaphysics, intimate family members who share meals and sleeping space are capable of the best and the worst acts towards one another. Fetishes manipulate forces that are considered very real and vital, yet they may be the predicament of one's social power versus one's terrifying deficiency or entanglement. Inasmuch as they take up this essential dialectics, fetishes and the references they entail to transgression call down the law of retaliation, stating that an abuse, immoderation or treachery calls for condemnation and revenge, thereby sustaining authority and maintaining society. Even the hallucinatory perceptions of various abusive uses of fetishes depict the law of retaliation, which might be phrased 'Whoever abuses the life of a member of his own group is finally turned on himself and will consume his own flesh and self-destruct'. In order to survive, an individual must acknowledge the law of blood's necessary reproduction in the ongoing familial saga, and thus the right of another to life and to a place in the kin-group.

Do Fetishes Kill?

I speculate that the lethal efficacy of the fetish derives from tying in the body, habitus, sentiment, sensation and imagination with the sub-symbolic imaginary order turned adrift in a flood of unbridled energy in direct and wild interference with the physical body, in particular the senses and libido. In the victim (and yet in every member who enlivens the group's imaginary), maleficent fetishes stir up the imaginary's stock of floating forces and imagoes or vital signs of all sorts, while tying them in with the affects or sensations of the victim's body below the grip of mediative discourse or cultural signification, and beyond the ethical order of law. Fetishes most freely explore the many virtualities of breaking down or fragmenting and disuniting taken-for-granted and multifaceted semiological divisions, such as internal/external, Self/Other, human/animal, life-giving/life-taking. Mobilising and disfiguring transpersonal body images of intercorporeality (Weiss 1999, Feldman 1997, Young 1997, Kirby 1996) – in particular, with regard to commensality, conjugality, birth-giving and the culturally defined body order, which is the order of the production of personhood par excellence – the fetish deconstructs the cultural and ethical order through extreme violation of the symbolic-classificatory terms and conventional rules of discourse, and through the disconnection or the medley of co-implicating meaning-bearing contexts, or the disruption of the order of anticipations or foreseen results. The fetish rules out any coherent pattern of boundaries and divisions proper to the body image and to the moral and symbolic order of a given cultural community. In the terms of Valentine Daniel (1997), it becomes apparent how much the fetish closes the user and victim up in their disfigured selves, in an unaccountable disconnection and terror.

Even if clients do not know the contents of the fetish, or the expert's incantations, the felt experience of ensorcellment is nevertheless pretraced, prefashioned. Through usage of the fetishes, the implicated sensual, symbolic and imaginary orders are 'inscribed' in the body as a kind of 'pictogramme' (Aulagnier 1975). Through the divinatory oracles, which draw on a common cosmology, the power objects become embodied experience. Their taboo becomes densely emotional because the forces entailed cohere with, and influence, the clients' bodies in ways prefigured or pretraced through sensuous channels.

The efficacy of the fetish, then, relies on the culture-specific consubstantiation in the body brought about in particular by initiatory rituals between the social and the individual (Das 1997a). Moreover, this efficacy of the fetish thrives on a specific, culturally shaped bodily predisposition, receptive to imagoes proper to the unconscious operating without the cognised mediation of the cultural symbolic. The fetish brings about an acting out in the body of a transference relation by which the recipient physically and emotionally identifies with, or incorporates, what he supposes he should become in the interaction with the specialist or the fetish: 'If I don't take this seriously, if I do not carry my fetish with me, misfortune will strike me in such and such a manner.' Through a most transgressive manipulation of sounds, odours, colours, shapes – all amalgamated in the enigmatic debris – the fetish socialises both the expectation and the illusion in the transference relation. Such a secret object invites the client to keep an open and alert mind, which could lead to questions such as 'Was it made to help or destroy me?' or 'Could the specialist really harm me?' The fetish, moreover, commits the client to the pursuit of a supersensual conformity to its unspeakable contents and, notwithstanding the deliriousness of these contents, to cling to the fetish's destructive capabilities and motions of negativity. The fetishes compel the body and senses to embody and live out the very terrifying motions that their abominable contents demonstrate. They deploy an unbounded libidinal id below the level of any social and symbolic order founded on the laws of filiation, political authority or a communal ethic. Like terror, fetishes unbind the universe of forces proper to the unconscious. They provide themselves an occasion to outgrow the symbolic order and live out, in direct or wild interference with the body, the sorcerous imaginary register in a flood of unbridled energy.

One of the most fundamental and intricate questions raised by ensorcellment and power objects is: How do they actually kill? My own hypothesis is that the ensorcelled person kills him- or herself, as it were, by embodying the mortal desires of intimidating others, or by introjecting the delirious references to destruction and death-giving, enabled and transmitted by the fetishes. The fetish, in other words, may suffocate or empty out the body-self by mobilising energies, imagoes and/or unconscious impulses of fatal attack: their traces are engrafted in commonly shared spheres that we only tentatively try to label, from various angles. In line with Kapferer (1997), Greenwood (2000) and Overing (1985, 1978), we venture to label, from a plurality of angles, these spheres, as well as the meltdown of their traces, as follows. Among others, they may entail, in either a distinct or a blurred order: (1) forms of intentionality involving spaces (of togetherness, work and reason) and time horizons (of origin, simultaneity, premonition, significance; past, present, future) that mobilise intentions and emotions between people and their life-worlds, or that fix inner identities; (2) culturally shaped, sensual, kinaesthetic (olfactory, aural, visual, tactile) arts, habits, dispositions to tie in with the other world and make it seem sensible and realistic; (3) culturally shaped fantasies, collective anxieties, symbolic traces (initiated by beliefs, stories, spells, incantations, paraphernalia and substances of the voluptuous, uncanny, nonsensical, void, destitute, deficient, wild, wicked, disastrous, horrifying) and the like.

Group members weakened in their body-self by virtue of their inferior position, affliction, illness, bad omens or threats may indeed succumb to a distressing situation and a shift to fatal anxieties. They may thus overly expose themselves, most vulnerably in their affect which tied in directly with their bodily condition, to the death wishes of certain relatives, that is, to a spiralling current of imagoes that is criss-crossed with libidinal energies of dual signification or break-up of predictable order, in an unstoppable whirling in which the death-forces empty out the life-forces to a point of no return, a point beyond regenerative capacity. In the subconscious domain of affects, the victim undergoes an increasingly grave and complex crisis and in time gradually abdicates his status as a subject; he believes that others are responsible for his misfortune and surrenders his weakened body to the uncontrollable events surrounding him. Such 'suicidal victimisation' under the spell of maleficent fetishes and ensorcellment is usually prevented through group control and the counter-attack of one's own dually charged fetishes. The victim, who surrenders his ability to make decisions and evaluations, gradually plunges into chaos, disorientation or despondency. Ultimately, the victim's physical body (*luutu*) and life-force or breath of life (*mooyi*, containing the elements of air and fire, illumination and energy; Devisch 1993) give over to crisis or even death. Lacking a cognised defence by the body-self (*muutu*; ibid.), the victim is vulnerable to angry spirits (which have no master and act on their own behalf), to his inner drives or to portions of his personality. And the victim exposes himself to the morbid desires unleashed by certain despotic relatives. The fatal desire of others (their dislike, hatred or aggression) is being incorporated by the victim, for in his bodily disposition and condition he has opened up to imagoes in which the forces of life and death, of love and hatred, of placebo and nocebo intersect and consume the life-resources of the individual. In brief, ensorcellment erodes and deterritorialises the victim, undermining his very bond with, or grasp on, life. The victim, in his imaginary, affects and body, is ultimately overpowered by the often deadly effect of the collective imaginary realm of forces. The dual signification of these forces (transmitted through fetishes, talk and intimidation on the part of people close to the victim) is supported by the processes of introjection-incorporation overruling the victim. So to be effective, the ensorcellment process does need to be brought to perceptibility in some way, but operates outside of the fully cognised or lawful order. This is the body beyond the grasp of conceptually mediated cognitive frameworks.

The victim's only recourse is to seek out a diviner and subsequently a therapist. In doing so, the victim is in fact breaking the fatal embrace of the forces by opening up to the symbolic, to the restoration of difference encoded by symbolic, hence metaphoric, thinking. He seeks a word, scenario or set of actors in the nebulous sphere of adversity and monstrosity that may help him to expel his own self-destructive inclinations or what may be described as his suicidal victimisation or self-conflagration as a victim or a living dead (Watson 1998: 42). A culturally authorised agency of fear is invading and suffocating the victim's life-forces, hence the body-self. In other cases, this agency of fear may assist the individual in confronting and overcoming the force of maleficent fetishes. We observe here what I would term a war between the impulses of life and death, a battle between meaning and its suspension, being waged within the victim himself.

To Conclude

My scrutiny of Yaka fetishes as hunters' props and plots unleashing annihilatory violence is thus an effort to develop an endogenously rooted epistemology for comprehending the not yet fully directed virtualities of the 'singular multiple' (Nancy 1996), of the putrefaction/fermentation of the life-world and society. The fetish invites us to look at Yaka life from the perspective of (nightly) frenzy, 'qui fait mousser la vie' (which stirs up life), as Kinois say, even as it may be at odds with modern institutions and capitalist profit-making (Devisch 1998, 1995). Indeed, an economy of affect forms the core of the Yaka realm of power objects, witchcraft and sorcery (De Boeck 1998, 1996). These beliefs and their dispositions, however, are often at odds with people's individual materialist aspirations, themselves exogenously unfolded as modern (in the sense of Western-entrepreneurial), if not Christian, virtue. Moreover, rumours and practices of fortune-seeking and sorcery most intensively mobilise and interweave local networks of trust and distrust in view of the harnessing of forces (intercorporeal and transworld, or ancestral and spirit) into vibrant body-politics.

ACKNOWLEDGEMENTS

Subsequent to university training in philosophy and in anthropology in Kinshasa, I participated in the daily life of Yaka people living in a settlement of villages in the northern Kwaango region along the Angolan border (in the Bandundu province of south-west Congo, some 450 kilometres from Kinshasa) in the period from January 1971 until October 1974 and again in April–May and September 1991. For approximately two to six weeks every year since 1986, I have been working among the Yaka in Kinshasa, in the suburban shantytowns where many families live in destitution, and in particular with Kongo healing communes and Yaka healers.

Further research that I have carried out or supervised, for briefer periods, has been located in Cairo, Tunis, northern Ghana, southern Ethiopia, southwestern Kenya, north-western Namibia, southern Nigeria, central and north-western Tanzania, and (Druze communities in) northern Israel.

My research among the Yaka in the 1990s has been carried out in the context of the programme of the Africa Research Centre, Department of Anthropology,

Catholic University of Louvain (Leuven), Belgium. It has been supported by the FWO (Fund for Scientific Research-Flanders), the EC (DG XII B4 Sector Health – STD2 0202-B and STD-TS3 CT94-0326) and the Harry-Frank Guggenheim Foundation, New York. I gladly acknowledge the valuable co-operation of my colleagues at the IMNC (Institute of the National Museums of Congo) and CER-DAS (Centre for the Co-ordination of Research and Documentation in Social Science for Africa South of the Sahara), both in Kinshasa. Finally, I want to record my grateful thanks to Peter Crossman and Paul Komba for their editorialship, as well as to those who shared their insights at presentations at the AAA Meetings at San Francisco in 2000, and at the Universities of Bergen, Kinshasa, Leuven, Pretoria and Uppsala.

NOTES

1. My use of the term 'imaginary' is similar to Lacan's (1949), not to the primary connotation of fiction. In Lacan's approach, the imaginary register is a mode of unconscious feeling and understanding of other people, as shaped by the partial projection of the subject's own affects of the body and psychic forces in the form of unconscious images or clichés, that is, imagoes (a notion evocative of Edmund Freud's *Sachvorstellung*). The images are transformed into the symbolic order inasmuch as they interpenetrate, in a shadowy in between zone, with the register of language (cf. Freud's notion of *Wortvorstellung*), social time and space, social exchange and dialogical intersubjectivity.
2. Jacobson-Widding (1979: 135) writes that for the neighbouring Kongo, 'the word *nkisi* belongs to the class of nouns which Laman, who was a linguist, calls the semi-person class of the class of trees' (see also MacGaffey 1991, 1977; Mahaniah 1982; Janzen 1978; Dupré 1975; Buakasa 1973).
3. The fetish is cyborg-like (Haraway 1990).
4. It is not surprising that Kinois people perceive the Internet as concretising the space-time virtualities attributed to fetishes.
5. This homeopathic logic itself is congruent with the premise of slash and burn agriculture.

BIBLIOGRAPHY

Appadurai, A. 'Dead Certainty: Ethnic Violence in the Era of Globalization.' *Public Culture* 10, no. 2 (1998): 225–47.
Aulagnier, P. *La Violence de l'Interprétation: Du Pictogramme à l'Enoncé*. Paris, 1975.
Baudrillard, J. *La Transparence du Mal: Essai sur les Phénomènes Extrêmes*. Paris, 1990.
Buakasa, T. *L'Impensé du Discours: Kindoki et Nkisi en Pays Kongo du Zaïre*. Kinshasa, 1973.
Bourdieu, P. *Le Sens Pratique*. Paris, 1980.
Butler, J. *Bodies that Matter: On the Discursive Limits of 'Sex'*. London, 1993.
Conrad, J. 'Heart of Darkness.' In *The Portable Conrad*, ed. L. Zabel. New York, 1965 [1902].
Corbey, R. *Wildheid en Beheersing: De Europese Verbeelding van Afrika*. Baarn, 1989.

Csordas, T., ed. *Embodiment and Experience: The Existential Ground of Culture and Self.* Cambridge, 1994.

Daniel, V. *Charred Lullabies: Chapters in an Anthropology of Violence.* Princeton, 1996.

Das, V. 'Sufferings, Theodicies, Disciplinary Practices, Appropriations.' *International Social Science Journal* 154 (1997a): 563–72.

———. 'Language and Body: Transactions in the Construction of Pain.' In *Social Suffering*, ed. A. Kleinman, V. Das and M. Lock, 67–92. Berkeley, 1997b.

De Beir, L. *Religion et Magie des Bayaka.* St. Augustin bei Bonn, 1975.

De Boeck, F. 'Beyond the Grave: History, Memory and Death in Postcolonial Congo/Zaire.' In *Memory and the Postcolony: African Anthropology and the Critique of Power*, ed. R. Werbner, 21–57. London, 1998.

———. 'Postcolonialism, Power and Identity: Local and Global Perspectives in Zaire.' In *Postcolonial Identities in Africa*, ed. R. Werbner and T. Ranger, 75–106. London, 1996.

Deleuze, G., and F. Guattari. *A Thousand Plateaus.* London, 1987.

de Surgy, A. *Nature et Fonction des Fétiches en Afrique Noire.* Paris, 1994.

Devisch, R. 'La Violence à Kinshasa, ou l'Institution en Négatif.' *Cahiers d'Etudes Africaines* 38, no. 2–4 (1998): 441–69.

———. '"Pillaging Jesus": Healing Churches and the Villagisation of Kinshasa.' *Africa* 66 (1996): 555–86.

———. 'Frenzy, Violence, and Ethical Renewal in Kinshasa.' *Public Culture* 7 (1995): 593–629.

———. *Weaving the Threads of Life: The Khita Gyn-Eco-Logical Healing Cult among the Yaka.* Chicago, 1993.

Devisch, R., and C. Brodeur. *The Law of the Lifegivers: The Domestication of Desire.* Amsterdam, 1999.

Dupré, M. 'Le Système des Forces *Nkisi* chez les Kongo, d'après le Troisième Volume de K. Laman.' *Africa* 41 (1975): 12–28.

Fanon, F. *Peau Noire Masques Blancs.* Paris, 1952.

———. *Les Mots, la Mort, les Sorts: La Sorcellerie dans le Bocage.* Paris, 1977.

Feldman, A. 'Violence and Vision: The Prosthetics and Aesthetics of Terror.' *Public Culture* 10, no. 1 (1997): 24–60.

———. *Formations of Violence: The Narrative of the Body and Political Terror in Northern Ireland.* Chicago, 1991.

Gil, J. *Métamorphoses du Corps.* Paris, 1985.

Greenwood, S. *Magic, Witchcraft and the Otherworld: An Anthropology.* Oxford, 2000.

Haraway, D. 'A Manifesto for Cyborgs: Science, Technology, and Socialist Feminism in the 1980s.' In *Feminism/Postmodernism*, ed. J. Nicholson, 190–233. London, 1990.

Huber, H. 'Magical Statuettes and Their Accessories among the Eastern Bayaka and Their Neighbors.' *Anthropos* 51 (1956): 265–90.

Jackson, M., ed. *Things as They Are: New Directions in Phenomenological Anthropology.* Bloomington, 1996.

Jacobson-Widding, A. *Red-White-Black as a Mode of Thought: A Study of Triadic Classification by Colours in the Ritual Symbolism and Cognitive Thought of the People of the Lower Congo.* Stockholm, 1979.

Janzen, J. *The Quest for Therapy: Medical Pluralism in Lower Zaire.* Berkeley, 1978.

Kacem, M.B. *Esthétique du Chaos.* Auch, 2000.

Kapferer, B. *The Feast of the Sorcerer: Practices of Consciousness and Power.* Chicago, 1997.

Kirby, K. *Indifferent Boundaries: Spatial Concepts of Human Subjectivity.* London, 1996.

Kristeva, J. *Pouvoir de l'Horreur: Essai sur l'Abjection.* Paris, 1980.

Krohn-Hansen, C. 'Magic, Money and Alterity among Dominicans.' *Social Anthropology* 3, no. 2 (1995): 129–46.

Lacan, J. 'Le Stade Miroir comme Formateur de la Fonction du Je.' *Revue Française de Psychanalyse* 13 (1949): 449–53.

Laderman, C., and M. Roseman. *The Performance of Healing*. London, 1996.

Lingis, A. *Dangerous Emotions*. Berkeley, 2000.

MacGaffey W. *Art and Healing of the Bakongo Commented by Themselves*. Stockholm, 1991.

———. 'Fetishism Revisited: Kongo *Nkisi* in Sociological Perspective.' *Africa* 47 (1977): 140–52.

Mahaniah, K. *La Maladie et la Guérison en Milieu Kongo*. Kinshasa, 1982.

Mudimbe, V. *The Invention of Africa: Gnosis, Philosophy, and the Order of Knowledge*. Bloomington, 1988.

Nancy, J.-L. *Être Singulier Pluriel*. Paris, 1996.

Overing, J. 'Introduction.' In *Reason and Morality*, ed. J. Overing, 1–28. London, 1985.

———. 'The Shaman as a Maker of Worlds: Nelson Goodman in the Amazon.' *Man* 25 (1978): 602–19.

Parkin, D., ed. *The Anthropology of Evil*. Oxford, 1985.

Pieterse, J.N., and B. Parekh, eds. *The Decolonization of Imagination: Culture, Knowledge and Power*. London, 1995.

Ricoeur, P. *The Symbolism of Evil*. Boston, 1967.

Stallybrass, P., and A. White. *The Politics and Poetics of Transgression*. London, 1986.

Stoller, P. *Sensuous Scholarship*. Philadelphia, 1997.

Stoller, P., and C. Olkes. *In Sorcery's Shadow*. Chicago, 1987.

Taussig, M. 'Transgression.' *Critical Terms for Religious Studies*, ed. M. Taylor, 349–64. Chicago, 1998.

Watson, S. 'The Neurobiology of Sorcery: Deleuze and Guattari's Brain.' *Body and Society* 4, no. 4 (1998): 23–45.

Weiss, G. *Body Images: Embodiment as Intercorporeality*. London, 1999.

Young, K. *Presence in the Flesh: The Body in Medicine*. Cambridge, 1997.

Top: Vodou ceremony (see chapter 2) in honour of the prophet Olivorio Mateo killed by military troops during the American occupation of the Dominican Republic (1916–24). Southern Dominican Republic, 1991. Photo: Marit Brendbekken.

Bottom: Female *brujo* calls on Olivorio Mateo by ringing a bell. Southern Dominican Republic, 1991. Photo: Marit Brendbekken.

Top: Altar table serving the spirits. Montaña Antigua, 1991. Photo: Marit Brendbekken.

Bottom: The preparation of biodynamic farm organisms as world-constitutive, anthroposophical practice (see chapter 2). Montaña Antigua, 1991. Photo: Marit Brendbekken.

Top: The Garap rite. The *klian* administers the potion that consists of water mixed with soil from the tomb of Wali Nyato', using a banyan leaf as a spoon (see chapter 3). Central Lombok, Indonesia, 1997. Photo: Kari Telle.

Bottom: The Suniyama rite. An exorcist dances before Mahasammata's palace (see chapter 4). Sri Lanka, 1993. Photo: Bruce Kapferer.

Top: This small men's house concealed behind fencing and sacred plants, where secret paraphernalia and remedies are hidden, is in North Ambrym, believed to be the heart of *kastom* and sorcery practices (see chapter 5). Vanuatu, 2000. Photo: Knut Rio.

Bottom: *Khosi* cult figurine for ritual (counter-)attack and protection (see chapter 7). Malaatu village, 1974. Photo: René Devisch.

Above: A Munnesvaram temple priest performs *puja* to the Meru Yantram image. The image ensures the efficacy of the temple's protective ritual, much of which can be considered to involve people seeking indirect protection from sorcery. (see chapter 6). Sri Lanka, 1985. Photo: Rohan Bastin.

Right: The inner sanctum of the Munnesvaram temple. To the side stands the statue of the goddess Ambal, also known as Pattini to many Sinhala Buddhists. Sri Lanka, 1985. Photo: Rohan Bastin.

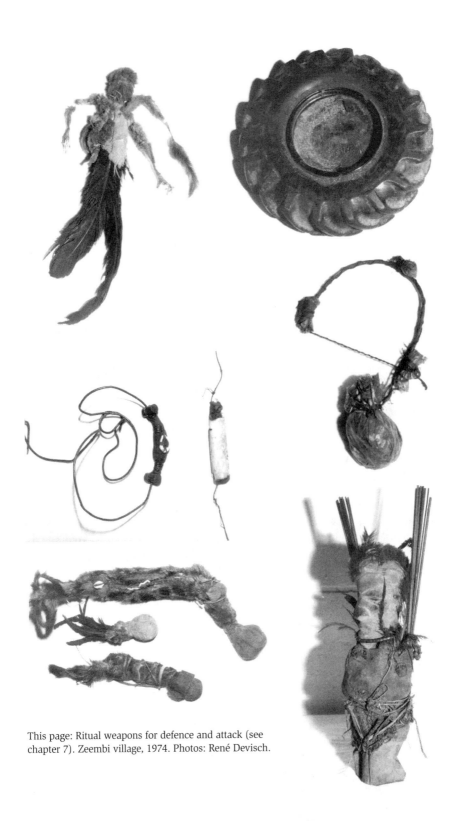

This page: Ritual weapons for defence and attack (see chapter 7). Zeembi village, 1974. Photos: René Devisch.

Chapter 8

FANTASY IN PRACTICE
Projection and Introjection, or
the Witch and the Spirit-Medium

Michael Lambek

> We become responsible agents when we can face the
> moral continuity of the familiar, conscious self with other
> strange, 'alien' psychic entities – our 'other selves'.... For
> we must accept responsibility for the 'acts' of these other
> selves; we must see these acts as *ours*.
>
> – Fingarette (1963: 180)

Whatever Happened to the Ego?

What is the relationship of psychoanalysis to questions of dignity, self-respect
and respect for others?[1] How, ultimately can we link Freud with Aristotelian concerns for eudaimonia – human flourishing – and for phronesis – sustained moral
judgement?[2] If Freud rightly tempers Aristotle's optimism, how might Aristotelian questions illuminate and complement Freudian forays into personhood?
If repression is defined as a state of disconnection and disavowal, of non-
acknowledgement of one's own thoughts and acts, then it is morally and politically problematic. Repression generates projection, in which accountability is
displaced onto others. However, I argue that in some instances, and given the
appropriate cultural means, it may provoke a dialectical return. Such introjection
provides the opportunity for gradual reconnection, recognition and, ideally, the
acknowledgement of responsibility.

I want to demonstrate the place of spirit possession in this 'work of culture'
(Obeyesekere 1990). My ideas derive from thinkers such as Fingarette, Loewald
and Schafer, who may be placed somewhere between the drive and relational
models of psychoanalysis (Mitchell 1988).[3] Anthropologists of a psychoanalytic
bent too often rely exclusively on the primary texts of Freud. Brilliant as these are,
they serve as the foundation, not the summation, of psychoanalytic thinking. Nor

is Lacan the only interesting thinker to follow Freud. If anthropology is to have a stronger voice in the dialogue with psychoanalysis, it needs to attend to developments within psychoanalytic theory and practice. The relational perspective, in which individuals are understood more emphatically as products of their engagement with others, affords cultural and social factors a more significant role. In particular, as I will argue, it enables us to see certain forms of religious practice as less illusory than Freud proposed.

Without wishing to discount the tremendous moral power in Freud's austere view, I am sceptical of those who dismiss relational models simply on the basis of their optimism.[4] If Freud's quest to understand human happiness led him to emphasise its always compromised nature, he also suggested the possibility of relative happiness and relative insight – these were surely the point of therapy – and there is no reason not to use psychoanalysis to demonstrate their presence, and not always simply their absence, in our subjects. Moreover, if psychoanalysis provides a lens to understand the significance of possession for those who undergo or encounter it, spirit possession in turn offers strong empirical support for relational perspectives, for the significance of processes of identification and introjection in building the ego, and hence for a view of ego strength that departs not only from excessive concern with boundaries and individuation, but also from the postmodern emphasis on fragmentation.

To make these points I draw on material collected since 1975 among Malagasy speakers on the island of Mayotte in the Mozambique Channel.[5] Periods of research have of course been intermittent, but the time depth has both enabled me to follow the course of spirits in people's lives and enabled my own ideas to mature.[6] Here I can offer only one piece of a dense, complex and subtle set of relations. I have been genuinely impressed by the spirit-mediums I have known in Mayotte and subsequently in Madagascar – by their strength, empathy and creativity; by their ability to express both joy and pain; and by their willingness to address ambivalence. While there is an element of idealisation in my portraits, remember that I am writing about people and practices who have suffered disparagement and misunderstanding by Westerners, people really 'in the shadow of modernity' (Meyer and van de Port 1999). By all means, let us use Freud to prick the complacent ideologies of the West, but let us also use him, against his own ethnocentrism, towards recognising the dignity of others.

Projection and Introjection

One of the signs or consequences of repression is denial, the disavowal or unrealisation of responsibility. This is evident in projection, the 'operations whereby qualities, feelings, wishes or even "objects", which the subject refuses to recognise or rejects in himself, are expelled from the self and located in another person or thing' (Laplanche and Pontalis 1973: 349).

I refer to those figures who are projected upon as witches. The witch serves as the vehicle for unacknowledged anti-social urges or unmet needs, notably excessive and inappropriately directed aggression and sexuality. And if the possibility of kinship is provided by repression, as Freud argued, witchcraft can be seen to form a kind of by-product, an inverted or perverted kinship characterised by the return of the repressed.

Introjection is the inverse of projection: '[I]n phantasy the subject transposes objects and their inherent qualities from the "outside" to the "inside" of himself' (Laplanche and Pontalis 1973: 229). As a form of taking in, introjection may be a means of recuperation of images, meanings or desire that had been held apart. Thus, an idea functioning as an object-representation shifts its function to become a self-representation (Fingarette 1963).

Whereas projection is usually seen as unhealthy and anti-social, a form of false consciousness, introjection may be both healthy – bolstering the Self or ego, rendering it more complex and multivalent – and socially positive, rendering the Self more connected and Other-oriented. From the perspective of relational psychoanalysis, introjection is central to human development and indeed to kinship. As Chodorow puts it: 'If a person is to develop at all, the self must come to include what were originally aspects of the other and the relation to the other.... We become a person ... in internal relation with the social world.... People inevitably incorporate one another; our sociality is built into our psychic structure and there is no easy separation of individual and society or possibility of the individual apart from society' (Chodorow 1989: 149).

Here I am not simply contrasting projection and introjection as distinct psychic functions, but rather, signalling the shift to an alternate paradigm from that of drive theory, with its central concept of repression, namely to a version of psychoanalysis that begins with relation and which has flourished under object-relational paradigms in the UK, and self-psychology in North America (Mitchell 1988). Relational approaches elaborate the psychic structures constitutive of greater maturity. Thus, for Loewald, whereas repression leads to the persistence of unconscious fantasies, internalisation can produce 'higher' levels of psychic structure and more 'mature' object relations (1980a: 77). Loewald attributes this view to Freud's reformulations in *The Ego and the Id* (1923): 'The point in this ... formulation is that it is not the fact of its being unconscious that characterizes the repressed (although it *is* unconscious), but the fact of its being split off from the coherent ego. What is internalized ... is not split off from the coherent ego but becomes ... an integral part of the coherent ego. While what is internalized and what is repressed are both unconscious (in the dynamic sense), the former is a structural element of the coherent ego, the latter, the repressed, is not' (Loewald 1980a: 78).

Loewald continues that in late Freud: 'The role of object ties and object relations ... is no longer that of being merely means for the achievement of satisfaction, that is, for the discharge of stimulus tension.... Object ties in the form of identifications and introjections become constitutive elements in psychic structure formation, in the formation of ego and superego seen not as defense structures against instinctual and environmental stimuli, but as more developed and more structured organizations of instinctual-interactive forces' (ibid.: 80).

Loewald's argument (1980a: 83) is clarified by his distinction between internalisation and identification:

> Identification tends to erase a difference: subject becomes object and object becomes subject. Identification is a way-station to internalization, but in internalization, if carried to completion, a redifferentiation has taken place by which both subject and object have been reconstituted, each on a new level of organization. When we speak of the internalization of object relations, such as in the resolution of the Oedipus complex and in the work of mourning, it is not ... a matter of maintaining identifications with the objects to be relinquished; the latter is the case in melancholia where the object and the identifications with the object cannot be given up. In internalization it is a matter of transforming these relations into an internal, intrapsychic, depersonified relationship, thus increasing and enriching psychic structure.... Internalization as a completed process implies an emancipation from the object. To the extent – always limited in the vicissitudes of human life – to which internalization comes to completion, the individual is enriched by the relationship he [or she] has had with the beloved object, not burdened by identification and fantasy relations with the object.... This ... is not simply freedom from old object ties that have been cast off, but an inner freedom we call maturity, achieved by internalization of old ties.

I argue that spirit possession enables movement towards internalisation as Loewald describes it.

Thus, we may distinguish the spirit-medium and the witch as two ideal 'nodes' in the flow of collective ideation. If the witch is a passive target for projection, the medium is an active receptor or appropriator of fantasy. In a sense, the medium is the vehicle of collective sublimation, while the witch is the vehicle of collective repression or 'de-repression'.[7]

In sum, I am proposing a model in which:

witch : medium :: projection : introjection :: object (victim) : subject (agent)

However, the psychological processes and cultural constructions at work make it look as if the witch were an active party (i.e. deliberately harming others) and the medium a passive vehicle (of invasive spirits).

Suleimana and the Transmutation of Aggression

What has particularly struck me about possession as I have observed it among northern Malagasy speakers is the dense web of interpersonal connections it establishes and invokes, interpersonal connections which exist not only between people but within them as well. Spirits mediate personal, domestic and professional relations, in particular as they shift between generations of mediums.[8]

Here I focus on the possession of Mohedja Salim by a spirit named Suleimana. Mohedja was in early middle age at the time of her first account to me in

1976 of events that dated back some 25 years earlier. She was a mother of six living children and numerous grandchildren, in a stable marriage to Tumbu. Their
household was one of average means that supported itself primarily by a mixture
of subsistence cultivation and cash-cropping. In 1976 Mohedja was active in village affairs and beginning to emerge as a respected healer.

The critical issue in understanding the personal or deep meaning of possession is knowing by whom the subject is possessed. The personal meaning of a
particular spirit for a host is shaped by its presence in other mediums.[9] Over the
course of her life, Mohedja has come to be possessed cumulatively by a number of spirits, each of whom entails a series of prior relationships. Thus, the
first spirit to possess her was a female *tromba* who had been present in her
mother from long before Mohedja's birth and who, Mohedja suggested, had
also been in Mohedja herself from birth.[10] This spirit, whom they shared, thus
expressed the mutual identification of mother and daughter. It first rose in
Mohedja – manifested through her dissociated state – just before her first marriage when her mother left her briefly in the village of her fiancé in order to
return to their home village to invite their kin to the wedding. Some 30 years
later, shortly before Mohedja's mother died, the spirit rose in the old woman for
a last time to announce that henceforward its clients should seek it exclusively
from Mohedja. Subsequent to the old woman's death, the female spirit began
appearing in several of her granddaughters.[11]

In the case of the *patros* spirit Suleimana, it is relevant that Mohedja says he
arrived simultaneously with another, more senior *patros* spirit who has been of
far greater importance to Mohedja and her immediate family.[12] The senior spirit,
Mze Bunu, represents for Mohedja her beloved and much respected elder half-
brother, who was himself possessed by this spirit's older brother. She says she
remembers seeing her brother possessed from her earliest consciousness. Mohedja's brother perhaps took the place of the father Mohedja had lost in early
childhood, and he too had to be partially given up when Mohedja was forced in
adolescence to move with her mother to the village where she married, which
was at some distance from her natal one. But subsequently internalised and
introjected as Mze Bunu, he has consistently provided brotherly/fatherly care to
Mohedja and her family. Mze Bunu has been entirely beneficent, and Mohedja's
husband Tumbu is particularly attached to him as a friend and a teacher.

Mohedja said that both Mze Bunu and Suleimana arrived during a severe illness following the birth of her first child, but also asserted that Mze Bunu was
the only one of her spirits never to have made her sick. The trauma was displaced entirely onto Suleimana. Mohedja stressed that Suleimana came to her
in quite another way from the older Mze Bunu – he was sent to her in order to
take her life. He wasn't successful at this, so he thought it best just to stay and
get food by rising in her and asking for it.

I will explore the specific meaning of Suleimana for Mohedja but I also want
to use Suleimana to make some general points about the way in which the experience of onslaught from an external source is gradually internalised in the subject's own terms. Through the emergence of the spirit and its voice, the subject

gains a means to articulate her concerns and transmute their valence. In both the subjective (intrapersonal) and objective (interpersonal) domains, possession enables a 'working through' of issues.

In this account I do not take sides in the heated debate about the origins of trauma. We will examine both external threats to Mohedja's person and the way that she characteristically imagines and experiences threat; these operate in dialectical relationship to each other. In some events in her life, the external source has more force, while in others, her own relational concerns and fantasies are primary. My point is that possession enables the medium to articulate and assimilate experience and so move ahead. This movement may be described as a series of projective-introjective processes.

Desire, intrusion and control are themes in early indications of possession. When Suleimana was first entering her, Mohedja said she would dream that someone came into the room and went under the bed and lifted it up so that she would fall off. Once, she shouted so loudly that her neighbour rushed in to see what was wrong. Suleimana appeared to Mohedja as a boy, wearing only black shorts and a black hat. He tried to frighten her, but she wasn't frightened. It was then he went under the bed and lifted it up.

Dreams of flying are a more common sign of receiving a spirit. When the spirits first entered her, Mohedja continually dreamt she was flying. A spirit would chase her and try to catch and hit her; as they fought, she was able to fly away just in time. These dreams were unlike the ones she had once mature relations were established with a spirit. In the latter, the spirits come of their own accord in order to tell Mohedja something. But she said that the dreams where she saw herself under attack came from her own soul (*rohu*).[13]

This is critical. In the dreams of attack Mohedja is warning and protecting herself by fighting off the spirit. The fact that she is chased but not vanquished is a sign of the relationship to come, one in which the spirit may bring suffering but where, in the end, the host remains strong. Spirit possession in which the host is able to negotiate a social relationship with her spirit (cf. Lambek 1981) is thus very different from being overwhelmed, going crazy and possibly even dying as a result of spirit attack. The dream is one of the first steps in the self-constitution of spirit possession, in which a host comes to realise that she is acquiring a spirit who will possess her and begins to set the terms of that relationship. While the initial arrival of the spirit is experienced as beyond the host's control, the dream is an indication that the will of the host has become involved and that she is beginning to look out and care for herself. Exactly as Mohedja puts it, it is the host's own *rohu* (mind or soul) that provides her with the dream and begins to exert control. Thus, while the spirit is always socially distinguished from the person of the host, the subjective process is one in which the host is involved from the start.

Fieldnotes, January 5, 1976. The person who sent Suleimana to kill Mohedja was Toihan, a distant cross cousin. When Mohedja was still young, he and his mother tried to procure an engagement between them. Mohedja disliked him from the first and refused outright. He sent her gifts, but she sent them all back; she was not about to keep anything from someone she did not like! Much later, when she had already married Tumbu, Toihan still wanted to marry her. Once he even tried to rape her. She completely rejected him.

Mohedja became sick. When the curer extracted the sorcery from her body, Suleimana rose in Mohedja and announced he had been sent by Toihan in order to kill her. Toihan had promised Suleimana a red chicken and some cloth when the job was completed. But, said the spirit, since he had been unsuccessful in doing what was requested, he had decided to rise in Mohedja instead. When the healer asked what he wanted of her, he replied a *patros* ceremony with a white goat and white cloth. Since the ceremony, Suleimana rises irregularly, much less often than Mze Bunu. Like other young spirits, he likes to dance and drink [goat's] blood.

Suleimana is from an underwater village, and since her initial possession he has taken Mohedja there to visit several times in her sleep. They travelled by bush taxi and canoe and entered a huge town with cement houses and tin roofs [at the time she told me the story, such houses were rare among ordinary citizens of Mayotte]. The town was full of people. Suleimana took her to his mother's house, where she was welcomed by his parents. They cooked and she ate alone, as is fitting for a guest. She saw many of his kin. When she had finished eating and chatting, she said her farewell. They rose in the canoe and took a taxi home. She has gone on this trip frequently, and Suleimana's family also visits her here in her sleep. She sees Suleimana in her dreams as a young man with nice features. She compares him to a handsome married man in the village.

June 1976. Mohedja also flies with Mze Bunu to his village. There, his is the only house inhabited and he lives alone. He brings out food and they eat together. He has a face like that of her older brother. Mze Bunu has no children; perhaps he is not married.

The general descriptions of the underwater villages are quite stereotypic, and I have heard stories of similar visits from other mediums. The *patros* spirits and their villages evoked the prosperity of a mercantile era prior to European arrival, although people were insistent that *patros* were not deceased humans.

What is personally articulated in the dream narratives is the establishment of strong, positive, reciprocal relations with powerful Others. Just as one would go to visit the family of a human friend, so too with the *patros* spirit. Mohedja indicates a comfortable, though somewhat formal, relationship in which she is accepted by Suleimana's family. The visits to Mze Bunu's have perhaps a hint of incest fantasy; they describe a more intimate relationship, a fact which corresponds to the way she talks about Mze Bunu in other contexts. Overall, these dreams demonstrate the strength of her identifications with the respective spirits. As in the initial dreams of being chased, there is a passive quality. Mohedja is taken on a trip; she doesn't set out by herself. At the same time, the dreams may be understood as an affirmation of the solidarity of her relations with her spirits and her sense of security with them.

In her relations with Suleimana we see Mohedja triumph over a man who had been harassing her. The aggression Mohedja experienced against her person was internalised, but at the same time its force was mitigated and turned to her own interests. The 'black' and 'red' were changed to 'white', and Suleimana rose infrequently to allow Mohedja her own chance to become an energetic, potentially dangerous young man. He also befriended her, taking her to meet his family. Suleimana was ultimately a better and more attractive person than the menacing Toihan.

That Suleimana did not appear much in her later life may mean that the emotional salience of Toihan and the issues he represented had declined for Mohedja. Stated more strongly, possession by Suleimana helped Mohedja work through and move beyond the trauma elicited by Toihan.[14] By contrast, the frequently present Mze Bunu drew from the much more profound relationship with her brother.

Suitors and Sorcery

Toihan was by no means the only rejected suitor in Mohedja's life. Persecution by such men was a motif that recurred several times as she recounted her life in 1975–6. There had been a number of incidents about which she experienced varying degrees of guilt or fear and, one may suspect, attraction. She handled the cases in different ways, not always by means of spirits. For example, harassed by one of Tumbu's kinsmen, she finally told her husband and let him address it.

Fieldnotes, July 28, 1975. Mohedja emphasised that Suleimana was the only one of her spirits who was sent to her by a sorcerer in order to kill her. All her other spirits came on their own initiative, that is, because they were attracted to her on their own account. However, she has been the object of sorcery several times by means of spirits who had to be exorcised rather than accommodated.

One sorcery attack took place when they were living out at their fields. She was very sick, delirious for 15 days. She was diagnosed by a cosmologer with a generalised 'evil spirit', rather than one that could come to possess people positively and by name, and once it was exorcised, she started improving. Before she was fully recovered, she asked Tumbu to take her to consult the *patros* spirit of her older brother. [Remember, the spirit is also the older brother of Mohedja's own trusted Mze Bunu.] The spirit said the source of her problem was sorcery [as the cosmologer had not], and he removed it. She learnt the identity of the perpetrator in a dream, and again it was a rejected suitor.

A year later, following the death of a woman suffering a post-partum psychosis, Mohedja again recalled the events that occurred when she lived in the fields.

She herself had no memory of the period of her illness, but heard about it later in conversation with her children. She was impaired for a month and thought it was the end. Her own *patros* rose and gave the name of the perpetrator, so she was told later. A lot of people heard the spirit shout it out. The perpetrator also lived at the fields. For some years he had been after her to leave Tumbu and

marry him. In the days when she was first falling sick she had a dream. Someone came and told her not to eat anything that this man might offer her. He
approached with something in his hand and invited her to eat. She refused, and
he opened his hand and she saw meat. He managed to force a tiny piece down
her throat, though she spat the rest out. She gagged and gagged. Then she
awoke. A few days later she fell really sick. She thought he sent the spirit
'because his longing for me could not be fulfilled'.

Mohedja's account shows an interesting implication of the rule that the healer
or diviner should not reveal the identity of the sorcerer. The curer's reticence
provides the victim the opportunity to construct her own interpretation, one
which is consistent, meaningful and psychologically relevant to her and which
will not be challenged in any public forum. Thus, the victims of sorcery inter-
nalise its meaning.

It is noteworthy that while some spirits arrive in their hosts as the result of
attacks of sorcery perpetrated by others, once established these same spirits can
provide a main source of protection against further sorcery and are a channel
through which sorcery accusations are rendered explicit. There is a positive
transformation from having been a victim to wielding a sure means of defence
and counter-attack. Mohedja regularly saw in her dreams the people who harboured evil intentions towards her. Sometimes she saw a sorcery packet buried
in the courtyard; the next day she would go to the spot and dig it up. Or else
the spirit would tell her in her sleep to get Tumbu to remove it.[15]

I do not wish to unduly psychologise Mohedja; rather, I start with the external sources of her problems – sexual harassment and post-partum illness – and
examine the ways she transcended them. However, there are motivational factors and projective processes at work. The local model that suggests illness may
be derived from sorcery provides a channel for an aggressive response, and, as
we have seen, it is Mohedja who identifies the sorcerer and in so doing it is she
who casts her hostility towards the suitors rather than elsewhere. Perhaps what
she fears is her own unacknowledged desire for them or perhaps it is a more
straightforward retaliation to what has been experienced by her as aggressive,
improper and unwelcome advances on their part. Such advances may refer
back to childhood events; for example, young girls often experience boundary
violations on the playground at night.

I don't know how to answer this. I restrict myself here to noting the similarity of Mohedja's interpretation of her afflictions to her account of another significant episode in her life, namely her first engagement. She and her fiancé
appear to have been in love. When his father cancelled the engagement, Mohedja was promised elsewhere, i.e. to Tumbu. By the time the fiancé discovered
what had happened, it was too late. He was so outraged by his father's behaviour that he went and deliberately made love to a virgin (a flagrant breach of
morality in Mayotte, virtually on par with incest) in order to shame his father.
Then, mad with grief at losing Mohedja, and not being able to stand the thought
of her with another man, he wrote her a final letter and left Mayotte forever.

Mohedja appears to bear guilt for what happened. Since then, each time that she rejected a suitor, however unsuitable he may have been, she was punished (perhaps identifying with the virgin violated by her former fiancé). Whereas her beloved fiancé dealt with the impasse by removing himself from the scene, the rejected suitors dealt with it by trying to remove Mohedja.

And yet, what is the result? After a period of suffering, she gains another spirit, another voice, another guardian – or an affirmation of those she already has – to help her. In a sense, she does accept the suitor, incorporating and gradually internalising him, but renders him acceptable by transforming him into the stronger and more desirable figure of Suleimana, who perhaps signifies the original fiancé. Projection is exchanged for introjection, and the position of being the object of unwelcome desire is exchanged for a new subject position. Loss has become gain.

Relational Dynamics

In classical metapsychology, writes Stephen Mitchell (1988: 134): '[H]uman experience is portrayed as a struggle to negotiate between the claims of body-based, asocial psychic tensions and the demands of social reality.... In each relational-model account the passions depicted characterize human longings and fears at all ages. The struggle between destructiveness and hopeful benevolence [Klein], the search for all-embracing love [Balint], the tension between self-expression and pandering [Winnicott], between autonomy and a longing to fuse [Mahler], the need for supportive recognition and admired heroes [Kohut] – these are fundamental dimensions of human relations, from infancy through senescence.'

The critical point and interest of Mohedja's practice lie less in what it may reveal about sexual longing, aggression or her ambivalence about these matters than about her relational development. Mohedja negotiates between dependence and autonomy, destructiveness and benevolence. She rejects male aggression yet welcomes and introjects strong figures to admire and depend on. The emergence of Suleimana and Mze Bunu demonstrate her need and ability to selectively reject or incorporate salient aspects of others and thereby transform her episodes of illness (whatever their etiology, in our theory or in hers) into occasions for growth, self-protection, articulation and increased connection.

My perspective draws much from Obeyesekere (1981), but I argue that individual spirits (as opposed to spirit types) are manifestations less of a person's drives or defences than of relations and relational issues. We may see the spirits as external expressions of these issues, but more important I think is the aspect of internalisation, identified long ago as critical for spirit possession by Crapanzano (1977). Phrased another way, there is a complex dialectic of externalisation and internalisation in which unclaimed or disclaimed aspects of the Self, manifest in Others, are appropriated, internalised and ultimately reclaimed (cf. Boddy 1989). Together, projection and introjection provide a dialectic of claims and disclaimers.

Spirit possession is more than static representation; it enables movement. In the best instances, the direction of this movement can be described in the following way: 'Paraphrasing Freud ... where fragmented internal objects were, there shall harmoniously related objects be; and where false, reactive self was, there shall true, agentic self be, with its relationally based capacity both to be alone and to participate in the transitional space between self and other self that creates play, intimacy, and culture' (Chodorow 1989: 159).[16]

Conclusion: The Illusions of Modernity

It is notable that for Freud (at least in *The Future of an Illusion*) mature self-understanding – insight – seems to exclude living in or with fantasy, and is certainly not to be achieved by means of fantasy. Reality and fantasy are opposed. But ethnography suggests that fantasy, suitably appropriated, may be a vehicle to psychic and social well-being – if not to happiness, then to moral responsibility. Relational models enable us to speak about psychic maturity, recognition of ambivalence, reflexive agency, personal integrity and mature playfulness, and about the local cultural means that enable some inspired individuals to reach, to a degree, a condition of eudaimonia, of human flourishing. I am speaking here, quite deliberately, about an Aristotelian this-worldly flourishing, not about the achievement of some superior numinous state at saintly distance from the ordinary world.

Mze Bunu and the other spirits are powerful beings. To become possessed by spirits one may first have encountered in one's senior kin – and then to act as and with them – is to take on their power. Is this to be understood as narcissistic illusion, and would such illusions be good or bad? Are they defences or do they enable? Mitchell (1988: 194) suggests that in healthy narcissism one enjoys illusions but readily relinquishes them; in pathological narcissism, illusions are taken too seriously. He draws attention to Loewald's etymology of illusion from *ludere* (to play): the capacity to play may be as critical a function of mental health as the capacities of loving and working that Freud emphasised. It is a matter, Mitchell suggests, of negotiating the delicate balance between illusion and reality, succumbing to the exclusivity of neither. The frame of possession – shifting between characters – provides a means for such negotiation and a space for play.

Consider also that the introjection of spirits corresponds to Kohut's (1977) internalisation of self-objects with their poles of grandiosity and idealisation. The grandiose pose of the spirit is mirrored by the audience and interlocutors, while the spirit provides an idealised authority for the host and her kin. In Kohut's view, these features, which Freud might consider illusions, are necessary for healthy development.

Let us grant that the aim of psychoanalytic treatment is insight, and let us agree that that is what we all seek through the work of culture as well. But insight is located not quite where Freud would have it; it is not necessarily fully discursive or 'rational'. The philosopher Fingarette (1963: 25) argues that insight 'is more than the suggestion of a new way of talking about one's life descriptively; it is the proposal to *experience* genuinely and *see* one's life in terms of the meaning-scheme suggested by the words'. In a profound argument, Fingarette links such integration of meaning to 'the psychological source of our capacity to will with responsibility and deliberateness'. In bringing behaviour within meaning schemes, it leads to the voluntary 'I wanted to do it' rather than 'it just happened' (ibid.: 38). Schafer (1976: 13) similarly argues that '[i]nsight is as much a way of looking as it is of seeing anything in particular'. Thus, insight is less an intellectual activity than it is a practical one. It is closely linked to acting responsibly and the true opposite to repression.

Loewald (1980b: 249) once wrote: 'Those who know ghosts tell us that they long to be released from their ghost life and led to rest as ancestors. As ancestors they live forth in the present generation, while as ghosts they are compelled to haunt the present generation with their shadow life.' 'Living forth' means that ancestors have become available for identification and internalisation. Likewise, religious figures – gods, saints, spirits – are not just projections to be dissolved in the light of rationality, not just the products or sites of wish fulfilment, but objects available for new patterns of internalisation (and for holding, mirroring, etc.).

The cultural repertoire of collective representations, public symbols and ritual practices provides vehicles for holding objects and the means for internalising them.[17] Like other artistic or religious traditions, spirit possession provides such a repertoire, which serves as a relatively durable resource for interpreting the human situation in all of its personal and historical specificity. Spirit possession may provide less reflective distance than does literature (though, despite what one might assume from discussions of mimesis, it is not without such distance), but it provides a more direct means for intimate introjection and self-transformation.

In Mohedja's case the sorcery or witchcraft gets transmuted in processes of identification and introjection. But, of course, this does not take place everywhere. For example, it seems missing in situations of collective witchcraft hysteria, such as that which grips much of southern Africa today. This is no longer witchcraft as simple projection; witchcraft grants the ostensive victims of social violence, i.e. the accusers, the right to violence, to produce victims of their own. This violence may be referred to as 'de-repression' (Žižek 1999), but what is notable is the way that social and economic violence – structural violence – gets displaced onto the interpersonal realm. Also notable here is the failure of ancestral mediation. Here 'ghosts' cannot be transformed or transmuted into 'ancestors' because the ancestors themselves seem to have withdrawn or been rendered impotent. It is the absence of elders who could be idealised or who could serve as idealising self-objects that is apparent, itself perhaps a consequence of the economic polarisation and social dislocation that Comaroff and Comaroff (1998) read as the subject of the witchcraft. Whereas Mohedja has the confidence to address attacks against her, to turn them around for herself and on her own behalf, the people of the townships appear unable to draw on similar means. Indeed, the ancestors may even be perceived to be actively blocking the progress of their descendants (J. Solway, personal communication) and become the objects of youthful rage.[18] The absence of ancestors – of a link between a valued past and a realisable future – leads people to respond to threats with greater violence of their own.

The epidemic of sexual and satanic abuse accusations that characterised North America in the last decade appears to have peaked. But comparison with Africa is possible (Comaroff 1997, Lambek 1997), especially in so far as we read the failure of positive ancestral identifications. A more general observation, then, is that if individuals are to receive help in directing their personal fantasies – which from a Freudian perspective are an inevitable part of growing up in a human family – in a positive direction and in avoiding the sort of repression that can lead with a little prompting to hysterical regression and accusations, the public symbolic domain must be involved. In order to curtail or transmute witchcraft projection, parents must have access to social values, and ancestors must be made available as powerful yet potentially benevolent figures who invite positive identification and fantasy.

Rather than asking whether some societies are more or less repressed, it seems wiser to turn to Obeyesekere's question concerning the public scope given to fantasy (1981). In societies where public vehicles for fantasy production *and* the means for positive identification – hence, transmuted realisation of fantasy – are widely available, the consequences of the universal human propensity and social need for repression will be distinct.

If I am right that internalisation of Others is critical for maturation and equanimity, then Freud's model of religion as exclusively illusionary – as produced by escaped repression or as a form of gratification – would need to be at least supplemented. When religion serves internalisation and integration, it becomes constitutive of the person or Self. To relinquish it via discursive insight would be to diminish the Self. In fact, to disavow relationality would be to reintroduce something like the effects of repression. The claim that my 'ancestors' are not a constitutive part of my agency is as false as the disavowal characteristic of repression that my 'ghosts' are not the ones wreaking havoc.

Under modernity, as envisioned by Freud, the repressed does not really have a ready means to make a positive return, to be introjected and to enlarge and enliven the Self. Freud's modern rational man is ultimately a highly individuated – indeed, lonely and alienated – thinker. I conclude that Freud is wrong to disvalue religion as illusion. Religion can provide suitable vehicles whereby projections can be lodged and whence introjections can be derived. And in so far as introjections are laid down as part of the psyche, they are no longer fantasy, no longer illusion, but rather part of psychological reality. Religious phenomena thereby take on a psychological reality in some sense analogous to what Durkheim understood as their social reality.

ACKNOWLEDGEMENTS

This essay was originally delivered as a paper at the international symposium 'The Repressed and Its Come Backs: Anthropology in the Shadows of Modernity', held in honour of Bonno Thoden van Velzen at the Amsterdam School for Social Science Research, 10–11 June 1999. I am deeply indebted to Birgit Meyer and Mattijs van de Port for the invitation and for detailed editorial comments, most of which (for reasons of timing) I have not been able to incorporate here. This conference was a lively event, and I remember with pleasure and gratitude the interventions of Melford Spiro, Judith Feher-Gurewich and Rafael Sanchez, in particular. I thank also Ruth Tugendhat-Guggenheim and Zwi Guggenheim for subsequently training their psychoanalytic vision on the argument.

NOTES

1. 'Whatever Happened to the Ego?' is meant to echo Spiro's (1979) query 'Whatever Happened to the Id?'
2. See Lear (2000).
3. Mitchell (1988: 91) depicts the relational perspective as one in which '[f]orms of relationship are seen as fundamental, and life is understood largely as an array of metaphors for expressing and playing out relational patterns: discovery, penetration, domination, surrender, control, longing, evasion, revelation, envelopment, merger, differentiation and so on. The body is still centrally important. Sexuality and bodily experiences are viewed as particularly apt arenas for this activity, since sexuality is enormously multiform and plastic. The number of different body parts, the variability of interactions, the poignancy of the sensations, the immense number of combinations – the almost infinite variety of human sexual possibilities makes this an enormously fertile reservoir of metaphors for expressing different types of relationships, different configurations of connections, between self and others'. He depicts the relational model as the inverse of drive model. For Freud, object relations are the realm in which drive impulses are expressed; for relational model theorists, 'sexuality and body processes are the realm in which relational configurations are expressed or defended against' (ibid.: 92). Mitchell's option is to see 'developmental continuity as a reflection of similarities in the kinds of problems human beings struggle with at all points in the life cycle. Being a self with others entails a constant dialectic between attachment and self-definition, between connection and differentiation, a continual negotiation between one's wishes and will and the wishes and will of others, between one's own subjective reality and a consensual reality of others with whom one lives' (ibid.: 149).
4. Relational models also have the virtue of eroding the authoritarian nature of psychoanalytic practice found in both the orthodox and Lacanian varieties.
5. This work has been funded by the NSF (1975–6), the National Geographic Foundation (1985) and, throughout my career, by the Social Science and Humanities Research Council of Canada, to whom I am much indebted. Mayotte is an island in the Comoro archipelago that was appropriated by France in 1841 and that passed from an oppressive regime of sugar plantations in the nineteenth century to free-hold subsistence and cash-cropping followed, in the 1980s, by the collapse of agriculture and the infusion of capital and infrastructure, as Mayotte edges towards complete integration within the French state.

6. My first book on possession (Lambek 1981) was gently criticised by Obeyesekere for omitting the subjective or deep motivational dimension. My second book (Lambek 1993a) moved from a structural account of possession to one that emphasised practice. This book certainly alluded to the psychic strength of certain mediums, a picture to which the current essay adds. Space does not permit me to demonstrate this as completely as I would like.

7. Poets and all those who take on the burden of historical witness might be included in the ideal type of the medium, while those who are objects of desire, laughter, etc., belong in the type of the witch. Mediumship expands the Self, whereas the witch suffers a loss.

8. Within possession as it is practised by Malagasy speakers, I see three movements or phases that provide opportunities for positive transmutations. The first concerns the onset of possession, often but not always as a response to trauma, or as a step towards articulating and acknowledging particular relations or relational issues. The second has to do with the way possession provides a unique and privileged communicational context in which something like the privacy and heightened transference of the analytic setting can be provided in a face-to-face community (Lambek 1993b, Antze and Lambek n.d.). The third concerns the way mediums integrate the presence of their spirits in their daily practice, especially by means of the observance of taboos (Lambek 1992). At all stages of possession, communication between host or medium and spirit is significant both directly, via dreams, and as mediated by third parties, who are often possessed mediums themselves. In what follows, I restrict myself largely to retroactive reports (from the third 'movement') of the first 'movement'. At the same time, the ethnography will escape the bounds of my schematic formulations.

9. Also relevant is the relationship of the spirit to spirits present in other mediums. In Mahajanga, Madagascar, even more critical is the historical identity of the spirit and its place in the royal genealogy (Lambek 2002, 1998).

10. *Tromba* are deceased Sakalava rulers and their associates.

11. For an analysis of this process as a form of articulating kin ties, see Lambek (1993a, 1988a).

12. *Patros* are spirits indigenous to Mayotte. Although human-like in many respects, they are a different category of being and assimilated to Islamic *jinn* (Lambek 1981).

13. A third possible source of dreams is the *rohu* of a dead person, typically a relative or friend who can come and tell you something.

14. In addition, Suleimana represented qualities of youthful male bravado, energy and violence, which Mohedja no longer wished to be a strong part of the persona she presented to the world. Some spirit-mediums continue to perform as youthful and at times outrageous male spirits until they are well on in years (Lambek 1988b).

15. On the complexities of healers extracting sorcery from themselves, see Lambek (1993a).

16. I do not take the 'true self' of this passage to refer to something essential, intrinsic, prior or complete.

17. In certain contexts, it may be apposite to refer to them as collective fantasy as well (e.g. Thoden Van Velzen 1995).

18. These processes may be connected in other ways. Bloch (1986) has argued that ancestral power is derived from capturing the vitality of youth and thus serves in part to channel or control it.

BIBLIOGRAPHY

Antze, P., and M. Lambek. 'Privileged Discourse: Reflections on Communicational Parallels in Psychoanalysis and Spirit Possession.' Unpublished manuscript. N.d.

Bloch, M. *From Blessing to Violence*. Cambridge, 1986.

Boddy, J. *Wombs and Alien Spirits*. Madison, 1989.

Chodorow, N.J. *Feminism and Psychoanalytic Theory*. New Haven, 1989.

Comaroff, J. 'Consuming Passions: Child Abuse, Fetishism, and the "New World Order."' *Culture* 17 (1997): 7–19.

Comaroff, J.L., and J. Comaroff. 'Occult Economies and the Violence of Abstraction: Notes from the South African Postcolony.' Max Gluckman Memorial Lecture, 1998.

Crapanzano, V. 'Introduction.' In *Case Studies in Spirit Possession*, ed. V. Crapanzano and V. Garrison, 1–40. New York, 1977.

Fingarette, H. *The Self in Transformation: Psychoanalysis, Philosophy, and the Life of the Spirit*. New York, 1963.

Freud, S. *The Future of an Illusion*. Trans. J. Strachey. New York, 1961 [1927].

Kohut, H. *The Restoration of the Self*. New York, 1977.

Lambek, M. *The Weight of the Past: Living with History in Mahajanga, Madagascar*. New York, 2002.

———. 'The Sakalava Poiesis of History: Realizing the Past through Spirit Possession in Madagascar.' *American Ethnologist* 25, no. 2 (1998): 106–27.

———. 'Monstrous Desires and Moral Disquiet: Reflections on Jean Comaroff's Consuming Passions: Child Abuse, Fetishism, and "The New World Order."' *Culture* 17 (1997): 19–25.

———. *Knowledge and Practice in Mayotte: Local Discourses of Islam, Sorcery, and Spirit Possession*. Toronto, 1993a.

———. 'Cultivating Critical Distance: Oracles and the Politics of Voice.' *Political and Legal Anthropology Review* 16, no. 2 (1993b): 9–18.

———. 'Taboo as Cultural Practice among Malagasy Speakers.' *Man* 27 (1992): 19–42.

———. 'Spirit Possession/Spirit Succession: Aspects of Social Continuity in Mayotte.' *American Ethnologist* 15, no. 4 (1988a): 710–31.

———. 'Graceful Exits: Spirit Possession as Personal Performance in Mayotte.' *Culture* 8, no. 1 (1988b): 59–69.

———. *Human Spirits: A Cultural Account of Trance in Mayotte*. New York, 1981.

Laplanche, J., and J.-B. Pontalis. *The Language of Psycho-Analysis*. Trans. D. Nicholson-Smith. New York, 1973 [1967].

Lear, J. *Happiness, Death, and the Remainder of Life*. Cambridge, Mass., 2000.

Loewald, H. 'On Internalization.' In *Papers on Psychoanalysis*, H. Loewald. New Haven, 1980a [1973].

———. 'On the Therapeutic Action of Psychoanalysis.' In *Papers on Psychoanalysis*, H. Loewald. New Haven, 1980b [1956–7].

Meyer, B., and M. van de Port. 'The Repressed and Its Come Backs: Anthropology in the Shadows of Modernity. Opening statement for the International Symposium.' University of Amsterdam, 10–11 June 1999.

Mitchell, S.A. *Relational Concepts in Psychoanalysis: An Integration*. Cambridge, 1988.

Obeyesekere, G. *The Work of Culture: Symbolic Transformation in Psychoanalysis and Anthropology*. Chicago, 1990.

———. *Medusa's Hair: An Essay on Personal Symbols and Religious Experience*. Chicago, 1981.

Schafer, R. *The Psychoanalytic Life History.* Freud Memorial Inaugural Lectures. University College, London, 1976.

Spiro, M. 'Whatever Happened to the Id?' *American Anthropologist* 81 (1979): 5–15.

Thoden Van Velzen, H.U.E. 'Revenants That Cannot Be Shaken: Collective Fantasies in a Maroon Society.' *American Anthropologist* 97, no. 4 (1995): 722–32.

Žižek, S. 'You May! Slavoj Zizek Writes about the Post-Modern Superego.' *London Review of Books*, 18 March 1999, 3–6.

Chapter 9

THE DISCOURSE OF 'RITUAL MURDER'

Popular Reaction to Political Leaders in Botswana

Ørnulf Gulbrandsen

In re-engaging the classic theme of sorcery and witchcraft in African anthropology, it is asserted that something new is happening in terms of the manifestation and magnitude of the phenomena that are commonly included in these notions.[1] Geschiere, for one, claims that 'nearly everywhere on the continent the state and politics seem to be true breeding grounds for modern transformations of witchcraft and sorcery' (1999: 6). And Jean and John Comaroff (1999) speak of escalations of what they label 'occult economies' in post-apartheid South Africa, escalations they also trace in other parts of the world, including the West and the post-communist East.

Although the intensity and public character of what seems to be going on in various parts of Africa apparently resemble the witch-hunting that took place during the colonial era, it has been argued that 'witchcraft' in post-colonial times is situated in a new kind of context that transforms it into something else. The Comaroffs, for example, maintain that '[i]n its late twentieth-century guise … witchcraft is a finely calibrated gauge of the impact of global culture and economic forces in local relations' (Comaroff and Comaroff 1993: xxviii–xxix). And Geschiere (1999: 214) enquires 'why there is such a strong tendency in many parts of post-colonial Africa to interpret modern processes of change in terms of "witchcraft"'. He argues that 'the paradoxical combination between, on the one hand, "globalization" with its connotations of open-endedness and unboundedness, and, on the other, "identity" seems to require definition and clarification that can help us to understand why "witchcraft" or related moral concerns play such a prominent part in people's perception of modernity' (ibid.: 216).

These statements are thought-provoking when addressing such a case as the present one: the heightening concern amongst people in Botswana about what is conceived as 'ritual murder'. Generalising notions of 'globalisation' and 'modernity' raise, however, a number of theoretical difficulties, amongst others because of their lack of analytical distinction. Case studies help to overcome some of these difficulties, as they speak more specifically about these notions in ways that also account more carefully for the dynamics internal to the phenomena in question.

In Botswana, celebrated virtues of European modernity – representational democracy, bureaucracy and commoditisation – have been introduced with great force by the post-colonial state. In replacing the allegedly arbitrary exercise of power by the rulers of the 'traditional', 'patrimonial' Tswana polities, these central elements of European modernity have been advocated as major instruments to ensure 'social justice' and 'development'. In this essay, I suggest that 'development' has, in reality, meant anything but 'social justice'. It has, most apparently, involved an escalation of wealth discrepancy, leaving almost half of the population below the official poverty line as spectators to the aggregation of power and wealth amongst a small elite (see, for example, Gulbrandsen 1996: 223ff., Good 1993). 'Development' in this case thus compares well with the European modernity in its sense of commodisation and individuation of the economy. This is a kind of development which is, to be sure, closely related to the highly exceptional (in an African context) integration of Botswana's political economy in global systems of beef and diamond trade (see Gulbrandsen 1996).

My concern here is how people's experiences of the major political and economic changes are reflected in specific conceptions of 'occult practices'. I will concentrate on their formation as a distinct discursive practice, resembling Scott's notion of 'hidden transcripts' (1990: 4). This discursive practice has been propelled by the peculiar ways in which Tswana notions of power abuse, as these are conceptualised through Tswana cosmologies of the kingship and of power, have been actualised in the contemporary contexts of representational democracy, bureaucracy and market economy.

If anything, notions of occult practices focus on the problematics of power, specifically their intensely constructive/destructive ambiguous dynamic. Because of this, they involve deep, existential moral concerns (Evans-Pritchard 1984: 51ff.). These aspects are accentuated in contemporary globalising processes. They find particular focus in the phenomenon of 'ritual murders', which, as I will show, enliven a discourse of empowerment among the poor and otherwise disadvantaged.

General forces of globalisation and modernity are a background to what I will argue. But a thorough understanding of current developments in Botswana demands that close attention be paid to the way the past is reconfigured in the present. Thus, the phenomenon of 'ritual murder' achieves its discursive force through post-colonial transformations in the structuring of power and its ideological legitimation. A reduction in analysis to general globalising processes would fail to comprehend the crucial mediating factors.

I shall anchor this analysis in an earlier study of Tswana kingships, in which I explained that ambiguities of power are located at the heart of the polity – the ruler being simultaneously the supreme benefactor (a benevolent despot) and the potentially most dangerous sorcerer (Gulbrandsen 1995: 421). I shall argue that this pervasive ambiguity of power reinforces people's alertness and strong concern about the personal character of any individual in a position of influence, high or low, 'traditional' or 'modern'. Above all, it constitutes a strong discursive practice that impacts upon popular reactions to power abuse.

The Tragic Death of Segametsi and Its Aftermath

The point of departure is the tragic death of a 14-year-old secondary school girl and the popular responses triggered by this event. On 6 November 1994, the body of Segametsi Mogomotsi was found outside a school fence in Mochudi, the major village of the Bakgatla, one of the Tswana-speaking peoples of southeastern Botswana. This village is located less than an hour's drive from the capital of Gaborone. While I was not in the field when the murder occurred, repercussions flowing from it and other similar cases were still strongly evident both later in 1994, when I returned to the field, and still in 2002, the time of my latest fieldwork. The continuing concern with Segametsi emphasises the significance of this case in the popular imagination.[2]

Among friends and acquaintances, the murder was often discussed, and everyone was prepared to proffer an opinion. 'We were all terribly shocked', one women told me, 'she had been killed in the most brutal manner ... the murderers had taken away her private parts.' This fact, often repeated, is the distinctive characteristic of what people generally identify as a ritual murder. Beyond expressions of tremendous anxiety caused by a young girl being murdered in the midst of the village, many of my informants were horrified by their own image of the brutality of such a murder: 'Do you know what these cruel people do? People say that they cut off the private parts while the person is still alive! They believe that it becomes even more powerful in that way. It is terrible! Terrible! People are so scared.'

It is a generally agreed opinion that the genitalia of a young girl comprise an extremely potent 'medicine', known as *muti*.[3] I heard numerous similar accounts of babies and young girls, especially, who had vanished. In the words of one man:

> The problem is that the police never find the bodies. People are terrified by what is going on; they are *so* afraid of leaving their children alone. People are disappearing in Botswana these days, I am telling you! Therefore, people have become very, very upset by this case, because this is not the only one. There are many, many! And do you know what? They are always increasing when election is approaching. Why? That is the time when the big politicians feels a need of strengthening themselves. They make themselves invulnerable and lucky in attracting electoral support – and they can make other politicians flat and useless.

Everyone I spoke to about this issue expressed very clearly that 'all of the disappearances', which have allegedly increased in number since independence, are connected to 'all those people who now go for riches, fame and power'. As one put it: 'We have no other way to explain how some people become very rich overnight.'

It was therefore certainly not to anyone's surprise that shortly after Segametsi's body had been found, the police arrested two prosperous businessmen who were also politicians. On the contrary, rumours that these particular individuals were involved in occult practices had already been circulating. However, the police were unable to establish sufficient evidence to keep them in custody, and they were released shortly afterwards. This was followed by the arrests of four other persons, three of whom were also both prosperous businessmen and involved in politics. The fourth was, in fact, Segametsi's father, who was kept in detention because it was claimed that he had confessed to being involved in the killing of his daughter. But the former three were also released due to lack of evidence. The three businessmen-cum-politicians allegedly celebrated their release – an occasion at which the paramount chief of the Bakgatla, *kgosi* Linchwe, was also believed to be a participant. We shall later see the significance of this.

The community was enormously provoked by the release of the suspects, as one newspaper report recounted:

> Enraged schoolchildren take to the streets, vowing to find the murderers of their schoolmate, Segametsi. The students are met by the police who try to disperse them, a few kilometres from the school. Hell breaks loose and a serious clash ensues. The students win the first round of the battle and proceed to Sekobye's (one of the suspected murderers [who was released]) and set his home alight. They also burn Kgetsi's home (another suspect [also released]) and as in Sekobye's house, nothing is retrieved from the house. Boulders, bushes, stumps and rubbish bins are used to block the roads. Soon the Molefhi Secondary School students join the fray, and the students fight the police, who have since been joined by the paramilitary riot squad.[4]

During the confrontations with the police, several youths were seriously wounded and one was killed.

Although the youths were the activists here (cf. Durham 1998), it was stressed to me by many of the adults in the village that the schoolchildren were encouraged by their parents. The release of the suspects inflamed more general sentiments relating to the widespread fear of ritual murder, which implicates those 'who become rich overnight' as the perpetrators of such crimes. A press article of an interview with one of the released suspects, touching on the reasons for his arrest, reported: '[I]t was because of rumours doing the rounds in Mochudi that he uses human parts to enhance his business. He said that the problem started after he had bought himself a Land Cruiser....' Defending himself, he 'challenged the Bakgatla to follow their custom by going to the grave of Segametsi and apply traditional medicine to determine the real culprit'.[5] It is significant that all of the people who were detained by the police and attacked by people were successful businessmen and politicians.

The political tension became such that one of the district councillors sued another on the grounds that the latter had interrupted his speech during a political rally, shouting 'Segametsi o kae? Segametsi o kae?' (Where is Segametsi?). He also complained that during another rally, the defendant had stated, with alleged reference to him: 'You are hereby warned to be on guard, because there is a lion on the loose in the village. The lion today masquerades as a sheep but when it reveals its true colours, it is capable of destroying you.'[6]

The force of popular anger directed towards prosperous business people was further expressed in subsequent riots (16–17 February 1995) by university and secondary school students in the streets of Gaborone, in which windows were broken and numerous stores damaged. Stories about occult practices amongst people who 'in ways we cannot otherwise explain' were becoming wealthy seem to have intensified during this period. They found confirmation some months later when a 25-year-old man from Kanye[7] was brought before the High Court and prosecuted for having murdered and dismembered a six-year-old child. The police discovered the forearms of the deceased behind the accused's sofa. In his confession, he reportedly stated that he had 'killed the child so that he could strengthen his liquor-selling business'.[8] About the same time, fears of ritual murder spread in Maun,[9] where a three-year-old girl went missing. In this case, 'the police together with tribal authorities called a *kgotla* meeting at the Maun *kgotla* to hear a group of traditional doctors throw bones and speak to the ancestors to determine what could have happened to the girl.... The doctor [said] she is not alive'.[10]

More than a year after Segametsi's murder, *The Botswana Guardian* informed an official in the district administration of the details of an alleged confession made by Segametsi's father a few days after the murder. Apparently, Segametsi's father, a relatively impoverished person, stated that he had been pestered by a businessman in Mochudi who promised him P 1200 (c. US$ 220) to find a child for *muti*, the purpose being to 'strengthen' his bottle store, which was about to be opened. They agreed that one of the businessman's employees should lure Segametsi away, and on the following night the father should appear at an agreed upon place to receive the money where '[I] found five people in the vehicle with the child. She was then bound.... When we got to the ponds, three of the men got off the vehicle and took a canvas material and Segametsi with them.... I could hear my child grunting pitifully in an attempt to scream....'[11] This disclosure, however, produced no further action in the disposition of the case; Segametsi's father was in fact judged insane and released from custody. Nonetheless, the news only reinforced the Bakgatla's suspicions not only of the father but also of the businessmen who had been arrested and then released.

The overall anxiety concerning ritual murder in Botswana that the Segametsi case aroused was elaborated in countless other stories describing the mysterious dimensions of the occult quality of such murders. A particular feature of the murders is that in almost all instances the body is never found. The body is so well hidden, people say, 'that even the flies cannot find it', meaning that the murder normally takes place far out in the bush, the body being buried deep into the Kalahari sand. The exceptional thing about the Segametsi case was that the body was actually found.

The fact that the youths acted as spearheads of a much broader popular movement against people of power and wealth is evident from the events that followed. The people of the village gathered in a major *kgotla* meeting, the *kgotla* being the popular assembly or council of the Tswana, headed in this case by the paramount chief since the meeting was held in the royal *kgotla*. They had come to meet with high government officials, including the attorney general and two cabinet ministers who arrived under heavy police protection. These officials made every effort to reassure the gathering that everything was being done to identify the murderers. No one, however, was convinced. Moreover, the paramount chief, the *kgosi*, was subjected to intense criticism and accused of having influenced the police in deciding to release those detained. This was substantiated, so the critics said, by the *kgosi*'s participation in a celebration held by the businessmen following their release: 'After all, he was known to be their close friend.' The situation became uncontrollable, and the governmental officials and the *kgosi* needed police protection in order to escape the crowd. As they drove away, their cars were stoned.

During this meeting, the attorney general declared that the government would call in Scotland Yard detectives to investigate the murder of Segametsi. A few days later, *kgosi* Linchwe called for a *kgotla* meeting in order to select a group of tribesmen to be made available for the detectives. But the debate again centred on the role of *kgosi* Linchwe. One of my informants, who had been present, related that 'the *kgosi* was so heavily attacked in the *kgotla* that he was weeping! We have never seen anything like that. His uncles declared, "We do not trust you anymore."' The press reported that co-operation with Scotland Yard was rejected on the grounds that the people 'did not have any confidence in them as they were being called in by the government, and therefore open to manipulation.... The meeting then reportedly ended in a stalemate'.[12] After the meeting, the people went on to destroy the property belonging to those allegedly implicated in the murder. Another riot ensued, culminating in confrontation with the police and heavily armed security forces.

These events triggered the mobilisation of university students in the capital of Gaborone. Joined by a number of other people from less wealthy sections of the city, they marched towards the Parliament where they forced their way into the members' chambers and ended up in a major battle with the police. The president's bodyguards were seriously injured, upon which soldiers entered the university campus and beat up students. This precipitated another street riot the following day, leading to another confrontation with the police and soldiers. A number of students were seriously injured.

The government was now under heavy attack in the press and otherwise for the harsh way in which state power had been implemented. In Mochudi this had even involved the killing of a youth. This case contributed, in due course, to polarising the relationship between the state and the public. All this was exacerbated by the fact that there was no progress with the Segametsi case. In due course, Segametsi's father was judged insane and released from custody, and the Scotland Yard report to date has not been released by the government. The whole situation encouraged widespread rumours, travelling well beyond Mochudi village, that the actual recipients of the *muti* derived from Segametsi's private parts were people located in high official positions.

The dramatic riots in the wake of Segametsi's murder were unique in the recent political history of Botswana. Nothing of the kind had happened before, and the people themselves were surprised – indeed, in a state of shock. The peaceful, harmonious order of political life in Botswana, an idealisation no doubt, seemed to them to have been completely shattered.

The tragic story of Segametsi continued to engage people as a central theme in private encounters, often giving rise to a number of other stories about vanished children whose disappearance was accounted for by reference to the occultic practices of the rich and powerful. About a year after the murder of Segametsi, a group of youngsters in the village of Mochudi performed a play 'about the ritual murder centred around a man who wishes to become rich and arranges the abduction of a young girl so that [she could be killed], only to find that the young girl they murder [is] his own daughter'.[13] The event certainly provided a general catalyst for the political action of youths in Botswana (see Burke 2000, Durham 1998). However, I shall concentrate on the significance of the events surrounding Segametsi's death in the critical discourses of Tswana politics.

Trust and Power

The discourse revolving around Segametsi's murder articulates contradictory aspects of ruler-subject relations at all levels of Tswana society. In order to understand this, it is necessary to outline the cultural construction of Tswana power relations as customarily centred in their kingship or 'chiefdoms', known as *morafe* (pl. *merafe*). At the time of Botswana's independence in 1966, most of the Botswana population were incorporated in eight such *merafe*. Until the mid-1980s, when processes of urbanisation accelerated, almost the entire population was living in rural villages, the major ones numbering in the tens of thousands. Each village is divided into wards responsible to a ward headman, and every ward is comprised of a number of patrilineal descent groups based on virilocal residence at marriage. The descent groups are each subject to the authority of the most senior agnate. The ward headman together with the senior agnates of the descent groups constitute a council that used to meet on a daily basis at the centre of the ward. The headmen are placed in a hierarchical sociopolitical order, with the king at the apex of the polity (see Schapera 1938; cf. Gulbrandsen 1996). These are polities that gained strength during the nineteenth century, due in large part to increasing interaction with the larger world (Gulbrandsen 1993). In many aspects, they were further reinforced during the colonial period within the context of the Bechualand Protectorate (Gulbrandsen forthcoming).

The supreme authority of the Tswana *kgosi* or paramount chief is acknowledged by the saying 'the king is the shepherd of the *morafe*'. The *kgosi* is not only rich but ideally generous, the source of wealth for all – he is *motswadintle* (the one from whom good things come). This benevolent ideal is stressed in such proverbs as 'kgosi ke mosadi wa morafe' (the king is the wife of the *morafe*) and 'moja morago kgosi' (the king eats last). The *kgosi* would dine daily 'in the open air, taking pieces of the boiled beef ... distributing them in his fingers to each one of the dozen rich men who always accompanied him.... The ritual advertised before all villagers the mutual dependency and ideal solidarity of the richest men of the realm' (Wylie 1990: 32; cf. Burchell 1824: 449). This custom signified the king and kingship as being at the centre of a political system founded in commensality and mutual dependency.

In order to perform the role as a benevolent, distributive and potent centre, the *kgosi* controlled the tribal herd and a common granary. The herd and the granary symbolised the condition of the Tswana polity. In Tswana thought, tension and conflict are closely associated with destructive forces and ancestral punishment, manifesting themselves at the level of the *morafe* in the form of drought and pestilence, resulting in the death of cattle and children. A ruler should be wise and forceful enough to preserve societal order in accordance with ancestral morality and to defend the people against external enemies. He must ensure *kagiso*, or peace and social harmony. The Tswana say that 'the dwellings of fierce men become ruins in ashes, the meek live quietly by reason of their meekness' but 'peace gives plenty of corn'.

Thus, people see their welfare, health, fertility and prosperity as being a matter where social tension and conflict are contained and virtually absent – the ideal state that Tswana call *kagiso* (harmony, peace). This condition is maintained by the unselfish exercise of authority. It depends on appropriate forms of the distribution of wealth in accordance with the hierarchical rules of rank and seniority, and is not subject to individual interest or favour. A failure in this economy of power generates animosity and jealousy, breaking the ideal of *kagiso*. Such an ideal is pursued through the institutions of the *kgotla* (public assemblies) and the *dingaka* (diviner/medium). The *kgotla* signed the grounding of the *kgosi*'s power as being in the social consensus of his subjects and his openness to the people. The *dingaka* was the instrument engaged to heal and, importantly, to protect the agents of power and their subject population.

This concern with *kagiso* is connected with the widespread horror of occult attacks, indigenously known as *boloi* (sorcery). Even the *kgosi* cannot easily escape them; on the contrary, he is believed to be a main target of powerful magic,[14] which aims to make him soft (*nolohala*) or, even worse, 'flat' (*papetla*), that is, politically impotent. In order to fortify the royal office (*bogosi*) and his own person, the *kgosi* is ideally entrusted with the most powerful doctors/magicians (*dingaka*, sing. *ngaka*) of the entire *morafe*. Most importantly, the *kgosi* extends such forms of protection to his subjects.

In explaining to me the value and importance of the hierarchical order, at the apex of which is the *kgosi*, some of my acquaintances told me how the *dingaka* of the *kgosi* supply forceful protective magic to the headmen, who pass it on to bolster the protective magic of ward headmen, heads of descent groups and family heads. Similarly, the most potent productive magic, especially the kind used to attract rain, is vested in the royal office, and its benefits pass to the people as a whole (Schapera 1971).

All of the practices connected with 'magic' are conceived as aspects of power inherent in all relations, including those of the family. These idealised and magical features of authority relations echo, to be sure, those of Weberian patriarchy, which have in many respects been ideologically continued as integral to the legitimacy of the republican state of Botswana. Such magically based authority is substantially different from that described for modern states (see Coronil 1997, Taussig 1997). The magicality of the contemporary Botswana state is grounded in cosmological meanings and practices that are integral to the everyday life in a 'traditional' but no less contemporary setting of Tswana life in rural areas.

In the above context, it must be stressed that the protective magic of the Tswana king and headmen is not primarily related to fear of external enemies. On the contrary, such damaging and destructive forces are predominantly perceived as intrinsic to the order itself. This has much to do with the protective and productive measures provided by the *dingaka*. Such measures are perceived as extremely vulnerable to destructive magic – to occult attacks – and efforts are thus always made to deal with them in secret. This is paradoxical in view of all the emphasis otherwise being placed upon openness, sociality and commensality, all of which are considered essential to *kagiso*.

What this means is that at the core of the political order – focused in persons of authority – are located the basic contradiction of the system: enemies of the social order are not, I repeat, necessarily external agencies of occult forces. On the contrary, in popular imagination, agents of dangerous occult forces might well be situated at the heart of the social order, driven by such highly disapproved motivations as greed, selfishness and jealousy. Even the supreme authority of the *kgosi* himself is closely monitored by his subjects, who are highly concerned with the potential for abuse of power. This concern is heightened by the fact that the *kgosi* is the major operator in the secretive dealings with the most powerful agents of magic – the *dingaka ya kgosi* (the king's doctors). This ambiguity is perfectly reflected in the proverb 'A king is like a knife; he might cut his sharpener', the sharpener (those who give him power) being his subjects.

In other words, this is a system that is perceived as inherently both highly necessary yet dangerous and threatening to human existence (cf. Gulbrandsen 1995: 423–4). The crux of the matter here is the fundamental distinction that the Tswana make between position and person, the ideals of a peaceful order and the always questionable character of its agents. These are realities of life that are not restricted to relations surrounding the royal office. They encompass all positions of authority of the *morafe*, including that of the family head. It is in the light of contradictions between collective responsibility and individual greed, care-taking and selfishness that I realised why people so often expressed the idea that 'it always depends upon the nature of the person', and why they so often engaged in extensive discussions about a person's character. This is reflected in the centrality of the popular discursive field of the *kgotla* in Tswana life-worlds and in their idealising of a life in the public space. That is a highly inclusive discursive field in which authority figures on all levels are committed to exercise their power in the open and are thus kept under surveillance on a daily basis. The perceived critical character of the open-hidden dimension in relation to the exercise of power is, as we have seen, epitomised by the occultic discourse which set the moral limits of the exercise of power.

The contradictions and tensions that this discursive practice catches up in the Tswana polity as it may have existed in pre-colonial times is, I suggest, intensified in colonial and especially post-colonial conditions. In the contemporary situation, occultic discourse now gathers up contradictions at the heart of the post-colonial state, whose political and bureaucratic processes are often more closed and removed form public surveillance than most processes once engaged by Tswana kingship and subordinate offices. In the post-colonial situation, this discursive practice transcends the limits of the Tswana *merafe* and gains, as I shall now explain, particular significance in terms of popular responses to political leaders within multiple contexts of the modern state.

Transformations of People's Everyday Lived-in-World

When I first came to Botswana in the mid-1970s, most people were still located in their natal villages within contexts similar to those that had existed for decades, if not centuries. To make a living, most people depended upon labour migration to South Africa, supplemented with subsistence farming. The modern state established itself on the basis of the existing socio-political hierarchy of the *merafe*. A pan-Tswana elite occupied state offices while retaining a firm footing in the *merafe*. The different forms of power were equally modern and interrelated.

During the two first decades of independence, until about the mid-1980s, Botswana was characterised by a great deal of optimism regarding its development. Wealthy people became increasingly wealthier, essentially because the state heavily subsidised their livestock production. Access to well-paid jobs in government and private industry was facilitated by government-supported higher education. The development of a modern state infrastructure and state social services, as well as programmes of urban development, cushioned the population against an economic downturn occasioned by South Africa's reduction of recruitment of migrant labourers, which had been a major support of Botswana's economy (Gulbrandsen 1994).

Expectations of the benefits of modernity were encouraged by political rhetoric buttressed, furthermore, by the increase in state resources as a result of foreign aid and the lucrative expansion of the diamond industry. However, developing from the early 1980s, I recorded an undercurrent of dissatisfaction, especially among those who remained as spectators to the immense accumulation of wealth among a small number of families. The relatively disadvantaged started to speak of government officials as 'fat stomachs', often wondering how relatively young people could afford their attractive cars and appear in such nice suits. Dissatisfaction amongst the vast number of unprivileged people was particularly apparent in urban areas. They expressed their discontent by withdrawing their electoral support of the ruling party.

The criticism of the new rich as persons who had manipulated social connections into the government was brought to the forefront of public consciousness in a series of corruption scandals in the early 1990s (Good 1994). Senior government officials were accused of illegally appropriating large tracts of extremely valuable residential land in the vicinity of the capital. During the succeeding years, a number of similar scandals followed. These cases nourished all kinds of other rumours of government-based corruption relating to the securing of government loans, access to otherwise unobtainable grazing and water rights, and so on. It is impossible to say how well founded these widely circulated rumours were. Nonetheless, throughout the 1990s, 'corruption' was on the lips of most. The feeling of general corruption has since gathered pace. It was associated with a current economic recession, reflected in a steep rise in unemployment among educated youth and further compounded by both the drying up of opportunities for migrant labour in South Africa and substantial job cuts in the urban construction industry at home. There is now a hiatus between the expectations encouraged by political rhetoric and the gathering harsh economic realities.

The discrepancy between expectation and harsh actuality is the condition in which an occultic discourse gathers its significance. But such discourse is not a mere expression of political and economic circumstances in the surface/depth sense that still prevails in much anthropological analysis. The occultic discourse is integral within social and political processes, as much a part of the ground as it is of the surface. It is more than a cognitive frame for the interpretation of experience, and plays a political and socially constitutive role, both creative of dimensions of the contexts of which it speaks and vital in structuring an emotional and passionate orientation of people in Botswana towards a situation in which they achieve some agency in changing their circumstances: a process in which the occultic discourse itself comes to have effect.

I have already explained that concerns about occult forces are intrinsic to the lived-in-world, at least in the rural context of the *morafe*. There is also a sense that magical potencies have to some extent broken free from their control and integration within hierarchical social orders. They are not subordinated to the social in the same way as they once were. It is commented upon that the *dingaka* are often now operating independently of the collective control of the *morafe*, the *kgotla* and extended kin, and are serving individual interests that stand in opposition to the social order as a whole. A discourse of urban/rural contrasts is one relation within which Batswana grasp the magical nature of current realities, many dangerous *dingaka* now being seen as resituated among urban neighbourhoods of strangers. Ambiguous enough as internal forces, they have intensified their danger, as it were, in their reconstitution as malevolent powers of the outside.

Here I note that a discourse of rural/urban contrasts (imaginary constructs of the nature of everyday realities) that centres on the role of *dingaka* might also be grasped as one that refers to a process whereby power, in its magical aspect, is perceived as having separated itself from the social body (the body of the people) and as now acting in opposition to the social body or the social order. More broadly, this is a development that works in favour of a state that is no longer in a constitutive relation to society, but is conceived as oriented destructively against it.

Thus, the town is regarded as the negative inversion of the idealised harmonious village life, much along the lines of an earlier functionalist anthropology that conceived of urban life as the dysfunctional image of rural existence. Such an imaginary is driven in political and economic actualities (e.g. of economic depression) that are particularly manifest in urban areas. This draws on factors that are sharply apparent on the surface and which are determined through a rural imaginary that is no less part of contemporary experience (constantly moving between town and country, urban Batswana continually make comparisons, describing the one as the alternative of the other). Some of the marked differences of urban life relate, for example, to the heterogeneity and geographical diversity of the population and the density of living conditions. The specific exigencies of urban living – problems with finding employment, navigating the local bureaucracy, gaining access to educational opportunities, acquiring property and establishing local security – result in these aspects of urban life being realised as negative qualities that demand the magical intervention of *dingaka*. The magical powers of *dingaka* are to a great extent associated with the negative dimensions of urban life and, paradoxically, are seen to intensify their potency and destructive possibilities in such contexts. They are, moreover, associated with the expanding social inequalities that are manifested acutely in urban space – individualised inequalities that themselves are imagined as the inverse of the idealised caretaking responsibilities vested in the hierarchical order of the *merafe*, as these are no less imaginatively conceived.

Power, Wealth and Suspicions of Occult Practices

The events surrounding the death of Segametsi gather much of their import as part of a general discourse concerning occult forces which sees them as a dimension of the negativities of recent political and economic developments. Vital within this discourse is a critique of the state, which is already within the construct of Tswana cosmologies of the state as these are articulated in relation to the kingship. The destructive magical force of power becomes dominant when such power separates from its social integument, from its embeddedness in social relations. This occurs when power withdraws from contexts in which it is subject to moral and social surveillance. If, as Foucault suggests, the power of European states is in their capacity for social surveillance (rather than being the object of surveillance), the Tswana kingship (as idealised and imagined) is a state which has its power controlled and limited in the surveillance of its agents by its subjects. As such, it is a polity that has some resonance with the idea that Pierre Clastres (1989) developed in his celebrated attempt to distinguish the nature of non-Western political orders from the ideas (in political science and in political anthropology) to which they were conventionally subordinated.

The point I pursue here is that the Segametsi case and related occultic discourse highlight the magical negativity of the modern state through conceptions relevant to the Tswana state as idealised. Furthermore, this idealisation or imaginary is a consequence of the fact that in contemporary Botswana, forms of social and political relations relevant to the pre-colonial state as idealised continued into modernity, and did so as a conscious ideological intention of the formation of the post-colonial state of the Republic of Botswana (Gulbrandsen forthcoming). Moreover, while social and economic discrepancies and inequities underpin the general anger that surrounded Segametsi's death, this anger expands its force and effect through a discourse of the occult that engages its feelings of outrage at the offence to Tswana political and moral value that the modern state has paradoxically harnessed to its own legitimation.

To ensure the legitimation of the republic, government officials engaged the village *kgotla*s in the establishment of the new order (Gulbrandsen forthcoming). The public was encouraged to present their needs in the forums of the *kgotla*s, at which government policy was also presented. During the formative period of the independent, post-colonial state, government agencies largely succeeded in establishing the state upon the socio-political order of the Tswana *merafe*. In particular, the first president of Botswana (Seretse Khama), the heir to one of the major Tswana kingdoms, quite successfully appropriated much of the symbolic wealth vested in these kingdoms. The state manifested itself as a *motswadintle* (the one from whom good things come), after the ideal of Tswana kingship (Gulbrandsen 1995).

Under the rule of President Khama, that is, until about 1980, the state established its legitimacy as the supreme agency of welfare and prosperity – and thus of *kagiso*. The nation-state appropriated to itself that moral space for the exercise of power previously restricted to the *merafe*. But, of course, the modern nation-state and its bureaucratic order constitute an entirely different socio-political construction to that which they ideologically appropriated and encompassed. The manner of the encompassment, however, exposed the agents and agencies of the modern state to a critical discourse that was once appropriate to the problematics of power in the circumstances of Tswana kingships. The discourse was now all the more intense because of the socio-economic contradictions of modernity. The organisation of power in modern states – and Botswana is no exception – is

bureaucratically hidden. In terms of the ideology of the *kgotla,* which the instruments of the state appropriated, such secrecy was indicative of abuse of power
(suggested by the refusal of state agents to be surveyed and morally controlled by
their subjects) and, further, of the involvement of state agents and their associates
in malevolent sorcery. Such a contradiction was generated and exacerbated in the
very contemporary scheme of things. Thus, the more officials used the *kgotla* as
a mechanism of public consultancy (as in the events surrounding Segametsi), the
more they became subject to the critical discourse of the occult which perceived
them as being engaged in dangerous, anti-social and secretive practices.

The state bureaucracy, idealised in Western discourse as a depersonalised
decision-making system in the sense of treating all citizens on an equal basis,
appears from the point of view of many Tswana as a field par excellence of the
secretive exercise of power, as a field beyond popular inspection and control. It
is thus the very antithesis to the idealised public space of decision-making, that
is, the *kgotla*, where the personal character (*botho*) of authority figures is monitored on a daily basis. In a bureaucratised polity, on the contrary, people see
few or no possibilities to gain information about the character of people to
whom they are subjected.

The hidden and therefore dangerous potential of the bureaucratic order of the
modern state is also conceived as a dimension of what is viewed as the mount-
ing individualisation of everyday life. In urban areas, people of power and wealth
live increasingly apart. To be sure, they remain located in kinship networks that
often include poor people, and they frequently visit their natal village where they
encounter unprivileged people. However, in their everyday life in urban areas,
they are mostly located in separate residential areas, moving around in luxury
cars and thus contrasting radically with the idealised traditional elite who used
to feature centrally in public life and who took pride in being approachable and
available to everyone. Hiding behind solid walls in gardens watched by vicious
dogs, these people increasingly manifest a symbolism of distance, superiority
and, indeed, exclusiveness. The warning sign on their gates – *tshaba ntswa*
(beware of the dog) – has gained considerable symbolic significance in popular
parlance. These features coincide with personal extravagance and the development of a culture of conspicuous consumption – epitomes of selfishness and
greed. Such persons are readily conceived as witches and sorcerers in a discourse
of the occult. In their individualised success they exceed the moral bounds of
that ideology founded in the ideals of the *kgotla* and *kagiso*.

The speed with which such people have risen to prominence is of particular
significance for comprehending the anger and anxiety that they inspire. For it
follows from notions of a hierarchy of forces and their agencies that such a
degree of success and prosperity is seen as necessarily depending upon access
to particularly powerful *muti* – that is, *muti* derived from human beings. This is
reflected in all the circulating stories – such as 'when election approaches, more
and more children are disappearing' – that reinforce this conception. The plots
contained by these narratives express, in my interpretation, a fundamental anxiety about being subjected to a state that is increasingly in the hands of people

who are governed by hidden agendas and engaged in secret combats from which they draw tremendous benefit, but which are highly destructive to the society as a whole. Many people share this anxiety and anger because they have, with considerable enthusiasm, approved the establishment of the state and, in many respects, placed their faith and destiny in this all-encompassing polity, on similar ideological terms as they were once subordinated to the *merafe*.

Overall, there is a sense of public betrayal by agents of the state. These agents have seemingly broken their compact with the people to an extent that makes moral questions related to the exercise of power increasingly acute, especially to all unprivileged people who remain spectators to those who rapidly accumulate wealth and conquer positions of power. This is a trend that contributes forcefully to the notion of a state leadership that 'eats our children', and, by virtue of rivalries for state resources, creates disruption producing destructive 'heat'. Such action negates the cooling potency of *kagiso*.

This aspect of Tswana modes of political thought, anchored in the cosmology of the *morafe*, is exemplified by the public attack on the once beloved *kgosi* Linchwe in the aftermath of Segametsi's murder. The anger directed towards *kgosi* Linchwe had much to do with the fact that he used to be the highly respected and much praised custodian of the moral order by virtue of chairing the royal *kgotla*, often appearing as a brave, eloquent challenger of senior governmental officials when they came to address his people. He had been recognised as a true protector of *kagiso*. For this reason, in particular, people were annoyed by his decision to leave the royal office to accept the president's offer of the chair of the customary court of appeal, a position firmly located in the central government.

In the wake of *kgosi* Linchwe's appointment, all kinds of suspicions developed about his being co-opted and corrupted by powerful governmental officials. His association with the alleged murderers only confirmed the view that he had lost his integrity. And it was rumoured that he was the one who secretly conveyed to 'people in high places' the *muti* derived from Segametsi's private parts. This allegation was, of course, grounded in the extremely ferocious way that the government had responded to the students' protests, in the rumour that *kgosi* Linchwe had influenced the police to release the suspects, and in the police force's apparent ineffectiveness in identifying and apprehending Segametsi's murderers. All this, and the potential malignancy of continuing government secrecy, was compounded in the government's refusal to disclose the findings of the Scotland Yard investigation.[15]

These various aspects relating to *kgosi* Linchwe's involvement in the Segametsi affair constitute what can be referred to as the 'hidden transcript' underlying the events. That is, contradictions relating to the hybridised structure and practice of the state were brought to the fore. *Kgosi* Linchwe was, for example, a focus of countervailing forces regarding the performance of power. Thus, his association with members of a new class and apparent secretive action of state bureaucracy exposed him to the criticism that he was abusing that power appropriate to the Tswana kingship authorised by ideals of openness and availability to public scrutiny. Integrated into the bureaucratic form of the modern state, the ideas of the *merafe* are no less integral to the modernity of the contemporary Botswana republic. And it is by this fact that a discourse of the occult achieves its force, by identifying agents of the state as the magical consumers of its symbols of beneficence – its children – and as being engaged in the sorcerous destruction of a social order that they should ideally generate.

Conclusion

Botswana is regarded by many as a success story of African democracy, in marked contrast to many other nation-states on the African continent. Furthermore, it has been able to weather many of the economic difficulties of other states because of the continuing importance of its cattle and diamonds on the world markets. Globalising forces, of course, still have their effect and undoubtedly influence the distinct processes in Botswana relating to social inequities that other scholars have discussed in the context of sorcery practices elsewhere. However, I have concentrated more on mediating conceptualisations and institutions of social and political power in the context of the modern state and their critical significance in grasping the import of occultic practice.

While some of the general statements that have been expressed by anthropologists concerning witchcraft or sorcery in Africa can be applied to my material, the Botswana data indicate some modification. Thus, Chiekawy and Geschiere state that witchcraft discourses have an 'amazing capacity ... to link global changes directly with local realities [because of] their *basic open-endedness*. Witchcraft discourse forces an opening of the village and the closed network: after all, it is *the basic interest of the witch to betray his or her victims to outsiders*. The image of the witch flying off to meet fellow conspirators and offer them relatives is a central one in African societies' (1998: 5, italics added; cf. Geschiere 1999: 215). This statement has some application to the material I have presented, but notions such as 'open-endedness' gloss too much and fail to consider sufficiently either the ideas that are embedded in sorcery or occult discourse, or their production in social and political transformations. I have concentrated on the way notions of sorcery and other malevolent ritualistic practices are related to specific cosmologies of power. In the Botswana situation, sorcery is part of a critical discursive field relating to a context in which the order of a contemporary bureaucratic state aims, to a considerable extent, to legitimise its practices through appropriating ideas and understandings pertinent to the imaginary of that state/society constituted in the terms of Tswana kingship.

These terms, I hasten to add, are not simply an invention of modernity or of the colonial era. The 'invention of tradition' arguments (Hobsbawn and Ranger 1983) miss the fact that in the Botswana situation ideas and practices relevant to Tswana kingship and the social relations of which it was the centre have continued into contemporary contexts as a modernity alongside – and, to a degree, in complementary relation with – the formation of the rational bureaucratic state order of the Western kind. This is a point I believe that scholars such as the Comaroffs (1993) would recognise. What I have pursued here is the contradictions that such continuities open up in the contemporary order of the Botswana state, and especially in the circumstances of the political and economic crises attendant on global developments leading to considerable discrepancies in wealth and life-chances. These processes work into a social and political world in which certain cosmologies of power are in play. The discourse surrounding ritual murders and the anxieties and fears that such discourse propels *in itself*, while conditioned in global economic and political processes, are not a mere expression of those processes. Rather, the discourses I have discussed engage particular orientations to social and political realities which see in them a specific kind of personally and socially dangerous significance. This significance is one that in a way deflects attention away from the global forces that are operating and focuses attention on no less real forces of contradiction that lie at the heart of the historical and political formation that is the contemporary Botswana state.

Undoubtedly, occult discourse in Botswana refracts individual uncertainties and vulnerabilities of an everyday nature that are often connected with unemployment and the many exigencies of urban life, as I have explained. But it is much more than this. It involves some serious problems of the legitimacy of political leadership within the context of the modern state, problems that are as much moral as material. One central feature of such a moral crisis is the fact that the rational order of the bureaucratic state involves practices that must contravene continuing Tswana notions (which agents of the state encourage) that power must be open to the public surveillance of the *kgotla*. The critical discourse surrounding sorcery and ritual murders builds in this kind of contravention that lies impossibly at the heart of the modern state.

Tswana occultic discourse is thus not an irrational expression of uncertainty. On the contrary, it is a response to the conflicting rationalities which are integral to the construction (and legitimation) of the Botswana state and the social order it encompasses. Further, the occultic discourse is directed explicitly to the problematics of power. Most particularly, it addresses the perceived abuse of power, such perception being driven in social inequities and incompatibilities created by Botswana's integration within larger global processes.

NOTES

1. Earlier versions of this article were presented at the 16th Satterthwaite Colloquium on Religion and Ritual in Africa and at the Research Seminar, Department of Social Anthropology, University of Bergen. I thank the participants for all the comments which have been most helpful for the revisions. In addition, I have benefited much from comments and criticism by John Comaroff, Wim van Binsbergen, Harri Englund, Deborah Durham, Suzette Heald, Judith Kapferer, Fred Klaits, Isaac Schapera, Bjarne Vandeskog, Pnina Werbner and Richard Werbner. In particular, I want to express my gratitude to Bruce Kapferer, who has been an important source of inspiration for this work. This work has been financially supported by the Norwegian Research Council.
2. Within the limits of the present essay, I shall pursue the issue of 'ritual murder' predominantly with reference to the particular case of Segametsi, while other cases will be dealt with in works in preparation.
3. *Muti* is a widely used word for 'medicine'. It is, perhaps, significant in this case that it is spoken of as a Zulu loan word. The sorcerous agency of *muti* is a potency of the outside.
4. *Mmegi* (The Reporter), vol. 12, no. 7, 24 February–2 March 1995.
5. *The Botswana Guardian*, 10 February 10 1995, p. 2.
6. *The Botswana Guardian*, 13 December 1996, p. 1.
7. The capital village of the Bangwaketse in the southern district.
8. *The Botswana Guardian*, 16 June 1995, pp. 1–2.
9. The capital village of the Batawana in the north-east district.
10. *The Botswana Guardian*, June 1995, pp. 1–2.
11. *The Botswana Guardian*, 1 March 1996, pp. 1–2.
12. *The Botswana Guardian*, 17 February 1995.
13. *The Botswana Guardian*, 22 September 1995.
14. There is vast historical evidence indicating the extent to which accusations of *boloi* have been a significant aspect of dynastic disputes. See, for example, Burchell (1824: 439, 457, 551–2), Campbell (1922: 166), Livingstone (1857: 118, 137–8) and Mackenzie (1971: 389–90, 404–6, 421–2).
15. As of 2002, the report was still not released, allegedly because identifying the murder(ers) would be detrimental.

BIBLIOGRAPHY

Burchell, W.J. *Travels in the Interior of Southern Africa*. Vol. 2. London, 1824.

Burke, C. 'They Cut Segametsi into Parts: Ritual Murder, Youth and the Politics of Knowledge in Botswana.' *Anthropological Quarterly* 73, no. 4 (2000): 204–14.

Campbell, J. *Travels in South Africa ... being a Narrative of a Second Journey*. 2 vols. London, 1922.

Chiekawy, D., and P. Geschiere. 'Containing Witchcraft: Conflicting Scenarios in Postcolonial Africa.' *African Studies Review* 41 (1998): 1–14.

Clastres, P. *Society against the State*. New York, 1989.

Comaroff, J., and J.L. Comaroff. 'Occult Economies and the Violence of Abstraction: Notes from the South African Postcolony.' *American Ethnologist* 26 (1999): 279–309.

———, eds. *Modernity and Its Malcontents: Ritual and Power in Postcolonial Africa*. Chicago, 1993.

Coronil, F. *The Magical State: Nature, Money and Modernity in Venezuela*. Chicago, 1997.

Durham, D. 'Missing Youth, Social Deictics, and the Social Imagination in Botswana.' Workshop paper, African Studies, University of Chicago, 1998.

Evans-Pritchard, E.E. *Witchcraft, Oracles and Magic among the Azande*. Abridged, with an introduction by E. Gillies. Oxford, 1984.

Good, K. 'Corruption and Mismanagement in Botswana: A Best Case Example?' *The Journal of Modern African Studies* 32, no. 3 (1994): 499–521.

———. 'At the Ends of the Ladder: Radical Inequalities in Botswana.' *The Journal of Modern African Studies* 31, no. 2 (1993): 203–30.

Geschiere, P. 'Globalization and the Power of Indeterminate Meaning: Witchcraft and Spirit Cults in Africa and East Africa.' In *Globalization and Identity: Dialectics of Flow and Closure*, ed. B. Meyer and P. Geschiere. Oxford, 1999.

Gulbrandsen, Ø. 'Positive Power as State Force of Control and Stability: The Case of Postcolonial Botswana.' Ms., Department of Social Anthropology, University of Bergen. Forthcoming.

———. 'Living Their Lives in Courts: The Counter-Hegemonic Force of the Tswana *Kgotla* in a Colonial Context.' In *Inside and Outside the Law*, ed. O. Harris, 125–6. London, 1996.

———. '"The King is King by the Grace of the People". Control and Exercise of Power in Subject-Ruler Relations.' *Comparative Studies in Society and History* 37 (1995): 415–44.

———. *Poverty in the Midst of Plenty: Socio-Economic Marginalization, Ecological Deterioration and Political Stability in a Tswana Society*. Bergen, 1994.

———. 'The Rise of the North-Western Tswana Kingdoms: The Dynamics of Interaction between Internal Relations and External Forces.' *Africa* 63 (1993): 550–82.

Hobsbawn, E.J., and T. Ranger. *The Invention of Tradition*. Cambridge, 1983.

Livingstone, D. *Missionary Travels and Researches in South Africa*. London, 1857.

Mackenzie, J. *Ten Years North of the Orange River, from 1859–1869*. London, 1971 [1871].

Schapera, I. *Rainmaking Rites of Tswana Tribes*. Leiden, 1971.

———. *A Handbook of Tswana Law and Custom*. London, 1938.

Scott, J.C. Domination and the Arts of Resistance: Hidden Transcripts. New Haven and London, 1990.

Taussig, M. *The Magic of the State*. New York, 1997.

Wylie, D. *A Little God: Twilight of Patriarchy in a Southern African Chiefdom*. Hanover, 1990.

Chapter 10

STRANGE FRUIT

The South African Truth Commission
and the Demonic Economies of Violence

Allen Feldman

At no other time more than in the present day has individual, social and institutional memory come under such concerted pressure, critique and exposure as
a fragile foundation for truth and facticity. This current reluctance to authenti-
cate social memory is intimately tied to well-known postmodernist depreda-
tions, which profoundly disenchanted the authority of tradition and authenticity,
and emptied core institutionalised myths of their temporal and semantic continuity. As institutionalised memory fails to provide overarching master narratives
that can win cultural consent, it has also become increasingly disjunctive with
previously unnarratable history and experience. Consider the synchronic fictions
of recent ethno-histories, the historians' debate in Germany on the facticity of
the Holocaust, or even the critique of post-traumatic stress disorder and other
recuperations of traumatic memory whose fictive psycho-medical legitimacy has
been challenged by Alan Young and Ian Hacking.[1]

One perceptual effect of this disenchantment of temporal continuity, ideas
of progress and authoritative historical presence is the flattening of the historical past, which now emerges as a synchronic series of orchestrated and mon-
taged images, of made-to-order and ready-to-wear opportunistic icons – an
endlessly refurbished collation of abbreviated texts and catchphrases. In late
modernity, the line of historical depth-perspective has fractured, which is to
say that a perspectival grasp or depth-vision of the historical eludes us or at
best is comprehended as stylised and illusionary, as artificially bounded as the
perspectival machinations of classical realist painting. Once the tendrils of linear historical time, ideally receding and converging onto a distant horizon of
origin points, became undone, the ability of any recuperative social memory to
travel this temporal ribbon to the counter-reality, the difference, the sheer
intractability of the diachronic was disrupted, if not rendered downright circular.[2] If the advent of mass-produced photography undid the currency of realist
painting, its perspectival artifice and narrative authority, what equivalent has

displaced linear recoupable history, also dependent on the formula of perspective and linear access to a temporal origin point? We may ask: Is the historical, like the realist image, merely a mass-produced artefact of the market necessities of the present?

Yet in tandem with these ahistorical semantic environments, and in the wake of recent campaigns of political terror, there emerges the transnational project of anamnesis, known as the war crimes tribunal and the truth commission, which is devoted to social justice and redress by way of the dignity-restoring and truth-claiming efficacy of historical recuperation. There have been more than 20 such projects since the end of the Second World War, and more are being planned each year in response to the myriad of low-intensity wars against civilian populations, ethnocidal projects and counter-insurgency campaigns, and unreconciled and non-rehabilitated colonial and post-colonial injuries.

Is history an anachronistic indulgence that only the previously oppressed Third World and Eastern European nations alone can afford? Are these truth commissions merely a prelude before such geopolitically marginalised countries sink into the plush sofas of short-term memory characteristic of the developed nations and stable mass media democracies? Alternatively, do these 'truth' projects provide access to critical historical memory, to a much-needed critical relationship to historicity itself? Do they have a wider appeal that transcends the local agenda to rectify former murky wrongs?

Perhaps these agendas of redress and rectification are not so local in their ramification, and the restoration of civil dignity by way of memory is a much wider transnational need than we suspect. Part and parcel of the pathologisation that is imposed on countries struggling with the aftermath of oppression, political terror and violence is that this very struggle with a dark past only further confirms the geopolitical pathogenic character of these former political emergency zones from the perspective of outsiders. As a consequence, this pathogenic stigma serves to ghettoise many countries in democratic transitions, which are busy confronting their past, and, not surprisingly, absolves many other supposedly more stable and long-term democratic nations from facing history. There has been a certain frisson in the developed nations envisioning epochal issues in terms of the turn of the millennium, while South Africa, Chile, Guatemala, Northern Ireland, Bosnia, Kosovo, Rwanda and Cambodia will have to confront the epochal turn in terms of what has passed for modern politics and state formation in the previous century. In pursuing their respective epochal enquiries, many of these post-violence societies are excavating much of the half-buried but still rotting and dimly comprehended geopolitical baggage that all nation-states have hauled with their respective political cultures into the present millennium. This contrast does not make the post-violent nation-states that are engaged in democratisation the historical or political unconscious of the 'West'; rather, it makes 'us' the unknowing bearers of their historical unconscious, for we still relegate to dream and fantasy the very historical material that these nation-states are awakening to with every passing day.

Critical memory, frequently allied with mourning, has become a symbolically powerful counterpoint both to the violence of anti-democratic regimes and other types of human rights violations, and to the incredible capacity of violent states and organisations to generate public forgetfulness and silence through fear, intimidation, communal trauma, disinformation and communicative distortion. Nation-building projects, reconciliation processes and movements for social justice have emerged energised by what can be called 'trauma-tropism'. 'Trauma-tropism' is a term I have borrowed and metaphorised from botany; in that science, it is defined as the reactive curvature of a plant or an organism resulting from a prior-inflicted wound. Single communities and entire societies can reorganise their identities, histories and projects around the curvature of chosen prior 'historical' wounding, and this would be a socially constructed trauma-tropism. Trauma-tropism is a form of collective memory; more specifically, it is a framework and methodology by which a collectivity recalls the past and places it in a dynamic and formative relationship to the interpretation of the present. Trauma-tropes are formations of memory that can cohere into formations of domination: institutional agendas, rules and prohibitions. Trauma-tropes are eventually prescriptive, even though they may initially indicate a point of historical stasis, a punctuation beyond which society cannot narrate itself. However, the stoppages and rupture incarnated in the trauma-trope can direct new narrative procedures, objects and solutions. And a set of ethical and governmental prerequisites have been institutionalised in the transnational discourse of human rights that organically links trauma-tropism to nomo-tropism, a curvature towards law, that is, the relocation of trauma, injury and pain from the individual and community to institutionalised memory, public culture, legal institutions and quasi-legal procedures of redress whereby persons and groups – 'victims of human rights violations' – are expected to overcome historical trauma through a repose in lawfulness.

Has the flattening of historical depth and the ambiguity of memory in part instigated a reactive recourse to trauma-tropism as a new vehicle for historical consciousness? In zones of present and former political emergency – such as South Africa and Northern Ireland, where I have conducted ethnographic research – there is an evident connection between the manipulative flattening, foreshortening and freezing of historical perspective and the turn to trauma-tropic practices, such as critical memory and truth commissions.[3] These political sites are characterised by the social production of memory out of violence on the one hand and, on the other, the state's concerted manipulation of the historical record and public memory of that violence as an instrument of counter-insurgency and of cultural hegemony. At these political sites, the orchestration of history is not solely part and parcel of the ambient perceptual immediacy and commodified media culture of late modernity or postmodernity, but a structural effect and strategy of chronic political terror and violence.

Apartheid-era South Africa was characterised by structural forgetfulness and the fragmentation of public recollection which was, and still is, an institutionally manipulated effect, emanating from: (1) the secret knowledge systems of the state and from once-clandestine oppositional political organisations; (2) the apartheid culture of deniability that extended from the upper echelons of apartheid's ruling organs – government, armed forces, police services and intelligence services – to the everyday class, racial and geographic insularity of most white South Africans; (3) the ghettoisation of social knowledge imposed upon communities of colour by apartheid's geographical sequestration, a race-based inequitable education system, linguistic stratification, the cultural decimation of violently urbanised rural populations; and (4) media censorship and deliberate disinformation campaigns. These factors created a public culture of knowledge fragmentation and forgetfulness, which overlaid a dense mosaic of privatised memories and local knowledge, subversive oral culture and cults of secrecy in both white and black communities.

The effect of information stratification by race, class and locale, and by disinformation and censorship, is still evident today. The fragmentation of social knowledge, historical recollection and cultural memory cannot be underestimated in post-apartheid South Africa. The South African Truth and Reconciliation Commission's (TRC's) mission and ethic of retrospective transparency by public institutions and political parties, of promoting a national session of confessional truth-telling, of opening secret archives and of institutionalising a culture in which victims give witness through its hearing process was a deliberate and ethically necessary attempt to address this legacy of fragmented social knowledge and memory. The transvaluation of the South African public sphere through disclosure, transparency and remembrance was considered to be a foundational stage of the state's democratisation and a core mission of The Truth Commission. The concealment of human rights violations and the sociological denial of the degree and depth of such violations were considered by the TRC to be as serious a moral offence as the actual acts of violence and atrocity themselves. The moral imperative of historical attentiveness, that is, the ethical responsibility to know and to be accountable for what is or can be known, underwrote the TRC's notion of truth and its project to interdict an institutional culture of deceit promulgated by the former apartheid state.

The following questions remain: What type of historical consciousness can be generated by a project to defragment historical knowledge, to redimensionalise historical experience through disclosure, confession, mourning and institutional redress? Through what methods will this defragmentation occur? Does this unification of historical knowledge and social cognition necessarily coincide with the unification of a polity as inferred by the concept and mandate of reconciliation? These are all issues in process in the contemporary public culture of South Africa, and the publication of the TRC's final report in October 1998 has not come close to resolving such conundrums.

In this essay, I shall discuss certain technologies of memory deployed by the TRC, particularly in its amnesty hearings. I will also show that mobilising memory is not only a vehicle for the recuperation of a violent past, but a technique, desire and performative achievement of the very political terror investigated by the TRC. Thus, social memory itself should be an object of contextualised human rights enquiry. Any truth commission's acts of recall and recuperation must necessarily contend with how social memory functioned in the midst of the very human rights violations and atrocities that the commission excavates, and this focus is particularly apt for understanding the cultural linkage between the socio-economic or structural violence and the transacted or performed violence of the apartheid regime – two levels of political domination that the TRC was often accused of artificially separating. If South Africa is to come to terms with a terror-ridden past, then it must be through a knowledge of how certain memory formations contributed to the creation of that violent past. We need here a socio-cultural history of anamnesis, a critical 'memory of memory' in order to remember a future that moves beyond the pathogenesis of political terror and human rights abuse.

A multiplex history of an era of human rights violations will need to take account of social memory as cultural form in all its incarnations, anchoring, utilities and affect, for it is from this dense and intractable material that any project of social justice and reconciliation must unfold. Consequently, in this essay I turn to alternative trauma-tropes, the history of violent labour discipline, sorcery-related practices and beliefs, and perceptions of the demonic in order to explore what is left out of the machinery of anamnesis activated by the liberal-rationalist historiography of the TRC. The uncovering of multiple and positioned readings of the same events is the prime task of this essay. However, in presenting alternative readings, I make no claim that the local level or diachronic reading of events is inherently more totalising and exhaustive than the TRC's reading of these same events. All of these readings are positioned and necessarily incomplete in so far as their current lack of interface and dialogue in South African public culture still refracts the after-effects of the apartheid era's sociological fragmentation of public memory and knowledge.

Truth commissions, like any historiographic project, are mediated by the trinity of time, place and person, and are thus exercises in authoritative and hegemonic, yet partial and skewed, historical memory and forgetfulness. It is politically crucial that normative frameworks, narrative structures and forms of witnessing are dissected, discussed and interrogated at the level of public policy and scholarly enquiry. At the same time, truth commissions cannot be simply critiqued and dismissed from the idealised and fantasised perspective of a non-existent and unrealised panoptic history. Idealistically dismissing truth commissions for the sin of capturing only partial historical truths and narratives is ultimately the sociology of the obvious; at the very least, what is seen as incompleteness is but the prelude to analysis, and should not serve as a dismissal and closure. By placing the public memory generated by the TRC in conversation with alternative historiographies, my goal is not to achieve a totalising history, but rather to contribute to a still necessarily incomplete and partial multidimensional cultural history of human rights abuse in South Africa.

Amnesty and the Ideology of Excuse

Due to its commitment to legal realism and the ad hoc therapeutics of 'the talking cure', what was the capacity of the TRC to approach the infliction and receipt of terror and violence as an organised continuum of meaning and identity, and not simply as a sequence of politically expedient or irrational or amoral acts that can be dismissed once publicised and condemned? Debates on these different interpretations were waged in public forums and associated with particular political parties and their respective strategies of remembrance and chosen historiography. Thus, the National Party and its supporters in the army and police depicted operatives of the state apparatus who perpetrated human rights violations as aberrant agents, whose stigmatisation would restore the integrity of the security forces while ensuring continued moral and political deniability for current opposition politicians and police and army upper command structures. Moreover, the psycho-theological tendencies of the TRC were used to reinforce such medicalising, psychologising and individualising interpretations of state-legitimised atrocities.

Amnesty hearings were the most controversial of the activities of the TRC. They were structured as modified adversarial adjudications in which the burden of proof rested with the applicant. The three criteria applicants had to meet were (1) full disclosure for the human rights violation for which indemnity was being requested; (2) demonstrated political motivation for the act; and (3) proportionality, that is, the moral ratio between the political goals and the violent methods used to realise those goals. The criteria of proportionality is potentially the most complex one to apply, as well as the most contentious. What measures can be applied to proportionality when it comes to acts of violence rationalised by arguments for a just war? In the context of amnesty hearings, the proportionality criteria could ideally foreground the irrationality of systemic institutionalised violence and recuperate the racialised socio-economic historical conditions that informed and patterned many of the atrocities committed by the state's security apparatus. However, the 'securocrats' of the former government were indemnified by demonstrating the first two criteria of full disclosure and political motivation. Where political motivation had been demonstrated in an amnesty application, no such application was denied for failing to meet the proportionality criteria. And although the killers of Steve Biko were characterised by the amnesty court as committing disproportionate violence, their amnesty application was officially denied on the grounds of failing to demonstrate 'political motivation' for their medical neglect of Biko. In effect, Biko's torture/interrogation was seen as politically motivated, but his post-torture medical neglect was not considered by the amnesty judges to be a political act. Can this division between the political and non-political be upheld, and can disproportionate or excessive violence be allowed to remain within the liminal conclusion 'lack of political motivation'?

One of the senior evidence leaders of the TRC's amnesty investigations had told me at the time of the Biko verdict that proportionality has been unofficially dropped as a criteria for denying amnesty, especially when political motivation is demonstrated. He and other evidence leaders had attempted to demonstrate lack of proportionality in hearings, to no avail, and this was borne out by the granting of amnesty in cases in which political motivation was demonstrated but the proportionality of the violence deployed in relation to mandated political agendas was clearly not evident. Indemnification based on political motivation situates most political violence within existing ideological rationales and does not challenge formal justifications for the use of force – it sanctions the truth claims of instrumental rationality in regards to political terror. For example, members of the former regime's security forces frequently cite anti-communism as a justifying motive for human rights abuses against youths and children (who never heard of this ideology) and for the practice of torture. In cases in which political motivation is not demonstrated, a normative void frames the act of violence at issue.

For much of the South African media, for a significant portion of the white public and for representatives of the former apartheid state, excessive state violence does not originate in the state apparatus or in the historical culture of racism, but rather in the behavioural and moral pathology of individual perpetrators – 'bad apples', as former General Magnus Malan put it under questioning by the TRC in October 1997 in Cape Town. This perspective obscures any clear understanding of institutionalised racism, its inflection of the terror of the counter-insurgency campaign. Conversely, granting amnesty based on the applicant's anti-communism can hardly be seen as the 'stripping away of the lofty excuses' of apartheid, as one apologist for this approach put it to me.[4] In my view, the signifying of racist violence in coded terms such as 'lack of political motivation' merely aids and abets existing social denial syndromes concerning racism in the white community and defaces the structural contexts of racist norms in the South African public sphere.[5]

Strange Fruit

(sung by Billie Holiday, words and music by Lewis Allen)

> Southern trees bear strange fruit
> Blood on the leaves
> Blood at the root
> Black bodies swinging in the southern breeze
> Strange fruit hanging from the poplar trees
> Pastoral scene of the gallow south
> The bulging eyes and the twisted mouth
> The scent of magnolia sweet and fresh
> Then the sudden smell of burning flesh
> Here is a fruit for the crows to pluck
> for the rain to gather
> for the wind to suck

for the sun to rot
for the tree to drop
Here is a strange and bitter crop

Amongst the numerous human rights violations and amnesty hearings dealt with by the TRC was the case of the Pebco Three. In this infamous incident of political 'elimination', three Black Civic Association activists were kidnapped by *askari* (double agents and informers), then beaten and executed by the police on 5 May 1985, near Cradock. One of the implicated policemen, Colonel Roelf Venter, described the scene of interrogation at an amnesty hearing held in October 1996:

> [W]e went to Cradock where Major Winter, the commander of the Cradock security branch took us to the place where the three captives were. It was an old police station in the Cradock area. We had a barbecue and had some drinks and the three captives were with us but their faces were covered so they were not able to see us. I could see them, and it had not appeared [that] they were in any way harmed.... I am not entirely sure what happened to these three ... persons nor did I hear afterwards what had happened to them.

The amnesty judge was fascinated with the positioning of the barbecue – or the *braai*, to give its local Afrikaans name – in the interrogation scenario.

> *Judge Wilson*: I've heard several cases where when people are being questioned the police who were doing the questioning are enjoying a braai, was that happening here?
> *Colonel Venter*: No. I did not interrogate them and I don't know whether they were being interrogated. They were in the vicinity but there was no interrogation conducted as we normally conducted interrogations.
> *Judge Wilson*: When you say in the vicinity were they outside where you were having a braai?
> *Colonel Venter*: Correct.
> *Judge Wilson*: Can you give any reason why they should have been brought out there, why they weren't kept shut up?
> *Col Venter*: No.

The Port Elizabeth paper *The City Press* of the 4 December 1994 does tell us what happened. It quotes a Sergeant X who made three statements regarding the Cradock incident. According to him, the Pebco Three were enticed by a telephone call to meet a British diplomat at the Port Elizabeth airport, and were driven straight to Cradock that very night by *askari*.[6] They were interrogated and assaulted with knobkerries (short, knobbed sticks) and pistol butts while the police held a barbecue, which was part of the scenario of the interrogation and not a postscript, as Venter claimed in order to remove himself from the scene of torture. Subsequently, the three activists were executed, their bodies burnt and the remains dumped in a river.

Anti-apartheid activists who had heard stories of interrogations or had undergone interrogations themselves understood the police *braai* as a code for assault and murder, as in the following case from Port Elizabeth in 1985.[7]

Mr Mpompi Melford Dlokolo: I could hear some cars driving in, these people (the police) had come to see this person and when Gerber came, he said 'So this is the Mpompi', then another foreigner from Port Elizabeth came –. He came and there were three whites with me and they were saying they were going to have a braai and I knew they were referring to me.... There is a farm not far from Humansdorp – as you go down there are also some bushes and then we go round those bushes and Faleni said I should go and collect wood. I said 'No, I am not going to'.
Rev. Xundu: Is Faleni the only person who you knew?
Mr Dlokolo: Yes, Faleni was the only black amongst whites. One of these white policemen was from Port Elizabeth. These were the two people who were torturing me. Faleni was asked to accompany me to go and collect wood so that they could make a braai, because we were heading for Uitenhage. Then I refused, I said there is grass, there is no wood. I didn't even plead, I just refused, so they made their braai next to the Kombi, then I had my thing, I was holding it fast and I was sure they were not going to do anything to me. So, we went to the police station, that is I was going to take an oath, before Kayamier who could see – Kayamier was a Judge in Humansdorp and they could see that I was bleeding.

The consumption and culinary imagery of the barbecue appears in the following testimony of T. Mvudle, given about his police interrogation in 1985 at Khutsong, where he was a leading member of the local youth/student organisation.[8]

At about one in the afternoon they called me. They said I seem to know a lot and I have been organising a lot. They requested information about the children who would go to Botswana and Zambia.... They took a shambok from the van.... They took our shirts off and then started assaulting us with shamboks. We kept on denying, saying we do not know. At about three they put a fire on. They had a braai. They would take us one by one. There was a forest nearby where they would take us. After coming back from the forest you just would not be able to talk. I would ask the others what happened. They would say no, we have been really beaten up at the forest.

At about four they took a group from amongst us. Four of us were left behind. The boys (his fellow captives) were braaiing meat. (the police) were saying they do not know what they are going to do about me because I had put them in trouble. Van Wyk was drinking brandy the whole time. He said that they are all the same. They took the fork that they used for the meat, and came to me. I was half-naked. He put it on my back. This mark is as a result of that assault. They burnt me. They said that I would tell the truth....

On other occasions, the police use the *braai* to humanise their relationship with their captives and insulate their own conscience from the violence, and as a cover-up strategy for recent acts of brutality, as evidenced in the amnesty hearings of the notorious torturer Jeffrey Benzien, here speaking to his victim:[9]

Mr Benzien: Could you remember the time that you had seen snow for the first time? Can you remember what happened in the snow? The husband and the wife and the two children who were taking photos of you playing in the snow along the N1? Your trip to Colesberg, where you braaied with me that night and with the rest of the Unit, therefore Mr Forbes, in the spirit of honesty and reconciliation, I am sure you are making a mistake about the 16th of every month [being] the day that I would assault you....

Mr Forbes: I would just like to say that these are all occurrences that I can clearly remember. But then to continue could I then ask Mr Benzien, apart from I think the impression that you are giving this Commission is that we went on these joy trips in the snow and for braais and so forth, can I put it to you that it was always after an assault of this nature, that we would be taken on these trips and that the intention of these trips was to ensure that the injuries would heal and that I would actually not get into contact with the District Surgeon?

Most of these acts of police cover-up took the form of burning the bodies of victims, in order to conceal both the acts themselves and the identities of the deceased. Charity Kondile, speaking on the kidnapping and execution of her son Sizwe, centres on the culinary aura of the disposal of her son's body.

Well, Dirk Coetzee goes on further to say that when he died, they put his body on a pile of wood with a tyre near the Komatiepoort River at night, where it took them nine hours to burn his body. Dirk Coetzee further states that twice they were burning his body, the flesh was smelling good and they were having beers at that time. So it was like a braai to them. As a mother I feel that, no matter whether it was politics, fighting for his land, I don't think he deserved all that treatment. I feel it was grossly inhuman. I feel they could have killed him and gave us the body or left it in the veld there, I feel that this was tantamount to cannibalism, or even Satanism.[10]

In July 1996 in Pretoria, investigators of the Fidelity Guards security firm and former policemen Hennie Gerber and Johan van Eyk petitioned for amnesty. The applicants claimed that they (along with co-investigator Frans Oosthuizen) had been in part acting on behalf of the National Party when they murdered suspected Pan-Africanist Congress member Samuel Kganakga on 21 May 1991. They had been investigating the robbery of R60,000 supposedly committed on behalf of the Azanian People's Liberation Army.[11] Advocates acting for the amnesty applicants told the TRC that Gerber's and Van Eyck's actions had been politically motivated and thus met the Commission's requirements for amnesty. The amnesty applicants regarded themselves as agents of the police against what was at the time seen as a communist-inspired onslaught against the state.[12]

Gerber, one of the amnesty applicants, described the abduction of the victim and the locale of the murder: 'He was ... taken by vehicle to this open field, I decided to go to Cleveland forest area where we usually had braais.' Their captive was bound and hoisted up by his legs so that he was hanging upside down. This was at about 9.00 a.m. Nkoana, an African employee of Fidelity Guards, witnessed the interrogation.

Mr Gerber ... came with a bag with some extra ropes in (it) also, it seemed like old telephone (wire). And then he instructed the deceased to sit down, tied his legs with a rope and used a piece of stone as the tree was very high, you know, to tie that stone to the rope and then throw it over the blue gum tree. They did that. They started hoisting the deceased upside down on that tree, and then after that they tied the rope on the tree. And they further untied his belt and ... they pulled his trousers up and took out this torturing machine (electric shock apparatus)[13] ... and started (connected) one wire on his finger and then the other piece of wire on his private parts.

Kganakga was questioned while the electricity was applied to his genitals. He continued to deny all knowledge of the robbery that he was suspected to have played a part in. Nkoana continued: 'I could see that the deceased was crying and starting jerking while hanging upside down and he was crying very badly. And while he was doing that, it seems they were enjoying the thing because they were laughing.'

After the application of the shocks, which lasted for about an hour, Kganakga was left hanging upside down on the tree for most of the day until about 5.00 p.m. He was lowered from time to time for more shock treatment but then hoisted back onto the tree. Nkoana was never told to ask Kganakga about his political affiliations. Later, Nkoana was sent by Gerber to buy 'cool drinks': '[T]hey said to me I must go to the shop to buy some cool drinks, because it seems maybe they have had enough (of torturing). They have been trying to get the information from Samuel, but all the time he was denying.'

When he returned, Gerber and van Eyk had retired to their vehicles about 200 metres from the tree. They were drinking whisky and vodka. Gerber explained the drinking of alcohol as follows: 'During these types of investigations and interrogations alcohol is always used. No right-thinking person can act in this way without your conscience plaguing you.' However, Gerber never made any reference to the laughing, the joking and the interrogators' connoisseur-like perusal of their handiwork that accompanied the torture and the alcohol consumption, which imbued the occasion with a recreational atmosphere.

Every now and then they returned to where Kganakga was hanging to continue the torture and questioning. During the course of the day, while Kganakga was hanging suspended from a tree, Van Eyck collected leaves that were lying in the vicinity and set a fire under the captive's head. It was his evidence that the intention was not to cause any injury to Kganakga but to further intimidate him by causing him to breathe in the smoke.

At 5.00 p.m. Nkoana was told he could go. Kganakga was lowered and brought back to the vehicles by the torturers. His face was swollen, his eyes were bloody and red; he could hardly walk, and he had marks and abrasions on his legs. Gerber then claimed that despite having hung upside down for most of the day, and in spite of his swollen legs and multiple abrasions, Kganakga was able to jump up, charge Johan van Eyck and grab him. 'That was when I realised that we had big problems', Gerber testified. As their captive ran in the direction of the mines, Kganakga was allegedly shot and killed while attempting to escape. It was decided to get rid of the body, and Gerber took the corpse to a deserted spot where he poured petrol over it and burnt it. Later, Gerber took the body and chopped off one arm, which had not been burnt, to prevent identification of the body. After the disposal of Kganakga's remains, the security guard put it about that one 'terrorist' had been killed during the course of the robbery. Nkoana reported for work the next day. He stated: 'On arrival at the office, the first person I met ... was Frans Oosthuizen. He then said in Afrikaans, "Moenie worry nie, ons het hom gebraai" [Don't worry, we have braaied him].' Thus, the disfigurement of Kganakga accompanied his categorical transformation and abstraction from an individual and co-worker of his torturers into a charred specimen of a fictive 'terrorist'.

Braai is Afrikaans and South African English for an outdoor barbecue, and *braaiing* is a ubiquitous weekend recreational practice throughout South Africa. Associated with sports competitions, hunting, the frontier geography of the bush, relaxation and alcohol consumption, it is also part of the political culture of white male dominance. *Braaivleis* is the name for the meat that is consumed at such events. It is my contention that at the *braai* and torture sites described above, consumption, commensality and violence were integrated, and that this synthesis seems to have become a convention – to the extent that one cannot immediately discern from Gerber's testimony of past *braais* held at the Cleveland Forest spot whether he refers to actual barbecues, to interrogations and torture, or to both.

This association of *braaiing* with torture and interrogation speaks to issues that have concerned theorists of torture and political terror since Arendt's meditation on Nazi banality. I refer to the incorporation of everyday life practices, objects and associations into extraordinary scenes of violence and terror, a dynamic which serves to normalise the violence for the perpetrators and which conversely refracts the increasing penetration of a culture of terror into the quotidian. At Kganakga's *braai* torture and those of others, consumption and commensality serve to normalise excessive brutality and to inure the perpetrators from the human consequences of their acts. Distancing and depersonalisation of the victims began with the hooding of the captive, the erasure of a face, of individual identity. Kganakga's disfigurement is further enhanced by inversion, by hanging him upside down, and this is elaborated by successive acts of disfiguring violence.

Torture has been universally described by its practitioners with the culinary imagery of 'softening' the suspects so that they will want to relinquish their information. Kganakga's body, for instance, was subjected to an elaborate and baroque series of culinary-type procedures that had little to do with the extraction of information: he was hung upside down like a piece of meat; he was 'softened' by electric shock attacks; he was smoked and cooked by fire; he was dismembered and butchered – his body transformed into leftover refuse. In the meantime, the laughing perpetrators consumed 'cool drinks' and alcohol.

These atrocities transformed Samuel Kganakga into an object of food consumption and recreation. Nkoana, one of two black witnesses, was obviously not part of this commensality. He misinterpreted the call for alcohol as the termination of torture and as a sign of the ex-policemen's frustration with their captive's denials; however, drinking was necessary to intensify the commensality of the violence. Gerber may have told the TRC that he drank due to a bad conscience, but it would not have advanced his amnesty application to advertise that he drank as a form of recreation and pleasure during torture. However, the inducement of anesthesia by alcohol, as claimed by Gerber, supports my point that the consumption practices and commensal dynamics of the torture served to inure the perpetrators from the consequences of their acts, from the pain they were causing. I would suggest that this physiological anesthesia is a component of a wider socio-cultural anesthesia which informed the racial treatment of Kganakga and which was manifested by the transmutation of the prisoner into something bestial – an artefact of consumption – and a racialised specimen and political commodity.

With regards to Kganakga's culinary dehumanisation, it is clear that the defacement of his personhood proceeded through a process of animalisation. Animalisation transforms the racial Other into prey, and in this instance communicates with the economic and food consumption metaphors of the *braai* that further deface – and by inference politically commodify – the victim's body. In Kganakga's case, the electric shock treatment, the hooding and hanging like a haunch of meat, and the attempt to burn the victim's head are techniques of racist cuisine, of changing the raw into the cooked, the individual into a specimen, Kganakga the security guard into a fictive terrorist and a political artefact that could be circulated as a triumph within the culture of securocrats.

In the TRC archives there are dozens of transcripts from the state security forces in which the act of *braaiing* features as commensal and recreational activity, as the site for casual police social gatherings, as a predominately male space, as a way of passing the time during the evenings in cross-border operations in the bush, and as a celebration of the completion of successful counter-insurgency operations. In reported incidents of human rights violations, the *braai* also appears in the midst of interrogation episodes entangled with the scene of torture, as an apparatus of torture and as a tool for covering up the tracks of torture and murder through the burning of bodies. These disposal fires are almost always termed *braais* or compared to a *braai* in TRC hearing testimony. The victims are always black; white anti-apartheid activists were the recipients of other forms of torture. Anti-apartheid activists who had heard stories of interrogations or had undergone interrogations themselves understood the police *braai* as a code for assault and murder. Being taken to a *braai* by the police meant that a black detainee would be severely ill-treated and possibly executed.

The Political Economy of Violence

> It is largely as a force of production that the body is invested with relations of
> power and domination, but on the other hand, its constitution as labour power
> is possible only if it is caught up in a system of subjection (in which need is
> also a political instrument.... [T]he body becomes a useful force only if it is
> both a subjected body and a productive body.[14]

In reference to consumption and commensality, anthropology has always
attended to *how* societies fashion the substances that sustain them, and here I
want to apply that perspective to bodies of colour as a sustaining substance of the
political terror and of the political economy of the apartheid regime. Consumption, food and commodification metaphors, as repositories of deep cultural memory, served to materially fashion acts of state and neo-state violence in South
Africa. I would propose that there is a mnemonic linkage of the *braai* tortures
described above with prior forms of labour coercion and the economic commodification and consumption of bodies of colour. This linkage can be discerned
at three levels: (1) the relationship of the forms of torture applied to Kganakga
and other victims of *braai* interrogations to the forms of labour discipline violence that ensured the continued commodification and compliance of black
labour in southern Africa from the seventeenth century to the 1980s; (2) the
depersonalisation and bestialisation of the victim's persona into an artefact of
consumption – *braaivleiss* – through culinary deformation and analogous forms
of bestialisation in labour discipline practices in the agricultural and mining
industries; and (3) the evocation of labour subordination performances in the
braai tortures. I would further suggest that the *braai* tortures were theatres that
mobilised antecedent forms of racialised interpersonal dominance and structural
subjugation that could not be practically sustained in the 1970s to 1980s in an
increasingly insurrectionary South Africa, and as such constitute acts of structural nostalgia. Thus, these interrogations, tortures, murders and body disposals,
irrespective of their practical political goals and content, legitimised excessive disproportionate violence that sustained and fed the perpetrators of these atrocities
at multiple levels of act, memory and meaning. These atrocities were re-enactments, material forms of anamnesis for the assailants that had only the most ten-
uous connection to anti-communist political or military strategies.

Here we must reflect on the process by which the racial Other, coercively
deployed as an instrument of economic production, is eventually transformed
into a medium of pleasurable consumption, a process that links violence and the
commodification of black labour with consumption/commensal practices that
elaborate white dominance within the economic culture of South Africa prior to
and during apartheid, and during the counter-insurgency campaign of the 1970s
to early 1990s. I stress the pleasures, fantasy material and satisfactions produced
by the chosen substance in these tortures, and in doing so seek to remedy the TRC
inability's to address disproportionate and racist violence in amnesty hearings.
And I will do so by deploying historical and ethnographic materials that speak to

a diversity of cultural memories linked to such violence that had no status with the TRC. Here one must point out that in South Africa, racism is historically not solely a psychological pathology but also an instrument of economic organisation and subjugation, crucial to the creation and disciplining of a labour force.

Both the violence applied to Kganakga's body and the locale of the torture harbour dense historical associations and genealogies that, I propose, are crucial to understanding the political economy of the body that is both refracted and re-enacted by such torture practices in South Africa during the 1970s and early 1990s. The methodology of torture and the ill-treatment of the body of victims in *braai* tortures and post-execution disposals access an economic memory, a culture of labour discipline, rituals of racial and class relatedness acted out on the terrain of the abused body of colour that are entwined with the cultural memories of white economic hegemony, an economy that was facing a growing political crisis in the 1970s and 1980s when state-enacted *braai* tortures emerged and became routine. The cultural fault line of this crisis, though aggravated by international sanctions and boycott, was situated in popular resistance, clandestine community organising and community-based insurrection that, from the perspective of a racist political economy, could only be viewed as a massive race- and class-based breakdown of labour discipline throughout South African society. Both in customary form and motivation, the *braai* tortures are archaeologically linked with the practices of labour discipline in colonial, post-colonial and apartheid-era South Africa. In turn, such evocations of labour discipline in practices of political torture can be viewed as mutually fashioning the embodiment, social identity and class position of both the aggressors and the victims.

It has been long established that societies do not leap from one economic mode and means of production to another; the latter are structurally related, not least by common ideological apparatuses such as labour discipline. I look to the means of production in three overlapping South African economic epochs to show the continuity and evolution of labour discipline ideologies and practices, tracking these practices as they eventually migrate to counter-insurgency practice. As evocative as it may be, I do not claim that the replication of labour discipline ideology and practices is symbolically expressive of the entire history of racist oppression in South Africa; no such totalisation is asserted here. I do make the link between the *braai* tortures and the discrete history of labour discipline, which does display a certain teleological profile as domination methods shift to and from different economic modes and relations of production that are pertinent here: (1) a slaveholding economy, (2) agrarian tenant/ sharecropping and white agrarian paternalism, and (3) industrial relations of production in the mineral industry. However, the migration of labour discipline practices to the field of counter-insurgency is not a teleological culmination of economic hegemony, but rather something contingent. The translation of labour discipline frameworks from economic domains to political-policing domains indicates that ideologies and structures of economic teleology and hegemony were in crisis in the period of *braai* tortures.

In the Cape Colony, at least one slave per month was publicly executed between 1680 and 1795. A full array of whippings, beatings and punitive amputations was mandated by law. One method of capital punishment was for the offending slave to be crucified hanging upside down from a tree, much in the same way Kganakga was suspended from the gum tree. The bodies of executed slaves were frequently left out in the bush to be devoured by carrion eaters. Slaves convicted of arson, a standard form of slave resistance and insurrection in the seventeenth and eighteenth centuries, were punished by being 'half-strangled and killed' on a 'slow' fire.[15]

The symbiosis between labour commodification and violence that was institutionalised with slavery in the Cape Colony in the seventeenth and eighteenth centuries was greatly expanded in terms of population and geographical scope following the emancipation of the slaves in the 1830s and the military annexation of trans-Ciskean territories in the 1840s and 1850s. It was finalised with the 1913 Land Act – that rapid and violent mass production of a rural proletariat composed of African tenant farmers who had staged an economic recovery in the latter half of the nineteenth century.[16]

Informal 'cajoling' and violent coercion of African labour resources under independent chiefly control was, from the eighteenth to the late nineteenth centuries, transformed into a coercive ideology of rural paternalism and a policing grid rooted in the compound system of the mineral industries. The right to corporeally discipline the underclass of colour had been vigorously defended by slaveholders in the Western Cape since the eighteenth century, when colonial governments had attempted to place half-hearted limits on these practices that were reasserted as part of the coercion of labour in the supposedly free labour market of post-emancipation South Africa. In the second third of the nineteenth century, white landowners, represented by such organisations as the Zuid-Afrikaansche Boeren Beschermings Vereeninging (BBV), promoted an ethic of farm-labor discipline based on patriarchal familial metaphors, a rural labour paternalism that was a key repressive apparatus enforcing class and racial distinctions. By the late nineteenth century, the white homestead, with its underclass of tenant and seasonal contract labourers, was seen as the ideological wellspring for the ethics of 'working, obeying and submitting' that organised racial interaction and class relatedness within disciplinary frameworks. This rural paternalism and its command of violence were advanced as a model in miniature for the South African nation-state as a whole.[17]

As the Comaroffs have extensively discussed, these views were part of a wider ensemble of 'moralised discourses' that posited the issue of African labour disciplining within policing, geographic, theological and medical frameworks. Nevertheless, brute violence existed alongside these ideological apparatuses in the enforcement of labour discipline, particularly in agricultural areas marked by labour scarcity. Rural paternalism was literal; white farmers looked upon and disciplined workers of colour as children, confining them to a world of domesticated subjugation. In the nineteenth century, the Natal Masters and Servants Act (1850) authorised the confinement and dietary punishment of offending farm labourers, and provided a legal framework for a customary law of beatings and floggings that were meted out to black contract labour.[18] The 1932 Native Service Contract Act, section 11, mandated the whipping of offending workers.[19] Based on the results of a study conducted between 1979 and 1981, the South African Council of Churches concluded that torture and other forms of violent disciplining of farm labourers was widespread. The study found a high incidence of workers being beaten naked, having their clothes cut from them before an assault, and having their sexual organs wounded; the Council urged the banning of sjamboks, a kind of whip. In 1986 the Association of Rural Advancement reported that the flogging of workers was considered a 'paternalistic rite' in rural Natal.[20]

The choice of an abandoned mine site as the locale for the interrogation of Kganakga can also be viewed as evoking an economic geography in a South Africa deeply entangled with the processes of violent labour discipline, proletarianisation and class formation. From the late nineteenth century onwards, the mines, with their heavily policed compounds, were essentially run as closed institutions. Further, the induction or initiation of black workers into mine labour resembled many of the more recent intimidation and sensory deprivation techniques used by the apartheid security apparatus in their treatment of political detainees. Mine training focused on coercive conditioning and the initiation of the black worker's body and mind to underground environments. The newly recruited workers were confined to heated, windowless 'acclimatisation chambers', where they received little or no food and water, and were compelled to do physical exercises.[21] Anti-apartheid activists describe being subjected to analogous sensory deprivation regimes in the 1970s and 1980s, involving position abuse, compulsory exercise, and food and sensory deprivation. The mine compounds in southern Africa were militarised sites patrolled by security officers who were recruited from ethnic groups different from those of the labourers. Boss boys, white miners and compound police frequently assaulted black labourers, resulting in large-scale desertions from the mines. In certain mines, recalcitrant workers were placed in cells equipped with 'stocks' and flogged. According to Van Onselen, the whippings were so vicious that it took more than one man to administer them.[22]

And as in the *braai* torture episodes, much of this violence was ideologically advanced through methods of depersonalisation and bestialisation. Ideologies of race-based bestialisation were crucial to the commodification of black labour. On the farms, contract black labourers were given the names of cattle or of wild beasts, such as Bobbejaan (baboon); farm holdings were referred to as being stocked with natives which had to be 'broken in'.[23] Mine workers were perceived by white managers as 'imported stock' that had to be acclimatised to the mines; instead of personal names, workers were known simply by their numbers. The Comaroffs state that the coercive commodification of the black population proceeded through animalistic imagery such as the trope 'beasts of burden'.

The selection of the bush as the locale for the interrogation of Kganakga can also be viewed as evoking a crucial stratigraphy in South African economic violence and labour discipline. Historically, the forced removal of individuals and communities of colour to the bush signified their subhuman and animalised status; the bush was where the bodies of recalcitrant slaves were disposed. The imagery of the bush is made up of contradictory and antagonistic cognitive maps. For Bantu cultures, the bush is positioned by traditional inside/outside polarities such as village/bush, the social/the wild. It is a liminal space for the ritual initiation of male youths and for traditional healers; the animals associated with the bush are symbolic mediators for the human world. However, the bush also resonates with the colonial history of the Xhosa and other African populations being pushed off of fertile lands to infertile margins by the British and Afrikaaners. In Cape Town, coloured working class memory interprets the forced relocation of coloured populations from city centres and nearby suburbs – such as District 6 and Mowbry in the 1960s to the remote Cape Flats – as tantamount to forced exile to the bush and as sealing their animalisation in the state's eyes. The bush was further elaborated as a geography of dehumanisation in the 1970s and 1980s, when it became the scene of clandestine state violence involving interrogation, torture and execution sites such as those described in the testimony cited above; this was a covert political geography that harboured remote execution farms that became the site of grisly forensic exhumations by the TRC. Police and army personnel operating in bush settings for long periods during operations such as cross-border raids referred to the state of being 'bush-fucked', a colloquial term for continued exposure to traumatic violence.

The performative infrastructure and semiotics of *braai* torture and the genealogy of punitive violence detailed above suggest that these episodes were ritualised re-enactments of racialised class relatedness mediated through the terrain of the black male body. The state's *braai* violence transcribed labour discipline codes onto the political template of the insurrectionary and insubordinate male body of colour. And this wholesale transfer of a symbolic economy of class and racial dominance/relatedness occurred when a once triumphant political economy was being challenged by 'labour' insubordination of previously unimaginable scope. In some *braai* tortures, the collapse of the mandated socio-economic and geographical discipline of apartheid was performatively encoded in customary forms of violent labour discipline. In other interrogations this was combined with overt rituals of labour service and structural nostalgia in which the prisoners prepared the *braai* that would later be used for their own torture. The disposal fires rendered many an aftermath of torture and execution into a scenario of commensality and celebration in which the victims were consumed at multiple symbolic levels. The imagined communist onslaught, with its explicit anti-capitalist associations, was the dream form through which the rupture in apartheid's symbolic economy was imagined and projected onto black bodies by the securocrats. It is now all the more curious – if not downright offensive to any human rights paradigm – that this fantasy served as the basis of indemnification in amnesty hearings.

The crime that Kganakga was accused of fit well into this fantasy material. Kganakga had been the black subordinate to Gerber and Van Eyck in their place of employment. The bank robbery attributed to him was a fantasised assault on South African capitalism in the form of violated labour discipline and expropriation of white wealth by clandestine agents of colour. Kganakga was assumed to be a member of the Pan-Africanist Congress, though he was never asked about it at any time during his torture. After his death, he was fictionalised as an unknown terrorist.

The construction of racial and class relatedness through labour discipline is apparent in the conjuncture of subjugated labour, the command of violence and consumption/commensality practice in the following account from Jabu James Malinga, speaking of his torture near Alexandra in 1978, which resembles the labour scenario of Dlokolo's torture described above.[24] In Malinga's testimony, the use of the term *kaffir* and the rehearsal of labour subservience serve to set both the scene of intimidation and the racial and class relatedness between the white policemen and their victim, all of which seem important to the policemen's interrogation protocol. The fact that, as in the Kganakga torture, policemen of colour either assist at or watch these atrocities further accentuates the dramaturgy of domination. We have here the doubled colonial optic of the bestialised black body, fit for punition, labour and burning, and the quasi-humanised black body wearing the endowed uniform, i.e. the discipline of its masters. Thus, the divide between bestiality and subhumanity is a labile one for people of colour in the *braai* theatre.

> And Mtibi and Skieter and ... Van der Linde (policemen), they were in a green Chevrolet. They called me, they said I must get into the car. I wanted to know why. They said, you kaffir, you mustn't ask a lot. Get in. Then I went inside the car and left off with them. They took me into some bush in Alexandra where it is a highway at the moment. They took some meat from the car, they said I must just go and get some wood for them. I did as I was told. And then they said I must make fire for them. Thereafter they said I must braai the meat for them as well. And thereafter they were eating and drinking alcohol.... Then they started beating me. They said I knew too much, they will show me something that I don't know. They handcuffed me and the fire was still burning at that time. They took me towards the fire, they threatened to burn me should I not be prepared to talk the truth. I didn't think that they would burn me or not. Whilst they were assaulting me and the other one lifted my leg they dragged me towards this fire. They started burning me, they said I must talk the truth. I refused because I knew that should I tell the truth they will kill all my companions. Then they burnt me. I was dressed in an overall. When they realised that I was burning they took something to extinguish the fire. They extinguished the fire. They said they wanted to know what we were doing on the 17th June. They wanted the truth. I still refused to tell them. I was just being kicked, I was not aware of what was happening, I was unconscious at that moment. I found myself at the clinic. That is when I became conscious. I can't remember what happened.

The rhetorical search for the truth by the torturers indicates that another type of truth than that of political secrets was being extracted from the abuse of Malinga's body. It is a truth that is not so much encased in what is said or silenced in an interrogation, but a truth and a discourse that was articulated in the methodologies and sequencing of acts of degradation and intimidation that moved Malinga and his interrogators through a series of stylised role sets organised by the iconography of forced labour, consumption and personal nullification.

In the aggression inflicted upon Samuel Kganakga, Jabu James Malinga, Melford Mpompi Dlokolo and other victims of *braai* tortures, the symbolic economy of performative violence and the violence of historically inscribed economic domination can be seen as integral to each other's ideological replication in consciousness and enactment. *Braai* tortures were a theatre of economic replay and nostalgia for old structural hierarchies that could be replicated in the present state of emergency only through the sensory associations of the masculinist and white barbecue. The *braai* torture was a pleasure-inducing experience in which the subordination of racial Others was explicitly linked to heightened moments of commensality, object-choice, and virtual or symbolic cannibalism.

The convergence of forced labour, violence and consumption practices also coincides with almost pan-African anti-colonial perceptions about European capitalist penetration and forced labour practices. This is particularly true for black labour in the mines, who view economic violence as a vast machinery for the consumption, cannibalisation, digestion and wastage of bodies of colour, a folk perception that coincides with west and southern African witch-craft-related beliefs concerning 'belly-eaters and soul-eaters'. The *braai* torture episodes give us a glimpse of this process from the other side of economic violence, that of the white *baas* (boss) and consumer of black subordination. We are dealing here with trauma-tropes, racial images and wounds that provoke commensal pleasures on the one hand, and acts of domination and violence that are encrypted by consumption symbols on the other hand, thereby indicating the presence of commodification logics at the core of both repressive and ideological apparatuses. It is precisely the capacity of *braai* tortures to evoke and replicate old hierarchies that enabled the perpetrators to extract power, pleasure and identity from these atrocities, essences that had little to do with the gathering of political intelligence but much to do with political, racial and class identity.

However, despite my focus on economic culture, this is not a traditional Marxist analysis, for there are other readings that intersect with the diachronic one I have just provided, and these readings directly address the excessiveness and disproportionality of the violence, its very lack of political utility, expediency and rationality. These facets must be attended to, for even contextual socio-economic explanations can overrationalise modalities of being and perception that begin on the historical stage of state political and economic instrumentality and terminate in an altogether different place, and that alternative site has been marked by the religious and medicinal beliefs of the communities from which the victims of *braai* torture came.

The Door of the Demonic

As a mother I feel that, no matter whether it was politics, fighting for his land, I don't think he deserved all that treatment. I feel it was grossly inhuman. I feel they could have killed him and gave us the body or left it in the veld there, I feel that this was tantamount to cannibalism, or even Satanism.

Charity Kondile, a Xhosa from Port Elizabeth and a member of the Zionist Church, whose testimony is mentioned above, had declared that the torture, execution and *braaiing* of her son Sizwe was a form of cannibalism and Satanism. It would be easy to dismiss her accusation of Satanism and the demonic as the expression of an understandably distraught mother. However, I have since discovered that the notion of the demonic reflects another, quite crucial cultural memory at play in the comprehension of state terror, this time from the perspective of South Africans of colour. I was recently sitting in the Cape Town office of a 'coloured' policeman seconded to the Amnesty Committee of the TRC.[25] He has been involved in numerous torture investigations, including *braai* tortures. A meticulous and methodical investigator and evidence analyst, and the right-hand man of the TRC's legal experts, he is also a member of the Seventh-day Adventist Church. He told me the following:

Sometimes when I read the amnesty applications, it really gets to me [that] it cuts me right to the bone, sometimes when I've read an application over a hundred times I still can't believe that men or humans can have been so evil going in and killing families, mothers, children, to me it was because they were just demonic, it is only a person who is controlled by demonic powers or forces who would do these evil deeds. Its evil! And I just hope and pray that they would find peace within themselves when they come and speak about this (at amnesty hearings).

I asked him what was the origin of the demonic.

I come from a police background it has been institutionalised that the police would braai every Friday, because of my religious background and my beliefs, I would not attend for at a braai they would discuss the women they slept with, the guys they assaulted. If you look at guys like de Kock, Coetzee, and other guys who braaied people, in normal human understanding you can never understand what would bring someone to do something like that, it's not the culture or the upbringing [-] it has to be some force or some demonic power because you are burning this person, while less than 20 metres from him, while this flesh is burning, you are actually having your meat, it's a Satanic ritual, you are offering this person to Satan, here is the trophy. If you look at it from [a] religious aspect it is actually some form of Satanism, 'you have given us this power (being above the law, being judge jury and executioner), so we are giving you back the sacrifice', it makes them feel powerful. By doing this they get that sense of power. If you look at it from a religious point it comes from Satan itself. They would never use those terms, but without realising it they are coming under the lordship of Satan himself because they are being controlled because of the evil deeds that they are doing.

Are they are extracting a sense of power from the act of sacrifice? I asked.

Naturally, yes, because if you do it once you will do it again. Blowing up one person into a 1,000 pieces, as one amnesty applicant put it, and the day after holding a braai and laughing about it, once doing that, they get that sense of power no matter who you are. It will take you up. And that power is demonic. It's not from God, for these men went to church, and they … never confessed the wrong they've done. Later on it becomes a normality, something they were just doing. They could argue the facts, but I could sit down with them and prove it to them, that they are totally under the control of the demonic forces. I would prove to them in a biblical sense and in a non-biblical sense. In the non-biblical sense, if you go to [a] certain place, certain places are under the stronghold of Satan because of the things that is happening there. If you go to Indonesia where they have a lot of witchcraft and a lot of rituals, they have voodoo, they have ouiji boards, these are all demonic powers. You that are living there are being controlled by demonic forces, that is from a non-biblical sense (non Christian). If you read the amnesty applications when they go to do torture they always go back to these certain spots, for instance a mine, a shooting range, because they feel safe there because no-one could see them. They realise this is really where we can exercise our powers. They open a door at that point because that place accumulates power, because sometimes when I step into a torture spot, I could feel its presence. I wasn't afraid, it even challenges me in my dreams, but I overcome it with the blood of Jesus.

I am still exploring how widespread these beliefs are, but the ethnic, religious and geographical differences between Mrs Kondile, a Xhosa from the Eastern Cape, and this Seventh-day Adventist policeman, of coloured or mixed race from the Western Cape, suggest an undercurrent of folk theorising on what the TRC would call disproportionate human rights violence. Like Charity Kondile, this TRC functionary, a former member of the same police force he is now investigating, sees the demonic in these acts of torture, a demonic that fashions power through ritualised violence, an act which is not simply the application of state power to the victim. The demonic is centred on the requirement and substance of the victim; it is not repressive violence that deletes or eliminates, it is a productive force akin to the apartheid economy. Like that economy, it is tied to a circuit of miasmic spaces which attract, magnetise and accumulate such acts of violence. The notion of the demonic speaks to embedded concepts of morbidity, of chronic evil, of sickness, possibly of possession and consequently of healing and redemption. We are in a religious and medically discursive territory here, but one that is far removed from the individualised confessional canons and talking cure of the TRC.

In order to explore the fuzzy terrain of the demonic and of moral sickness and healing, I turned to *Umntu Omhlophe*, the 'white people' popularly known by the

Zulu term *isangomas*, carrying my case files of atrocities to male and female tra-ditional healers from KTC and Crossroads shanty towns where I was conducting community-based fieldwork. I was interested in the notion of miasmic space that can attract further acts of violence as discussed by the policeman and as inferred by Mrs Kondile. Xhosa *isangomas* by trade are intimate with such spots, which are usually associated with roads, especially crossroads where fatal highway accidents have occurred, and particularly with mine shafts, where industrial acci-dents and deaths have taken place. There are sites where 'a lot of people have lost their souls', I was told. The recurrent phrase was that these were magnetic spots that 'pulled', 'dragged' or 'invited' souls – *ukutsala imiphefumlo*, in Xhosa. *Umphefumlo* is a soul (the prefix *imi-* indicates the plural form), and *phefumla*, the verb form, means 'to breathe'. *Phefumla* has a moral connotation, for to breathe is also to speak of painful events that weigh on someone; it can also mean the strong, empowered speech of the traditional healer. A person in mourn-ing or a person harbouring great suffering and emotional trauma experiences a heavy weight on the chest and shoulders, and cannot breathe easily.

These miasmic spots are places where the spirit leaves the person, as indi-cated by the many souls lost at these locales. In such a miasmic spot, one is no longer *umphefumlo*, that is, with a soul; once the soul is gone, one can no longer breathe, for what made one breathe is absent. At this juncture, the souls that are 'dragged' from the person are transformed into *imimoya emibi*, trou-bled, restless spirits that gravitate to the miasmic site. *Kwelemimoya* (spirit-place) is a term used to describe the locations of dragged spirits. Since 'bad' untimely death is frequent in the mines, it is customary amongst the miners to commission *isangomas* to go down into the mines every six months to talk to the spirits at a spot where someone has died. Cows and goats are slaughtered, and white beads and tobacco are left, as this propitiation ensures a renewed level of safety for the miners. Roads where car accidents have been frequent receive the same ceremonial attention.

I held extensive discussions with the *Umntu Omhlophe* (the 'white people') about what was occurring psychologically, physiologically and metaphysically in the *braai* tortures. In these discussions, the term used for the victim was *ixhoba*, which can mean prey or target. To *braai* is *ukosa*, or *ukoja*. In their diagnoses, the *isangomas* focused on the exposure of the torturers to the aroma of burning human fat, a substance that is used by a few healers in their treat-ments, though most utilise animal fat. According to the healers, the aroma and smoke of burning human fat will encourage the torturer to kill again and to burn more victims to re-experience this aroma. The more the perpetrators inhaled burning human fat, they more they were compelled to commit the same act. One healer declared that the police were 'poisoned', and concluded they were 'like animals' or animalistic. The term for animals in Xhosa is *isilwanyana*. The phrase used by the healers is *babu-lwanyana*(rha); *babu* is plural for peo-ple, and the entire term means literally 'animalish people'. Here the trope of bes-tialisation is associated with the torturers and not with the tortured. By treating people as prey and food, the police had bestialised themselves, and this was both a moral and physiological condition, if such a distinction would be made by the healers, considering the perpetrators' addiction. Referring to the Christian characterisation of indigenous African belief systems, one *isangoma* described the police as 'animists', thus appropriating a white moralising discourse on primitivity and reassigning it to the police.

The concept of an addicting aroma is crucial here for many reasons. To be addicted is to crave (*ukurhaleia/ukubawa*). It can also be described as an itching (*ukurhawuzelela*). This term connotes being discomforted by an alien presence, and was often used by ANC activists when they were suspicious that an informer was in their midst. As described to me: 'It is such a level of discomfort that you have to remove that person by killing him. They feel it in the blood that an informer is around.' This deadly aroma of burnt human fat, which is either inhaled through the nostrils or absorbed through the pores of the skin, intersects with the notion of *umphefumlo* or soul as akin to breath. It can imply toxification of the assailants' souls, as well as their bodies. As one healer described it to me: 'The human fat is in their blood. It has penetrated their bodies and requires cleansing. They are polluted.'

Being addicted to killing would be seen as the multiplication of the pollution. *Isinyama*, pollution or curse, is a moral concept applied to Xhosa who are sent to jail and who consequently require ritual cleansing after their release. Before they decommissioned their weapons, former resistance fighters I met with in Katlehong in Gauteng hired an *isangoma* to clean (*umgqwaliso*) the *isinyama* associated with their weaponry. Another form of *isinyama* is associated with calendrical killing sprees: if a person kills at a certain time of year and is not cleansed (*ukususa isinyama*), the Xhosa believe he will kill again in the next year during the same season, in a kind of temporal duplication or addiction that complements the notion of miasmic space.

According to a Xhosa healer: 'This craving makes them want to smell that aroma again, they gain a pleasure from smelling human flesh.' This is a miasmic and an empowering process all at once. According to the *isangomas*, it can be viewed as a particularly morbid form of *intelezi*, or medicine. *Intelezi* is the name for certain types of medicines used by herbalists and *isangomas*; it can also mean a specific herb. *Intelezi* is frequently administered through exposing the body to herbal steam: the medicine is simmered in water, and the person taking the *intelezi* sits over the pot on a chair covered with blankets. It is important that there is no ventilation so that stream penetrates as much of the body as possible. The patient sits there until feeling dizzy, which is the sign that the medicine has entered the body through both the pores and the nostrils. Steaming is *ukufutha*, and the process described above is referred to as 'cooking yourself' or *ukupheka*.

Ferdy Barnard, an infamous policeman who terrorised the KTC squatter camp near Cape Town and who was supposed have been allied with certain anti-ANC herbalists, was rumoured to have practised witchcraft, and was considered as having 'cooked himself' (*wazipheka*) with multiple empowering *intelezi*. This process of 'cooking' closely resembles what the healers described

as occurring in the *braai* tortures, when the odour of burning human fat penetrated the bodies of the torturers. Indeed, one *isangoma* declared that the police
in the Kganakga torture had 'cooked themselves' (*bazipheka*) in the odour of
human fat. Cooking is also associated with a herbal hardening of the body. It
can be said that the police cooked themselves with empowering substances that
intensified their propensity not only for violence but also for human atrocity.

Heat symbolism also features in the *isangomas*'s sensing of a place inhabited by *imimoya emibi,* or troubled or bad spirits, the spatial phrase being *imi-
moya-abantu abahambayo ye.* In the aftermath of Nelson Mandela declaring
Robben Island a national memorial, a place of nation-building remembrance, a
federation of *isangomas* went to Robben Island to ritually cleanse it of some of
those accumulated memories. They did so after a representative of Mandela, a
well-known female ANC activist, was raped in her cottage by an unidentified
white male when she stayed overnight on the island as part of an inspection
tour commissioned by Mandela. The only white men on the island that night
were policemen. I asked one *isangoma* who performed the cleansing how she
felt when she first set foot on the island where anti-colonial and anti-apartheid
resisters had been incarcerated, abused and died, including eighteenth-century
insurrectionary Indonesian Muslim clerics, nineteenth-century Xhosa chieftains
and many of the current ANC leadership, and where this rape had just occurred.
She replied:

> [She] wrote us a letter telling us about the incident, we went together to clean
> the place to pray to ensure that this time even sangomas would gain access to
> the museum as in the past were not allowed, not unless one will first consult
> with the ancestors, for we believe that museums are not clean. When we first set
> our foot there to inspect the place we came back with broken hearts as we saw
> the place as not suitable for human beings. We felt the troubled spirits [*imimoya
> emibi*] in our blood. Your body tells you by 'choking'; you feel that way when
> you suspect someone of being a witch – or – even if a person is sick your body
> will tell you the type of sickness they have, it's the same when a place is sick. A
> heavy heartbeat and a choking weight on your chest is the first thing you feel.
> You can barely breathe, and the air you breathe is hot and you feel like uttering
> something but something is preventing you.

The notions of the sick place and of the hot choking air reappear in the healers' diagnosis of what is morally, spiritually and physiologically taking place in
the *braai* tortures. A sick place of this type is embedded with its own memories, affective residues of excessive violence and negativity that have occurred
there. Consequently, until they are healed, such sites exist outside of historical
time. The past is endlessly replayed at these locales, and even those who come
from the present, such as Mandela's representative, can be sucked into this ful-
crum of temporally static pain and violence. There can be no new beginnings
at such locations, no reorigination of identity and purpose, since only the violent past circulates there.

Conclusion

Through South Africa's history of political economy, I have shown that chronic and excessive political violence can be motivated by the momentary provision of a retrospective mythography – the dependency of apartheid on the reality and spectacle of spatially and industrially disciplined and ultimately consumable black bodies. This framework allows us to see how oppressive states and para-state organisations may repeatedly use violence to materially provision and reshape the social world into momentary idealities, desired historiographic stage-sets and scenarios of nostalgic subjugation that can have no sustainable existence in the everyday world and which cannot be achieved without the use of further mirroring violence. This framework can also explain the persistent reuse of certain types of violence despite their inability to instrumentally further the stated political agenda of the perpetrators in any pragmatic fashion.

My analysis also brings the two poles of structural violence and transacted violence into greater proximity through the very tissue of historical memory that animated the *braai* violence. In the debates that have surrounded the South African Truth and Reconciliation Commission, there has been much comment about the TRC's focus on 'exceptional', 'extreme' and 'gross' acts of human rights violations, as well as concern that the enquiry risks normalising and backgrounding the underlying structural violence of apartheid's socio-economic institutions in South Africa. From certain perspectives, the emphasis on 'gross human rights violations' is seen as an artificial separation of the political dimensions of the apartheid regime from its economic character and structural underpinnings. However, once analysed from the perspective of both the commodification of the body and critical race theory, such acts as Kganakga's torture and murder come into focus as present-day expressions of a depth archaeology. At different stages in the history of the colonial and post-colonial political economy, transacted violence and structural violence served as symbolic lubricants for each other. Severe labour discipline, as an act, a threat and a spectacle, facilitated the ideological and structural reproduction of the colonial economy. Structural nostalgia for this class and racial hierarchy haunted the re-enactments of *braai* violence as a form of historical desire, magic and fantasy that found expression in disfigurement and pain, and which rechannelled the violated and consumed black body as a renewed productive fuel for state power.

In accessing alternative memory, I was compelled to inject the absent notion of racially fetishised violence into the amnesty deliberations of the TRC, for the concept of racialised violence I employ contains embedded layers of historical and somatic meaning that were filtered out of the TRC's engagement with state violence due to its juridical-positivist approach to history. In this context, I view racism not as a form of civil rights discrimination or as a psychological pathology, but rather as the fetishisation of the body of colour in the labour objectification/coercion of colonially subjugated populations. I argue that European regimes of labour discipline in colonial and post-colonial South Africa deployed the body of colour as an instrumental-economic substance and a magical substance. I show that in South Africa the performative signifiers of race- and class-based economic domination were eventually, in a time of hegemonic crisis, transposed into the sphere of state political ritual, thereby symbolically ordering counter-insurgency performance and consequently normalising and legitimating what has been termed 'gross' human rights violations. Hence, the cultural memory of 'white' economic dominance was mobilised as a self-conscious political vehicle that translated the residual economy of the colonial body into emerging economies of transacted political violence. This dynamic of transposition by which the so-called 'instrumental' practice of the political economy was refigured as the legitimating semiology of domination in state violence points to the magical invocation of the memory of economic domination in the material culture of political repression. I strategically deploy racialised somatic fetishism as an alternative analytic to the liberal-rationalist reductions of the TRC concerning politically motivated, and thus indemnifiable, human rights violations. I do not completely reject the norm of human rights that animated the TRC; rather, I connect the suppressed discussion of racialised violence to the equally avoided human rights norm of 'disproportionate violence' that was originally mandated, yet conveniently forgotten, by the TRC. Racialised violence and disproportionate violence form an excluded locus of a fundamental contradiction within the liberal-rationalist historiography of the TRC, and have thus become subject to structural forgetfulness by the human rights paradigm. As juridical blind spots, they are historical recesses where alternative historical memories and political experiences can be accessed.

In part, my goal in this essay has been to examine how the history of certain memory formations mediated the reproduction of certain types of excessive and racialised violence, which were given short shrift by the TRC. By treating memory as a utilitarian and unproblematic transparency largely residing in individuals or fragmented communities, or as a neutral juridical technology, the TRC ignored social memory as a normative institutionalised formation with its own political history. In doing so, the TRC ended up stressing memory's therapeutic possibilities at the expense of establishing its pathogenic connection to institutional violence and that violence's inherence in economic racism, a connection that would more explicitly relate the TRC's project with the historical evisceration of apartheid's economic and spatial violence. In neglecting the hegemonic contours of institutional memory, the TRC failed to develop a self-reflexive relationship to its own technologies of memory and failed to confront the human rights danger in not recalling the disproportionate character of so-called politically motivated institutional violence. The TRC has left an ambivalent and contradictory moral legacy to the degree that it has ceded to future generations an important archive of political terror and violence, witnessed largely from the previously unwritten perspective of black history and embodiment, and yet has failed to adequately confront the institutional procedures that reproduce and bureaucratically routinise such violence – an important prophylaxis for future democratic institution-building in South Africa.

I have triangulated racialised victim fetishism by the state apparatus – a form of state sorcery – with the human rights notion of disproportionate, surplus/excessive violence and with specific historical-economic co-ordinates of production and symbolic consumption. In effect, for the TRC, disproportionate and excessive violence functioned as a cipher or code for unnarrated, unrecognised and unwanted historical memory, perception and experience. By accessing alternative historiographies, located in labour history, local moral geographies, indigenous norms of healing, and 'folk' theories of sorcery and the demonic, I posed and began to answer the difficult question of how a political culture fashions power (symbolic and pragmatic) from violent techniques of production and human substances of consumption – a question any truth commission could benefit from contemplating. If not addressed, this is a question that will leave all truth commissions in a morass of symptomology and ad hoc moral condemnation that will ultimately make human rights discourse a laughing stock or a circus-like spectacle. At the same time, the salvaging of historical memory tied to excessive and officially unnarrated political violence can promote the subjecthood and agency of those communities and individuals who have been the recipients of consuming colonial and post-colonial intrusions of their person and embodiment. And is not the dignified restoration of subjecthood and personhood one of the primary goals of human rights enquiry and redress?

While excluded from the proceedings of the TRC, the respective yet related discourses on the demonic by Xhosa healers and Christianised Africans attempt to address exactly what is disproportionate in this violence through the concept of miasma, the Satanic or *isinyama*, depending on the commentators' belief systems. In the nexus of demonic narratives, the disproportionate is always defined by its chronic character, by its predilection for duplication and by its instigation of endless dissatisfaction. It is characterised by an inability on the part of the assailant to master the surrogate victim at the very moment of the latter's annihilation, for such is the moral lesson of the craving, toxic dependency and poisoning induced by burning human fat. Through the imagery of medicinal cooking, of *intelezi*, and the moral inversion of its healing powers, the culinary ambiance of the *braai* tortures is clarified: at the moment of cooking and consuming his victim, the perpetrator himself is cooked and consumed by the very addiction that empowers and drives his violence. It is an Africanised Hegelian symbiosis of the master and the subjugated, in which the latter becomes toxic to the former. That, too, is a certain type of social justice.

The discourse on the demonic discussed in this essay holds forth the promise of various processes of healing in the blood of Christ, if one is a Seventh-day Adventist or Zionist, or through the ritual cleansing of person, weapon and space, if one attends to the Xhosa healers. Nevertheless, the notion of what needs to be healed is determined by the concept of miasmic contiguity and contact, and people are not the only subjects of healing – or rather, personal healing is a heavily mediated and eminently material process. The agents and actors of healing are multiple; weapons need to be cleansed, and geography previously desecrated by chronic 'bad' death requires detoxification. Healing, here, is not a psychological, confessional process, or solely a dyadic relationship between perpetrator and victim. Further, the discourse on the demonic, whether that of the evangelical Christian or the herbal healer, does not excuse the institutional dynamics that foster the inhumane. The spatialisation of the demonic extends from the locales of *braai* torture to the corridors of the apartheid state; it is a diffusion of the miasmic and not an individualising medicalisation and psycholigisation of the guilty. Finally, the terminal power of the violent state is morally nullified in the discourse of the demonic by its emphasis on the reversibility of evil. Both Robben Island, prior to its cleansing, and the various locales where resisters were tortured and disposed off through *braaing* and other nefarious methods constitute a continuum of enchained memory spaces. This architecture of memory is not only psychological but also structural and geographical. It constitutes a moral geography, a cartography of past national destruction, and thus is a potential archipelago of national reconstruction for a people still waiting to exhale the cooling breath of historical redemption.

ACKNOWLEDGEMENTS

I am grateful to the Harry Frank Guggenheim Foundation for the Study of Violence and Aggression for providing funding for both the research and write-up of this material. I would like to acknowledge the crucial role of Western Cape Action Tours of Cape Town for brokering introduction to the *isangomas*. I am grateful to the Cape Town witness handling/briefing team, particularly George Molebatsi, of the Human Rights Violations Committee of the Truth and Reconciliation Commission for allowing me to sit in on their pre- and post-hearing briefing sessions, and for allowing me to share meals with witnesses during the course of the hearings. Many evidence analysers of the TRC provided me with generous access to deep background materials and contextualising perspectives. I would also like to thank Mitzpah Botho, my Xhosa translator, who was willing to absorb some ethnographic education from me, as I absorbed her complex, nuanced and eminently ethnographic understanding of the multiplex speech of the healers. The translations are the product of our dialogues. I am in debt to René Devisch, Paul Stoller and Conerly Casey for providing me with a rich comparative perspective from West Africa, and to Pamela Reynolds, David Bunn, Steve Robbins, Karen Colvard, Jane Harries and Bruce Kapferer for providing stimulating theoretical questions.

NOTES

1. For discussion of cultural contouring of memory and historiography, see Connerton (1989), Ricoeur (1988), Koselleck (1985), Johnson (1982), White (1978) and Veyne (1976).
2. See Lyotard (1973) for the analysis of historiographic representation as an exercise in realist perspective; see also Feldman (1997, 1996) on the intersection of historical perception and the history of perception.
3. There is no truth commission per se operating in Northern Ireland, but the recently mandated commission to reinvestigate the causes of the Bloody Sunday Massacre has much of the functions and reconciliation ethics of a truth commission, although it focuses on only one event. It is hard to imagine that this type of enquiry into Northern Ireland's recent past will stop at this incident.
4. The following statement from General Magnus Malan, former minister of defence, is illustrative of the theodicy of communism that justified the scope and degree of the violence of the security forces:

> Although it is difficult to appreciate the threat which communism posed to the free world, and South Africa in particular, especially after the demise of communism in Eastern Europe during 1989, for purposes of a proper analysis of the policies and actions of the South African government during the 1980s, it is necessary to take a brief look at its actual position during that time. I shall endeavour to give a short summary of the international climate as interpreted by the government of the day, and against which that government's action should be seen.
>
> The threat was the expansion of Marxism by fomenting revolution in southern Africa. Its aim was perceived to be, first, the overthrow of the white regimes in southern Africa so that the militant Africa bloc could realise its aspirations with regard to the destruction of so-called colonialism and racialism and the establishment of Pan-Africanism. In its desire to destroy alleged racism, the Arab bloc can, with certain exceptions, be regarded as the partner of the Africa bloc in its hostile actions, as far as this serves its own purposes. Marxism's second aim was seen to be the striving after an indirect strategy in order to unleash revolutionary warfare in southern Africa and, by means of isolation, to force the Republic of South Africa to change its domestic policy in favour of Pan-Africanism.
>
> These are not my ex post facto interpretations or perceptions. These sentiments have been repeatedly stated over the years.

5. In giving little due to the adjudication of political motivation based on anti-communism, and critiquing the TRC for failing to develop moral measures for the proportionality of human rights violations, it may be suggested I am in danger of aestheticising violence because I do not allow a significant role for instrumental rationality. In reference to torture, I have critiqued instrumental rationality as a legitimisation strategy and truth claim precisely because it elevates, sterilises, dematerialises and thus effectively aestheticises sordid acts of institutionalised dysfunctional cruelty. Marcuse and Adorno saw the technical rationality of National Socialism and its racial imaginaries as two sides of a uniform process of mythification – each strand realised in the other, in a particularly German adaptation to modernity. The mobilisation of racial or ethnic myth and phobia through rationalised institutional procedures and ideologies is, in fact, the aesthetic facade that hides and legitimises the sordidness of irrationally applied violence. I would suggest that more historical, political and cultural content can be gleaned from the form or performative infrastructure of such episodes than from the ostensible goal orientation of such interrogations – the obtaining of a confession.

Further, the predication of state violence by bureaucratic command structures, psychopathology or anti-communism does not exhaust the comprehension of chronic violence and state terror by the communities who were the recipients of these violations.

There is a surplus memory of these events that mobilises cosmologies and theodicies that have little admissibility in the TRC hearings and investigations, and which bypass institutional rationalities to directly address the issue of the disproportionate in state violence in the cultural form of the demonic.

6. *Askari* were captured members of liberation organisations who were 'turned' by the Afrikaans security forces and worked as double agents for the police and army.

7. *Truth and Reconciliation Commission Human Rights Violations Submissions – Questions and Answers.* Date: 26–28 August 1996. Name: Mpompi Melfred Dlokolo. Case: Ec/96 Uitenhage – Day 1.

8. *Truth and Reconciliation Commission Human Rights Violations Submissions – Questions and Answers.* Date: 11 November 1996. Name: T. Mvudle. Case: Krugersdorp.

9. *Truth and Reconciliation Commission Amnesty Hearing.* Date: 14 July 1997. Name: Jeffery Benzien. Day 1.

10. *Truth and Reconciliation Human Rights Violations Submissions – Questions and Answer.* Date: 17 April 1996. Name: Charity Kondile. Case: Ec0021/96 – East London, Day 3.

11. All statements are taken from TRC transcripts of amnesty hearings held in Pretoria in July 1996.

12. *Pretoria Amnesty Hearings*, 15–19 July 1996, J.A. Van Eyck (0070/96); H. Gerber (0071/ 96) murder of Samuel Kganakga on 21 May 1991.

13 All ellipses and parenthesis are added by author.

14. Foucault (1979).

15. This was reserved by the company's slaves; private slave owners were not allowed to flog slaves. For discussion of these statistics and of slave punition in the Cape Colony, see Shell (1994: 193, 206–11, 215–16; 265–6) on punition of slave arsonists. For a comparative discussion of punishment of Khoisan farm labourers and Cape Colony slaves, see Newton-King (1994: 257–8). On ideologies of labour discipline and the application of violence, see Mason (1994: 48–52).

16. See Comaroff and Comaroff (1997), Keegan (1996), Van Onselen (1982), and Philip and Plaatje (1916).

17. See Gilommee (1989).

18. See Lacey (1981: 169–71).

19. See Bradford (1987: 51–3).

20. For a fuller discussion, see Kraak (1993: 37–30).

21. See Kraak (1993: 95–7).

22. For a detailed discussion of mine labour discipline and the social structure of the compound system in Southern Africa from the late nineteenth to mid twentieth century, see Van Onselen (1976: 137–57).

23. Bradford (1987: 42–3).

24. *Truth and Reconciliation Commission Human Rights Violations Submissions – Questions and Answer.* Date: 28 August 1996. Place: Alexandra. Name: Jabu James Malinga.

25. 'Coloured' usually refers to the descendants of the slave populations of the Western Cape, although it can also refer to those of mixed race and to Indians.

BIBLIOGRAPHY

Bradford, H. *A Taste of Freedom: The ICU in Rural South Africa 1924–1930.* New Haven, 1987.

Comaroff, J.L. and Comaroff, J. *Of Revelation and Revolution: The Dialectics of Modernity on a South African Frontier.* Chicago, 1997.

Connerton, P. *How Societies Remember.* Cambridge, 1989.

Feldman, A. 'Violence and Vision: The Prosthetics, Aesthetics of Terror.' *Public Culture* 10, no. 1 (1997).

———. 'On Cultural Anesthesia: From Desert Storm to Rodney King.' In *The Senses Still: Memory and Perception as Material Culture in Modernity,* ed. C.N. Seremetakis. Chicago, 1996.

Foucault, M. *Discipline and Punish: The Birth of the Prison.* New York, 1979.

Gilommee, H. 'Aspect of the Rise of Afrikaaner Capital and Afrikaaner Nationalism.' In *The Angry Divide: Social and Economic History of the Western Cape,* ed. J. Wilmott and M. Simons. Cape Town, 1989.

Johnson, R. 'Popular Memory: Theory, Politics, Method.' In *Making Histories: Studies in History-Writing and Politics,* ed. R. Johnson. London, 1982.

Keegan, T. *Colonial South Africa and the Origins of Racial Order.* Cape Town, 1996.

Koselleck, R. *Futures Past: On the Semantics of Historical Time.* Cambridge, Mass., 1985.

Kraak, G. *Breaking the Chains: Labour in South Africa in the 1970s and 1980s.* London, 1993.

Lacey, M. *Working for Boroko: The Origins of a Coercive Labour System in South Africa.* Johannesburg, 1981.

Lyotard, J.F. *Des Dispositifs Pulsionnels.* Paris, 1973.

Mason, J.E. 'Paternalism under Siege.' In *Breaking the Chains: Slavery and Its Legacy in the Nineteenth-Century Cape Colony,* ed. N. Worden and C. Craig. Johannesburg, 1994.

Newton-King, S. 'The Enemy Within.' In *Breaking the Chains: Slavery and Its Legacy in the Nineteenth-Century Cape Colony,* ed. N. Worden and C. Craig, 257–8. Johannesburg, 1994.

Philip, D. and Plaatje, S. *Native Life in South Africa: Before and Since the European War and the Boer Republic.* London, 1916.

Ricoeur, P. *Time and Narrative.* Vol. 3. Chicago, 1988.

Shell, R.C.H. *Children of Bondage: A Social History of the Slave Society at the Cape of Good Hope, 1652–1838.* Johannesburg, 1994.

Van Onselen, C. *Studies in the Social and Economic History of the Witswatersrand, 1886–1914.* Johannesburg, 1982.

———. *Chibaro: African Mine Labour in Southern Rhodesia 1900–1935.* London, 1976.

Veyne, P. *L' Inventaire des Differences.* Paris, 1976.

White, H. *The Tropics of Discourse.* Baltimore, 1978.

Contributors

Rohan Bastin teaches anthropology and is Head of the School of Anthropology, Archaeology and Sociology at James Cook University, Australia. He has conducted research in Sri Lanka since 1984, and more recently has pursued research interests in Kerala, in southern India. His publications include *The Domain of Constant Excess: Plural Worship at the Munnesvaram Temples in Sri Lanka* (2002).

Marit Brendbekken is a Research Fellow at the Department of Social Anthropology, University of Bergen. She is finalising her Ph.D. dissertation based on long-term fieldwork in the Dominican-Haitian borderlands. She has also conducted fieldwork in urban slum areas of the Dominican Republic, among peasants in northern rural Haiti and Rastafarians on Dominica, and among anthroposophists in Järna, Sweden. She is the author of 'Hablando con la mata. Las plantas y la identidad campesina' (1998).

René Devisch is Professor of Social Anthropology at Catholic University of Louvain (Leuven). He has conducted (medical-)anthropological fieldwork among the Yaka people in south-western Congo (1971–4) and Kinshasa (three to six weeks annually since 1986), and has supervised doctoral research in 10 African countries in the context of the programme of the Africa Research Centre, Department of Anthropology, Catholic University of Louvain, Belgium. He is the author of *Weaving the Threads of Life: The Khita Gyn-eco-logical Healing Cult among the Yaka* (Chicago 1993), and the co-author, with Claude Brodeur, of *The Law of the Lifegivers: The Domestication of Desire* (Amsterdam 1999).

Allen Feldman is a political/medical anthropologist and the author of *Formations of Violence: The Narrative of the Body and Political Terror in Northern Ireland*, now in its third printing; *On Cultural Anesthesia: From Desert Storm to Rodney King*; *Vision and Violence: The Prosthetics and Aesthetics of Terror*; and other numerous articles on the political anthropology of the body and the senses. He is Visiting Faculty at the Anthropology of Everyday Life Program at the Institute for the Studies of the Humanities, Ljubljana, and at the International Trauma Studies Program NYU and is a Principle Investigator for AIDS, homelessness and policing at the Postgraduate Center for Mental Health, New York.

Ørnulf Gulbrandsen is Professor of Social Anthropology at the University of Bergen. He has done fieldwork in Norway and amongst the Tswana of Botswana and is currently starting new fieldwork on Sardinia. He has published on a wide range of topics, including industrial anthropology, religion, kinship/marriage, politics and cultural ecology. He is currently working on the relationship between the state and Tswana kingdoms, addressing, in particular, the exceptionality of Botswana's political and societal stability in a wider African context.

Bruce Kapferer is Professor of Social Anthropology at the Department of Social Anthropology, University of Bergen, and has held chairs at several other institutions, including the University of Adelaide and University College London. He has conducted extensive fieldwork in southern Africa, Sri Lanka, India and Australia, and has published several monographs on themes including forms of ritual healing, sorcery, nationalism and urbanisation, among them *Legends of People, Myths of State* (1998 [1988]), *The Feast of the Sorcerer* (1997) and *A Celebration of Demons* (1991 [1983].

Michael Lambek is Professor of Anthropology at the University of Toronto and has carried out fieldwork in Mayotte and Madagascar. He is the author of *The Weight of the Past: Living with History in Mahajanga, Madagascar* (2002); *Knowledge and Practice in Mayotte: Local Discourses of Islam, Sorcery and Spirit Possession* (1993); *Human Spirits: A Cultural Account of Trance in Mayotte* (1981); editor of *A Reader in the Anthropology of Religion* (2002); and co-editor of several other works. As Toronto co-editor of *Social Analysis* for several years, he oversaw several special issues.

Knut Rio is a Research Fellow at the Department of Social Anthropology, University of Bergen, where he has submitted his doctoral dissertation 'The Third Man: Manifestations of Agency on Ambrym Island, Vanuatu'. In it, he considers how the social articulation in kinship, agriculture, ceremonial exchange and sorcery hinges on the importance of outsiders and third parties, and how this triadic model of sociality has influenced colonial encounters and the local development of hierarchy.

Kari G. Telle is a Ph.D. candidate at the Department of Social Anthropology, University of Bergen. Her dissertation deals with notions of place, ritual and the politics of religion among the Sasak, with a strong focus on gender. Her research interests also include state-civil society relationships and political violence in Indonesia. Her article 'Feeding the Dead: Reformulating Sasak Mortuary Practices' appeared in 2000 (Bijdragen tot de Taal-, Land-en Volkenkunde).

Authors Index

Subject Index